Social Work Research

Social Work Research

Methods for the
Helping
Professions

Revised Edition

Edited by

Norman A. Polansky

The University of
Chicago Press

Chicago and London

The University of Chicago Press, Chicago 60637
The University of Chicago Press, Ltd., London

© 1960, 1975 by The University of Chicago
All rights reserved. Published 1975
Printed in the United States of America

Library of Congress Cataloging in Publication Data

Polansky, Norman Alburt, 1918–   ed.
   Social work research.

   Includes index.
   1. Social service—Research. I. Title.
HV11.P64 1975   361'.007'2   74–26798
ISBN 0–226–67219–0

Contents

069031

Preface

The first edition of *Social Work Research* appeared nearly fifteen years ago. Not all that has happened to the world and to social work since then has been for the best. Nevertheless, our book, which was billed as "the first compendium of method and methodology in social work research," substantially succeeded in what was hoped of it. A codification of what had been learned until then about the design and conduct of studies in our field, it served to disseminate this synthesis to practitioners, administrators, fellow researchers, and especially to students.

Over the years, the book went through six printings and was widely used for the teaching of research at both the master's and the doctoral level in social work. We discovered that it received additional acceptance in companion disciplines who share our conundra about providing the new knowledge needed by an essentially practice-oriented profession. Students from counseling, music therapy, nursing, psychiatry, medical sociology, and other fields have received parts of their training with our book. Hopefully, the present revision will continue to be of use also beyond our professional boundaries, as it has in the past. All of us, after all, adapt to our immediate needs the logic and methods originating in psychology, sociology, social psychology, and the other "basic" behavioral sciences. Indeed, most of the authors of this volume, as of the last, have had at least part of their training in these disciplines. Yet we have found that the rigorous pursuit of theoretical advances is more, rather than less, complex in fields like ours. Reality is not as orderly as is knowledge organized into traditional academic disciplines.

As a text, the first edition was found by many students to be serviceable but difficult. Indeed, the editor acquired a conditioned wince in response to the greeting by a stranger at a national conference, "Are you the Norman Polansky who . . . ?" Some of the difficulty derived unavoidably from the subject matter, for most of what is humorous about research is visible only to its in-group. Part of our difficulty came from the ambition we had at the time, which was to write a combination handbook and text. A rather high level of abstraction was imposed by the fact that we did not yet have enough social work research with which to provide as many concrete illustrations of general principles as we would have liked.

There is no reason that books which are informative ought not also be readable. The present revision has tried to move in that direction. It is now more definitely a textbook geared to the advanced undergraduate or first-year graduate student. The volume has been shortened somewhat, and we have attempted to even out the level of the writing. There are now examples of relevant current research so that in many chapters *what* has been found out adds to the learning of *how* it was discovered. The references are themselves a major guide to further study.

Once again, I feel very fortunate to have secured the collaboration of a distinguished group of colleagues in putting together more knowledge than any one of us pretends to have alone. They have worked seriously, promptly, and well, and have subjected themselves to a discipline uncommon in compendia—i.e., writing in terms of what seems most needed for an integrated teaching tool, rather than in line with one's own predilections. There have been changes in the cast of authors based on a variety of factors which it would be tedious to recount. None was dropped lightly from the original list, and it is a source of satisfaction to know that their contributions are readily accessible in the many copies of the first edition which survive. If I appear more prominently as a writer of this version than of the first, the reason does not lie in any sudden access of wisdom or energy. It simply seemed that among a group of mature and willful colleagues, the person most likely to be amenable to convictions I had developed about new content needed, style, and the keeping of deadlines would probably be me. Which is not to say that to get something the way you want it, you must do it yourself. To the contrary, the other authors of this book are here because what they write is nearer my heart's desire than what I would have written if I had done it all.

The original impetus for a handbook came out of the Committee on Methodology of the Research Section of the National Association of Social Workers, a well-loved body long since lost in the welter of compulsive reorganization to which the association is addicted. The chairperson (then chairman!) of that committee was Ethel G. Harrison. Work on the first edition took place during the period when Margaret Blenkner, Lillian Ripple, and Henry Maas were successively heads of the section, and Lili Sweat our staff person from NASW. Mary Macdonald, Leonard Kogan, and Genevieve Carter served with the present editor as an editorial board to produce the first edition, and their beneficial influence survives in this revision, I am sure. This edition is no longer under the aegis of NASW, having been freed of inevitable accompanying constraints by the thoughtfulness of its Publications Committee, chaired by David Fanshel before the revision was undertaken. Responsibility for the net readability of the present version is even more my own. Let me add, therefore, that this textbook is designated to accompany and support the efforts of the gifted classroom teachers who will use it and will surely elucidate whatever still remains obscure.

My thanks are very much due to my wife, Nancy Finley Polansky, whose love and concrete assistance helped with the revision in all its many phases, and to my children Grace Rachael Vaughn Polansky (a fellow social worker) and Jonathan Rolfe Polansky, for keeping the future meaningful.

Athens, Georgia   NORMAN A. POLANSKY

Introduction: Social and Historical Context

We live in the era of the knowledge explosion. There are estimates that 95 percent of all the scientists who have ever lived are presently at work. It is a commonplace that whole new industries—television, atomic power, artificial fibers—rest on the breakthroughs in theory that made them possible. Less noticed is the fact that generating knowledge has itself become a major industry. Setting out systematically to find out how the world works is called by many names. Its most familiar title is research.

This book is about research as it is done in social work. The intention is to provide a compact introduction to the goals, the rationale, the methods, and their applications to social work research. We will begin with an image of the place of research in our field, how the knowledge industry relates to social work.

THE FUNCTION OF RESEARCH IN SOCIAL WORK

In disciplines like archaeology and astronomy it would be redundant to spell out the need for research. Archaeology and astronomy are, or hope to become, sciences. Any science is dedicated to obtaining information, ordering it into laws, and then disseminating it throughout society. Social workers, on the other hand, are not primarily knowers; they are doers. They are not astronomers nor even weathermen. Although the practitioner sometimes finds himself passively observing what he is helpless to influence, he does not watch for the sake of being informed. Marx remarked that the aim of the game was not to understand the world but to change it. Most social workers believe that understanding makes for efficiency in the change process, and hopefully a less feverish, violent atmosphere than Marx foresaw. But, as practitioners, they accept the same proposition; they intend to make a difference. When the practitioner harnesses verified laws to improve the efficiency of his work we speak of scientifically based practice. The fruits of research are then blended with good will into modern social work.

Prediction

Few argue openly for a social work operating on ignorance. Still, it is necessary to specify the ways in which research may contribute to practice, for knowing is not the same as doing.

Kurt Lewin, the great social psychologist, set down a famous prescription for rational social management. Intelligent intervention, he said, requires three phases, repeated over and over: planning, execution, and fact finding or feedback (Lewin 1948). In other words, the practitioner decides what he hopes to achieve and how, takes the actions called for, and checks to see if his actions have worked as he had hoped. Then he is ready to take the next step.

Social workers have learned the hard way that, in professions where people are heavily burdened and mean well, they are apt to skip the phase of fact finding. Definite arrangements are needed to guarantee the feedback. Otherwise, an inept course of social treatment will continue uncorrected. So one way in which tested knowledge makes an important contribution to practice is feedback; sometimes this is organized into evaluative research (see chapter 8).

The more important phase at which science enters rational social practice is planning. In a profession, planning involves imagining ahead to estimate alternative chains of events. Here is an age-old dilemma: if I give relief, Mr. Jones will probably never return to work; if I don't, his children will certainly go short on food. What can I do to better the odds that he will go to work—and get the children fed? What will happen if I do nothing at all? Faced with this puzzle, generations of social workers have given relief, recoiled in despair, or referred the case elsewhere. Provided they did not try to evade the whole issue, their planning was founded on one or more *predictions*.

A major motive for wanting knowledge is to increase our sense of mastery. Just as infants fear the dark, the unknown stirs anxiety in all of us; mapping one's surroundings helps dispel it. Unfortunately, a feeling of mastery can be achieved by maneuvers that are completely internal transactions, such as thinking up neat categories into which to file ideas, or other games of obsessive rumination. The social worker needs realistic mastery in the world of observable facts. He feels he has it when he bases his interventions on predictions that prove to be reliable.

The whole aim of research in the profession, therefore, is to improve our feeble ability to predict the course of events. Our concern is with knowledge for use; foresight is crucial to effective practice. It is no wonder that successful prediction is the major criterion of whether a law one thinks he has discovered is "valid." This is as true for science in general as it is for each profession.

Roads to Knowledge

How does a group accumulate the information, rules, and beliefs by which it guides its practice? Things seldom begin with organized research; the group starts its life with a job to do and goes on from there. It is well that social work, for example, did not wait to base its practice on scientific findings, for to this day we have barely enough of these to steer 10 percent of an average worker's day. Fortunately, learning happens in many ways.

Those entering a profession learn from being taught verbally, in lectures, discussions, conversations. They read; they observe; they engage in trial and error under supervision. As if by osmosis, they are acculturated into the tradition of "what social workers stand for." Important pieces of professional equipment are taken on unconsciously by identification with admired teachers and senior colleagues. And, if one asks how the profession as a whole acquired its beliefs, the answers are very similar.

A great deal of professional practice comes from incidental learning. When we move to a new neighborhood, we do not typically make conscious listings of shops and their locations. Yet, if we need a druggist, we will perhaps have noticed one en route to the grocery. Incidental learning, then, is one source of knowledge. A profession is not the same as a science, but it does have the major advantage of being actively immersed in its subject matter. Some claim each practice effort is "a small experiment," but of course this stretches the meaning of the term. It is true that one of the very best ways to understand man is to try to change him. Intelligent members of the profession are enriched from studying their failures, analyzing what they did wrong.

For all these reasons, the university has served the profession typically as a repository and transmitter of knowledge rather than as a generator of it. Most that is new comes from those on the firing line of direct practice. Probably this is as it should be.

There is, then, no royal road to knowledge, and it adds up gradually by various means. Like a science, a profession is a group effort, a social process, and one of the great satisfactions life holds is the feeling that one may have helped move his field forward. What is, then, the purpose of organized research? Simply this: to try to hurry, even force, the accumulation of knowledge. Research does this by following a set of guidelines and procedures which have slowly evolved since the Renaissance and which we term the scientific method (see chapter 1). The scientific method is a codification of the logic and style used by gifted men through which they discovered the theory that leads to dependable prediction. In other words, we know from experience that through using this method of seeking and confirming laws we hasten the rate of discovery far beyond the pace at which it otherwise occurs. That is why we now can have a knowledge explosion, and why a profession is said to be "scientific" to the extent that its practice is based on laws tested by the scientific method.

In a field that is a pure science, everyone seeks information and the discovery of new laws as his major interest. In professions like medicine, engineering, and social work, most people, most of the time, are involved in applying what has already been found out. Knowledge seeking tends to become the chief concern of certain specialized people. Most social workers, like most physicians, never do research. Some do it at certain periods of their lives; and some make it their main occupation. But everyone has a stake in what it may produce, and that is why every member of a profession needs a basic grasp of how the scientific method is applied in his field.

THE SUBJECT MATTER OF SOCIAL WORK RESEARCH

Defining Social Work

Social work research concerns itself with all the many areas in which social workers are professionally involved. It is nearly impossible to set down a concise definition of what the areas constitute. The most recent *Social Work Encyclopedia* illustrates in over 1,600 pages the range of subject matters, and it does not profess to be complete (Morris 1971). One possible definition of social work might be "the processes by which persons relate themselves to one another and simultaneously to other aspects of their environment." The quotation, however, is from Theodore Newcomb (1953), who goes on to say, "This writer likes to apply the label 'social psychology' to this area of investigation" (p. 8).

In any event, a profession's boundaries are not laid down by being defined once and for all. They evolve. Students entering law schools in this generation in the hope of furthering civil rights certainly have a different conception of their profession than does a retired corporation counsel. It will be adequate for present purposes, therefore, to define social work as a field that does things for people who are in difficulties, or in danger of coming into difficulties, and which views their social situation as potentially contributory. As noted, there is tremendous variety within this broad area. One frame of reference used to classify a particular study, therefore, is the subject matter to which it especially relates, for example, services to children, poverty, social aspects of health, supervision.

Points of Application

Another framework for categorizing a study has to do with the point in the helping process to which we envisage its contributing. Borrowing from medical terminology, we may describe a study as aiming to clarify *pathology*, to improve *therapeutics*, or to advance *general theory*.

The constituent sciences on which social work rests—e.g., psychology, sociology, psychoanalysis, anthropology, economics, etc.—have as their end goals concise abstractions about individual and societal behavior to which we refer as *general theory* (see chapter 1). In a field dedicated to active service, abstract laws are more likely to be drawn upon than formulated. So social work research has seldom undertaken to advance general theory as such. Nevertheless, any practical problem which is studied long enough sooner or later leads one back to fundamental issues about the nature of man and his group life. Investigators trained in a general theory are likely to recognize its relevance to all sorts of practical concerns. As a result, the distinction between "pure" and "applied" research is not sharp, and at least a few social work researchers have simultaneously advanced general knowledge in an underlying science. For example, a classic study of sociometric phenomena by Newstetter and others (1938) is more frequently cited in the literature of social psychology than in that of social work. The same is true of an investigation in which this writer participated, on behavioral contagion in children's groups (Polansky, Lippitt, and Redl 1950).

The more typical instigator of studies in our field is the question, What has gone wrong, and why? How come this family is trapped in a "cycle of poverty"? What caused that youngster to become a heroin addict? Such questions seek the roots of *pathology*. And with good reason. Very often, if we know enough about the causes of a disease, we can then infer how to treat it or even to prevent it. Naturally, a large proportion of social work research has gone into advancing pathology.

If one has a complete and general theory of human behavior, and can pinpoint what has gone wrong, deciding what to do about it should be merely a matter of deduction. No new information would be needed. Unfortunately, at this stage of the art, our knowledge of pathology and our general theory are seldom that advanced. Social and individual *therapeutics*, methods of treatment, require discoveries in their own right. Historically, nearly all treatment innovations have come from direct practice. Research has been brought in to offer a reassuring answer to the question, Are we doing any good? The outcomes of evaluation have not always been encouraging, to put it mildly.

A major contribution to therapeutics, combining it with pathology, has been in studies of *need for service*, target populations at greatest risk, and the like. Of course, there is no reason organized knowledge seeking cannot also be directed at issues of technique, and a number of us have made beginnings in that direction (Miller 1958; Polansky 1971a). The hope is that research will contribute more substantially to practice theory in the future.

INTELLECTUAL PREDECESSORS

We have been describing the purposes and content of social work research. How did it arrive where it is now? There is a French saying, with which most members of my generation gladly concur: It is safer to write history than to make it. But, it has also been said that those who neglect history are doomed to repeat it. Many of our intellectual ancestors were highly intelligent and perceptive, and the issues that engaged them are still with us.

Actually, on one side we come from a proud line of snoopers, busybodies, and folks addicted to minding other people's business. Not only that, but they were judgmental and not at all reluctant to push for change. On the other side, we have a cousinly relationship with most behavioral science disciplines through common ancestors. There was a time when physics was known as natural philosophy, and in some ancient universities it is still so known. Similarly, many sociological problems were discussed as moral (later social) philosophy, and for many years those at work in social agencies attended the same national conventions as did those in university sociology departments. Since we all evolved from the same philosophical matrix, it is no wonder we borrow back and forth from each other, in research methods and in theory.

The Polemicists

Usually unrecognized as such, but definitely in the family tree of social work, were the great English polemicists. Jonathan Swift's *Gulliver's Travels* (1726) is regarded by many as a tale for children, but it is more than that. Swift (1667–1745) was also an outstanding moralist who fought for social justice. In the days before television, *Robinson Crusoe* (1717) enlivened our reading. We usually did not know or care that Daniel Defoe (1660–1731), its author, had also pamphleteered at great personal risk on behalf of the lower classes of his day. Scrooge is brought to mind every Christmas, and Charles Dickens (1812–70), who created him, won fame as humorist and storyteller. But Dickens was very seriously engaged in bringing to the middle and upper classes a vivid picture of lower class life in the England of the latter nineteenth century—its orphans' homes, slums, workhouses (see *Oliver Twist*, 1838). Having begotten a large brood and had the gall to bring a young mistress into his own home in his middle age, Dickens also found time for active personal involvement in philanthropy. Thus he used his connections among wealthy admirers to raise funds for some of the earliest "model tenements" which, for better *and* for worse, were the precursors of our huge low-income housing developments. A magnificent polemicist was Samuel Clemens (1835–1910), Mark Twain, whose *Huckleberry Finn* (1885) is of course a classic. As social workers, we may well review it for the manner in which it portrays such older evils as slavery, family feuds, and, especially, the perils of a neglected boy with a drunken, abusive father whom no law controlled in those days.

The polemicists were primarily communicators, but they were also observers and social critics, and they were interpreting what they observed in the hope of evoking action.

The Scholar-Reformers

Men like Dickens and Clemens collected impressions, but they did not pretend to do this systematically. Close to them in spirit, somewhat closer to the modern researcher in method, is the group one might label scholar-reformers. Their pursuit of facts was more organized. However, one might well wonder whether they persevered in data collection in order to draw conclusions, or to add to the weight of evidence that would hammer home convictions at which they had already arrived.

Prominent in the history of prison reform is John Howard (1726–90) (Macdonald 1960, p. 6). Serving as sheriff of an English county, he saw men acquitted of a crime, only to be returned to prison for debt—for the food they had eaten while awaiting trial! Stirred by other staggering observations, Howard devoted the remainder of his life to exposing jail conditions in Britain and on the Continent. He counted numbers of men being held, depicted their housing and the food given them, and so forth. Searching for intimate information, he had himself placed in several prisons and hospitals. Indeed, he eventually died of a fever contracted while investigating military hospitals in Russia. Howard stands as an inspiration to all later scholars by demonstrating the power of carefully recorded facts and detailed observations to mobilize social change—at least in the British Parliament of his day.

An American whose achievements surpassed even Howard's was Dorothea Lynde Dix (1802–87). Miss Dix's life is a challenge to all middle-aged retirees. Her dramatic career as muckraker and lobbyist began only after she had already given up operating her private school—supposedly because of ill health! Dix's concern was the mistreatment of the mentally ill. She devoted eight years to traveling early nineteenth-century America, covering sixty thousand miles of primitive roads to enumerate the insane and to describe the conditions under which they were being kept or tethered.

In 1848 she petitioned the Congress for federal aid to help mental patients, since she had enough evidence to be able to estimate that such facilities as were available could not accommodate more than a twelfth of those needing care. She had enormous eloquence in backing her statistics with vivid illustrations, penetrating the bland indifference of the politicians of her day. Who could have believed Dix's work would lead to our system of state hospitals, which themselves were the targets for reform in the 1950s?

> I have myself seen more than *nine thousand idiots, epileptics,* and *insane, in these United States* . . . in *jails*, in *poorhouses*, and in *private dwellings*, there have been hundreds, nay rather thousands, bound with galling chains, bowed beneath fetters and heavy iron balls, attached to drag-chains, lacerated with ropes, scourged with rods, and terrified be-

neath storms of profane execrations and cruel blows [Macdonald 1960, p. 9].

The constructive fanaticism of this noble spinster typifies so many of our predecessors who meddled to others' advantage. They were moved by the passion and compassion one still seeks in social work research. Another, similar, campaigner was Thomas Mott Osborne (1859–1926), who is recalled in connection with his attempts at rehabilitation of felons.

In England, the scholar-reformers were usually much involved in contemporary politics, especially the Fabian Socialists, who also counted George Bernard Shaw (1856–1950), H. G. Wells (1866–1946), and other writers in their number. Outstanding in the group was Beatrice Webb (1858–1943). Born into a wealthy English family, Webb was early involved in the plight of the poor from listening to the discussions of her father's associates among intellectuals and politicians of his day (Cole 1946). She served her youngest apprenticeship as a "visitor," acting as rent collector and manageress of a model tenement, but was driven from that career partly by the smells of the slums (particularly near the common toilets, of which there was only one on each building floor). Later she worked with Charles Booth in his surveys (see below). Eventually, in an overall investigation of the evils of the welfare system, she and her husband, Charles, made a historical survey of the operation of the English Poor Law—a survey which still stands as a scholarly monument. Their research, and their efforts, contributed heavily to the emergence in Britain of the insurance systems we now know as social security.

The Survey Movement

Artists, political philosophers, reformers recur in the intellectual ancestry of social work research. Their motives were often very close to our own. Science, however, also implies zeal for accuracy, and this demands suitable methods. We come next to the survey movement. Both in the advances and the pitfalls it brought with it, the movement is surprisingly contemporary.

An early figure was the Belgian, Frédéric Le Play (1806–82). Le Play reasoned that the way people live is well revealed by where they spend their incomes. Detailed compilations of family expenditures, therefore, should offer a quantified picture of the lives of European workers. Through interviews and direct observations, he compiled workers' budgets. It also occurred to him to cross-check the information he was given for accuracy by questioning neighbors and others who knew the family intimately. (This would now be termed a validity check.) Le Play was not completely original; even before him, citizens of Hamburg charged with administering charity had made surveys of earnings and expenditures of the self-supporting poor. The purpose was to set relief grants at a point below minimal earned income, according to the principle of least eligibility. Le Play extended the studies to a broader group of society, of course. None will fault his conviction that social reform ought be based on detailed knowledge of a society.

A heroic figure in the development of techniques for social surveys was Charles Booth (1840–1916). Many of the gentlemen scholars of nineteenth-century England owed the leisure to pursue their work to inherited incomes. Booth, however, rose from poverty to comfort by his own efforts as merchant and shipowner. The Charity Organization Society movement had been founded in London shortly after our own Civil War. When Booth was a man in his middle years, there was still a great deal of public debate about the causes and possible remedies of poverty. Booth decided to go beyond argumentation to find out directly just who were "the poor," how they lived, and the like. The results of his work from about 1889 to 1897 emerged in the seventeen volumes called *The Life and Labour of the People of London* (1891–1903).

Booth intended to make a complete picture of East London, notable for its slums. He gathered facts about the number of its people, how they earned their livings, the manner of their existence—e.g., numbers of persons per room, availability of running water, toilets and other amenities which are still of interest in housing surveys. The task was ambitious; he went at it with enormous energy and great intelligence. Much of his data came from local officials familiar with the residents of their districts, but these reports were complemented with interviews by Booth's staff. Indeed, he conducted many interviews himself, and eventually moved into East London for a time in order to have the advantage of participant observation. Among the assistants Booth hired, or attracted as volunteers, was the young gentlewoman who combined charitable with scholarly impulses, Beatrice Webb.

Realizing the need to reduce his mass of data to indices one could more easily keep in mind, Booth participated in inventing the field we now call descriptive statistics. For example, he used rough measures of central tendency and correlation coefficients. The eight terms he set up for categorizing people along what we would now call a scale for socioeconomic status are: (A) The lowest class of occasional labourers, loafers, and semi-criminals; (B) Casual earnings—'very poor'; (C) Intermittent earnings, and (D) Small regular earnings (together, the 'poor'); (E) Regular standard earnings—above the line of poverty; (F) Higher class labour; (G) Lower middle class; (H) Upper middle class" (Booth, *Life and Labour*, as cited in Macdonald 1960, p. 7). Especially for refining distinctions in the lower end of the status scale, Booth's listing is more apt for poverty research than modern schemes that distinguish only lower-lower from upper-lower classes.

Like Emile Durkheim (1858–1917), who was engaged at around the same time in bringing sociology out of its era of armchair speculation, Booth was a genius, and his work had enormous impact. He enjoyed—

and suffered—the flattery of imitation. Benjamin Rowntree (1871–1954) did a somewhat similar survey in York, England, in which he was able to demonstrate that appropriately chosen samples do, in fact, permit one to make dependable projections about a total population of interest.

In the United States, the outstanding example of Booth's all-encompassing approach was the investigation which came to be known as the Pittsburgh Survey. The study was led by Paul U. Kellogg (1879–1958), a newspaperman turned social worker through having served for a time as assistant editor of an early journal called *Charities*. The Pittsburgh Survey was conducted from 1909 to 1914, and it aimed at an exhaustive description of the effects of industrialization and urbanization on a modern city. Statistics on the distribution of income, crime, disease, and the like, were tabulated and ingeniously represented in charts, maps, and the other visual aids that have come to be associated with urban research. The enormous study was eventually published in a series of volumes. Its results are said to have been instrumental in reducing the work day to eight hours in major industry, and in abolishing the seven-day work week. In short, Kellogg succeeded to an extent in using the weight of evidence to produce conviction and consequent social reform, although it is doubtful he had much influence on the Fricks, the Mellons, and others whose huge fortunes were being sweated out in Pittsburgh's mills.

The later history of the community survey movement found it spreading across the country, welcomed for the twin purposes of rational social planning and social reform. There was even a social work journal, *Survey*, edited by Kellogg for many years. Unfortunately, with the passage of time, Booth's creation decreased in effectiveness as a means for stimulating social change. The reason lay partly in the inherent limitations of the large-scale survey; diminishing effectiveness also is a fact of life in all social movements.

Community surveys were typically launched, in the first place, in a mood of reform—"Let's get the facts and do something about them." Gradually the data collection became institutionalized and routinized. A typical research department in the Council of Social Agencies of a large midwestern city in the early 1950s was likely to consist of a director, his full-time assistant, and a clerk-typist. The staff occupied themselves with securing lists of people seen by the welfare department, apprehended by the police, or registered with the health department for venereal disease or because of death, and so on. These "cases" were then plotted on huge maps of the city so that the rates (incidence or prevalence) of social problems for each census tract in the city could be computed. For the benefit of consumers who had difficulty reading numbers, there were visual aids, like maps with degrees of shading to indicate density of each problem. It was dangerous to move into a neighborhood whose delinquency rate was such that it was depicted in black.

From correlating indices according to census tract, it was easy to demonstrate for the umpteenth time that all sorts of social problems tended to concentrate in the same part of town. Expectable results reiterated year after year lost their shock value; moreover, they usually added little to what the practitioners already knew. The worst census tracts are intractable. As Sarason (1970, p. xiii) has so aptly put it, "In the end there is the word, whereas in the beginning there was the idea." What began as an intellectual adventure wound down into social bookkeeping.

The scientific limitation of the community survey was inherent in it from the beginning. Imagine designing a study so great in scope as to title it *The Life and Labour of the People of* . . . anywhere? The number of dimensions the human mind can invent is evidently infinite; hence, the *exhaustive* description of any concrete object is impossible. A community survey is inevitably diffuse. One can live with studies like this when a field is new and not much is known. But when knowledge starts to accumulate, broad swathe studies cease to add anything new and appear increasingly superficial. The pressure is on for research that is more refined, more precisely focused to answer pointed questions that have already emerged, more oriented to theoretical issues. The substantive results and methodological advances of the community survey are now standard equipment in the behavioral sciences, although the movement itself has been in eclipse for several decades. However, a recent interest in discovering social indices for measuring the "quality of life" in our metropolises may lead to its reemergence in new dress.

Another offshoot stems from a discovery that was made in the process of conducting community surveys. It was found that when the leadership of a city involved themselves in initiating, funding, and facilitating a survey, they felt more concern about its outcome and were more likely to take action on the basis of its findings. The principle is the same as that in investigatory casework or psychotherapy. So a permutation came into vogue, to be known as the "community self-study." The "expert" brought in to conduct the study tries to elicit maximum local participation in its conduct. Participation is envisaged from the beginning as an early phase of marshaling action. The basic facts about what is wrong in cities are often so glaring that precision in their collection is of less significance than the concern they elicit. Finally, self-studies are also employed to avoid taking action, but this form of social evasiveness is research only by happenstance. Any other committee maneuver might serve as well.

Through the work of Robert Park (1864–1944), Ernest W. Burgess (1886–1966), and others of the Chicago school, the work begun by Booth was used to help construct a model of urban growth and decay, and entered general sociology. In order to constitute a major advance, a specific style of research need not survive unaltered. With this awareness, we shall now mention a group of people not usually credited with contributing to social work research, but who seem very much part of its heritage.

The Clinician-Scholars

Social work knowledge, as noted, has three points of application: general theory, pathology, and therapeutics. Practitioners who spend their lives face to face with clients are well situated to make observations relevant to pathology and especially to therapeutics. The question is whether their observations remain private experience, or are converted by them into rules that find general usefulness in the field. Much depends on the talents and intelligence of the practitioner; much also depends on whether he even tries to articulate what he is learning into general principles—whether he "conceptualizes" it.

The field of social work would have little to transmit to new generations if it had not had some unusual practitioners. They experimented in their work; they appraised the results critically; they tried to distill principles from their observations and those of others; and they were able to articulate the end result in a form from which others might benefit. They were our clinician-scholars. Regardless of whether their methods of fact gathering would survive rigorous criticism by a modern methodologist, what they were doing is clearly in the important traditions of science. One has, for example, only to read a description by Freud (1856–1939) of the steps by which he altered his theories in the light of new evidence (Freud 1953) to acknowledge that he was not only an imaginative genius but a scrupulous scientist.

For decades, the set of techniques we call casework was the heartland of our field. Casework was a long time in evolving—several centuries, as a matter of fact. In 1917 Mary Richmond (1861–1928) published *Social Diagnosis*. Her book sets forth principles for the conduct of what was then termed a "social investigation" of the client family. Richmond integrated her own experiences with those of others, and set down a landmark in the professionalization of social work. Subsequent writers on casework like Gordon Hamilton (1892–1967), Charlotte Towle (1896–1966), Annette Garrett (1898–1957), and Virginia Robinson (1883–   ) were primarily teachers when they made their contributions; they acted as treasurers of knowledge rather than creators of it, but the work of analysis and conceptualization in which they engaged is also to be seen as a kind of research.

Work with face-to-face groups had been in process of development since the days of Toynbee Hall (founded 1885) and Hull House (1889). But, it remained for such products of wisdom research as Grace Longwell Coyle's (1892–1962) *Group Work with American Youth*, published in 1948, and Wilson and Ryland's *Social Group Work Practice*, published the following year, to do the textbook's job of codifying practice in this newer field. Thousands of practitioners have made analogous contributions in the form of journal articles on more limited topics, setting forth their observations and innovations. It is on their collective wisdom that textbook writers rely.

The ideal in a practice field like social work is really in the image of Freud—clinician, theoretician, researcher, and teacher. Few in our field have sustained all these roles. An exemplar is Fritz Redl (1902–   ), who was trained originally in pedagogy and then in psychoanalysis, who made work with severely disturbed children a lifelong preoccupation, and taught social group work for many years. The two books that Redl wrote with David Wineman, *Children Who Hate* (1951) and *Controls from Within* (1952), are models of a type of clinical research. In attempting new strategies of treatment, they contribute not only to therapeutics (e.g., "the life-space interview") but also to the elucidation of ego mechanisms not previously identified and classified. Their studies under social work auspices have been widely read by students of psychoanalysis, child psychiatry, education, and psychology. A number of other social workers have made comparably general contributions, and it is of interest that at this level of discourse distinctions among disciplines lose their relevancy. Experts out of all sorts of backgrounds come together on general theory.

In view of the many commonalities, one may well ask whether social work research has, in fact, made any unique contribution to research method in the behavioral sciences. The answer is not easily given. For one thing, a number of social work researchers are also expert in academic disciplines and have held joint appointments in them. The specific problems to which we address ourselves and the nature of the data with which we deal have at least led to emphases which amount to specializations. An example of this is in the coding of narrative documents (see chapter 5). The availability of case recordings and group records naturally led to the wish to use them for advancing knowledge. Even though narrative documents had previously been categorized and reduced to quantifiable terms for purposes ranging from propaganda analysis to attitude surveys, social work research has carried the art of content analysis to a high level, to meet its peculiar needs.

RESEARCH AS A FIELD OF PRACTICE

Continuities

As was earlier noted, it is typical of a profession, as opposed to a science, that relatively few of its members spend full time on organized research. Research, therefore, is something of a specialty. Yet the world is the same, the people are the same one knows in practice. On entering this new arena, one keeps everything he already knows. The interviewing skills learned for diagnosis and treatment in casework are also relevant to the interview survey. And the knowledge gleaned in organized research is expected to accord with that from all other sources available. The mystique popularly associated with science is not meant to dazzle but to illuminate.

Expectations of the Modern Researcher

There was a time, not long ago, when social workers put their trust in the all-purpose researcher. Armed with the scientific method and what he liked to call his "research-mindedness," he was supposed to be able to advance knowledge in any field he touched. Progress in our own and related disciplines has outmoded the utility expert, for the same reason the community survey lost usefulness. As all the obvious things become known, it is harder to make an increment. To push back the subtler and more complex boundaries of our ignorance requires content expertise as well as method, as in any other science.

Moreover, it is necessary nowadays to be sufficiently versatile that one can fit his method to the problem. In the field of group dynamics, for example, Freed Bales (1951) devoted years to evolving a system for recording group interaction which would apply to all human groups. His instrument, indeed his method of observation, is helpless to pick up the exchanges that go on in a group of aggressive and delinquent ten-year-olds, even if they are willing to remain in the room. The modern behavioral scientist, therefore, is expected to be able to move with some confidence from survey research, to a laboratory experiment, to exploiting mass statistics. He should know many available instruments for data collection and be willing to invent his own if none already fits his needs.

Nor do most sophisticated practitioners believe that "facts speak for themselves." They speak a tongue one is prepared to hear, and to the deaf they say nothing at all. As Darwin noted, all facts speak for or against some doctrine. Hence, the modern researcher is inevitably involved with hypotheses and theoretical advance. The theory may not be at a very high level; it may be still in its formative stages; but it is expected to be present in every study.

Finally, there are many areas of social work research in which it is necessary to be a practitioner in order to sustain creativity. It is nearly impossible to come up with advances in treatment tactics which are both imaginative and realistic when one never sees clients. On the other hand, it is relatively easy to be struck with new insights into group functioning if one is still very actively engaged with groups, as in community organizing or group work. The ideal researcher, therefore, is either still in practice or lives very close to it. He knows the theory that guides practice and his research, and it is very real to him if he wants to contribute to "practice-theory." Many attempts have been made to substitute for this combination, since it takes so long for any person to acquire all the requisite experience and skills. The most familiar substitution is the inter-disciplinary team of researchers and clinicians. All now agree, alas, that the best integration in an interdisciplinary approach seems to come from having two disciplines within a single skull. Medicine has faced similar issues and arrived at about the same conclusions. The most fruitful scientific career seems to include practice, research, and teaching, or alternating among the three.

THE PROCESS OF RESEARCH

What is it like to do research? What does the actual study process look like? Two answers must be given: there is the ideal image, the form in which things are typically reported in scholarly journals; and then there is the way things actually happen. No cynicism is intended. Journal articles are not filled with deceit. The fact is that research, like the rest of living, seldom proceeds according to plan. It would be inefficient for busy readers and wasteful of scarce journal space to recount all the false starts, the backing and filling that researchers customarily undergo, so the reporting follows a fairly standard format (see chapter 12). A won-derfully entertaining account of a study that won the Nobel prize for closing in on the origin of life is given in a book by Watson (1969), one of the prizewinners.

A paradigm of the research process would look like this:

1. A researchable problem is located, sharpened, and related to theory (conceptualized); since this is an applied field, its practical sig-nificance is also stated;
2. The logic by which conclusions will be drawn is specified (study design);
3. Potential subjects of the study are identified (sampling design);
4. Instruments for collecting information from or about the subjects are borrowed from others or created (method of data-collection):
5. Data are collected (study execution);
6. The data are analysed statistically and/or qualitatively (analysis of results);
7. Results are compared with the problem originally posed so that conclusions may be drawn;
8. Larger implications for theory and for practice are inferred;
9. The significant elements of the whole process are summarized into an intelligible report to be disseminated to colleagues.

This is the idealized image. As often as not, one takes two or three tentative steps, but finds the next impossible. For example, all may go swimmingly until one discovers there is no method he can borrow or invent to measure what he wants to measure. Then it becomes necessary to turn back and try a different tack. One may have to recast the statement of the problem into something close to, but not quite the same, as he had initially in mind. Some very meaningful problems prove unapproachable, and we are forced, like disappointed mountain climbers, to leave them to the next generation to tackle. But what we have listed is a fair map of the steps that have to be followed, and pretty much in the order indicated.

It is also a map of this book.

REFERENCES

Bales, R. F. 1951. *Interaction process analysis.* Cambridge, Mass.: Addison-Wesley.

Cole, M. 1946. *Beatrice Webb.* New York: Harcourt, Brace.

Coyle, G. L. 1948. *Group work with American youth.* New York: Harper.

Freud, S. 1953. On psychotherapy. In *Collected papers,* ed. E. Jones, 1: 249–63. London: Hogarth.

Lewin, K. 1948. *Resolving social conflicts.* New York: Harper.

Macdonald, M. E. 1960. Social work research: A perspective. In *Social work research,* ed. N. A. Polansky, pp. 1–23. Chicago: Univ. of Chicago Press.

Miller, R. 1958. An experimental study of the observational process in casework. *Social Work* 3:96–102.

Morris, R. 1971. Preface. In *Encyclopedia of social work,* ed. R. Morris, pp. ix–xv. New York: National Assoc. of Social Workers.

Newcomb, T. M. 1953. The interdependence of social-psychological theory and methods: A brief overview. In *Research methods in the behavioral sciences,* ed. L. Festinger and D. Katz, pp. 1–12. New York: Dryden.

Newstetter, W. I.; Feldstein, M. J.; and Newcomb, T. M. 1938. *Group adjustment—a study in experimental sociology.* Cleveland: School of Applied Social Sciences, Case Western Reserve University.

Polansky, N. A. 1971*a.* *Ego psychology and communication.* Chicago: Aldine-Atherton.

―――. 1971*b.* Research in social work. In *Encyclopedia of social work,* ed. R. Morris, pp. 1098–1106. New York: National Assoc. of Social Workers.

Polansky, N.; Lippitt, R.; and Redl, F. 1950. An investigation of behavioral contagion in groups. *Human Relations* 3:319–48.

Redl, F., and Wineman, D. 1951. *Children who hate.* Glencoe, Ill.: Free Press.

―――. 1952. *Controls from within.* Glencoe, Ill.: Free Press.

Richmond, M. E. 1917. *Social diagnosis.* New York: Russell Sage Foundation.

Rowntree, B. S. 1901. *Poverty: A study of town life.* London: Thomas Nelson.

Sarason, S. B. 1970. Foreword to *A social history of helping services,* by M. Levine and A. Levine, pp. xi–xiii. New York: Appleton-Century-Crofts.

Watson, J. D. 1969. *The double helix.* New York: Atheneum.

Wilson, G., and Ryland, G. 1949. *Social group work practice.* Boston: Houghton Mifflin.

1

Theory Construction and the Scientific Method

Norman A. Polansky

Most of those who work within the guidelines and precepts we call the scientific method are well aware of its proper place in the total enterprise, but this is not true of all. It is easy to become so enthralled with technology as to lose sight of one's goal. It is unfortunate when this happens in any field; it is especially disturbing in social work research, because the needs of those we serve are enormous, and our resources, especially for research, are always thin. So when one meets a virtuoso of trivia who computes medians and rank-difference correlations to five useless decimals, who devotes six months to analyzing data that were patently untrustworthy to begin with, or who slavishly states hypotheses in the null form, then dismay competes with amusement. Even a newcomer picks up the scent of much ado about nothing.

The best way to keep a comfortable grasp on the scientific method is by the handle of what it is meant to achieve. The aim of the game is the discovery of natural laws which can be articulated into bodies of theory. So, let us start this explication with some fundamentals about theory construction that are generally accepted among working scientists. We shall simplify the description as befits an introduction to a much-argued subject. The reader who wants to go further will do well to consult the wise book of Abraham Kaplan, *The Conduct of Inquiry* (1964), with which this writer is in substantial agreement. Other useful references are those of Wallace (1971), Glaser and Strauss (1967), and the well-known work of Beveridge (1950).

THE FUNCTIONS OF THEORY

Psychological Functions

One can draw an analogy between an infant and the investigator whose science is in its infancy. To the infant, all seems a great, buzzing confusion. He hardly knows where he ends and his mother begins. His earliest responses are similarly undifferentiated. A loud noise, a tickled foot, a hunger pang all have the same outcome: he wriggles and screams. As he matures, however, actions become more efficiently matched to stimuli, so there is pulling away from heat, smiling at mother, and so on. At a certain point, the infant anticipates his hunger and asks to be fed by making special noises. By now, the baby's world is acquiring more clarity; he is beginning to master it with conditioned responses which are very much like predictions. The adult's ego is vastly more differentiated with respect to processing stimuli, anticipating, and taking action, but it also operates mostly automatically. What is the function of theory? In a profession dealing with complicated problems, it is the function of theory to help the practitioner perform with conscious attentiveness what he does routinely in ordinary living. Theory helps him process information efficiently to increase his mastery over the world. A good theory simplifies life.

Anyone who has struggled to grasp an unfamiliar theory of human behavior finds it hard to believe that theory simplifies anything. What is the basis for our statement? In the final analysis, all fields of knowledge concern themselves with data from raw experience. But raw experience is mostly chaotic. Scientists assume that there is, in fact, an underlying orderliness in nature, and that the chaos is more apparent than real. A good theory, therefore, serves to reduce the chaos by laying bare the hidden regularities on which we depend to do our work. All this is in line with the positivist position, which regards theory as mental shorthand in which experience is recorded.

Just as there are many ways to go about seeking knowledge, so are there a number of ways to summarize it into a theory. Obviously, some modes of theory construction have proved more efficient than others; not all propositions peddled to the unwary under the label of theory prove equally useful. We can illustrate with a couple of issues. One can achieve a sense that the world is orderly by setting up a system for filing things into mental pigeonholes. People are extroverts, or else they are introverts; they are pyknic, athletic, and asthenic; and so forth. This sort of classificatory scheme is not as useful to social work, certainly, as is a dynamic theory. Any dynamic theory deals with regularities among *sequences of events*, physical, social, or psychological. For example, we may say that when a defense is stripped away, anxiety is likely to show itself; or, that behavior that is consistently unrewarded will become extinguished. These are psychodynamic theories. Propositions about sequences lead to predictions, with their potential for manipulation and control. All theory involves categorizing, but a *dynamic* theory is best suited to the psychological functions we have been describing.

A good theory must also be *empirical*. That is, it must deal with the world external to one's own mind. (We cannot logically prove there is such a world, but we find it useful to assume there is an objective reality.) A rather good test of whether a hypothesis deals with things "out there" is whether or not it could be wrong. Some theories concern themselves mostly with defined relationships. For example, $2 + 2 = 4$ is a proposition that is always true because we have agreed to accept stated conventions about the relations among the symbols. Our only certainty is in the world of the mind. Nature is infinitely more subtle and complex than the thought of men, and an empirical theory accepts the challenge of matching itself against more than its own internal logic. According to the "verifiability theory of meaning," a statement is meaningful only if it is capable of empirical verification. In fact, as Kaplan has pointed out, if deductions made "logically" from theory do not fit what we observe about our world, we are quite justified in questioning the system of logic—as well as the theory (1964, p. 8). So, as a beginning we may say that the brand of theory likely to be useful to social work is *empirical* as well as dynamic.

Social Functions

Along with its usefulness to the individual craftsman, theory serves a number of functions we may label as social. No man can, unassisted, master a whole field of knowledge—i.e., map its boundaries and discover its relevant laws. Freud was a genius, an innovator, and a prodigious worker, but he did not create psychoanalysis single-handed. He cultivated a coterie of colleagues and disciples, if only to seek consensual validation of his formulations. Einstein was also an imaginative genius and a tremendous synthesizer, who progressed from fairly limited studies of color to insights into the fundamental relations among light, energy, and matter ($e=mc^2$). All the practical work of subjecting his theory of relativity to the test of external reality was done by others.

Not only is it necessary to have the help of others to build an extensive theory, but, for most scholars, even if one could do it alone, it would not be as much fun. The joys of show-and-tell would be missing; there would be none of the competition that motivates much scientific work. So that there can be more than one player, indeed, so that there can be teams of players, an essential function of theory is to provide a scoreboard on which all can follow the game.

Another social function lies in the fact that the fruits of inquiry are meant to be generally useful—not only to those who discover them, but to all men. To be sure, this attitude involves a value which all do not share. Huge corporations guard trivial technical inventions for profit; concern for secrecy is so great that many processes in the chemical industry are not even patented. It is not essential to successful knowledge seeking that one believe it to be for the common good, even though most major scholars have lived and died by that conviction. More to the point is the fact that control over important parts of our environment requires the coordinated effort of large groups of men and women. Recently there was a threat that several of our astronauts would be marooned in a crippled space module. Three thousand technicians were immediately set to work to ready a rescue mission. How many people would it take to mount a nationwide effort to eliminate child neglect? One of the shortcomings in President Johnson's skirmish with poverty was its lack of a coordinating theory, and most of those at work in it had no dynamic theory at all. It has been observed in psychiatric hospitals that when a staff is following a consistent theory, even one that is not quite accurate, the hospital is more likely to cure patients than are the many places that exist without an "overall philosophy" (as their treatment theory is miscalled). So a mutually accepted theory helps coordinate services which are offered by groups of people; and, as noted, it guides the joint search for new knowledge.

Science, then, is a *social undertaking*. Many of the elements of what we call the "scientific method" follow from this fact. Laws must be intelligible to others (communicability); observations and the methods of observation must be able to be shared (interobserver reliability); studies and their results must be able to be repeated by other investigators (replicability). Communicability, reliability, replicability—these are all often treated as if they were matters of aesthetics among journal editors, or moral questions. They ought be neither, for they follow simply from the fact that science is a social process.

Of course, the fact that studies are done by people, with other people, for other people brings all-too-human phenomena in its wake. Scientists seek fame during their own lifetimes, and many manifest a greed for immortality resembling the futuristic narcissism seen in politicians. Valuable time and energy have been wasted on unrequited claims to priority. Whole schools of thought are cultivated into existence by academic entrepreneurs eager to acquire followings and reputations. For such people, it is better to be at the center of a well-known controversy than to find anything out, and their claims to fame are often based on garbling principles originally discovered by Freud many decades since. Such happenings are beside the point with regard to what science is all about. But they are part of the human condition, and the student is naïve who lets himself be taken in by pseudotheoreticians. Adlai Stevenson once remarked that American journalists "separate the wheat from the chaff, and publish the chaff." Sophistication about theory construction will help the student guard against wallowing in chaff.

CONSTITUENTS OF A THEORY

Most of the terms to be discussed in the following pages have been defined variously, depending on which authority one follows. However, it is important for the newcomer to research to start with the way terms are generally used, regardless of precise nuances. We begin by emphasizing that a theory is not the same as external reality; indeed, it may prove not to correspond at all to the world "out there." A theory is a system of *ideas* put together in a coherent way; hence it includes rules for relating its ideas both to external reality and to each other.

The Ideal Image of a Theory

Ideally, a *general theory* seeks to embrace all, or a substantial part, of the phenomena of a whole field of discourse. Again, ideally, it is formed like a pyramid—resting on specific facts at its base, with abstractions signifying these facts next above, and generalizations that are increasingly comprehensive as one approaches the apex. The grand achievements of a successful science are expressed in a few terse propositions writ large atop the pyramid. The goal is to be able to understand, even predict, most of what goes on that is of interest to the science from a few major laws.

Fortunately, a theory may be very revealing even if it does not yet meet this standard. There are propositions which, while not yet fulfilling the grand design, nevertheless succeed in synthesizing substantial segments of discourse. Take the statement, "Power is a goal-structured field; therefore, most average expectable people will be motivated to move upward in it." When this is borne in mind, a number of observations fall neatly into place: the resemblance between the announcement of an engagement on the society page and the report of blood lines in a racing form; the proclivity of those with power to show they have it; the fact that the behavior of high-power members of children's groups is contagious to other members, who use imitation as a form of substitute social movement (Lippitt et al., 1968). There are many propositions in social science which are limited in scope but very helpful. Pleading their respectability, Merton (1967) has called them "theory of the middle-range."

Oddly enough, a proposition is often valuable even if it is not precisely true. That smoking "causes" lung cancer is now generally accepted. The specific carcinogenic factor remains obscure. Probably it is not the free nitrogen inhaled through a cigarette, for nitrogen makes up four-fifths of the air we breathe all the time. Not all heavy smokers get cancer; some get heart disease. Yet the statement, although imprecise, obviously points in the right direction. Eventually the details of the process will stand revealed, and meanwhile it is wise to forego smoking.

Kurt Lewin (1951, p. 21) referred to the business of honing and further specifying propositions as the "method of gradual approximation." Most scientists operate well below the genius level, and most of our time is devoted to polishing our insight lenses. Gradual approximation is the major activity of what Kuhn (1970) has termed "normal science." Newton had no notion of the possible transmutation of mass into energy, but Newtonian mechanics has proved perfectly competent for building enormous suspension bridges. Because personality is usually all of a piece, you can help a person give up a symptom, and, even if you do not really know why the treatment worked, its benefits may generalize to other aspects of his life. Which is all that rescues all the bad therapists in our midst! We may take it for granted that most of our theories in social work are approximations at best, but this does not mean they are not serviceable. If nothing else, they coordinate group effort.

So theories of the middle range, and even half-baked theories, are accepted, *faute de mieux*. One job for social work research is to put the broad generalizations of practitioners under scrutiny in order to pinpoint the circumstances in which they are true—and those in which they are not. The effort to link clinical observations with research findings sometimes reveals deeper regularities which underlie both.

Concepts

A concept may be defined as a name or symbol given to a group of objects, people, or events having something in common. Students gain the impression that the development of concepts must be very difficult; in fact, it is very easy for most who are capable of graduate work. Asked what label to apply to a chair, a table, a sideboard, a tea cart, one would say "furniture." More specifically, one could say "dining room furniture." Joy, happiness, gladness, affection are all "cheerful emotions." If anger is added to the list, we might call them simply "emotions." We see, then, that concepts are abstractions which everyone of normal intelligence uses, in our culture. Contrary to some older anthropological theorizing, there is reason to believe that members of preliterate tribes also use them (Cole et al., 1971). Concepts differ in how abstract they are, and breadth of coverage is accompanied by loss of detail as we move up the scale of abstractness. Sex and age are common concepts in sociological studies; they are also at a very low level of abstraction. Many of us wonder if they deserve to be dignified in theories, or if they should not be treated simply as descriptive adjectives. Finally, we should note that in a dynamic theory the concepts that are of interest deal with events.

Concepts are the basic building blocks of theory. Inventing concepts is not hard. What *is* hard is finding just those abstractions that are most efficient for facilitating prediction and mastery over a wide range of events. Here is work for genius.

Operational Definition

Most sophisticated scientists of this generation accept that every concept embedded in a system of theory requires two definitions—a conceptual one and an operational one. The *operational* definition consists of the steps, actions, "operations" one performs in order to relate the concept to events in the real world. For example, a mother is upset about whether

her infant is ill, and decides to check his temperature. (Temperature happens to vary with circumstances, and so may be called a *variable*.) What does she do? She feels the baby's forehead with the palm of her hand and discovers his skin is warm to touch; that means it is warmer than hers. She has now tried one possible operational definition but believes it is too crude, since it has left her more anxious than informed.

The mother now takes a further step, in which she exploits the familiar fact that most metals expand when their temperatures rise. In her medicine cabinet, she happens to have a thin column of mercury. Conveniently, it is enclosed in a glass tube into which it was sealed at a known air pressure (sea level). The mother takes this gadget and inserts the mercury end into the infant's rectum, holds it there for several minutes, and then looks to see how far the mercury has expanded along a numerical scale which is etched onto the glass vial. The mercury has reached a point marked 102, and mama now telephones this somewhat frightening fact to her baby's physician. For she has operationally defined the infant's body heat, using a thermometer.

The notion of operational definition was urged earlier in this century by the Harvard physicist Bridgman (1927). Eager to break with a tradition of seeking Platonic "essences," which was still confusing theoreticians, Bridgman proposed that any concept is simply a label for the measurements it entails. Operationalism had a great vogue in the behavioral sciences, and was represented by such statements as, "Intelligence is whatever intelligence tests test." Some adhered to this variety of rank empiricism out of impatience with all the obsessive, hairsplitting verbosity that preceded it in academe; some, because it seemed innovative and grandly pragmatic; and some, naturally, because they were too simpleminded to absorb theory at a high order of abstraction and complexity.

Fortunately, even though no funeral announcements have been published, the fashion has passed on. Taken to its logical conclusion, radical operationalism is simply silly. As Gustav Bergmann has asked, if one moves his apparatus to another part of the room, where presumably it works a tiny bit differently, is he now measuring (ergo, defining) a new concept (Kaplan 1964, p. 41)? Obviously, even the worried mother who lays no claim to being a scientist has something more enduring in her mind than that. Indeed, she uses two *alternative* operational definitions of body heat: the inserting of metal, and the laying on of hands.

Operational definition, then, need not be as simple as directly touching or looking; it can involve a chain of logic and require several steps. Its purpose, however, is always to relate the "world out there" to the idea we have in our minds. Two questions now follow naturally. How do you invent an operational definition? And, how do you decide whether the way you are linking your concept to reality is a good one? The latter question—how well an operational definition fits its concept—is the issue of *validity*, and will be dealt with in chapter 3. Finally, there are symbols used in theory whose presence in a causational process is inferred. Such ideas are called *constructs* or, with a somewhat different nuance, *intervening variables*. Take the sequence in which a man was spurned by a woman he loved but, with the passage of time, "forgot" her and went on to others. One day he came upon her unexpectedly, felt dizzy, and nearly fainted. It now became obvious that the conflictual feelings were there all the time; the "forgetting" was actually an instance of defensive detachment in the service of repression. Although *repression* may not have been directly observed, we have reason to believe it occurred. In this particular example, the concept *repression* is used as a construct.

Conceptual Definition

In contrast to operational definition, *conceptual definition* deals with the relationship between the concept we have in mind and the other concepts that make up the theory of which it is a part. The old formulation that the ego is the part of the personality that mediates between the id, the superego, and external reality is not a hypothesis. It is a conceptual definition, just like saying $2 + 2 = 4$. On the other hand, saying that the superego is the part of the personality most readily dissolved in alcohol is an operational definition. Any substantial theory necessarily involves many concepts. As we commented earlier, some of these are linked in nature so that their connections have to be discovered, but there are other linkages consisting of conventions. We term these conceptual definitions.

Hypotheses

Assuming we are not dealing with mere conventions, we can now define what we mean by a hypothesis. A hypothesis is a proposition linking two or more concepts. In the kind of theory that interests us, the propositions typically have an "if . . . then . . ." form, such as, if A happens, then B will happen—or, at least, B is very likely.

Like concepts, hypotheses vary in abstraction and generality. The statement that people who are made anxious by sexual feelings are very likely to be prudish is less general than the proposition that anxiety-laden impulses are likely to be defended against. Hypotheses also vary in form, even in the implicit images they convey. Most members of the writer's generation were taught to look for *cause-effect* relations. We would say that high cohesiveness causes a group to try to achieve uniformity of opinions. That male alcoholics frequently have childish, long-suffering, but accusatory wives was also seen as a cause-effect phenomenon, with the wife exacerbating her husband's problems. The cause-effect model, however, does not fit all instances in which two variables are associated.

This is true of intelligence and social class—how are we to decide which "causes" which? For a time, therefore, thinking in terms of cause-effect was given up by most social scientists.

An idea which was substituted was the notion of dependence. Speaking mathematically, we have *dependence* when a change of state in *A* is regularly accompanied by a change in state in *B*. The two variables can be in a roughly symmetrical dependence, as in the covariation of poverty and family breakdown. Or the two may have an interdependence which is *a*symmetrical. For example, it does not seem likely that juvenile delinquency influences maternal coldness very much, but the converse is highly believable. Another way to describe the association is to call child neglect the *independent* variable, and the child's delinquency the *dependent*. Situations of mutual interdependence among variables are common in nature; one is better not to be locked into the rigid idea that, "The cue-ball hits the eight-ball into the corner pocket."

One version of strict determinism, which believes there are no accidents in nature, is to assume that for every cause there is an effect, for every effect there is a cause, and that this is a one-to-one correspondence which must eventually be teased out. Yet we also know that the same outcome can have varied causes, a point beautifully illustrated by Selye's conception of the general adaptation syndrome (1956). A severe injury, a heart attack, an emotional shock may each set off nearly identical physiological responses, including a dangerous drop in blood pressure. There is also the Freudian notion of *overdetermination*: a long-time symptom will serve more than one psychological purpose. So there were good reasons for relinquishing our infatuation with seeking "single cause—single effect" relationships.

Yet this conceptual model still serves a useful purpose, even when it is used with reservations. It underlies, really, the familiar logic of the experiment in science. And, as Lazarsfeld (1945, p. viii) has commented, the controlled experiment "is really the central concept for any systematic thinking on problems of social causation." Even to understand unique events we must perform hypothetical controlled experiments. "If we want to know what the Battle of Marathon did to Greek history or how a specific radio advertisement influenced the buying habits of an individual listener, we shall have to visualize what might have happened under different conditions" (p. ix). It may pay to pursue unitary cause-effect connections, therefore, even though one knows he will not always find them. Meanwhile, hypotheses can be stated in any of the forms we have indicated.

Laws and Theories

The discovery of one or more natural laws is the capstone of any scientist's career. What is a law? Like a dynamic hypothesis, it states an expectable relationship between two or more classes of events. However, in the generally accepted meaning, two additional things must also be true: (*a*) a hypothesis is not elevated to the status of a law unless it states a connection of some *generality*. Statements about limited ranges of events are not dignified as "laws," except in jest. (e.g., Polansky's Law states that research costs more, takes longer, and finds out less than you plan for. This is only a specific instance of the general law of the futility of effort.) (*b*) The relationship stated as a law must be very dependable and have been observed repeatedly.

The term *theory* is used loosely. Often it is simply a synonym for a hunch. A group leader may announce, "I have the theory that Tony won't be here next week." For most scientists, however, the term refers to a body of concepts, each with its operational and conceptual definitions, which are articulated into a set of laws sufficient to cover a range of discourse. Freud's personality theory is very general, in this sense; a more limited theory, a theory of the middle range, might be the set of ideas organized by Festinger (1957) around the notion of cognitive-dissonance. Within Freudian psychology, Festinger's line of research would be placed within ego psychology, and subsumed further under studies of the synthetic function of the ego.

Criteria of a Good Theory

As was earlier mentioned, social work needs theory that is empirical as well as dynamic. Another criterion of good theory would be relevance. And, should it be questioned how relevance may be judged, one can only answer, with apologies to Portia, that the quality of relevance is not strained.

If a theory is to simplify life, it should fit the *rule of parsimony*. Parsimony in theory means that one should add propositions grudgingly. The same thought is embodied in the principle called "Occam's razor": "That entities should not be multiplied beyond necessity" (Cohen and Nagel 1934, p. 395). Before proposing a new concept or a new law, one asks: Cannot this discovery be explained by theory already in existence? Is there not an existing law which might be modified to embrace not only the new finding, but also what was previously known? Occam's razor prunes toward the magnificent terseness and pyramidal shape which are the marks of parsimonious theory.

By way of contrast, we have the ad hoc hypothesis, which is just what it sounds like, an explanation advanced on the spur of the moment to account for limited results. There are "Discussions" appended to grossly empirical investigations consisting of long paragraphs saying, "It could have been this . . . It could have been that . . ." Belatedly, the investigator is trying to rationalize not only what he found, but why he looked for it in the first place. Ad hoc explanation is the mark of the dilettante; far from simplifying thought, it adds clutter. It was not just personal pique which led Freud to invite a series of schismatics to leave the psychoanalytic movement when he felt their pet theories were introducing more complexity than advance (Polansky 1971). All the ambitious clinicians who seek to erect a general theory on the shaky foundation of a single advance in therapeutics are also violating the rule of parsimony.

But one can also err in the opposite direction, by jumping to premature conclusions, overlooking the complexities in nature in our search for grand laws. The aphorism of Oscar Wilde comes to mind, "Truth is never pure and rarely simple." Oversimplified theory has the effect of satisfying curiosity when it ought to be whetting it. Premature closure conflicts with another criterion advanced for assessing theory, its fruitfulness. A theory's *fruitfulness* refers to the degree to which it opens new vistas, and stimulates bursts of creative work. The *psychological* study of instincts, for example, had come to a drab standstill until the work on ethology of Lorenz (1961) and some fellow biologists imbued it with new life. Kaiser (Fierman 1965) advanced the principle that the key to successful therapy is whatever will help the client stand behind his words. His idea stimulated the writer's interest in *verbal accessibility* as a character trait, and led to a series of studies of its etiology, dynamics, and consequences (Polansky 1971; Polansky, Borgman, and DeSaix 1972).

Hypothesis Generation

Fruitfulness has much to do with another issue: How are new hypotheses generated? A fruitful theory is one that rapidly gives rise to a series of hypotheses which seem worth verifying toward the end of reducing a whole segment of reality to a new orderliness. In the hope of ensuring this will happen, it has occurred to some scientists that if all theory were, like physics, cast in the form of mathematical relations, new hypotheses could be derived by simply solving equations. The calculus certainly did a great deal for physics; and vice versa!

So the machinery of mathematical logic is hauled in, and the demand is that all theory be cast to follow the form of a *hypothetico-logico-deductive* system. Such elegance requires that the investigator, especially if he is a doctoral student, phrase his magnum opus in the form of "Postulate 1 . . . ; Postulate 2 . . . ; Derivation A . . . ," and so forth.

There is, alas, not yet a single example that this kind of obsessive rumination has advanced any social science. Our best ideas do not come from derivation as much as inspiration. And no one knows, really, how insights leading to brilliant hypotheses can best be stimulated. There are bright, earnest, mathematically gifted investigators who have little insight, and no amount of formal elegance rescues their work from routine plodding. On the other hand, there are scientists who begrudge the time they work, but who spin fascinating hypotheses, and they live in leisure on this gift, like well-paid entertainers. Like the rest of life, science really is unfair, even to hypothetico-logico-deductive systems. Social work research may well eschew such elegance for the foreseeable future.

Having faced the fact that brilliant hypotheses are works of genius, where do the rest of us get them? Logical *deduction*, reasoning from the general to the particular, is one means, of course. Another is the obverse, *induction*, reasoning from the particular to the general. In a recent study of the role of the maternal personality in determining the child's standard of care, it was found that the less competent mothers are likely also to have the less successful husbands. This implies that it is not common for poor mothering to be compensated by superior fathering; such children are doubly deprived. It also suggests a much broader possibility, namely, that people who choose each other for marriage are likely to be very similar in their emotional maturity, whatever the variations in surface manifestations between them (Polansky, Borgman, and DeSaix 1972). Those who research for a profession suffer the disadvantage of being too involved to sustain theoretical preoccupations to the extent possible for those who are in "pure" science; they enjoy the advantage, however, of being rather consistently bombarded by raw data. Hence, induction seems the method of hypothesis generation most apt to social work research.

Conceptualizing is a term tossed about in social work. It refers to the process of phrasing a problem or an event that concerns us in the concepts and laws of a (usually) already well-established general theory. Conceptualization requires some talent for relating the ephemeral and concrete to the enduring and more abstract. Essentially, it demands that the investigator be familiar with one or more general theories possibly relevant to his area—and that he believe generalization is worth the effort.

Much else might be added concerning issues faced by a serious theoretician. The roles of metaphors and models, the influences of metatheory and metaphysics, all have their place. Hopefully, however, what has been given will serve as a compact introduction to the terminology and some of the issues involved. Most of the issues are readily understandable to those social workers who find such airy problems a welcome change, say, from dealing with child abuse. It must by now be clear, too, that the distinction between "basic" as opposed to "applied" research is far more evident to some who grant funds than it is to serious scientists. On the one hand, we can see that a study that is severely limited in scope, kept at a low level of generality, and determined to be immediately usable, might be called "applied." On the other hand, all problems impinge on fundamental scientific concerns. The Wright brothers, and Thomas Edison, did "basic" research. Is it possible that anyone who does not have to restrain himself from basic research ought not be entrusted with any investigation at all? Especially in a field as complex as social work?

PROBLEM FORMULATION

Like most aphorisms, the saying that "a problem well formulated is half solved" is more pleasing than accurate. It does serve to clarify that effort spent on defining *what is to be studied* is a significant phase of the whole research process. Properly choosing and clarifying one's objectives do not promise certain research success; but poor problem formulation guarantees disappointment.

As well as in the world of reality, research also begins in dreams and nightmares—a fact that seems unbelievable when reading the tedious prose in which it is reported. Of course, the typical origin of questions for study varies with the field. More than in most "academic" fields, current reality determines the issues that engage social work researchers. The desperate needs of our clients and our ignorance in the face of them immerse us constantly in questions begging solution. All that are needed to motivate us are a modicum of sensitivity and skepticism about principles being taken for granted. The challenge, therefore, is not so much to find something that needs work as to phrase it into a question that *can be studied with hope of adding to relevant knowledge.* This is not easy, and, to a large extent, adeptness in problem formulation requires a talent that can be cultivated rather than a skill that can be taught. However, there are some guidelines that do help.

An Ideal Problem

What would a promising problem for study look like? Ideally, it would be cast in theoretical terms (i.e., conceptualized) so that its results might contribute not only to one agency or community but to theory for the field at large, and even beyond social work. At the same time, because this is research for a profession, the hope is to have results that are of immediate, or almost immediate, relevance to helping clients. In most academic fields, when it comes time to report a study, the rationale consists simply of describing the theory that led to the research. In social work research, there are ideally twin rationales: the immediate, or "practical" occasion for the study; and its potential, theoretical significance. There are those, even in the social sciences, who think this an impossibly difficult demand. Perhaps they overlook the extent to which our major conceptualizers dealt also with very practical matters, as Durkheim (1897) did in his study of suicide. Similarly, one can make a descriptive study of clients who prematurely break off treatment, or one can try to develop a theoretical framework within which this would be only one phenomenon to be explained (Shyne, Kogan, and Wasser 1957; Ripple 1957). Naturally, the latter type of study is sometimes possible only after a descriptive study has been done. But as Breedlove (1972, p. 55) also points out, "The underlying problem for professional practice, curriculum development as well as evaluative research, is the failure to give serious attention to the development and testing of practice theory."

What else do we look for in assessing a research proposal? It is not enough that a question be posed well. It must be susceptible to answer. This means it must be so limited in scope that the investigator has reason to expect he can achieve results within the time and resources at his disposal; it must also be limited enough that its chief terms can be related to reality, operationally defined. Hypotheses like "Man is essentially a loving being" do not seem to lend themselves to research. The necessity that one's question be so formulated that it is susceptible to an empirical answer has been generally discussed by Selltiz et al. (1959); and Ripple (1960) has related the principle to the realities of social work.

Nonresearchable Questions

Our positive guides to problem formulation are broad and, of course, too general to be of much help. Fortunately, it is possible to be more explicit on the negative side. What sorts of questions do *not* lend themselves to empirical research? Here is a partial list.

1. Matters of definition. It has been remarked that the question, 2 + 2 =? is not susceptible to empirical testing. By agreement, we have accepted that $2 + 2 = 4$. When the same issue is expressed as $(x + y)^2 = ?$, however, one may have to check the impulse that the answer this time is not simply a convention learned in high school! The same is true of questions that add up to, "Is it valid to regard mothers of delinquents as delinquogenic?" or, "How do tramps differ from hobos?" (Any way they want to.) A cue that his question simply concerns definitions is the researcher's fantasy that absolute certainty will be found.

2. Questions of values. "Is it worthwhile to keep malformed babies alive?" The answer is obviously a value judgment. How about, "What is the cost/benefit ratio of services that accompany relief?" This sounds more practical with adumbrations to good words like accountability thrown in, until a small voice whispers: (*a*) The cheapest solution is to let the poor starve to death; even administering relief involves a value judgment; (*b*) It is ridiculous to talk about cost/benefit ratios when the cost is to one group (taxpayers) and the benefit is to another (clients), and the two are in very, very different situations!

3. Questions with only one acceptable answer. Not many agency executives can accept a negative answer to the question most often posed, "Are we doing any good?" One might as well let the staff vote. If the clients are still there, and their problems are still there, one has to keep trying to help them. Answers that just destroy the effort to help are psychologically unacceptable. Other questions are logically unanswerable, at least in the *form* in which they are posed. "Is delinquency preventable?" Basic to our whole theory of probability is the notion that, in principle, *anything*

is possible. Even when a multimillion dollar demonstration fails, all that is shown is that this staff, using this technique, with these clients, did not succeed. Very often, a question has only one logical answer, but even experts fail to notice. Studying a preliterate group in Liberia, Cole and his associates (1971, p. 213) ask, "Is evidence from ethnographic analysis relevant to understanding individual psychological processes?" This is silly. What would it mean if one were to say, "No, never, of course not!"

4. Questions of insidious intent. A local fund-raising body has decided to merge two agencies, but first they call in a researcher. Question: "What savings will be effected by a merger?" Answer: "Fire one executive, but raise the salary of the one remaining and hire him two assistants." Research is supposed to go beyond common sense, but it certainly is no substitute for it, nor for the willingness to make decisions.

5. Matters susceptible to factual answers but not feasible for study. Some matters are, in principle, able to be studied, but they are beyond us because the necessary technology does not exist at the time we want it. Then it is up to the investigator either to develop new methods of data collection himself, or else to abandon the problem. It is because so many blocks in our road to knowledge are of this sort that technological breakthroughs are greeted with excitement by scientists, even if their significance is not at all apparent to outsiders. Every method which will be described in later chapters was, in its time, a new development; the most mundane were once exciting.

There are other bases of nonfeasibility, many of which will also become obvious later in the book. If the researcher cannot find a way to get the cooperation from the subjects that he needs, his study may be washed out. Some studies cost too much in time and money to be within the grasp of most investigators, and certainly of most graduate students. There is even the study that takes so much out of one that he never wants to repeat it himself, and he notices no one else replicates it either. Even Bertrand Russell (1951) complained that never again, after his work with Whitehead on the *Principia Mathematica*, was he able to undertake serious effort in mathematical logic—the field he did so much to invent!

Fortunately, most serious researchers easily evade these caveats, designing studies of problems that are meaningful and feasible. When his field is well enough advanced, the researcher phrases his problem in conceptual terms, and in the form of an hypothesis; when it is not, he may start with a fairly simple question. The thing to bear in mind is that high-level conceptualization may obscure the fact that one is dealing in nonsense; nor does good, plain English guarantee he is not. Finally, it is a good idea to see whether, before beginning any study, one can articulate what it is about in a single declarative sentence. If this proves impossible, it is very likely the researcher either has not decided, or does not know, what he is about.

PROGRAMMATIC RESEARCH

Sooner or later, a responsible scientist recognizes that conducting a single study, unrelated to his other work, is like tossing a rock in a pond. It is not that it makes no difference at all; it is that it makes so little difference as to be hardly worth doing. It used to be customary to end a study with some variation of, "And thus, we see, more research is needed . . ." In fields still as thinly staffed as social work research, if one does not stoop to retrieve his own gauntlet, himself, no one else picks up the challenge. So, it is a sign of maturity in both the scientist and his science when problems are increasingly formulated in terms of a program, or a potential program of studies. A *program* consists of a group of studies interlocked in such fashion that they lead to increasing depth and comprehensiveness in theory, and in study design.

A program may be pursued by an investigator working alone, by an investigator and his students, by a group of researchers, or even by colleagues who keep up with each other's work from distant parts of the world. There has by now been a number of research programs in social work research. We have even had a far-sighted and influential funder of research, Charles Gershenson, who persuaded the government to make a few open-ended research grants to established investigators when he was director of research for the Children's Bureau. Examination of the various ways studies are articulated into programs also serves to illustrate the process of problem formulation.

1. Increasing *abstraction* and *generality*. How are laws of increasing generality arrived at? One way is by the demonstration that a particular finding is but one instance of a more basic issue. An example which will be familiar to many is the work by Adorno and others, *The Authoritarian Personality* (1950). The authors' initial question was whether there was anything distinctive about the personalities of those who hate Jews. They found that anti-Semites did not confine their disfavors; they were likely to be suspicious of all racial and religious groups outside their own, a pattern labeled "ethnocentric." Why the xenophobia? An even more generalized scale was developed which picks up a set of rigid, unconsciously bitter and power-obsessed traits the authors aptly term "authoritarian," and it was found that ethnocentrism is but one expression of generalized authoritarianism. By now, the pattern perceived was at such depth that there was speculation whether, in fact, one would not find extreme left-wingers (e.g., Communists) resembling right-wingers (e.g., Fascists) on this set of traits. Further pursuit of the question, Why? led from social psychology to psychoanalytic theory. The authoritarian personality surely has much in common with the paranoid character (Polansky 1971); the data on their early life experiences suggest the need for studies in the theory of object relations. What we see in this sequence, then, is the push

toward more and more fundamental questions through repeatedly asking, Why? This is what Lewin had in mind with his notion of gradual approximation in theory and empirical work.

Another way to establish generality is by repeating one's own or another's study, but with changing samples. Thus, Kadushin and Wieringa (1960) replicated in Holland a study Thomas, Polansky and Kounin (1955) had done in Detroit, and found Dutch college students used substantially similar cues in assessing the motivations of a potential helping person.

2. Increasing *specificity* through control. The notion that each cause has a single effect is not really tenable, but it does encourage the search for precision about relationships through increasing control over what are termed "extraneous variables"—other factors that clutter the picture and make it hard to draw clear conclusions. The aim in "introducing controls" is to eliminate as many extraneous variables as possible. Festinger, Schachter, and Back (1950) did a classic field study in a housing project. In one setting it was found that the more socially cohesive the members of a court, the more their attitudes on a relevant issue were uniform. But, in a field study there are always many possible interpretations of the reasons for any correlation. In this instance, causal direction was unknown. Had people in the highly cohesive courts become more friendly as they found they agreed on things ("Birds of a feather flock together")? Or—a more interesting possibility—did cohesiveness give rise to spontaneous pressures in the group to achieve consensus? To check the latter hypothesis, Back (1951) conducted a laboratory experiment. He found that if groups are substantially matched to begin with, and their cohesiveness is then manipulated experimentally, the more cohesive groups do, in fact, strive harder to effect uniformity of opinions.

The shift from the field study to the laboratory is only one way specificity may be striven for. Other forms of control include matching of cases while sampling, partial correlational techniques, improvement of measurement instruments, and so forth.

3. Pursuit of the varied *determinants* of a dependent variable of interest. Programs of research may also strive to answer, What are the factors that influence how much X is present? Focusing on a variable that is reasonably univocal, the aim is to specify the things that affect it. Geismar (1973) recently published the latest in a series concerned with "family functioning," a concept for which he and his colleagues have developed an extensive measurement technique. The latest book reports the influence of racial, class, and other influences on family functioning among a large group of young families in Newark, New Jersey.

4. Pursuit of the consequences of an independent variable of interest. A program may take an obverse tack to that above, and ask What *other*

things are determined by X? What, for example, happens to the children of drug addicts? What are all the effects of urbanization?

5. Checking out and *improving a measurement technique*. A very famous series of studies in social work research was conducted by Hunt, Kogan (1952), and others at the New York Community Service Society in the 1950s. Its aim was to develop a valid scale for measuring change among clients seen in casework. Such a scale was obviously needed in order for a series of other questions to be answered—e.g., What *proportion* of clients are helped, and how much? What treatment *methods* are most effective? Which *kinds of clients* are able to be helped by methods currently in use? And so forth. The necessity of breakthroughs in instrumentation for progress in many scientific areas has been noted. Therefore, it is quite expectable that we would find whole programs with methodological advance as their major objective.

There are mixed patterns in which studies are linked programmatically. Most large-scale programs include instrument development, for example, as at least a minor theme. But perhaps these examples will suffice for an image of what this level of research planning is like. It epitomizes the whole scientific enterprise.

POSTSCRIPT

This chapter began with an analogy between the development of the infant's ego and the evolution of a science. The relatively normal process of learning to cope with oneself in one's environment requires at least some organization, looking ahead, controlling impulses. As with any normal ego operation, however, these functions may become pathologically exaggerated when used in the service of defense. The severe obsessive-compulsive, after all, is a very anxious person. Aware that much of his energy is tied up in maintaining defenses, he peers fearfully ahead, trying to foresee and prepare, lest he be struck by an emergency which will make demands he cannot meet. To many, therefore, it must appear that a science is simply a group-rationalized obsession, with most methods serving the function of compulsive rituals. Not only is this possible but, as we have emphasized, it can easily become true.

That a process can be exaggerated into a symptom does not mean it ought to be eliminated. How can one preserve the imaginativeness and relaxed willingness to expose oneself to new experience that leads to incidental learning, while gaining the efficiency that comes from careful collection of facts, which are then processed in logical, communicable sequences? "This is a problem which cannot be solved by the erection of procedures into defensive maneuvers. But neither does the research worker propose to revert to a reassuring, infantile world of undifferentiated gen-

eralizations and magical solutions in the face of a chaotic environment"
(Polansky 1952, p. 152).

This chapter has laid out the mission and some of the strategy of the
scientific method. For tactics, *vide infra*.

REFERENCES

Adorno, T. W.; Frenkel-Brunswik, E.; Levinson, D. J.; and Sanford, R. N.
1950. *The authoritarian personality.* New York: Harper.
Back, K. W. 1951. The exertion of influence through social communica-
tion. *Journal of Abnormal and Social Psychology* 46:9–23.
Beveridge, W. I. B. 1950. *The art of scientific investigation.* New York:
Random House.
Breedlove, J. L. 1972. Theory development as a task for the evaluator.
In *Evaluation of social intervention*, ed. E. J. Mullen and R. R. Dump-
son, pp. 55–70. San Francisco: Jossey-Bass.
Bridgman, P. W. 1927. *The logic of modern physics.* New York: Mac-
millan.
Cohen, M. R., and Nagel, E. 1934. *An introduction to logic and scientific
method.* New York: Harcourt, Brace.
Cole, M.; Gay, J.; Glick, J. A.; and Sharp, D. W. 1971. *The cultural con-
text of learning and thinking.* New York: Basic Books.
Durkheim, E. 1966. Orig. 1897. *Suicide: A study in sociology.* New York:
Free Press of Glencoe.
Festinger, L. 1957. *A theory of cognitive dissonance.* Stanford, Calif.:
Stanford Univ. Press.
Festinger, L.; Schachter, S.; and Back, K. 1950. *Social pressures in infor-
mal groups.* New York: Harper.
Fierman, L. B. 1965. *Effective psychotherapy: The contribution of Hell-
muth Kaiser.* New York: Free Press of Glencoe.
Geismar, L. L. 1973. *555 Families: A social-psychological study of young
families in transition.* New Brunswick, N. J.: Transaction.
Gibbs, J. 1972. *Sociological theory construction.* Hinsdale, Ill.: Dryden.
Glaser, B. G., and Strauss, A. L. 1967. *The discovery of grounded theory.*
Chicago: Aldine.
Hunt, J. McV., and Kogan, L. S. 1952. *Measuring results in social case-
work: A manual on judging movement.* Rev. ed. New York: Family
Service Assoc. of America.
Kadushin, A., and Wieringa, C. F. 1960. A comparison: Dutch and Amer-
ican expectations regarding behavior of the caseworker. *Social Case-
work* 41:503–11.
Kaplan, A. 1964. *The conduct of inquiry.* San Francisco: Chandler.
Kuhn, T. 1970. *The structure of scientific revolutions.* 2d ed. Chicago:
Univ. of Chicago Press.

Lazarsfeld, P. 1945. Foreword to *Experimental sociology*, by E. Greenwood. New York: King's Crown.

Lewin, K. 1951. *Field theory in social science*. New York: Harper.

Lippitt, R.; Polansky, N.; Redl, F.; and Rosen, S. 1968. The dynamics of power. In *Group dynamics*, ed. D. Cartwright and A. Zander, pp. 236–50. New York: Harper & Row.

Lorenz, K. 1961. Imprinting. In *Instinct*, ed. R. C. Birney and R. C. Teevan, pp. 65–77. Princeton, N.J.: Van Nostrand.

Merton, R. K. 1967. *On theoretical sociology*. New York: Free Press of Glencoe.

Polansky, N. A. 1952. Why research in the social work curriculum? *Smith College Studies in Social Work* 22:147–53.

———. 1971. *Ego psychology and communication*. Chicago: Aldine-Atherton.

———; Borgman, R. D.; and De Saix, C. 1972. *Roots of futility*. San Francisco: Jossey-Bass.

Ripple, L. 1957. Factors associated with continuance in casework service. *Social Work* 2:87–94.

———. 1960. Problem identification and formulation. In *Social work research*, ed. N. A. Polansky, pp. 24–47. Chicago: Univ. of Chicago Press.

Russell, B. 1951. *The autobiography of Bertrand Russell*. Boston: Little-Brown.

Selltiz, C.; Jahoda, M.; Deutsch, M.; and Cook, S. 1959. *Research methods in social relations*. Rev. ed. New York: Henry Holt.

Selye, H. 1956. *The stress of life*. New York: McGraw-Hill.

Shyne, A. W.; Kogan, L. S.; and Wasser, E. 1957. *The short-term case in the family agency*. New York: Family Service Assoc. of America.

Thomas, E.; Polansky, N.; and Kounin, J. 1955. The expected behavior of a potentially helpful person. *Human Relations* 8:165–74.

Wallace, W. L. 1971. *The logic of science in sociology*. Chicago: Aldine-Atherton.

Samuel Finestone
and Alfred J. Kahn

2
The Design
of Research

DESIGN AS THE LOGICAL STRATEGY OF A STUDY

All research begins with the identification of gaps in knowledge and the formulation of problems for research. A set of decisions then becomes necessary to establish guidelines for the investigation of the problem. These planning decisions constitute the design of the study; they make up the logical strategy for accomplishing the purposes of the study. The design in turn becomes the basis for more specific preparation for research activity, usually including the detailing of measurement techniques and the construction of instruments for collecting data. There follows the actual collection of data by whatever means have been decided. With raw data available, a stage of analysis and interpretation is necessary to produce findings on the questions or hypotheses originally posed. Finally, a report is prepared to communicate the entire process and the results of the process.

To be sure, the process is never as tidy and uncomplicated as this brief overview suggests. However, the function of a research design becomes clear. It guides logical arrangements for collection and analysis of data so that conclusions may be drawn.

The Substance of Research Design

The substance of research design has been referred to as a set of decisions. But decisions about what? The answer varies with the particular study, but usually the following kinds of strategic decisions have to be made.

1. *What are appropriate sources of information?* Human subjects? Of any particular type? Documents or literature? Already existing statistical tables?
2. *What is the sampling strategy?* That is, what is the appropriate population from which to draw data, how are units to be selected from this population to constitute the sample for the study, how many?
3. *By what methods will the information be obtained from the sources selected?* If human subjects are the appropriate source, are they to be interviewed, asked to complete a questionnaire, tested, observed? If documents, case records, or statistical compilations are the source, how will they be treated?

4. *What is the general strategy for measuring, counting, or classifying the data?* This question is closely related to the variables of central concern to the study. While some variables are straightforward (e.g., age), others are more complex (morale, productivity, coping level, etc.). Indicators are needed for these latter types of variables. Rules may have to be worked out for combining the indicators into one or more general indices.

5. *How will the process of obtaining data be patterned?* The patterned arrangements for obtaining data vary with the level of the study. Where the state of knowledge is at a beginning point, exploration of the general phenomenon is needed, rather than precise description, analysis of relationships between data, or testing of cause-effect relationships. On the other hand, if variables are clearly known, a more precise pattern may be called for. One may even be ready to use an experimental design.

6. *How will the data be analyzed?* It is necessary to foresee, for each of the questions of the study, what data are relevant, how they are to be combined, and how they are to be treated statistically so that appropriate conclusions may be drawn. In a descriptive survey (e.g., the opinions of a selected sample), the responses bearing upon particular issues have to be identified, and statistical measures chosen which will summarize the opinions. In an explanatory survey, where the interest is in seeing how variables are related to each other, a preview of the selected relationships, identification of relevant data, and decisions on statistical procedures for studying the relationships are needed. In an experimental study, certain differences have to be identified for statistical treatment; for example, the differences in results between groups exposed and not exposed to treatment.

Since statistics of various kinds are basic in expressing the results of research, a knowledge of statistics is necessary to foresee possibilities in the phase of designing it. Raw data emerging from large-scale research will usually be processed by computers, nowadays according to computer programs. The electronic data-processing strategy should, therefore, also be kept in mind.

Not all decisions are made in the phase of designing research. Specific details come up as one proceeds. But broad guidelines will ensure clear direction.

An Example of a Research Design

To make this listing of decisions more concrete, an example is offered of a particular study of interest to social workers. It should be remembered that, since studies are of different types, the design to be described cannot be generalized to all studies.

The authors (Reid and Shyne 1966) were interested primarily in comparing the outcomes of brief casework service of fixed duration with traditional service of open-ended duration. Although other important variables were included in their complex study, our discussion of design decisions will refer only to the central variable, brief versus extended service.

What are the appropriate sources of information? The primary source selected was the clients who would receive either of the two types of service; a secondary source was the caseworkers providing the service. Research interviews with clients were planned at three points in time; at completion of intake, at termination of service, and three months after termination. Data from caseworkers were secured through written schedules at intake and closing covering the same points included in the research interviews with clients, as a way of supplementing and checking on the information and judgments derived from those interviews.

What about the general sampling plan? Since the project called for intensive study, a particular voluntary, nonsectarian family agency was selected as the setting. First-time applicants to this agency who stayed through the intake process and accepted an offer of service during a particular period constituted the sample of 120 clients on whom Reid and Shyne focused. A smaller number of caseworkers serving these clients were also involved in the study. Reid and Shyne note that the sample had particular characteristics, for example, youth, education, absence of gross pathology, to which study findings were related (p. 53). For generalization to other types of clients, research studies with other populations would be necessary.

The strategy of measurement and classification had to be thought out in terms of what was to be measured, namely, the two central variables of type of treatment and outcome. For the measurement of outcome, measures of individual and family change had to be selected. Sixteen key ratings were eventually used, including research interviewer ratings of changes in family outcome, ratings of changes in various aspects of family functioning, etc., with a check of such ratings by research observers based on tape recordings of client-worker interviews. Caseworker ratings and client ratings of change were also used. In general, from a number of sources, the extent of change in the problem situation was rated as considerably alleviated, slightly alleviated, unchanged, or aggravated. Rules for assigning clients to one or another of these categories had to be worked out.

The patterning of the process of obtaining data was a crucial element of the design. Basically, a "two-group comparative experimental design" was selected. Clients accepting service were randomly assigned to one of the two major types of service; either to planned short-term service or to traditional open-ended continued service. *Random assignment* meant that, by intent, no consideration was to be given to preselecting the type of service considered appropriate for particular clients. The wheel of chance determined which type of treatment a client would get. Thus, the two groups were as likely to be matched on all characteristics as chance permitted. Two other points may be noted about the pattern of experimental design. Since the study was comparative in nature, there was no true control group, that is, no nontreatment group. Therefore, results could only apply to comparisons between these two forms of treatment, and not to the effect of treatment as compared with no treatment. Second, since the experiment was to be conducted in a real-life agency, it may be characterized as a field experiment under operating conditions rather than a specially contrived *laboratory experiment*.

A final decision in the design is the strategy for analyzing data. The basic strategy in our example was simple: the comparison of change in the two groups. Also, statistical tests of significance had to be selected which would indicate the extent to which differences in results between the two groups would be beyond what might be expected from chance. Some of the tactics of analysis and statistical procedures emerged as the data were worked with, but it may be presumed that the broad strategy was thought out in the design phase of the study.

The Importance of Early Design Clarity

While design decisions require much thought and ingenuity, there are still important details to work out which are extensions of, but not part of, research design per se. For example, if the design decisions require that social work graduates of a particular period be mailed questionnaires to elicit information on their current positions, responsibilities, and tasks, it will be necessary to construct a mail questionnaire instrument. The terms "position," "responsibility," "task" will have to be defined; translated into items for the questionnaire. The format of the questionnaire will have to be worked out, and the instrument pretested with a small sample for its clarity, feasibility, and effectiveness in gathering the required information. And, of course, the precise sampling plan will have to be worked out: graduates of which years, how many graduates, how selected, and so on.

Why, if a broad statement of design leaves so much unsettled, is it so important? First, because nothing reveals so clearly the adequacy of the proposed study as a means of providing information, as a way of answering questions, or as a way of testing hypotheses as does the bare design. Details of procedure rest upon decisions about a study's fundamental logical strategy. It is not unusual for a fuzzy design to generate specific procedures for data gathering and analysis that produce results which do not really address the original problem. For example, studies of the effectiveness of social work based on interviews with social workers will not really provide evidence of effectiveness, even though such studies can give precise answers to what social workers *believe* their effectiveness is. Studies which attempt to assess children in foster care by studying all those in it on a particular day give a distorted picture. The children who remain in foster care are a special part of the population who entered it; namely, those who could not return to their own families. Indeed, the sources of bias which pose threats to the validity of conclusions are many, and must be protected against. Design decisions should protect against or "control for" factors which may introduce bias in the search for knowledge.

SOURCES OF BIAS IN RESEARCH

Understanding sources of bias and how they may be controlled to a reasonable degree (there is no perfect research!) is obviously important for any researcher. Understanding is also important for other professional social workers, since they are consumers and users of research.

In this section, we are concentrating on biasing factors which should be considered in the design phase of research. An organized and definitive account of such factors is provided by Campbell and Stanley (1963).

Bias Derived from the External Context

Specific events occurring shortly before research began or while it is being conducted may bias results. In a descriptive survey of public attitudes toward public assistance recipients, for example, the results will be influenced if there has been a wave of publicity about "malingerers" and "cheaters." The designer of research can consider building in questionnaire items which distinguish between those who have and those who have not been exposed to the publicity so that he may take account of the effects of exposure, or he can conduct waves of interviews at intervals of several months to identify variations.

Suppose we wish to investigate whether a social work program makes a difference in the extent to which families participate in community activities. The usual procedure is to measure the extent of community participation before and after the program begins and to calculate the amount of change. But external events in the community which occur between the "before" and "after" measurements (e.g., the raising of an issue of great interest) may well introduce an effect, and the result is that it is not possible to separate the effect of this rival explanation of change from that of the social work program. How can such an external source of bias be controlled for? Instead of a single experimental group, the research design may include a comparable control group. Both are measured before and after the social work program, but the control group is not exposed to the program. Any change in community participation in the experimental group is then a result both of the social work program *and* of external events; any change in the control group is a result of external events alone. The strategy of analysis is to subtract the control group changes from the experimental group changes. The difference represents the gain (if any) resulting from the social work program.

To be sure, this is a simplified example, for there are other problems in controlling for bias. Outside events may be so much more powerful that they swamp the effect of a social work program. This is one reason why efforts to test the effects of social work programs directed to a relatively limited portion of all the factors impinging upon the lives of people have difficulty in showing significant results.

When an experiment is completed in a very short period in a laboratory, the effect of external events is not likely to be significant. But even here, unusual distractions (noise, etc.) may make a difference which will confound results.

Bias Derived from Sampling Decisions

The choice of a population and the method for selecting a sample from that population may produce an unusual group and thus bias results.

The problem of *experimental mortality* may also be mentioned in considering sampling bias. Subjects in an experiment may drop out; those who remain may not be representative of the original group. This problem particularly plagues panel studies, where a small group is studied over a fairly long period. Any rehabilitation-vocational training program which gives results only for those who complete the program is not giving a true picture of results. The research design must protect against these dangers as much as possible, or the results must be frankly qualified.

Bias Derived from the Involvement of Subjects

The results obtained in an experiment may depend upon the attention paid the participants rather than upon the specific treatment being tested. Drugs may produce improvements not because of their specific pharmacological effect but because of response by patients to any sign of attention. The *placebo effect* (a placebo is a neutral pill) has to be taken into account. A research design may control for this effect by setting up three groups: one which is exposed to an experimental drug, one without any drug exposure, and one with a placebo not known as such to the subjects or even to those administering the drug. With measurements "before" and "after" for each group, the gain of drug over no drug may be assessed after the gain due to the placebo alone is subtracted. It is intriguing to consider how the placebo effect can be controlled for in social work treatment evaluation.

The *Hawthorne effect* takes its name from experiments conducted in the wiring room of a Western Electric plant in Hawthorne, New Jersey, in which the interest was in the relation between better lighting and productivity (Roethlisberger and Dickson 1939). The attention paid the experimental group produced results independent of the changes in illumination.

One of the authors of this chapter found an analogous situation in organizational change research in a public welfare center. The staff wanted to do better, show better results, simply because they were part of an experiment and not because of the specific organizational changes introduced. One staff member even offered to see to it that the statistics on home visits would be doctored to show positive results! It was necessary to play down the interaction of researchers with staff, and to discourage the Hawthorne effects. Ideally, the research design should have included another welfare center where the changes could be introduced in as neutral a way as possible without the special aura of an experiment. Of course, in some situations, the effect of being at the center of a study may produce negative as well as positive motivations.

Bias Derived from Natural Processes

Processes occurring within people (growing older, more tired, etc.), rather than the independent variables being tested, may produce results. If children are treated over a period of years and positive change is found, how much is due to treatment and how much to maturation? When detached workers are assigned to gangs, how much of subsequent change is due to gang members' "settling down" as part of normal adolescent development? A useful feature of a research design is the provision of a control group not exposed to treatment. Since maturation occurs in both the experimental and the control groups, its effects are "canceled out." Some conditions are characterized by *spontaneous remission*; that is, the conditions often disappear without specific treatment. We all know the old saying that six days of drug dosage will cure a cold, while it takes half a dozen days without a drug. In a research design where maturation or spontaneous remission may be plausible explanations for improvement, a control group is a necessary feature.

Bias Derived from Initial Tests or Experimental Programs

Measurement may itself affect subsequent behavior, and thus produce a rival explanation for effects of the treatment program. Consider what taking a "test" on attitudes toward sexual behavior may produce, especially if the subjects have not thought about the items before. The results of a second test, administered after a program, may be hard to interpret, since any differences could be partly a result of taking the initial test. What design strategies can control for this difficulty? A simple one is to eliminate the "before" test and have an "after only" test for both the experimental and control groups.

Another, more complex, solution is proposed (Solomon 1949), in which an experimental group is measured before and after exposure to an experimental stimulus or program, and in which there are also *three* control groups, all measured afterward. One control group is measured before but not exposed to the stimulus, another is not measured before but is exposed to the stimulus, and the third is neither measured before nor exposed to the stimulus. Statistical comparisons of the results of the four "after" measures make it possible to take into account the possible effects of the initial measurement.

An initial test may also interact with subject characteristics in a way which introduces bias. For example, intelligence tests may have built-in cultural or language biases and may be reacted to differently by different cultural groups. Such interactive effects limit the generalizability of results. Characteristics of the tester or interviewer may interact differentially with those of particular cultural groups. In an early study, black soldiers were less likely to tell white interviewers that they believed the army was discriminatory than they were to tell black interviewers. Experimental programs may also interact with characteristics of subjects. Verbal therapies, for example, seem to work better with some cultural groups than others. The construction of *culture-free* tests or interviews, or design features which control for influences of the kinds described above, are important concerns of the researcher. The critical reader wishing to evaluate research conclusions, will want to examine whether such interactive effects are likely, and whether they are taken into account in the research design.

Bias Derived from Final Tests

If the research design includes a test before and after an intervention (e.g., a test of knowledge before and after an experimental educational program) then the improvement may be due in various degrees not to the educational program but the sheer *practice effect* in taking the same test twice. Using an alternate form for the final test, equivalent but not identical to the initial one, may reduce the danger of this kind of bias. Another factor jeopardizing validity is *instrument decay*. Standards in a posttest may be unintentionally different from those in the pretest, so that changes are due not only to an intervening experimental program but also to altered measurement. Research interviewers may have greater skill in post- than in preinterviews, judges may become fatigued in marking essays or making observations by the end of a study.

Bias Derived from Statistical Regression

When initial tests yield extreme (very low or very high) scores, there is a tendency for scores to be closer to the middle on subsequent tests—a change that has nothing to do with the experimental program. High scorers may have had some good luck on the initial test; low scorers some bad. Scores at any given moment, though they may represent accurate measurements, also include a component of chance (unsystematic, random) error. But luck is capricious, and, on the average, extreme errors modulate in subsequent tests. Thus pretest to posttest differences would be reduced. Statistical regression is especially of concern in studies where selected *extreme groups* are compared before and after an experimental program.

LEVELS OF RESEARCH DESIGN

It is useful to distinguish four levels of research design. The first level is a preresearch phase. It is that *unplanned observation* which stirs curiosity and suggests leads for planned exploration, description, or investigation of relationships—but only in the prepared mind. Next comes the *formulative-exploratory level* (the terms are used interchangeably) whose objective is to prepare for other levels of research in various ways. A third, *descriptive* level of research aims to describe how selected variables are distributed in a population or a phenomenon or a situation. Finally, there is the level of *investigating and testing relationships between and among variables*, either through retrospective explanatory surveys, longitudinal studies, or projected experimental designs.

Although the ultimate objective of research is to build theory through arriving at related sets of propositions about relationships among concepts, especially among variables, it does not follow that variable-relationship levels of research are always the most appropriate. The point is that the state of preexisting knowledge may in one case call for exploratory research, in another for describing the distribution of characteristics in a population. At other times, the state of theory and the prior history of the problem are such as to make wasteful all research design levels short of the experimental testing of variable relationships.

Although these four levels will be discussed separately below, it should be recognized that they represent arbitrary points on a continuum. Many studies are at some point between the "pure" points which have been given names. Furthermore, it is common for a particular research undertaking to begin with one level (e.g., an exploratory phase) and go on to another level in which descriptive studies or investigation of relationships between variables are carried on.

Unplanned Observation

Accidental events may suggest insights for further investigation. A piece of radioactive rock was accidentally left on a photographic plate overnight. It caused changes in the plate which stirred Madame Curie's curiosity about reasons for the change. Her curiosity eventually led to the discovery of radium. Newton was hit on the head by an apple falling from a tree, and the incident stimulated his search for the laws governing gravity. The untrained, unprepared, and incurious observer would not have been stirred by these accidental occurrences. It is precisely because the unprepared mind does not recognize "good things" that the social work researcher is motivated to retain close ties to development in social work practice and theory.

Exploratory or Formulative Studies

Studies to clarify later, more systematic research are often needed in social work. Suppose the participation of parents of mentally retarded children in programs which serve them is to be studied. What factors should be considered? How shall mental retardation services or "participation" be defined? How, and on what basis, will such parents be interested in cooperating with such a study? The area of interest—parent participation in mental retardation programs—is not yet a research problem. It can be transformed into one only through a period of exploratory study which lays the basis for further research. Or suppose one notes high failure rates in certain types of residential treatment, or frequent personnel turnover in specific types of agencies. In the absence of conceptual leads or strongly held hypotheses, some type of exploratory study is the best strategy for a beginning.

Many different methods are used in exploratory research. Usually there is a flexible following up of leads, moving from one phase to another. Selltiz and his associates (1959) speak of *surveying the literature* as a way of building on the research of others; particularly to identify hypotheses. Novels and critical writings may suggest leads for study. An *experience survey* may be used to tap the opinions and insights of those familiar with the phenomenon. Interviews with practitioners or administrators may, for example, provide leads for a study of preventive approaches to child abuse. Sometimes systematic application of social science conceptualization may be profitable.

The *critical incident technique* merits attention as a fruitful approach in an exploratory-formulative study, though it may be used in other ways. To quote from an initial formulation (Flanagan 1954, p. 32):

> By incident is meant any observable human activity that is sufficiently complete in itself to permit inferences and predictions to be made about the person performing the act. To be critical, an incident must occur in a situation where the purpose and intent of the act seems fairly clear to the observer, and where its consequences are sufficiently definite to leave little doubt concerning its effects.

An example of the use of critical incident technique is a study in a residential treatment setting for children (Goodrich and Boomer 1958).

Eager to tap available know-how in work with hyperaggressive children, all staff who had contact with children were interviewed periodically and were asked for an incident in which they had done something good or bad for children in the light of accepted goals. Staff were asked to tell of the child's behavior which prompted some intervention on their part, what they did or said, whether it was a positive or negative intervention, and what treatment was involved. Following the collection and recording of the incidents, the researchers classified them, formulated concepts, re-sorted and related categories to each other, etc. In effect, they undertook an organized process of induction which ultimately produced thirty-one basic interventive principles subsumed under four major headings. These principles then became available for testing through experimental designs. The critical-incident technique of data gathering may also be used for descriptive research. For example, social workers in a hospital asked what led family members or relatives to hospitalize a patient who was apparently emotionally disturbed. A series of logical categories were developed so that related incidents could be grouped together. Similarly, McGowan (1973) collected a series of incidents in which child advocacy activities were carried out. It was then possible to derive *operational definitions* for various types of child advocacy activities.

Glaser and Strauss (1967) suggest a strategy of comparative analysis, in which critical incidents are examined and classified until a pattern emerges, and further examples of incidents are studied for elaboration of the theoretical categories and relationships among them until no new ones emerge. The "constant comparative method of qualitative analysis" may be seen from their investigation of dying patients, and the concept of "social loss" in relation to the way such patients are treated (Glaser and Strauss 1964).

Another method used in exploratory-formulative studies includes the *manipulation of an independent variable*, for example, a particular kind of treatment program. One schizophrenic patient in a mental hospital was selected who stole food, hoarded towels, and wore an excessive amount of clothing (Ayllon 1963). Initial measurements on the amount of such behavior were taken, a program of various kinds of positive and negative reinforcement techniques was used with the patient, and subsequently the same behavior was observed. Results included the elimination of food stealing with consequent weight reduction, and the elimination of hoarding and of wearing excessive clothing. The net outcome of such clinical exploration is not a tested relationship between treatment technique and symptom reduction, but it provides a plausible hypothesis for further testing with larger samples and more controls.

A final type of exploratory research has the purpose of *preparing basic tools for research*. Some selected examples of particular interest to social work include the development of a "movement scale" for measurement of change in casework treatment (Hunt, Blenkner, and Kogan 1950), a classification of casework techniques (Hollis 1967), family functioning scales (Geismar 1971), and an inventory of child behavior characteristics (Borgatta and Fanshel 1967). All of these scales involve complex conceptualization and the empirical demonstration of reliability. They have been, and continue to be, used in social work research.

There is a debate among social researchers: should they concentrate on evaluating the results of social work (does it work? what works?) through experimental designs, or should they devote themselves to more exploratory and descriptive kinds of research focusing on intensive studies of the nature of social work practice? To some extent, it is a matter of preferences and judgments of what research is most needed. There is a need for all levels of research in order to expand the knowledge base of social work practice.

Descriptive Studies

Descriptive studies vary in the units of study (individuals, groups, families, organizations, communities, the nation) and in the simplicity or complexity of the phenomenon to be described. In all descriptive studies, however, sampling plans and procedures call for rigorous consideration of representativeness and sampling size.

In the simplest form, such studies describe a population by reporting characteristics (variables) one at a time. More complicated descriptive studies consider two or more variables simultaneously for greater precision and concreteness. When *causal* relationships among variables are of interest, we speak of *explanatory surveys* (Hyman 1955). Sometimes this distinction is difficult to make, since the difference between describing characteristics of a population and investigating causal relationships among these characteristics is a relative one.

Examples of surveys in which the phenomena to be investigated are relatively simple include census studies and opinion poll studies. Yet, either total populations (as in the U.S. census) or rigorous sampling plans and procedures are necessary. Administrative statistics in an agency reporting numbers of cases, numbers of interviews, numbers of workers, etc., are of this type. Consider, however, a study which attempts to assess attitudes to mental illness or, indeed, the mental health status of a population (Langner et al. 1969). Complex conceptualization as well as rigorous sampling are necessary even though the aim remains descriptive rather than explanatory.

The Council on Social Work Education regularly reports on statistics on social work education, an example of compilation whose aim is not explanatory or theoretical, but important in planning and funding development. Because these statistics are issued annually, it becomes possible to study changes over time in numbers of students, graduates and schools; numbers and sizes of different types of educational programs, etc. The Family Service Association of America has completed a 1970 census of its clients, including demographic characteristics and program utilization (Beck and Jones 1973). Comparison with characteristics of the general population through census data add another dimension to this study, permitting statements of similarity and differences between FSAA client population and the general population. The question, Are family agencies disengaged from the poor? can be answered at least in terms of the kinds of clients attracted. Another feature is the use of client and working ratings on satisfaction with treatment.

The use of *social indicators* to measure the state of social well-being may be discussed under the heading of descriptive research. The development, gathering, and evaluation of social indicators is of distinct interest to social workers concerned not only with individual cases, but with the general social welfare (Kahn 1969, pp. 88–93). There is a growing literature on social indicators (Bauer 1966; Sheldon and Moore 1968; U.S. Department of HEW 1969). As descriptive studies, social indicators are often ends in themselves, especially for planners, policy makers, and administrators.

Explanatory Surveys

The development of behavioral theory (why people or collectivities behave as they do) or of practice theory (whether, how and why social work interventions work in a variety of problem situations) ultimately calls for a level of research design aimed at investigation of *causal relationships among variables*. As in a descriptive survey, the explanatory survey is ex post facto, after the fact. In experiments, on the other hand, the researcher introduces the causal variables (for example, a treatment program) and measures the effect directly. In a word, explanatory surveys are retrospective, experiments are projective.

Explanatory surveys are conducted when:

1. There has already been sufficient conceptualization in the science of the phenomenon and the variables to be considered for investigation to take place without a prior phase of exploratory-formulative study.
2. The purposes of the study go beyond description of the variables or of noncausal correlations (as in a descriptive study) to an analysis of causal relationships among variables. Sometimes the specific relationships to be sought are hypothesized before the data are gathered and analyzed; sometimes the hypotheses are formulated later after preliminary processing of the data suggests various leads for analysis. Very often there is a combination of the two.

3. The causal factors are not manipulated by the investigator. For example, if there is an interest in the psychological and social consequences of different diseases, it is neither practical nor ethical (in our culture) to use a projected experimental design. The *experimental* logic would call for selection of a sample of subjects, random assignment to different groups each of which will be inoculated with particular diseases (possibly with one "no disease" group), and then measurement and comparison of the consequences. Obviously this kind of problem can only be investigated after the diseases and their consequences have taken place in a "natural" way. This is why explanatory surveys are sometimes called *natural experiments*, as opposed to *contrived experiments*.

Similarly, an interest in differential consequences of various lengths of foster care for children could not be approached except in an ex post facto way. It is neither feasible nor ethical to set up groups of children who will be randomly and arbitrarily assigned to foster care for different lengths of time for research purposes.

4. The measurement techniques have been worked out. For example, if "adjustment" is to be measured, reliable and valid scales need to exist for measurement.

The four conditions (preconceptualization of variables, interest in causal relationships between and among variables, nonmanipulability of the causal variable, existence of measurement techniques) underlie the selection of an explanatory survey design. The basic logic includes the selection of a relevant population, a sampling strategy, a strategy for measuring variables, and strategies for data reduction and analysis. While some variables pose no difficulty in measurement, others require much preliminary work in developing reliable and valid scales.

There are limitations in explanatory surveys which should be made explicit. Let us return to our example of research directed to the assessment of consequences of various lengths of foster care. The very practical advantages of an ex post facto design are accompanied by disadvantages. One, mentioned earlier, is that we cannot get a pure population of those exposed to foster care, only those who have remained in it up to the time of the survey interviews. Thus, conclusions about the level of adjustment of foster children are colored by the absence of those who have already returned home or those who were adopted, and may give a more pathological picture of foster care consequences in general than is actually the case (Fanshel 1972).

A second difficulty is that sometimes the time order between variables presumed to constitute cause and effect is ambiguous. If we are interested in the relationship between marital stability-instability and individual adjustment, which causes which? Asking questions about premarital adjustment can help sort out the time order, but responses to interviews requiring long-term retrospection have questionable accuracy.

A general problem is that not one but many variables are often associated with a particular effect. The introduction of an additional variable into the analysis of an original two-variable relationship may indicate that the original relationship is not substantively significant, or that it exists only because of the influence of the third variable, or that it varies depending on the third variable. The elaboration of relationships between two variables by one or more additional variables has been intensively studied (Lazarsfeld 1955; Hyman 1955; Zeisel 1968, pp. 118–52; Rosenberg 1968). Only a highly condensed and oversimplified discussion is possible here.

The problem starts when we have an apparent causal relationship between an independent (causal) variable and a dependent (effect) variable. A third, *antecedent variable* introduced into the analysis may occur in time before both the original variables and influence both. Hence the original relationship is found to be *spurious*. An example is the finding that the number of fire engines sent to a fire correlates directly with the amount of fire damage. This seems to indicate that the fire engines are a causative factor in fire damage. Suppose a third variable, the severity of the fire, is next introduced into the analysis. This variable *antecedes* both the original variables and influences both. The apparent relationship between fire engines and damage is spurious. The real situation is that the severity of the fire influences both the number of fire engines and the amount of damage.

Another situation exists when the third variable occurs in time between the independent and dependent variables, and again an apparent correlation disappears upon further scrutiny. An example (Zeisel 1968, pp. 136–37) starts with the relationship between marital status of employed women and proportion of working days absent. Apparently, married women have more absences. A third variable, amount of housework, is then introduced into the analysis, and the apparent relationship is partially explained. This *intervening* variable is not an antecedent variable as in the previous example. It occurs between marital status and work absence. The more refined interpretation is that married women have more housework than do single women, on the average, and that women with more housework have more work absences.

A third situation occurs when the additional variable is a *contingent variable* rather than an antecedent or intervening variable. In a study of staff reactions (Brager 1969), one finding was that those staff members who had high commitment to original goals and values of the agency were much more disapproving of the way the agency handled a crisis in which government officials attacked the political radicalism of staff than were staff members with low commitment to original goals and values. A third variable was introduced into the analysis; whether or not staff members felt under direct personal stress as a result of the attack. Statistical elaboration showed that where no personal stress was involved, there was an even greater tendency for highly committed staff to disapprove the agency strategy than among staff with low commitment. Under conditions of personal stress, there was still a difference between staff with high and staff with low commitment with respect to disapproval of agency strategy, but the difference was much less than originally appeared. Thus, the original difference related to degree of commitment was further specified: higher under the contingency of no personal stress, lower under the contingency of personal stress. (This is called an *interaction* in statistics; see chapter 9). In general, the designer of an explanatory survey should consider these elaborations of original relationships in laying out the strategy of analysis. The critical reader of research should consider whether attention has been paid to necessary elaborations in analysis, so that original two-variable relationships are not taken for granted, but logically related additional variables are indeed introduced into the analysis. Such additional variables may demonstrate an original relationship as *spurious* (explain it away), may show that it can be *explained* by an intervening variable, or may *specify* the conditions under which it may be higher or lower.

Longitudinal or Cohort Studies

While cross-tabulations may take into account the possible effect of additional variables, other limitations remain. This is the reason for the development of other than ex post facto designs, particularly the longitudinal or cohort design. A population is selected, and is studied over a long period of time through successive waves of data gathering. Then processes of change can be studied as they occur, rather than through a one-shot, retrospective survey. There does not have to be dependence upon memory of the past. Also, the problem of a population which at one point in time is different from the population at an earlier period is minimized. The longitudinal, developmental study is therefore superior to the cross-sectional survey in many instances. Why, then, is there not more use of the longitudinal survey? The answer lies in the magnitude of the research effort; the time, energy, expense, and complexity of analysis; and the high rate of sample attrition.

There are some examples of longitudinal studies of great interest to social workers. One study covered a period of five years in the life of

American Indian children from the point of adoption by white parents through five waves of interviews with the adoptive parents (Fanshel 1972). How the children fared; the motivations, life styles, and parental practices of the adoptive parents were assessed and the interrelationships of the many variables involved were studied. Of equal or greater complexity are the studies of a sample of 600 children entering foster care in New York City in the same year, who were followed for five years. The children, the natural parents, and the agencies involved all had successive waves of interviews or questionnaires or testing throughout the period. Children who left foster care for return to own home or adoption were followed up. An initial volume (Jenkins 1972) and articles have been published, and more are to follow. Given the mountain of data, and the very large number of relationships possible to investigate, statistical techniques such as factor analysis and multiple regression were necessary. Another example of a cohort study is the one on all British children born during a specific week 3–9 March 1958. (Kellmer Pringle, Butler, and Davie, 1966).

Experimental Designs

The purpose of experimental design is similar to that of the explanatory survey; to draw causal inferences about the relationships among variables. Some of the conditions necessary for an experimental design are similar to those necessary for an explanatory survey. There are, however, three important differences. Whereas an explanatory survey may or may not have hypotheses formulated in advance of data collection and analysis, it is essential that a hypothesis be formulated in advance of experimental activity. The hypothesis must be conceptually clear and testable through available technical means. A good deal of emphasis is usually placed on the relationship of the hypothesis to theory; that is, the hypothesis should have connections to preexisting theory and have the potential for building upon that theory. However, the theoretical emphasis may be somewhat less in evaluative experiments where the more practical issue of whether programs are effective is the question (Mullen, Dumpson, and Associates 1972). The distinction is not always as sharp as this, for evaluative experiments may be formulated in a way which makes a contribution to general theory.

The second condition, unique to the experiment, is that the causal variable must be manipulable by the researcher. Finally, neither the causal variable nor the effect variables preexist, as they do in the explanatory survey. The researcher introduces the causal variable and measures its effect.

Examples of experimental designs are given in the next section, where various experimental patterns are discussed.

Major Experimental Design Patterns

While all experiments have the purpose of testing the effects of independent variables introduced by the investigator, there are many different design patterns by which the testing is accomplished (Selltiz et al. 1959; Campbell and Stanley 1963; Phillips 1966). Patterns are based on combinations of three elements: the number of groups involved, the kinds of stimuli, and the number and timing of measurements. Groups may vary from one to many. The independent or causal variable introduced by the investigator may be *experimental* (e.g., a new kind of treatment), *conventional* (e.g., the usual kind of treatment), *placebo* (e.g., a pseudo-stimulus), or simply the absence of any kind of deliberately induced stimulus as with a true control group. The measurements may be "after only" (made after exposure to the stimulus), "before and after" (made both before and after the exposure), or "multiple after" (made at more than one period after exposure).

The Classic Control Group Pattern

The classic pattern has two groups; one exposed to an experimental stimulus, and one not exposed, with before and after measures for both groups. A simple diagram may illustrate:

1. *B X A*
2. *B — A*

where *B* is the before measure, *X* is the experimental stimulus, *A* is the after measure, and the dash indicates the lack of an experimental stimulus.

An important feature is that persons are assigned *randomly* to either the experimental or control group. Only chance dictates whether any particular person is assigned to one or another group. The toss of a coin, or other randomizing procedures, may be used. Neither the subject nor the researcher selects the group on the basis of what is presumed to be "good." Random assignment may be approximated by *individual matching* procedures, by which each person assigned to the experimental group is matched with another person with equivalent characteristics (e.g., age, sex, income group, social adjustment status). Another approximation to random assignment is *frequency matching*, in which the experimental and control groups are set up so that the characteristics of the groups on the whole are equivalent (e.g., mean age, percentage female, percentage low-economic class). Generally speaking, the random assignment of subjects is preferred, because there are logical and statistical difficulties in applying the results of an experiment beyond the original subjects involved after individual or frequency matching procedures are used.

Suppose we wish to test the hypothesis that patients released from a mental hospital who receive follow-up care from social workers achieve greater gains in social adjustment than equivalent patients without follow-up care. In a classic experimental design, patients are assigned randomly to an experimental group (with follow-up care) and a control group (without it). Two ratings of social adjustment are made for *each* group; at the point of release and after a selected period in which only the experimental group has received follow-up care. The *gain* in social adjustment is calculated for both groups by comparing initial and final ratings for each. The gain of the experimental group is compared with that of the control group. If the gain of the experimental group is larger than that of the control group, to a degree greater than can be expected by chance alone, the original hypothesis is supported or, more exactly, cannot be rejected. If not, the original hypothesis is rejected.

The After-Only Pattern

In a modification of the classic pattern, the before measures are eliminated. Thus, we have a posttest only with two groups, one experimental, and one control. A simple diagram will illustrate:

1. — X A (experimental group)
2. — — A (control group)

This pattern may be used where pretests are unavailable, inconvenient, or likely to produce biasing effects with subjects. Thus, practice effects of testing are controlled, since there is only one test. The assumption is made that the groups are equivalent in all important respects. This pattern cannot be as sensitive to initial differences as the classic pattern, since the latter includes a pretest. However, it is often more practical.

An example of the application of this pattern in social work research is an experiment in which applicants for public assistance were randomly chosen for participation in orientation groups, while others did not participate (Finestone 1967). The orientation covered client rights, procedures, requirements, etc. Both groups were later "measured" indirectly through questionnaires filled out by social workers who conducted eligibility home investigations after the application process. The questionnaires covered such factors as the degree to which clients understood the requirements and services available to them, their freedom in asking questions, their cooperation in providing necessary information and documents. The eligibility workers did not know which clients had been in the orientation groups and which not. Before measures would have been unrealistic in this case, since the phenomena to be measured could best be obtained after the eligibility study. It would not have been impossible to construct some before measures, but the gains would not have been commensurate with the effort and would have introduced other problems, particularly in a field experiment in an operating public assistance agency.

The Comparative Pattern

In the comparative pattern, the purpose is to compare the outcomes of alternative forms of treatment. This design pattern does *not* provide evidence of the gain of treatment over no treatment at all. A simple diagram would be:

1. — $X_1 A$
2. — $X_2 A$

Where X_1 *and* X_2 are two forms of treatment, the same after measures are applied to both, and there are no before measures. It is quite conceivable that there may be before measures, in which case we have:

1. $B X_1 A$
2. $B X_2 A$

Or, in some approximation of before measures, there may be ratings of the amount of change between the opening and closing of cases. This procedure is somewhat different than a straight before-after comparison and yet is not merely an after measure. It is possible, too, to combine a comparative pattern with a classic or after-only pattern, by including a no-treatment group along with different treatment groups. We would then have:

1. $B X_1 A$
2. $B X_2 A$
3. $B — A$

Still other pattern variations can be constructed by different combinations of the elements.

Considering the difficulties of getting a true control group for social work research activity and the hesitancy about leaving some clients without any service (although it can and has been done), the carefully constructed comparative pattern has much to commend it. An example of social work research using a comparative pattern has already been noted, in which differences in outcome for clients randomly assigned to planned short-term treatment and conventional extended service treatment were measured (Reid and Shyne 1969). Since the research was conducted in an operating agency, it may be termed a field comparative experiment. In a simplified form we have:

1. — $X A$
2. — $C A$

where C indicates conventional extended treatment.

An interesting example of a comparative *laboratory experiment* is a study of social workers' reactions to different kinds of clients (Rosen and Liberman 1972). In this study, two kinds of social workers (professionally trained and untrained) were "exposed" to two kinds of clients (aggressive and compliant) in an interview situation. The "clients" were

portrayed by an actress, trained for the task, who played the different
kinds of client roles. Thus, what was involved was an *experimental
analogue* or simulation of client interviews. The advantage of simulation
is that the interview stimuli were relatively standardized (relatively the
same for all workers), rather than unstandardized as in the situation of
different clients. The social workers' performance in interviewing was
the "effect" or after measure—specifically, the responsiveness and relevance of workers' comments were measured. It might be said that the
causal variable introduced by the researcher was a combined variable
producing four experimental groups (trained workers with aggressive
clients, trained with compliant clients, untrained with aggressive clients,
untrained with compliant clients), and the "effect" variable was a measure
of interview quality.

The pattern might be represented by:

1. $— X_1 A$
2. $— X_2 A$
3. $— X_3 A$
4. $— X_4 A$

Other simulations have been used in social work employing actress-
portrayed clients (Kounin et al. 1956; Thomas and McLeod 1960) and
a filmed interview (Miller 1958).

Other Multiple-Group Patterns

These design patterns are employed to take into account placebo effects
or interactive testing effects. They have been little used in social work
research, perhaps because in social work activity it is difficult to concep-
tualize what a placebo would be. Formal tests are sometimes used, though
the equivalent measures through rating scales based on data are often
employed. A diagram for a placebo design pattern would be:

1. $B X A$
2. $B — A$
3. $B P A$

The point of the third group would be that the effect of the placebo alone
could be subtracted from the difference in gain achieved by the experimental group over the control group. For example, there has been experimentation with the effect of certain drugs in reducing the hyperactive
behavior of school-age children. From a population of such children,
subjects were randomly assigned to three groups: one got the drug, one
got nothing, and one got a placebo. Neither the doctors nor the children
knew which pill was the drug and which the placebo. Before and after
measurements of the extent of hyperactive behavior were made.

This kind of experiment raises sharply issues concerning the rights of
human subjects (the children and their parents) to participate voluntarily
on the basis of full explanations of the experimental procedures, to be

protected against exposure to risks which would outweigh benefits, and to be assured of anonymity. These considerations are important in any research in which people are subjects.

Previous mention has been made of the Solomon four-group design pattern, constructed to take account of the interactive and practice effects of testing. Because there are no current examples of its use in social work research (though it could be used), the design pattern is not included here. Description and analysis of this design may be found elsewhere (Selltiz, et al. 1959; Campbell and Stanley 1963).

The Successional Design Pattern

In the successional pattern (before and after with a single group) we have the top half of the classic pattern. Diagrammatically:

$B\ X\ A$

The successional pattern is weaker than the classic pattern, for there is a problem in attributing any gains (A minus B) to the stimulus. How do we know that the gains might not have occurred without the stimulus? How do we know that rival explanations for the change are not plausible —for example, the maturation of subjects or the influence of outside events? The evidence that any change is due to the stimulus is not strong. Yet a case can be made for using the successional design in which the single group is considered its own control group. An example is the early Saint Paul Family Centered Project, which gave a special kind of "reaching out" casework to disorganized problem families (Geismar and Ayres 1958). From previous experience, there was no reason to expect these families to improve if left untreated.

Somewhat more confidence can be given to results of successional design patterns if use is made of comparisons with existing norms. For example, in a study of the effect of treating delinquent children in a community program as an alternative to the regular court procedures, the proportion of community-treated children who got into further trouble with the law was ascertained. Although there was no formal control group or comparison group, the gains made by children in the community program were compared with the known statistical norms of recidivism found with court-treated children (Jones 1973). The use of applicable norms for comparison approximates, in a somewhat weaker way, the use of the control or comparative group. Sometimes this is the more practical way to proceed; the resulting evidence may be persuasive even if not conclusive. Where stronger design patterns are not practical of implementation, the use of comparative norms gives more evidence than would otherwise be available. However, such a point of view might be disputed by some researchers who doubt the value of all but the most rigorous patterns of research design.

Other Variations in Design Pattern

It should be clear that, while there are broad guidelines for design patterns, the choice is often a balance between what is desirable for maximum control of biasing factors, and practical difficulties in achieving such control. Ingenuity in doing whatever is possible is illustrated in a study of an innovation in a medical education program (Kendall 1972). In this study, the effect of a course in comprehensive medicine upon medical student attitudes to families was to be tested. From a design point of view, a classic design pattern was indicated in which one randomly selected group would get the course and another would not, with a before-after comparison. However, the educational administrators would not agree that any medical students should be denied the opportunity of taking the comprehensive medicine course, which emphasized patient contacts as a source of learning about and helping families, as well as learning medicine. A design pattern was constructed to get around this difficulty and still allow access to whatever evidence was available on the effect of the new course. It was arranged for one group of students to take the new course in the first half of the fourth year and the other to take it in second half. Measurements in both groups on attitudes to families were made at the end of the third year (before the new course had begun), in the middle of the fourth year (after one group had taken the new course while the other had taken the regular courses in surgery, obstetrics-gynecology and electives), and at the end of the fourth year (after the second group had taken the new course). There were then comparisons of achievements between the first and second groups at three points in time. The pattern may be diagrammed in this way:

From end of third year to middle of fourth year
1. $B \, X \, A$
2. $B \, C \, A$ (where C is the conventional course)
From middle of fourth year to end of fourth year
1. $B \, C \, A$
2. $B \, X \, A$

Several comparisons could then be made. In the first period, the gains (A minus B) of the experimental group could be compared with those of the conventional group. (The experimental group had gained while the conventional group had not.) The same comparison could be made in the second period, even though the groups were reversed. Finally, by comparisons of gains in period 1 and period 2, reasonable inferences could be drawn about the duration of effects.

Even in a single-group design, results can be regarded with more confidence, as we have said, if measures are made at various times, not simply before and after. A series of measurements in an organization at several points before a new structure or procedure is introduced, and again at several points after it has been introduced, is more persuasive than a single pair of before and after measures. For example, suppose there are productivity or quality measures available at a number of points in time before a "team structure" is introduced in an agency, and at several points after introduction. The evidence is not as conclusive as if there were comparison with a current "no team" structure, but it is better than a simple before-after measure.

There have been some experiments in which only a single case is involved. Of course, both internal validity (freedom from bias in making conclusions specific to the case) and external validity (extension of conclusions to other cases) are seriously in question. Yet even here there is value in intensive study of the single case, certainly as a way of understanding the phenomenon (an exploratory level of design). Some researchers have pointed out that there are a great many items of behavior in a single subject, and that all the items may be considered as a "population" of units and subjected to statistical analysis at various points in time before and after the introduction or withdrawal of treatment measures (Davidson and Costello 1969). The difficulties of generalizing results from single cases are too great to classify such studies as other than exploratory, in our opinion. The relative value of such studies, however, should be recognized, particularly among social workers (see chapter 11).

A Suggested Typology of Research Design

Several dimensions of design have been discussed in previous sections. It may be helpful to summarize this discussion in the form of a classification of major types of research designs. The particular classification offered differs slightly from that proposed by others (Selltiz et al. 1959; Tripodi 1969). Readers are encouraged to apply this typology in classifying the major types of research design used in social work. Such classification will make it easier to grasp the essential elements of design and to appreciate strengths and limitations.

1. Exploratory Studies

The general purpose is to prepare for more systematic research in an undeveloped field.

Specific purposes include the conceptual definition of variables and ways to measure them, the search for useful hypotheses, the development of methodological approaches, and the investigation of the feasibility of research.

Designs and methods vary greatly, and there may be a combination of approaches. Most often, the design and methods are flexible and informal. Small samples, not rigorously representative, are often used for in-depth study in arriving at insights for later confirmation by other levels of research.

2. Descriptive Surveys

The general purpose is to describe the characteristics of a population or phenomenon when the characteristics of interest are known.

There are no prior hypotheses about causal relationships between variables, or testing of such relationships. However, there may be simultaneous consideration of two or more variables for more precise description.

The design requires carefully defined populations and representative samples (see chapter 4). Data may be gathered from questionnaires, interviews, observation, or available statistical reports. Such studies are usually ends in themselves (policy, planning, administration) but also generate hypotheses.

3. Explanatory Surveys

The general purpose is to test hypotheses about cause-effect relationships.

The variables are not introduced or manipulated by the researcher; events have already taken place.

Approximations to control groups or comparison groups are achieved by statistical analyses after the data have been collected.

The subtypes of explanatory surveys include (a) hypothesis-testing explanatory surveys in which hypotheses are stated in advance of data collection; (b) search-for-relationships explanatory surveys, in which hypotheses are not stated in advance, but emerge and are tested in the process of data analysis.

4. Panel or Longitudinal Studies

The general purpose is to study the way change occurs in a selected group through successive measurements over an extended period of time. Factors related to the changes may also be investigated.

Variables are not manipulated by the investigator; they occur "naturally" and are studied as they occur.

Panel studies differ from explanatory studies in that phenomena can be studied as they occur rather than after they have occurred, and from experimental studies in that the causal factors are not introduced or manipulated by the researcher.

5. Projected Experimental Research

The general purpose is to test cause-effect hypotheses.

Independent (causal) variables are manipulated by the investigator.

The design *patterns* vary but generally include experimental and control groups with random assignment of subjects to each, or approximations to control groups.

Major subtypes of experimental designs (ignoring the variety of design patterns) include:

1. *Laboratory experiments.* These are conducted in a specially contrived situation and employ random assignment of subjects to experimental and control groups. The study setting is typically one unfamiliar or foreign to the subjects.

2. *Field experiments.* These are conducted in existing institutional settings and employ random assignment of subjects to experimental and control groups.

3. *Approximations to laboratory or field experiments.* These employ other than random assignments to experimental groups (e.g., individual or frequency matching), or use the experimental group as its own control group, or use other approximations.

Some Concluding Observations on Research Design

The design of social research is primarily a technical enterprise. Research planning decisions are based on knowledge of sources of bias and error, and on arrangements for collecting and analyzing data which minimize bias and error. By no means does this imply that there are standardized solutions to design problems. Ingenuity and judgment are required to construct designs, drawing upon knowledge of a range of design alternatives and of their relative strengths and weaknesses.

There are, however, requirements for a research design that go beyond the technical issues. It must be geared to the substantive and conceptual interest expressed in the way the research problem is formulated. A research design should not become a Procrustean bed upon which professional issues become truncated or distorted. The matter of conceptual and substantive fit is a special consideration in research on social work practice or program. For example, if individualized service activity is to be studied, design decisions should not convert what is being studied into nonindividualized activity because the latter is easier to research by conventional designs.

Social work research is also a social enterprise. Very often it involves relationships with administrators or staff in organizations, and with human subjects whose behavior and attitudinal responses constitute the research data of interest. In the real world in which social researchers operate, technical, substantive, and social considerations influence the design of research. Some researchers view nontechnical influences as undesirable barriers to scientifically rigorous research, while others accept them as legitimate influences. In this latter view, research design represents the best compromise between technical and nontechnical considerations.

In organizational research, particularly evaluative research, there may well be a lack of fit between classic experimental research designs which emphasize a before-after strategy including a control group, and the need of the organization to find out how to improve its program and practice. A single "good or no good" decision may be unrealistic and unhelpful. A better fit may be provided by a serial feedback or loop design, in which the results of one stage of research are fed back to improve program and practice, leading to successive phases of research and feedback.

The involvement of human subjects in research raises a number of ethical and practical issues. Experimental animals or inorganic substances are not asked whether they wish to participate in research; there is no need to consider whether results should be given in nonidentifying or confidential terms; and the risks of experimental procedures or measurement techniques are not really an ultimate consideration. But human subjects have rights which have been affirmed by scientific bodies and in federal guidelines for funding of projects. Ethical values hold that human research subjects—not research objects—should participate on the basis of informed consent, that reporting of results should preserve individual privacy unless expressly waived, and that risks should be carefully assessed against the estimated benefits of research (U.S. Department of Health, Education, and Welfare, Public Health Service 1971).

These ethical constraints do indeed affect the design of research. A sample of human subjects may really be a sample of those willing to supply information or to participate in experiments rather than a purely random sample. There are ways to reduce the bias which may be thus introduced.

There has been a good deal of attention, in social programming, to the participation of those who will be affected by the program. Without making a case for universal participation or for any particular form of consumer or subject participation, there may be research situations in which such participation may be useful and, indeed, essential if there is to be any cooperation.

In summary, three broad questions face designers of social work research and critical readers of research:

1. To what extent does the research design control for potential bias and error?
2. To what extent does the research design fit the substantive and conceptual requirements of the research problem?
3. To what extent does the research design fit the social and ethical requirements of the research process?

REFERENCES

Ayllon, T. 1963. Intensive treatment of psychotic behavior by stimulus satiation and food reinforcement. In *Exemplars of social research*, ed. P. Fellin, T. Tripodi, and H. J. Meyer. Itasca, Ill.: F. E. Peacock.

Bauer, R. A., ed. 1966. *Social indicators.* Cambridge, Mass.: MIT Press.

Beck, D. F., and Jones, M. A. 1973. *Progress on family problems: A nationwide study of clients' and counsellors' views of family agency services.* New York: Family Service Assoc. of America.

Borgatta, E. F., and Fanshel, D. 1970. The child behavior characteristics (CBC) form: Revised age-specific form. *Multivariate behavioral research* 5:49–82.

Brager, G. 1969. Commitment and conflict in a normative organization. *American Sociological Review* 34:482–91.

Campbell, D. T., and Stanley, J. C. 1963. Experimental and quasi-experimental designs for research on teaching. In *Handbook of research on teaching,* ed. N. L. Gage, pp. 171–247. Chicago: Rand McNally.

Davidson, P. O., and Costello, C. G. 1969. *N = 1: Experimental studies of single cases.* New York: Van Nostrand Reinhold.

Fanshel, D. 1972a. *Far from the reservation: The transracial adoption of American Indian children.* Metuchen, N.J.: Scarecrow Press.

———. 1972b. *Repeated assessment of mental abilities over a five-year period.* Mimeographed. New York: Columbia University School of Social Work.

Finestone, S. 1967. Final progress report of the experimental welfare center project. Mimeographed. New York: Research Center, Columbia University School of Social Work.

———; Lukoff, I.; and Whiteman, M. 1960. *The demand for dog guides and the travel adjustment of blind persons.* Research Center, New York School of Social Work, Columbia University. New York: Equity Press.

Flanagan, J. C. 1954. The critical incident technique. *Psychological Bulletin* 51:327–58.

Geismar, L. I. 1971. *Family and community functioning: A manual of measurement for social work practice and policy.* Metuchen, N.J.: Scarecrow Press.

———, and Ayres, B. 1958. *Families in trouble.* St. Paul, Minn.: Family Centered Project.

Glaser, B. G., and Strauss, A. L. 1967. *The discovery of grounded theory.* Chicago: Aldine.

———. 1964. The social loss of dying patients. *American Journal of Nursing* 64:119–22.

Goodrich, W., and Boomer, D. S. 1958. Some concepts about therapeutic interventions with hyperaggressive children. *Social Casework* 39:207–13; 286–92.

Hollis, F. 1967. Explorations in the development of a typology of casework treatment. *Social casework* 84:335–41.

Hunt, J. McV.; Blenkner, M.; and Kogan, L. S. 1950. *Testing results in social casework.* New York: Family Service Assoc. of America.

Hyman, H. H. 1955. *Survey design and analysis.* Glencoe, Ill.: Free Press.

Jenkins, S., and Norman, E. 1972. *Filial deprivation and foster care.* New York: Columbia Univ. Press.

Jones, J. 1973. Second year evaluation report: Neighborhood youth diversion program. Mimeographed. New York: Center for Research and Demonstration, Columbia University School of Social Work.

Kahn, A. J. 1969. *Theory and practice of social planning.* New York: Russell Sage Foundation.

Kellmer Pringle, M. L.; Butler, R. N.; and Davie, R. 1966. *Eleven thousand seven-year olds.* London: Longman.

Kendall, P. 1972. Evaluating an experiment in medical education. In *Continuities in the language of social research,* ed. P. E. Lazarsfeld, A. K. Pasanella, and M. Rosenberg, pp. 452–63. New York: Free Press of Glencoe.

Kounin, J., et al. 1956. Experimental studies of clients' reactions to initial interviews. *Human Relations* 9:265–93.

Langner, T. S., et al. 1969. Psychiatric impairment in welfare and nonwelfare children. *Welfare in Review* 3:10–21.

Lazarsfeld, P. F. 1955. Interpretation of statistical relations as a research operation. In *The language of social research,* ed. P. F. Lazarsfeld and M. Rosenberg. Glencoe, Ill.: Free Press.

McGowan, B. 1973. Child advocacy: Methods and techniques. Ph.D. dissertation, Columbia University School of Social Work.

Miller, R. R. 1958. An experimental study of observational processes in casework. *Social Casework* 3:96–102.

Mullen, E. M.; Dumpson, J. R.; and Associates. 1972. *Evaluation of social intervention.* San Francisco: Jossey-Bass.

Phillips, B. S. 1966. *Social research: Strategy and tactics.* New York: Macmillan.

Reid, W. J., and Shyne, A. W. 1969. *Brief and extended casework.* New York: Columbia Univ. Press.

Roethlisberger, F. J., and Dickson, W. J. 1939. *Management and the worker.* Cambridge, Mass.: Harvard Univ. Press.

Rosen, A., and Liberman, D. 1972. The experimental evaluation of interview performance of social workers. *Social Service Review* 46:395–412.

Rosenberg, M. 1968. *The logic of survey analysis.* New York: Basic Books.

Schwartz, E. E., and Sample, W. C. 1967. First findings from mid-way. *Social Service Review* 41:1–39.

Selltiz, C.; Jahoda, M.; Deutsch, M.; and Cook, S. W. 1959. *Research methods in social relations.* Rev. ed. New York: Henry Holt.

Sheldon, E. B., and Moore, W. E. eds. 1968. *Indicators of social change.* New York: Russell Sage Foundation.

Solomon, R. L. 1949. Extension of control group design. *Psychological Bulletin* 46:137–50.

Thomas, E. J., and McLeod, D. L. 1960. *In-service training and reduced workloads: Experiments in a state department of welfare.* New York: Russell Sage Foundation.

Tripodi, T.; Fellin, P.; and Meyer, H. J. 1969. *The assessment of social research.* Itasca, Ill.: F. E. Peacock.

U.S. Department of Health, Education, and Welfare. 1969. *Toward a social report.* Washington, D.C.

——. 1971. *The institutional guide to DHEW policy on protection of human subjects.* Washington, D.C.

Zeisel, H. 1968. Say it with figures. Rev. ed. New York: Harper & Row.

3
Principles
of Measurement

The business of the researcher is to contribute toward the answering of questions, the testing of hypotheses, and the making of decisions. These objectives are, of course, shared with many others who are not considered to be researchers. An agency administrator, for example, may answer more questions, test more hypotheses, and make more decisions in a single day than a researcher may do in a year.

What is the difference between persons who are designated as researchers and others who commonly share the same general aims? It may be suggested that, in addition to concern with developing theory, the methods by which the researcher goes about his or her business account for much of the difference. Although his methods may at times be regarded as finicky or fussy, the researcher prefers to describe them as systematic and scientific. As this book well testifies, the conscientious researcher is a strong advocate of the old adage "Look before you leap!" Although the pressure of circumstances may force departure from ideals, the researcher tends to worry about such things as the definition of concepts, the specification of populations, the framing of sampling plans, and the explication of underlying assumptions. Of all the things the researcher worries about, one of the most important is the area of concern commonly referred to as *measurement*.

Philosophically speaking, the researcher may be regarded as a naïve interactionist who shuttles between the so-called real world and the world of ideas or concepts. To a large degree the *theory of measurement* has to do with delineating rules and procedures whose application is designed to increase the probability that goings-on in the world of concepts will correspond to goings-on in the world of reality. The philosopher of science might describe this correspondence as the degree of homomorphism between the empirical or object system on the one hand and the abstract or model system on the other.

The Purpose and Function of Measurement

As might be expected, definitions of measurement vary. Perhaps the most commonly cited authority in this connection is the mathematical physicist, N. R. Campbell, who defined measurement as "the process of assigning numbers to represent qualities" (1920, p. 267). Another classical definition is that of the mathematician-philosopher Bertrand Russell (1938, p. 176), to whom "measurement of magnitudes is, in its most general sense, any method by which a unique and reciprocal correspondence is established between all or some of the magnitudes of a kind and all or some of the numbers, integral, rational, or real as the case may be." In more recent years, and with special influence on concepts of measurement in the social and behavioral sciences, there is the psychologist S. S. Stevens's definition of measurement as "the assignment of numerals to objects or events according to rules" (1951, p. 22). Later, Stevens stated, very appealingly, "In its broadest sense, measurement is the business of pinning numbers on things" (1958, p. 384). He added, "More specifically, it is the assignment of numbers to objects or events in accordance with a rule of some sort." In the same year, Torgerson agreed essentially with Campbell and Russell in contending that measurement refers to the properties of objects rather than to the objects themselves: "Measurement of a property . . . involves the assignment of numbers to systems to represent that property" (1958, p. 14).

These definitions all agree that measurement involves the assigning of symbols to things or, more precisely, to the properties of things according to specified rules and operations. This idea is very close to what we ordinarily mean by language, and, in a broad sense, the use of collective nouns, adjectives, and adverbs is a first step in the development of measurement procedures. More narrowly, the type of language usually associated with the concept of measurement is that of numerals and, even more narrowly, that of numbers. Just as there is room for discussion about whether there can logically be such a thing as nonnumerical measurement, there is also debate about what may properly be included in the thing to be measured. Classical measurement theory, by and large, is concerned with the world of physics, i.e., with "fundamental" dimensions such as length, weight, and time duration or "derived" dimensions such as density and velocity. While the world of physics plays a most important role in social work and its concerns (for example, the age and weight of a child or the area of his bedroom), the social worker is also concerned with many other "worlds"—the psychological world, the sociological world, the economic world. The social worker must, perforce, deal with data from any or all of these worlds, and hence we must assume that what is to be measured in social work research includes the properties of such things as physical objects, persons, groups, institutions, and geographic areas.

All this does not mean, however, that measurement procedures are identical as we move from one domain to another. Within physics, as Campbell notes, measuring temperature is not the same as measuring length. The length of an object can be measured directly by placing a foot rule alongside it, but temperature is measured indirectly by noting the height of a column of mercury in a tube. The foot is a small piece (standard unit) of length, but one degree as shown by a thermometer is not a small piece of temperature in the same direct sense.

Although the social work researcher will be dealing frequently with physical magnitudes, perhaps more often he will be interested in psychological, sociological, and economic variables in such realms as motivation, racial conflict, and family friction. One of the "real world" systems which he commonly encounters is money. Objectively speaking, money has many of the characteristics of length; i.e., as one foot plus one foot equals two feet, so one dollar plus one dollar equals two dollars. Nevertheless, in psychological and sociological (not to mention economic) terms, we know that the value of a dollar does not remain constant. Thus, one dollar added to an income of $25,000 scarcely means the same as a dollar added to an income of $250. Moreover, psychologically speaking, even height and length can not be assumed to have constant significance, viz., a woman who is six feet tall may not be as pleased to be that tall as would a man of the same height.

The Role of Measurement in Scientific Research

The assignment of reference symbols to the properties of "objects" results in several major kinds of data. This is discussed in more detail below under "Scales of Measurement." The first kind involves situations in which the measurement operation is one of classification and the data consist of "counts" or frequency per class. Such data are commonly referred to as attributive, classificatory, qualitative, or *enumerative*. A second major kind of data occurs when it is possible to assume that the property being studied varies from less to more, either discretely or along a continuum, and the numbers assigned to various "amounts" of the property depict their ordering or magnitude. The measurement operation in this case consists of ranking the objects with respect to the specified property or assigning numbers which indicate the relative or absolute "amounts" of the property each object possesses. Data resulting from these operations are called quantitative, a further distinction being made between *ordered and metric data*.

Progress in a particular area of research can often be judged roughly by the prevalence of classificatory, ordering, or metrical concepts in the field. We say roughly because at times the introduction of apparent quantification cannot be justified in terms of the "sensitivity" of available techniques. However, when there is adequate theoretical and experimental justification, the benefits to be derived are marked. Among the advantages are the following:

Increased precision of description. Although classification is probably the first significant step in the development of a science, it is often useful to distinguish among things which are grouped together in a given classification. A certain group of parents, for example, might be categorized as "rejecting," but it would be of greater value to describe each parent in terms of the degree to which such behavior is exhibited. In this instance attention is directed to observations within a category. In other instances attention may be given to differences between categories. To call one set of cases short-term and another long-term simply tells us that they differ at some arbitrary point such as five client interviews. The number of interviews per case would tell us not only that one group of cases received more contact than another but also how much more.

Increased communicability of research operations and results. In general, as we move from classificatory to metric concepts, it becomes necessary to be more rigorous in specifying measurement procedures. This results both in greater possibility for exact repetition of studies and in greater clarity of presentation and interpretation of findings. It is commonly said that numbers are the only universal language. We can infer more about the standard of living of a particular family when we know family income, expenditures, rent, etc., than when we know only that the family is or is not receiving public assistance.

Increased possibilities for discovering and establishing relationships among phenomena. The long-run objective of scientific research is to develop principles which will account for what has already been observed in the empirical world and predict what has not yet been observed. Again, as one moves from classificatory to metric data, there is greater opportunity for discovering regularities and patterns in our data. With classificatory data it is possible to detect nonrandom associations between classifications. Ranked data permit general statements regarding strength and direction of association. Metric data allow for the quantitative expression of functional relationships. Numbers, when properly applied to empirical phenomena, make possible the use of the full armamentarium of mathematics in constructing and testing theories aimed at explaining, predicting, or controlling the phenomena of the "real world."

ELEMENTS OF MEASUREMENT THEORY

The purpose of this section is to present an overview of the conceptual framework which, whether recognized or not, lies behind the application of measurement procedures. It is a curious world, really three interpenetrating worlds, of theoretical models, number systems, and empirical data.

Theoretical Models and the World of Reality

As noted above, the researcher shuttles between the real world and the world of concepts. The real world provides his empirical evidence, the world of concepts a scheme or map for "making sense" out of the portion of the real world which he is seeking to account for, explain, or predict. The conceptual scheme or map is known as a theoretical model. Depending on the stage of development of the particular science or area of research, the model consists of more or less clearly defined constructs and more or less logical relationships or connections among the constructs. If the theoretical model is to be useful, there is the necessity of specifying rules connecting at least some part of the conceptual system with the world of reality. If all works well, these rules permit passage between the world of reality and the hypothetical world of the theoretical model. Then the connections within the theoretical model permit further passage among the constructs, finally emerging as *predictions* about some other part of the empirical system. If the predictions are found to be substantially correct, the theoretical model is strengthened; otherwise, there is need to check where it went wrong and make corrections.

Rules of Correspondence

The semantic definitions connecting the theoretical model and the world of reality are called *rules of correspondence* (Torgerson 1958). It is largely with regard to these rules that measurement plays its significant role. At their weakest, the rules of correspondence between concepts in the model and empirical observations are ad hoc assumptions on the part of the investigator; at their best, the rules take the form of rigorous operational definitions which specify the connections between the concepts and the relevant observations. A strong contribution to such rigor is possible when the properties of the empirical system can be "measured" to permit the expression of the concept in numerical terms.

Postulates Basic to the Real Number System and Complete Measurement

The ideal situation in measurement exists when numbers can be assigned to the properties of "objects" and the numbers can then be manipulated according to the rules of mathematics. The traditional viewpoint in measurement, as expressed by Campbell, is that justification for treating data as numbers—i.e., addition and the derivative procedures of subtraction, multiplication, and division—occurs when operations with objects in the physical world can be carried out which duplicate the additive properties of the number system. Thus, for example, it is possible to "prove" that a line four feet in length plus a line two feet in length equals a line six feet in length by placing the two lines end to end and applying a foot rule to the new line. Such possibilities for direct attack on measuring the properties of objects are very limited (length, weight, time) and in the physical world most properties are measured in an indirect fashion.

Within the scope of this chapter no attempt will be made to present a detailed account of the properties of numbers and the concomitant requirements for so-called complete measurement. In general, the postulates underlying the real number system may be grouped into three major classes having to do, respectively, with equivalence, order, and additivity.

Some postulates regarding equivalence
(a) Either $A = B$ or $A \neq B$ (equivalence, nonequivalence)
(b) If $A = B$, then $B = A$ (symmetry)
(c) If $A = B$ and $B = C$, then $A = C$ (transitivity)

Some postulates regarding ordinality
(a) If $A \neq B$, then either $A > B$ or $A < B$ (connectedness)
(b) If $A > B$, then $B \not> A$ (asymmetry)
(c) If $A > B$ and $B > C$, then $A > C$ (transitivity)

Some postulates regarding additivity
(a) $A + B = B + A$ (commutative law)
(b) If $A = P$ and $B = Q$, then $A + B = P + Q$ (axiom of equals)
(c) $A + (B + C) = (A + B) + C$ (associative law)

(In the statements given, the symbol $\neq$ means "not equal to"; $>$ means "greater than"; $<$ means "smaller than"; and $\not>$ means "not greater than.")

The reader who is not aversively conditioned against simple equations should immediately conclude that the propositions stated above are self-evident (the labels for the propositions are for reference purposes and should not be allowed to influence this conclusion). And the propositions are indeed self-evident to anyone familiar with elementary arithmetic. In general, this suggests that difficulties in problems of measurement do not occur within the self-contained realm of numbers but in formulating rules of correspondence between the numerical model and the "thing" measured which permit the model to be tested empirically.

SCALES OF MEASUREMENT

Torgerson (1958) summarizes the major characteristics of the number series, some of which were stated as postulates in the preceding section, as follows:

Numbers are ordered.

Differences between numbers are ordered. That is, the difference between any pair of numbers is greater than, equal to, or less than the difference between any other pair of numbers.

The series has a unique origin indicated by the number 0.

These Torgerson calls, respectively, the characteristics of *order*, *distance*, and *origin*. They are based on the fact that numbers form a sequence going from lesser to greater; that differences (distances) between numbers may be directly compared, e.g., $6 - 4 = 3 - 1$; and, finally, that numbers begin at zero, so that any number represents the distance from zero to the number. To these three characteristics may be added the elementary characteristic of uniqueness or nonequivalence, namely, that different numbers are not equal to each other. Torgerson, following Campbell and Russell, rejects classification of objects or events as a form of measurement. In this he is in disagreement with the well-known views of Stevens (1946, 1951, 1958, 1968), who conceives of classification as the most primitive form of measurement. Torgerson's main point is that in measurement the numbers assigned should refer to relative degrees of a property shown by different objects and not to the objects themselves. We shall agree with the more liberal point of view and assume that classification does warrant conception as a measurement procedure.

Elaborating the classification of scales given by Torgerson to include Stevens's nominal scale, but calling it *nominal classification*, we present six major types of scales in table 1. The type of scale is based on the characteristics of the number system possessed by the scale.

TABLE 1
Six Major Types of Scales of Measurement

	Nonequivalence	Order	Distance
No natural origin	Nominal classification	Ordinal scale with arbitrary origin	Interval scale
Natural origin	None/Some scale	Ordinal scale with natural origin	Ratio scale

Order includes the property of nonequivalence; distance includes the properties of nonequivalence and order. Stevens's system of classification consists of the nominal scale, the ordinal scale (without regard to origin), the interval scale, and the ratio scale. Torgerson omits the column labeled "Nonequivalence." Adapted from Torgerson (1958).

Nominal classification. In the so-called nominal scale, numerals are assigned to objects or classes of objects. A nominal scale, for example, may be used to identify different objects within a group, e.g., baseball players with various numbers; or different classes of objects which contain comparable items, e.g., groups of individuals labeled with various numerals according to religion or ethnic identification. Another example would be the use of numerals to designate various diagnostic categories of a psychiatric or psychosocial classification.

A slightly more complicated example of assigning numerals to objects would be the use of a five-digit number to identify different cases carried by a large social agency. Thus a particular case might be numbered 11376.

If, within each case, the father were further assigned the numerals 01, the mother 02, the oldest child 03, and so on, each individual's number might be regarded as having a major classification in which the first five numerals are assigned to different families, while a numeral in the sixth and seventh place would identify different members of each family and constitute a minor classification. The utility of such a use of numerals can be seen when it is noted, for example, that all individuals receiving a 0 and a 2 in the sixth and seventh positions of the number would be mothers.

While identification of things which are alike and discrimination between things which are unlike are the basic operations underlying all measurement, there are several reasons why the usual nominal scale should probably be regarded simply as a classification system and not as a scale in the sense that the remaining five categories in table 1 refer to scales. In the first place, the numerals used for distinguishing different classes exhibit none of the properties or relationships of real numbers except the tautology that no two different numbers are alike. This means that any other set of different symbols, e.g., letters of the alphabet or different colors, could be utilized to label the classes rather than numbers. The advantage of numerals is their convenience and large supply.

In the second place, and somewhat paradoxically, a nominal classification containing more than two classes is too complicated to be regarded as a scale. This is because there is no restriction on the kind or number of properties which may be used in establishing the classification system. Thus, a commonly used psychiatric classification (American Psychiatric Association, 1966) is based on consideration of many properties such as symptoms, occurrence of trauma, course of development, and so on. Although this is an extreme example, it serves to illustrate that classification is not necessarily simpler than measurement or scaling.

The key to the matter is the term *unidimensional scale*. Before one attempts to deal with measurement problems concerned with more than one property at a time, it is logical to discuss scales which deal with only a single property. Except for nominal classification, the scales designated in table 1 refer to the use of numbers to represent differing degrees or amounts of a particular property.

The none/some scale. The simplest scale dealing with a single property appears to be what may be called an absence/presence or none/some scale. It is simply a dichotomous or two-category affair, one category for objects which are characterized by absence of a given property and the second category for objects which possess that property. In its most literal form, the first category should represent "zero amount" of the property and the second category "100 percent amount" of the property. However, since few objects of research interest show such "all or none" characteristics with respect to a particular property, objects are usually assigned to the first category if they possess none or a negligible amount of the given property and to the second category if they show a discriminable or minimal amount of the property. Thus, a number of sounds may be classified as "not audible" or "audible," a group of individuals may be classified as "not casework clients" or "casework clients," or a group of cases in a family agency may be divided into those which have closed on an unplanned basis versus those which have closed on a planned basis.

A nominal classification consisting of more than two categories may be resolved into a group of none/some scales by considering each category successively as the "some" category and combining all other categories into a single "none" category. To give an oversimplified example, an investigator may have classified a group of cases into three categories, depending on whether the major problem was in the economic area, the family relationships area, or the physical health area. This three-category classification may be represented by three none/some scales—one, for example, based on cases which do not show an economic problem and cases which do show an economic problem. This example also illustrates a useful device for handling a classification system in which a given case may fall into more than one category. Thus, some cases may have been regarded as possessing not only an economic problem but a physical health problem and perhaps also a family relationships problem. In such instances, where the total count in a classification system may exceed the number of cases, the entries in each none/some scale consist of the number of cases falling into a particular category, e.g., possessing an economic problem, while the number of cases in the second category consists of the difference in count between the total number of cases and those which fall into the specified category.

According to the logic of the none/some scale, many commonly used dichotomies, such as male-female, aggressive-passive, or accepting-rejecting, may be reducible to unidimensional none/some form by designating one of the categories as the none category and the other one as the some category. Thus, a male-female classification becomes a none/some scale if the categories are taken to represent nonfemales and females.

In instances where utilization of a none/some scale is applicable, it is common to assign the number 0 to the none category and the number 1 to the some category. Whereas the use of the number 0 is inherent within the system, the second number may be arbitrarily chosen as any number but zero. In many uses both numbers may be chosen arbitrarily, with the same results so far as relationship of the dichotomous variable to other variables is concerned. However, in addition to the computational convenience, which is provided by use of 0 and 1 for the value of each category, the resulting frequency distribution is immediately interpretable in terms of proportions or percentages. It might also be noted that the utilization of none/some scales—often called coded or dummy variables—has been shown to facilitate analysis of complex data by multiple regression methods (Cohen 1968; Kerlinger and Pedhazur 1973).

Ordinal scale with arbitrary origin. In measurement with an ordinal scale, the numbers used for representing various amounts or degrees of a given property correspond to order of magnitude. Thus, a group of children might be arranged in order of height from left to right along a wall, with the smallest child assigned the number 1, the next-to-smallest child number 2, and so on. The numbers would indicate the rank order of the children with respect to height.

Examples of situations where a set of objects is ordered with respect to degree or magnitude of a particular property are very common. Horses are ranked in order of finishing a race. Chickens in a barnyard may be ranked in order of who pecks whom. Students, unfortunately, are often ranked in terms of how well they please the teacher.

The foregoing examples represent situations in which separate objects are completely ranked. In other instances, classes of objects rather than single objects are ranked or ordered in terms of a particular characteristic or property. An oft-cited example is Mohs's ten-step scale of the comparative hardness of minerals (what will scratch what), in which talc has rank 1, gypsum has rank 2, all the way to diamond, with rank 10. The sociological literature on social stratification abounds in scales purporting to rank different individuals in terms of social class, such as Warner's index of status characteristics (Warner, Meeker, and Eels 1949) or Hollingshead's index of social position (Hollingshead and Redlich 1958).

Ordinal scale with natural origin. Torgerson (1958) points out that in some instances one of the classes of an ordinal scale may logically be assigned the number 0 to represent zero amount of the property under consideration. A commonly used type of item in research schedules is one which describes the relative frequency of a particular kind of behavior in terms of "never occurs," "occurs rarely," "occurs occasionally," and so on. With such a ranking scale it would be logical to assign the number 0 to the category "never occurs."

In other cases, the category which could logically be assigned the number 0 might occur somewhere toward the middle of the scale rather than at the lower end. For example, the steps on an attitude scale may run from "dislikes very much" at one end to "likes very much" at the other end, with a neutral point in the middle representing the attitude "neither likes nor dislikes." The neutral attitude may be considered the natural origin of the scale and be assigned the number 0. Scales of this kind are commonly referred to as *bipolar* in nature.

Interval scale. In measurement with an interval scale (sometimes called a *cardinal scale*), not only does the order of the numbers in the scale correspond to the order of magnitude of the property, but the difference between the pair of numbers assigned to two magnitudes bears a functional relationship to the difference between the two magnitudes. Such scales are said to have a common unit of measurement so that it is permissible to say that one object has less or more of a given property than a second object and how many units less or more.

Many examples of interval scales exist in the physical world. Temperature as measured either by the centigrade or the Fahrenheit scale is one example. In the centigrade scale the unit of measurement is the degree, representing 1/100 of the distance between the freezing point of water set at 0° and the boiling point of water set at 100°. The arbitrariness of the magnitude of the unit of measurement scale is seen from the fact that in the Fahrenheit scale each degree represents 1/180 of the distance between the freezing point of water (set at 32°) and the boiling point of water (set at 212°).

Calendar time is also measured by an interval scale, with arbitrary origin at the birth of Christ. The common unit of measurement is the year, which allows us to say that the same amount of time elapsed between A.D. 1700 and A.D. 1800 as between A.D. 1850 and A.D. 1950. Surplus or deficit in family income as compared with public assistance budget standards could similarly be regarded as distances on an interval scale.

Ratio scale. If an interval scale has a natural origin at number 0, representing zero amount of the property being measured, the scale is called a ratio scale. In this case, the numbers assigned to various degrees or amounts of the property bear a direct relationship to the absolute amount of the property. With such a scale we can say not only that one object has so many units more of a property than a second object but also that the first object is so many times as "big" as the second object. Thus, a tree one hundred feet in height is twice as tall as a tree fifty feet in height, or a boy who weighs one hundred pounds is twice as heavy as a boy who weighs fifty pounds. This is in contrast, for example, to the ordinary temperature scale, where it is not meaningful to say that a temperature of 50°F. is twice as hot as a temperature of 25°F.

Interestingly enough, the counting of objects generally gives rise to ratio scale measurement. Thus, a social worker with a caseload of twenty cases has twice as large a caseload as one with ten cases. The property of the group of objects in this connection is *numerosity*. Numerosity is an especially interesting property because it illustrates so clearly the process of abstracting from "nature" which is characteristic of research data. In counting, the number 1 is assigned to each object, and each is added. In most research uses of counts, e.g., items per class in a nominal classification or frequencies per class interval in a frequency distribution, the objects counted are alike in some property under consideration, but generally they differ in other properties with which the investigator is not concerned. Just as the individual who has fifty dollars is not usually concerned with differences in the serial numbers or state of cleanliness of the bills, so the decision above that a worker with twenty cases has twice as large a caseload as one with ten cases would take no cognizance, for example, of the fact that the second worker may be seeing clients twice as often as the first one.

Unidimensionality, Indexes, and Multidimensional Scaling

Except for nominal classification, the preceding discussion of scales of measurement was concerned with the concept of the *unidimensional* scale. Scaling methods have been primarily directed at the scaling of stimuli, persons, and responses but have also been used to scale attributes of "large" entities such as institutions, cities, and nations. Specific scaling techniques including pair comparisons, successive intervals, equal-appearing intervals, and many others are described in Guilford (1954) and Torgerson (1958). An especially rich variety of scaling methods has been developed for the scaling of attitudes (Edwards 1957; Summers 1970; Dawes 1972).

Perhaps the most rigorous technique for building unidimensionality into a scale is that developed by Guttman (1950). The basic notion of the Guttman scale is that a person who agrees with an item at a given location on the scale will agree with all items below that location. Deviation from such a "perfect" scale is evaluated by a coefficient of reproducibility, and it is generally accepted that a "good" scale will show a coefficient in excess of 85 to 90 percent. An example of such a scale is the four-item Benefactress of Children Scale developed by Fanshel (1966) for ordering foster mothers with regard to their satisfaction from providing care for neglected children.

Although it is possible to apply direct scaling methods to a large range of phenomena—attitude statements, personality characteristics, severity of crime, similarity of occupations, and so on—in many areas of research such so-called *representational* measurement may not be feasible and the investigator frequently resorts to *index* measurement (Coombs 1964; Dawes 1972). A common example of index measurement is the cognitive or ability test, where the testee's score is based on adding points for correct answers. In social work, many indexes of *social need* are similarly derived from the combination of two or more variables (Zimbalist 1957).

A common problem in social work research is finding that usual measures of socioeconomic status or social class (Hollingshead and Redlich 1958; Warner, Meeker, and Eels 1949) do not differentiate impoverished households which tend to cluster in the lowest category. Approaches to "spreading out" such cases in a meaningful way by development of indexes are seen in two recent studies. Polansky, Borgman, and De Saix (1972), working with a rural Appalachian sample, developed a Childhood Level of Living Scale consisting of a final set of eighty-nine items—e.g., water is piped into the house—in twenty-one subscales, which were rated by welfare workers. For biological families of children who entered foster care in New York City, Jenkins and Norman (1972) formulated an Index of Socioeconomic Circumstances based on a weighted combination of five subscales, including main source of support, education, income rank of neighborhood, juvenile delinquency rank of neighborhood, and number of negative housing conditions.

In some instances, where investigators have combined several different variables into a single index which is then treated as a unidimensional measure, it may be useful to attempt to delineate a more detailed pattern or structure in the data.

Such an approach is provided by multidimensional scaling which has many similarities to the mapping of a designated geographic area. More generally, the problem of multidimensional scaling has to do with the assignment of a set of numbers to represent varying orders or amounts of two or more properties possessed by a group of objects and the relationships among the properties. To give a simple geometric illustration suggested by Green (1954) in terms of a portion of the theoretical framework postulated by Ripple (1955), a client's motivation may be considered to be a function of both his discomfort and his hope. The variable (property) under consideration is *motivation*. In terms of motivation, let us assume that three clients, A, B, and C, have been judged (assuming further that this complex variable could be measured on an interval scale) to show the following differences: $A - B = 4$, $B - C = 3$, and $A - C = 5$. These differences could obviously not occur (except in error) if motivation were a unidimensional variable, i.e., if A, B, and C were points on a single straight line. However, if A, B, and C are actually located at the vertexes of a right triangle (in two-dimensional space), the differences become consistent (the rule of Pythagoras says so!). Thus, A and B differ 4 units in discomfort but not at all in hope, B and C differ 3 units in hope but not at all in discomfort, and A and C differ in both discomfort and hope.

Problems relating to multidimensional scaling can take many forms. In some cases the objective may be to analyze complex variables into a set of unidimensional variables, e.g., by factor analysis (Shyne and Kogan 1958). In other cases the problem is more directly related to unidimensional scaling; that is, the establishment of order among values or of distances between values is the aim of the investigator. Further discussion of this topic is beyond the scope of this chapter. The interested reader is directed to the classic treatment by Torgerson (1958) and the recent compilation by Shepard, Romney, and Nerlove (1972).

Measurement Scales and Statistics

The classical requirements for complete measurement necessitate empirical demonstration that various degrees of a specified property behave in the same manner as the number system. This could be interpreted to mean that the property's characteristic of additivity of quantities should be confirmable experimentally. As noted previously, this requirement is probably directly demonstrable by physical operations for only a few so-called extensive dimensions in the physical world, such as length and weight.

What possibilities are then left with regard to measurement in the nonphysical world? The stock-in-trade of the social work researcher, as well as of his colleagues in such related fields as psychology and sociology, abounds in properties of persons and groups, such as attitude toward receiving help or family cohesiveness. That such properties are not amenable to complete measurement in the classical sense of physically demonstrable additivity seems hardly debatable. Stated in such terms, most nonphysical properties of objects, persons, or events can probably at best meet requirements for ordinality.

There is, indeed, a body of opinion that psychological and sociological variables having to do with aptitudes, attitudes, personality characteristics, properties of groups, and the like can be measured at best on ordinal scales. This opinion commonly takes the form of insistence that only certain types of statistical procedures are permissible depending on the strength of measurement, i.e., type of scale, of the variables involved. Table 2 lists examples of "permissible" statistics given by Stevens (1958, 1968) in the framework of his hierarchy of scales. In each instance, statistics permissible for a given type of scale are permissible for "stronger" scales, i.e., the median is permissible not only for the ordinal scale but also for the interval and ratio scales.

Specifically, much discussion has centered on the so-called misuse of interval scale statistics for numerical data in which equality of units has not been clearly established. For example, a group of children may be ranked by means of an IQ test, but differences in their actual scores should not be taken seriously. At its extreme, this point of view as represented in table 2 would hold that computing means, standard deviations, and product moment correlation coefficients cannot be justified for most psychological and sociological variables, nor can it be justified for the same or related data in social work research (Bush 1959). In terms of tests of "significance" and other methods of statistical inference, the

TABLE 2
Type of Scale and Permissible Statistics

Scale	Permissible Statistics
Nominal	Mode "Information" measures Chi square
Ordinal	Median Percentile Rank correlation
Interval	Mean Standard deviation t-test F-test Product moment correlation
Ratio	Geometric mean Harmonic mean Percent variation

Based on Stevens (1958, 1968)

same point of view would advocate the abandonment of classic *parametric* statistical methods largely based on normal distribution assumptions in favor of *nonparametric* or distribution-free methods, which to a considerable extent make use of classifications or ranks rather than scores. A contrary point of view holds that classic parametric procedures are generally *robust*, i.e., provide reasonable inferences even in the face of violation of underlying assumptions.

Whether statistical methods must always be consistent with the scale properties of the attribute being analyzed is debatable, especially when analysis is concerned with summary measures for groups of subjects. Statistical methods, whether parametric or nonparametric, like mathematics in general, are self-contained systems basically independent of reality considerations. Nevertheless, the value of statistical procedures when applied in research depends on the degree to which the results of the statistical manipulations lead to useful and meaningful decisions or contributions to knowledge. The "safe" approach, since in general fewer assumptions are made, may appear to be to use nonparametric rather than parametric techniques whenever a relevant method is available. At the same time, the investigator must be aware that in adopting the safe approach, he may be discarding data and weakening his chances of detecting significant differences or relationships (see chapter 9). In addition, most nonparametric methods do not lend themselves to a combination of variables or to estimation of the magnitude of experimental effects or strength of relationships.

Perhaps in the future a clearer rationale will be developed for the choice of particular statistical techniques for particular kinds of data. At present it appears that on a practical level, *especially for larger samples*, differences in conclusions reached by the employment of non-parametric or parametric methods are usually negligible. Questions of what to measure and how to measure, as well as problems of sampling, control, and relevance to theory, are more pressing.

ASSESSING THE ADEQUACY OF MEASUREMENT PROCEDURES

Up to this point it has generally been assumed that the operation of classification, ordering, or quantification has been carried out without error, and that the aims of the investigator have been achieved. These two considerations—the degree to which the measures are free from error, and the degree to which the measures reflect what one is looking for—have been referred to as the *reliability* and *validity* of measurement. Over the years each of these terms has accrued many synonyms (Kogan 1959). In addition to these two basic considerations, the adequacy of a particular measurement procedure must also be evaluated in terms of certain more mundane criteria which may be grouped under such headings as *practicality* and *feasibility*.

Practicality and feasibility have to do with such things as cost in time, money, and effort in using the procedure, the need for special training, and the ease of scoring and interpretation of results. They also include attention to matters of ethics in collecting information or seeing that a research procedure does not interfere with treatment aims or administrative policies with respect to the group of clients, groups, or institutions being studied. We shall not elaborate further on these matters except to emphasize that the research worker's technical competence often founders on the twin reefs of practicality and feasibility.

The General Concept of Reliability

Although secondary to problems of the validity or relevance of measures, we shall speak of reliability first, since reliability is a necessary if not sufficient condition for the establishment of adequate validity. Here we are primarily concerned not with what is being measured but rather *how well* whatever is being measured is measured. We may ask of our data, for example, how close we would come to the same results if we repeated the measurements a number of times. Would each of a group of boys have remained classified as delinquent or nondelinquent? Would a sample of families have been ranked in the same order with respect to social class status? Would a group of clients have been judged to show the same amount of movement? In each instance, it may be noted, the particular procedures used may not have done a good job of "getting at" delinquency, social class, or movement, but in considering reliability of measurement we are postponing this crucial question and are concerned only with the reproducibility, repeatability, or generalizability of our results.

In most theoretical discussions of reliability it is assumed that the measurements involved are in the form of scores which can be handled by the usual processes of arithmetic. As a matter of fact, the measurements most common to such discussions are based on so-called objective tests, in which an individual is presented with a number of items from which a score is derived by counting the number of correct responses. In the light of the preceding description of requirements for measurement, one may question the degree to which distributions of such scores approach interval-scale form, based as they are on assumptions such as the normal distribution of traits. However, for purposes of the present discussion of reliability and validity, we will assume that the results of the measurement procedure have been expressed in the form of scores and will note that, generally, the principles involved can also be applied to classification or ranking.

Theoretical Definition of Reliability and Standard Error of Measurement

All measurement is characterized by error or, more accurately, by variability. Hypothetically, one might take an infinite number of measurements of a particular property of a particular thing and reasonably assume that some measure of central tendency for the set of measurements represents the "true value" for the thing measured, and that some measure of variability can be used to summarize the variations around the true value. For a property expressed in scores, the true value could be represented by the mean of the repeated measures and the variability or errors of measurement by the standard deviation of the repeated measures.

A related approach to the concept of reliability begins with a similar postulate: that any observed score can be thought of as consisting of two parts expressed by the equation:

$$X_o = X_t + X_e ,$$

(where X_o = the observed score; X_t = the true score; and X_e = the "error" component). If it is then assumed that the errors in a set of measures are distributed independently and randomly, it is easy to show that the variance (square of the standard deviation) of the observed scores is equal to the variance of the "true" scores plus the variance of the errors, or, in equation form:

$$\sigma_o{}^2 = \sigma_t{}^2 + \sigma_e{}^2$$

With slight manipulation this equation will read:

$$\frac{\sigma_t^2}{\sigma_o^2} = 1 - \frac{\sigma_e^2}{\sigma_o^2}.$$

The reliability of a set of measures (symbolized by r_{11}) is then defined as either side of the above equation, i.e.,

$$r_{11} = \frac{\sigma_t^2}{\sigma_o^2} = 1 - \frac{\sigma_e^2}{\sigma_o^2}$$

(definition of coefficient of reliability), or, in words, the coefficient of reliability of a set of measures is defined as the ratio of the true variance to the observed variance. Further manipulation would indicate that

$$\sigma_e^2 = \sigma_o^2 (1 - r_{11})$$

and

$$\sigma_e = \sigma_o \sqrt{1 - r_{11}}$$

(definition of standard error of measurement).

The two definitions above, i.e., the coefficient of reliability and the standard error of measurement, represent the two most common ways in which the reliability of a set of measures is expressed when the measures are in the form of scores. The coefficient of reliability expresses reliability in terms of a ratio of variances, implicitly interpretable as an index of association between pairs of repeated measurements, while the standard error of measurement expresses reliability as the standard deviation of the distribution of "errors" of measurement.

Methods of Estimating Reliability

It should be emphasized that the above definitions of the coefficient of reliability and the closely related standard error of measurement are completely hypothetical. In the development and application of measurement procedures, we can at best estimate hypothetical reliability. The number of approaches to estimation of reliability are almost legion, depending on such factors as the nature of the measurement instrument, the possibilities for repeated measurement, the effect on the object of repeated measurement, the conditions under which measurement occurs, and so on.

In the realm of objective psychological tests, the estimation of a coefficient of reliability is most commonly based on one or the other of five major methods: (1) immediate retest with the same test; (2) delayed retest with the same test; (3) immediate retest with an equivalent or parallel form of the original test; (4) delayed retest with an equivalent or parallel form of the original test; and (5) internal analysis of a test given on one occasion.

Comparison of these methods would quickly reveal that one should not expect to obtain the same coefficient from each of them. For example, one might reasonably expect that a correlation based on retesting a group of subjects with the *same* test would tend to be higher than a correlation based on retesting with an equivalent but *different* form of the test. The magnitude of a particular estimate of reliability depends, as will be recalled from the theoretical definition, on the relative proportions of the observed variance assigned to "true" variance and "error" variance. In the example above, retesting a group of subjects with the same test means that the content of the test has been held constant, and this condition will tend in general to "inflate" the estimate of true variance while lowering the estimate of error variance.

Thorndike and Hagen (1969) have described the relationships between the five principal methods for estimating test reliability and three major sources of variation in obtained scores. Table 3 is a slightly modified version of one of their tables, showing a summary comparison of the different procedures. This table shows clearly that each procedure, in estimating reliability, takes account of certain sources of variation while neglecting others. It may be noted that in this analysis of relations between procedures for estimating reliability and sources of variation, the method of using immediate retest with a parallel form is similar to estimation based on a single test.

TABLE 3
SOURCES OF VARIATION REPRESENTED IN DIFFERENT PROCEDURES
FOR ESTIMATING RELIABILITY

Procedures for Estimating Reliability	Sources of Variation in Scores		
	Variation Arising within Measurement Procedure Itself	Changes in the Individual from Day to Day	Changes in the Specific Sample of Items
Immediate retest (same test)	X		
Retest after interval (same test)	X	X	
Parallel test form (without time interval)	X		X
Parallel test form (with time interval)	X	X	X
Subdivision or item analysis of single test	X		X

Based on Thorndike and Hagen (1969).

The sources of variation indicated in table 3 may be subdivided and extended almost without end. Thorndike's original table also includes changes in the individual's speed of work, which are pertinent for a timed test. Other possible sources of variation, for example, might be differences due to different testers or to different scorers of the test. In other contexts sources of variation might be referred to as interviewer, observer, judge, or case reader "error," leading, for example, to the concept of *interjudge reliability*, generally measured by some coefficient of agreement between independent judges.

Enough has certainly been said to convince the reader that reliability is a very general concept covering a wide range of possibilities for estimation and interpretation. And yet it must be emphasized that only the surface of the subject of reliability has been scratched. Other factors such as the variability and general level of the group on the particular property or characteristic, as well as the number of items used in obtaining the score for an individual, are also reflected in the estimate of reliability (Anastasi 1968; Cronbach 1970, 1972; Lord and Novick 1968; Thorndike 1971). A reliability coefficient standing by itself tells us very little about the dependability of measurement with a particular instrument or research procedure. In order properly to evaluate a quantitative statement about the reliability of a measurement procedure, we should know in detail the method used for estimating the reliability, the characteristics of the persons, objects, or events comprising the sample studied, the conditions under which measures were obtained, and any other information pertinent to application and interpretation of the procedure. As noted at the beginning of this section, reliability of measurement is secondary in importance to the validity of measures (to be discussed below). High reliability or precision does not guarantee a measure's relevance to the purpose at hand; but negligible or low reliability of a measure may destroy relevance.

The Concept of Validity

In a broad sense the validity or relevance of a measurement procedure is based on the degree to which the aims or purposes of making the measurements are accomplished. Since the aims of making a set of measurements may vary in number, kind, and scope, it follows that in general we must speak of the *validities* rather than the *validity* of a measurement procedure.

Many attempts have been made to classify the major types of validity underlying measurement procedures. Upon analysis, such attempts at classifying types of validity appear to be efforts at classifying major purposes of measurement. The types of validity refer in turn to the kinds of evidence one should collect in order to demonstrate that the specified purpose or purposes have been met.

Evidence for validity usually comes from one or both of two major sources. On one hand, there is what may be called the *logical* or *rational* approach to problems of validity. Secondly, there is the *empirical* or *statistical* approach, in which one seeks evidence by determining the relationship of one's measures to other measures or variables.

Logical or rational approaches to determination of validity involve critical examination and analysis of the form, structure, and content of the measurement procedure in terms of what the investigator has aimed or claimed to measure. We may ask, for example, How clear and unambiguous are any definitions or instructions used? Was the sequence of steps taken by the investigator in developing the instrument a logical, well-planned sequence?

The empirical or statistical approach to validity is based on determining the relationship of the measures in hand to something outside the measures themselves. The "something outside" is called a *criterion*. Psychological testers have long devoted themselves to the construction of instruments designed to have a diagnostic or prognostic function. It is well known that aptitude and ability tests have been developed which "predict" with reasonable success how well an individual will do in college, in medical school, or on the job. Most often empirical validity is reported in terms of a correlation known as a *validity coefficient*.

A very useful contribution toward clarification of the conceptual framework of validity was made some years ago by a joint committee of the American Psychological Association, the American Educational Research Association, and the National Council on Measurements Used in Education (1974). The purpose of this group was to develop a manual specifying the kinds of information which should accompany publication of tests and other devices for diagnosis and evaluation.

The conclusions of the committee about major aspects of validity are presented in modified summary form in table 4.

TABLE 4
MAJOR TYPES OF VALIDITY

Types of Validity	Evidence Required
Criterion-related validity	
Concurrent	Measures correspond to concurrent criterion performance or status.
Predictive	Predictions made from measurement procedure are confirmed by data gathered at some subsequent time.
Content validity	Measurement procedure samples universe of situations or subject matter about which conclusions are to be drawn.
Construct validity	Certain explanatory constructs or concepts, i.e., theory, account for measures obtained.

Based on American Psychological Association (1974).

It will be noted that empirical or criterion-related validity is subdivided into *concurrent* or *predictive* validity, depending on whether the criterion data are coexistent with or subsequent in time to the measures being validated. The distinction between concurrent and predictive validity is important primarily for practical reasons such as the necessity of follow-up to establish predictive validity. To complete subclassification of criterion-related validity on the basis of the temporal relation between the measures and the criterion, one might add *postdictive validity* to the list to designate situations in which the aim is to "predict" prior events or conditions, e.g., testing an adult male and then comparing results with known facts about his relationship to his mother during his childhood.

It may seem at first glance that what was previously referred to as rational or logical validity has been subdivided into *content* validity and *construct* validity. But this is not the case. Although content and construct validity depend to considerable degree on rational analysis and judgment, they are strengthened by empirical data-gathering operations. In social casework research, for example, Hunt and Kogan (1952) have described both the logical considerations and empirical procedures underlying the development of the *Movement Scale*, and Ripple (1955) has summarized how an instrument was designed to measure motivation, capacity, and opportunity in relation to clients' use of casework service. It should be noted that in the opinion of some investigators the most useful method of determining the construct validity of an instrument is by the procedures of factor analysis (Harman 1967).

The various concepts embraced under the rubric of *validity of measurement* are of basic importance because they force us to think *behind* as well as *beyond* the particular measures obtained from a particular procedure. They focus our attention not only on clarifying *what* is being measured but the connections between what is measured and other phenomena in the world. The ultimate criteria of the adequacy of measurement and, indeed, the adequacy of research in general, stem from the utility of what is done. Measurement in social work research should produce accurate information which is meaningful and useful for theory, practice, and progress in social work.

SUMMARY

Measurement, as described in this chapter, refers to the process of using numbers to represent properties of objects according to specified rules. In the context of social work research, the "objects" whose properties are the subject of measurement may be persons, groups, institutions, and the like. Depending on which characteristics of the number system (non-equivalence, order, distance, origin) the measures can be shown to possess, scales of measurement may be classified into six major categories: nominal classification, none/some scale, ordinal scale with arbitrary origin, ordinal scale with natural origin, interval scale, and ratio scale. All but the first of these categories refer to unidimensional scales.

Measurement considerations play a significant role in the formulation and testing of theoretical models as well as in the choice of appropriate methods of statistical analysis. In general, as one moves from classificatory to metric procedures, one gains in terms of increased precision, communicability, and possibilities for discovering and establishing relationships among variables.

In addition to the scale of measurement attainable, the adequacy of a measurement technique should be assessed for practicability, feasibility, reliability, and validity. Reliability refers to a cluster of concepts relating to the precision, dependability, or stability of a set of measures. Validity or relevance depends on how well the purposes of the measurement procedure are met and is based on a combination of rational and empirical operations. Finally, the success of a measurement technique must be judged according to its demonstrated utilities.

REFERENCES

American Psychiatric Association. 1966. *Diagnostic and statistical manual of mental disorders.* 2d ed. Washington, D.C.: American Psychiatric Assoc.

American Psychological Association. 1974. *Standards for educational and psychological tests.* Washington, D.C.: American Psychological Assoc.

Anastasi, A. 1968. *Psychological testing.* 3d ed. New York: Macmillan.

Bush, R. 1959. The new look in measurement theory. In *Use of judgments as data in social work research,* ed. A. Shyne. New York: National Assoc. of Social Workers.

Campbell, N. 1920. *Physics: The elements.* Cambridge: Cambridge University Press. (Reprinted 1957 as *Foundations of science.* New York: Dover.)

Cohen, J. 1968. Multiple regression as a general data analytic system. *Psychological Bulletin* 70:426–43.

Coombs, C. 1964. *A theory of data.* New York: Wiley.

Cronbach, L. 1970. *Essentials of psychological testing.* 3d ed. New York: Harper & Row.

————, et al. 1972. *The dependability of behavioral measurements.* New York: Wiley.

Dawes, R. 1972. *Fundamentals of attitude measurement.* New York: Wiley.

Dotson, L., and Summers, G. 1970. Elaboration of Guttman scaling techniques. In *Attitude measurement,* ed. G. Summers. Chicago: Rand McNally.

Edwards, A. 1957. *Techniques of attitude scale construction.* New York: Appleton-Century-Crofts.

Fanshel, D. 1966. *Foster parenthood.* Minneapolis: Univ. Minnesota Press.

Green, B. 1954. Attitude measurement. In *Handbook of social psychology*, ed. G. Lindzey. Cambridge, Mass.: Addison-Wesley.

Guilford, J. 1954. *Psychometric methods*. 2d ed. New York: McGraw-Hill.

Guttman, L. 1950. The basis for scalogram construction. In *Measurement and prediction*, by S. Stouffer et al. Princeton, N.J.: Princeton Univ. Press.

Harman, H. 1967. *Modern factor analysis*. 2d ed. Chicago: Univ. of Chicago Press.

Hollingshead, A., and Redlich, F. 1958. *Social class and mental disease*. New York: Wiley.

Hunt, J. McV., and Kogan, L. 1952. *Measuring results in social casework: A manual on judging measurement*. Rev. ed. New York: Family Service Assoc. of America.

Jenkins, S., and Norman, E. 1972. *Filial deprivation and foster care*. New York: Columbia Univ. Press.

Kerlinger, F., and Pedhazur, E. 1973 *Multiple regression in behavioral research*. New York: Holt, Rinehart & Winston.

Kogan, L. 1959. Validity, reliability, and related considerations. In *Use of judgments as data in social work research*, ed. A. Shyne. New York: National Assoc. of Social Workers.

Lord, F., and Novick, M. 1968. *Statistical theory of mental test scores*. Reading, Mass.: Addison-Wesley.

Polansky, N.; Borgman, R.; and De Saix, C. 1972. *Roots of futility*. San Francisco: Jossey-Bass.

Ripple, L. 1955. Motivation, capacity and opportunity as related to use of casework service. *Social Service Review* 29:172–93.

Russell, B. 1938. *Principles of mathematics*. 2d ed. New York: Norton.

Shepard, R.; Romney, A.; and Nerlove, S., eds. 1972. *Multidimensional scaling*. New York: Seminar Press.

Shyne, A., and Kogan, L. 1958. A study of components of movement. *Social Casework* 39:333–42.

Stevens, S. 1946. On the theory of scales of measurement. *Science* 103: 677–80.

———. 1951. Mathematics, measurement, and psychophysics. In *Handbook of experimental psychology*, ed. S. Stevens. New York: Wiley.

———. 1958. Measurement and man. *Science* 127:383–89.

———. 1968. Measurement, statistics, and the schemapiric view. *Science* 161:849–56.

Summers, G., ed. 1970. *Attitude measurement*. Chicago: Rand McNally.

Thorndike, R., ed. 1971. *Educational measurement*. 2d ed. Washington, D.C.: American Council of Education.

———, and Hagen, E. 1969. *Measurement and evaluation in psychology and education*. 3d ed. New York: Wiley.

Torgerson, W. 1958. *Theory and methods of scaling.* New York: Wiley.
Warner, W.; Meeker, M.; and Eels, K. 1949. *Social class in America.*
  Chicago: Science Research Associates.
Zimbalist, S. 1957. Index-making in social work. *Social Service Review*
  31:245–57.

4
Some Principles and Methods of Sampling

Margaret Yeakel
and Grace Ganter

Sampling is a powerful tool in social research. A *sample* is a group of subjects selected from a larger group and including less than all the subjects in that larger group. It is a number of cases, or instances of behavior, pulled out from a much larger number. Sampling procedures not only make it possible to secure information about a large number of subjects without studying all of them; they also make it possible to know how much confidence one can have that the information gathered is similar to the information that would have been gathered if one had studied everyone in the larger group. To the extent the sample is like or unlike the larger group from which it is drawn, it is said to be more or less representative of that group. If study of a relatively small number of subjects can put an investigator in a position to make assertions about a much larger number, it is clearly uneconomical for him to put time, money, and effort into collecting data from all subjects in the total *population*. Sampling obviously has to do with the scientific aim of *generalizing*.

There are still a number of widely held theories which have not been tested to see whether the behavior they encompass is representative of the general population of human beings. Such theories were often the result of pioneer work in the understanding of human behavior, but the early trailblazers lacked knowledge of the rest of the terrain to which their explanations have sometimes been applied. Indeed, our respect for such pioneer work has continued to make it difficult for some social work practitioners to accept the findings from additional studies which clarify the measure of error in the original sampling procedures. For example, some of the disciples of Sigmund Freud continue to explain a great deal of human behavior as deriving from Oedipal strivings, without regard for additional studies which question the generality of the Oedipus complex in other cultures.

The current adversary situation between members of the psychiatric profession and members of the homosexual community illustrates some of the implications of sampling error. Prior to 1957, research in this area dealt with two specific samples of homosexuals—psychiatric patients and prison inmates. The results of this research revealed that the subjects were psychologically impaired, and homosexual object choice was presumed to be a result of deeply internalized pathology. Subsequent to 1957, a large number of additional studies employing quite different

samples—nonpatient homosexual and nonpatient heterosexual subjects—
revealed no significant differences in these two groups of subjects with
regard to degree and variety of pathology (Silverstein 1973). Despite
this contrary evidence, many members of the psychiatric profession continue to regard homosexuality as a category of mental illness.

It seems likely that preconceived beliefs about the meaning of homosexual object choice influenced the sampling procedures employed by
investigators prior to 1957. It is also likely that all investigators are especially vulnerable to bias in studies of groups whose behavior is seen as
deviating from the behavior of the majority of the members of a society.
Whether or not we accept Silverstein's view that deviance is not in the
behavior of the offender but in the perception of his audience, we are
frequently biased by our own perceptions of deviance in the subjects, or
human events, we select to investigate. All of us need some system of
sampling selection which operates to control bias in choosing cases for
study—a system to prevent us from being guided by our preconceived
beliefs. The principles of sampling provide the investigator with one way
to anticipate biases that are bound to enter into research, and to minimize
them. It is for this reason that the sampling process is a most powerful
tool in our continuing effort to build general knowledge which is critical
to social work practice.

In our own experience as research teachers we have noticed that some
students are turned off before they begin the study of sampling theory
because they do not have an opportunity to associate it with their own
practice. Perhaps it also touches on some of the difficulties which we all
experience as we struggle to raise to consciousness our own sampling
errors in our assessments of social reality. Most of us find it threatening
to hold opinions which differ from those of others. Consequently, we
spend a good deal of our life energy sampling other people's opinions in
order to get confirmation for our own. The sampling methods most often
used in this process are relatively unsystematic and, of course, highly
selective with regard to whose opinions we sample! The discipline required
of the researcher is quite a different matter, but ultimately it is worthwhile
to learn the difference.

THE ISSUE OF REPRESENTATIVENESS

Choosing the individuals (or groups, or events, or situations) about whom
the information that will constitute the data of the study will be secured,
is the sampling process. This process is carried out on the basis of a
sampling plan, or *design*, that is developed before the sample itself is
sought out. The sampling plan includes specifying the study population,
deciding on a sampling method or technique, actually recruiting or locat-

ing the sample, and providing a means for using data from the sample to estimate the presence in the population of the particular characteristics or attributes that are being studied.

As has been mentioned, the problem of illegitimate or mistaken generalizations shows up in the critical issue of the sample's *representativeness*. The characteristic of representativeness, as that term is used to describe a sample, means that an obtained sample is, in effect, a miniature edition of the whole study population in all major respects that are significant to the study's purpose. The degree of the sample's representativeness is the key to establishing a legitimate claim that a study's findings are likely to approximate closely what could have been learned had the entire population been studied. For this reason, representativeness is a highly valued characteristic of a sample, and is what the sampler tries to achieve through the way he or she chooses it.

Moynihan's description of the family structure of black Americans as "matriarchal" depended on defining "matriarchal" as "female-headed" families; so far as sampling was concerned, the description rested on an undocumented assumption that black, female-headed families who were public assistance recipients were representative of black families generally (Moynihan 1965). Mead's study *Sex and Temperament in Three Primitive Societies* illustrated the fallacy of generalizing about the nature of femininity and masculinity from evidence based on samples that are quite unrepresentative of the very different expectations held in other cultures (Mead 1935). Kinsey's early report *Sexual Behavior in the Human Female* was inaccurately titled; it was actually a report of a study of some 5,940 white American females, 75% of whom were college educated, almost all of whom were Protestant, and who were largely residing in the three states of Illinois, Florida, and California (Kinsey et al. 1953).

DEFINITIONS

We shall, in the balance of the chapter, be using familiar words with more precise meanings than they have in ordinary usage.

The term *population* is used, in research, to refer to a collection of cases that fit certain defined limits, made explicit by the investigator. The term *case* is used in a very general sense to signify an individual member of a population—whether a population of persons, of objects, of events, of case records, or of groups of cases regarded as units. When an investigator begins to think of a study, and to clarify and explicate the concepts in which he will formulate his study question, he begins to envision a population. He may think, for example, of studying the effects on children of watching violence on television. The concept "children" implies a population of children differentiated from nonchildren but otherwise as yet not defined. The study also implies a population of effects, a population of TV sets, and a population of television pictures of violent activities or behaviors. Thus, each concept implies a population.

The population thus envisioned is going to have to be hunted up, or waylaid somehow, at specified places during a specified period of time. The study question, as it develops, may impose qualifications that help to delineate the study population more explicitly. The investigator then sets up boundaries that define the study population more specifically and explicitly. Following is an example of this point.

Geismar and his associates were interested in studying family functioning of young urban families, a heading that would include a great many families in the United States and elsewhere. The actual study population, however, was defined by the investigators as the list of Newark families for whom the birth of a first child had been recorded, over a sixteen-month period in 1964–65, in the Bureau of Vital Statistics of the Department of Health and Welfare in New Jersey. It is to this population that the results of the study could be legitimately applied, or generalized. This is not to say that the study's findings might not very well describe other young, urban families, but such a generalization could not be extended on the basis only of Geismar's findings (Geismar 1973).

Figures, or sets of figures, that are used to summarize the description of a study population are called *parameters*. The figures may be averages, percentages, ratios, or other numerical statements. Population data available from a variety of surveys and censuses are examples of parameters. The following examples will further clarify the term.

In 1962, the Public Health Service reported that 74% of the population of the United States had hospital insurance (U.S. Department of Health, Education, and Welfare 1962). The figure 74% is a parameter of the population of the United States in 1963. In the same year, a study of a rehabilitation project at the Sidney Hillman Health Center was carried out by the Amalgamated Clothing Workers. Their study population was the membership of their union. This study population reported 92% hospital insurance coverage (H.E.W. 1963). The 92%, then, was a parameter of the union population, and differed from the comparable parameter of the total population of the United States.

When an *average* is used as a population parameter, an additional parameter—a figure used to summarize the spread or "dispersion" of the population around the average—should also be reported. This figure takes account of the fact that the extent of the variations among members of a population around the summarizing figure is not communicated through the report of an average.

As we have said, a sample is a portion of the study population. We have emphasized the goal of sample representativeness. There is a practical implication of representativeness which might be of help in further defining a sample. There is frequently a difference between the sample that is *drawn* and the sample that is finally *obtained*. This raises a question, in the mind of the investigator, about the extent to which the obtained sample is representative of the study population. For example, Geismar began with a study population composed of 3,585 names; the sample that was drawn consisted of 1,800 names picked out of the original list. Locating people from a list of names can present difficulties, leading to considerable shrinkage. In Geismar's study, 49% of the sample drawn could not be located; moreover, the study was planned to follow a portion of the sampled families over a period of five years, during which some of the 51% of the families drawn and located in the study's initial stages moved away or were otherwise lost. The *final sample obtained*, for whom complete data were available, consisted of 555 families (Geismar 1973).

Another dedicated investigator, Henshel, reported vividly the obstacles encountered in an attempt to locate a sample for a study of Anglo and Chicano retardates, in order to "present the individual's story in his own words." After four months of intensive searching, only a few of a list of 174 names of individuals who had been clients of a state rehabilitation commission, and who met criteria for sample inclusion, had been located (Henshel 1972). Geographic mobility, lack of lasting social ties, evasiveness of former acquaintances who were suspicious of interviewers' motives, inaccurate addresses, were some of the major obstacles the investigators encountered. The obstacles are suggestive of some of the economic and social barriers a researcher may anticipate in planning a study of one of the socially undervalued subpopulations in our society.

Refusal by individuals to participate in the research, like nonreturns of mailed questionnaires, is a fairly frequently encountered source of *erosion* or attrition of a sample that has been drawn. Refusal to participate may itself signal some significant difference between those who consent to participate and those who do not. Geismar sought intensively, and was able to contact during the period after his study had begun, 77% of the cases missing from the sample that had originally been drawn. He found that these omitted cases differed materially from those that had been located on the criterion variable—family functioning—but not on demographic variables. Henshel compared available file data for unlocated individuals with similar data for those located; the two groups were fairly comparable except in the extent of their contact with the rehabilitation agency that furnished the listing. So the issue is whether the bias introduced by sample erosion is relevant to the research aims.

A *statistic* is a figure, or set of figures, that summarizes the description of a sample. It is the counterpart of the parameter of the large collection. If a sample is representative of its underlying population, the statistics that describe the sample should resemble the parameters that describe the population. Thus, if two-thirds of a sample are married and one-third single, and the population from which the sample was drawn has a similar proportion of married and single individuals, the sample is representative of the population at least with regard to marital status. And if it is representative on something that can be checked, this offers some reassurance that it is also representative on other dimensions.

Sample selection defines a wide variety of standard methods of sampling which have been developed and adapted to many kinds of research problems. The "best" sample design depends on how the study population is physically distributed, the resources available to the researcher, the particular characteristic that is to be studied, and the objective of the research. The investigator wishes to move from the known to the unknown. The data obtained about the sample are to be used to estimate an unknown parameter. The selection of a particular sampling design generally has, as its aim, to achieve representativeness and to maximize precision in the estimate of the "true" value of the parameter, for a given cost. Since few social workers are experts in sampling, students and practitioners should be prepared to find, and to use, the advice and suggestions of people who are sampling experts before they crystallize any plan for a costly project. Practitioners whose work requires some depth of knowledge of sampling theory will find an increasing number of available research texts with more extensive and technical discussions of sampling theory than is attempted here. We have listed a number of useful texts at the end of this chapter.

RANDOM CHOICE AND REPRESENTATIVENESS

With the objective of achieving representativeness, a sample is to be chosen from a defined study population. The essential qualification for the selection technique is that the investigator use some system to prevent his own subjectivity, or that of others, from determining which of the study population are selected. The objective of achieving representativeness is commonly approached by introducing chance, or luck, into the selection process. Random choice may be achieved in a variety of ways. If a population has been listed, and a complete, accurate, and unduplicated list is available, the safest way to introduce chance is to assign each unit of the population a number, and use a *table of random numbers* to determine which of the units will be drawn for the sample. Any system that has nothing to do with the cases one is working with can be applied; names can be drawn from a hat or from a revolving drum as in a lottery; letters of the alphabet can be used.

Randomness is not valuable in itself: representativeness is what is desired. The most certain way to achieve representativeness is to follow some system that allows chance to determine which of the population shall be selected. The mathematical definition of a *random sample* is a sample drawn in such a way that each and every case has an equal chance of being chosen at each drawing. Strict definition requires that sampling be done "with replacement"—that is, any case once drawn at random is returned to the population "pool" and may be drawn again if the number of that case again turns up randomly. This allows every possible combination of a given size to have an equal chance of selection. For a variety of reasons, sampling in social research is generally "without replacement." One does not interview the same person twice, for example.

A sample may be randomly drawn without being a random *probability* sample, since the probability of an element's being chosen must already be known to meet the definition of a random probability sample, and this depends on a prior complete listing of all the cases from which the sample, of a given size, is to be selected. Thus, random selection is not a guarantor of a probability sample, and is not undertaken with achievement of known probability of selection as a goal. Rather, control of investigator bias and achievement of representativeness are at stake. Random selection does not guarantee representativeness. But a large body of experience has shown that samples that have been randomly chosen tend to be representative. This is why random assignment is used in setting up experimental groups. If both experimental and control groups are representative of the same underlying population, they resemble each other.

Representativeness is a relative matter, in the final analysis. However, representativeness of the obtained sample, as we have noted, should be estimated and reported to clarify for readers whether conclusions based on the sample do, indeed, apply to the population originally specified or to the sample alone. The investigator should make some estimate of how far nonreturns, refusals to participate, and inability to locate cases may distort findings. Even when the sample is representative of the study population, it is frequently desirable to remind readers of the limits of that population.

Sampling Error

We have thus far referred to errors of inference against which the researcher seeks protection through random sample selection and population specification. Now we will discuss briefly another type of error, whose effects can be assessed and controlled for when probability sampling is employed.

Any sample is only one particular combination, out of many, of the cases or subjects in the population. The particular statistic used to summarize the description of a sample is called an *estimator*. Usually this is some form of an average, or a ratio. An obtained sample provides the investigator, through measurements of a given characteristic, an estimator of a particular numerical value. This value is called an estimate because it is used in the *estimation of a parameter* of that characteristic.

Clearly, the value of an estimate obtained from a random sample has partly been determined by chance. With many repetitions, many estimates would have been provided, covering a range of values. The value, in each case, would have partly been due to chance.

Having obtained his estimate, the investigator now thinks of a statistical population of estimates, his own among them. Since each reflects, in part, the operation of chance, it is expectable that a certain amount of error will characterize the entire distribution of the estimates.

How much chance error to expect in such a statistical distribution is a question of mathematical probability, which is concerned with recurrent events. Since chance will operate in random sampling to produce fluctuations in estimates, these fluctuations will also recur. Over a very long run, they will stabilize; and a standard, or expectable, value can be calculated for the distribution of errors of chance that is subsumed in the distribution of the estimates.

Mathematicians and statisticians have created probability tables and formulas whose usefulness for the sampler is as follows. From an obtained random sample, the investigator is in position to use the estimate provided by his single sample to project the corresponding parameter of the statistical distribution of all possible estimates. He can also compare the variability of individual scores in his sample with the variability expected, on the basis of chance alone, for the distribution of all possible estimates. Using the formulas provided for the type and size of sample he has and the kind of estimator he is using, he can draw two inferences: (1) about approximately what value the parameter he is searching for will take, in the long run, and (2) about how much confidence he has that, over a long run, a given proportion of other approximations, derived from repetitions of the study, would be different from his own. For instance, in national public opinion polls it is possible to estimate a margin of error on a straw vote for president. Thus, if a 3% margin of error is estimated for a predicted vote of 51% for the Democratic candidate, the vote is being projected as somewhere between 49½% and 52½% for that candidate—in which case that candidate's election cannot really be predicted.

The sampling error of a distribution of sample estimates is a kind of systematic error built into a particular sampling plan. It refers to the kind of error that is reflected in any statistic by virtue of the fact that something less than the whole collection of cases has been studied, and that chance has entered into sample selection. For different sampling methods with different kinds of estimators, and for samples of different sizes, the expectable size of the sampling error will also differ. This enables an investigator to weigh the merits of different sampling alternatives and choose those that will best fit both his purpose and his purse.

PRECISION AND SAMPLE SIZE

Between two samples equally representative of a population, it would seem to be common sense to choose the larger, to give a picture of a population that is both accurate and precise. The larger the sample, however, the more difficult it sometimes is to avoid distortions stemming from superficial coverage, or inability to control conditions under which observations will be made. Such distortions affect the accuracy of study results; they are difficult to estimate, since they are not mathematically calculable. So one may opt for better coverage of fewer cases.

Sampling errors, in the mathematical sense described above, condition the *precision* of the estimate a sample yields about the parameter. The sample size enters into the calculation of amount of error due to chance variations in the statistics of randomly drawn samples. A large sample is less subject to such error than a small sample. Variability is a function of sample size; it would take more repetitions of small samples to arrive at the same degree of precision in estimating a parameter than would be required for larger samples. The general formula that expresses this is $s/\sqrt{n}$. The precision of a statistic is inversely related to the square root of the size of the sample. To reduce error from sampling, one must square the proportion of error desired, and increase the sample by this square. If one wished to reduce sampling error by two units, it would be necessary to multiply the size of the sample by four.

If only a small margin of error is tolerable, with regard to making a prediction based on the results obtained from a sample, a very large sample is required. On the other hand, gains in sampling precision may be offset by losses in validity of data obtained; with a given amount of money, the researcher must decide where to put his priorities.

SAMPLING TECHNIQUES

Several standard random-probability techniques of sampling have been developed and tested. They are based on the use of tables of random numbers. Each is a variation of the method of simple random sampling with replacement. In this section we shall discuss several of the most common: simple random sampling without replacement, stratified sampling, systematic sampling, and area sampling.

Simple Random Sampling without Replacement

Starting with a complete, accurate, unduplicated list of subjects, the investigator assigns each subject a number. He uses a "table of random numbers" to determine the selection of units, up to a predetermined sample size. Each subject is selected once, and only once.

Sampling from a Stratified Population

When the subjects in a study population can be grouped into subclasses or strata and *the proportion in each subclass is already known*, each stratum is sampled independently.

The familiar reference to subpopulations classified with respect to socio-economic class is an example of *stratification*. The term is not restricted to socioeconomic variables but can be applied with respect to any characteristic for which two or more mutually exclusive subcategories can be designated. Samples may be stratified by time intervals as well as social or geographic characteristics.

If a population is stratified along the lines of several variables, the number of strata formed will be equal to the product of the number of subcategories identified for each variable. A population stratified by sex into two strata, and by academic year into four, will be subdivided into eight strata—first-year men, first-year women, second-year men, and so on. Each stratum identifies a percentage of the population; the sum of the percentages of all the strata is 100%. Each stratum is homogeneous with respect to the particular subcategory of the variable employed for stratifying. Stratification thus increases representativeness.

In *proportionate stratified sampling*, each stratum is randomly sampled independently of the other strata, taking enough cases from a given stratum to make its size in the total sample proportionate to the percentage of subjects known to be included in that stratum in the population. Suppose, for example, that a sample of 100 workers is to be drawn from a study population of 500 social workers, stratified by years of experience and by type of employment agency, and distributed as follows:

	YEARS OF EXPERIENCE			
Agency	Under 5 years	5 to 9 years	10 years	Total
Public	25%	15%	10%	50%
Private	25%	15%	10%	50%
Total	50%	30%	20%	100%

The list of workers would be divided into six subpopulations, one for each cell in the table. The stratum "public agency workers with less than 5 years experience" includes 25% of the workers; 125 names would be listed to be sampled for this cell. The total sample is to include one-fifth of the total population (100 of 500 cases). The sampling fraction for each stratum, then, is one-fifth. Choosing one-fifth of the 125 public agency workers with less than five years of experience would provide 25 of these workers for the final sample; this is 25% of the total sample of 100 workers.

In *disproportionate,* or *nonproportional, stratified sampling,* strata are sampled independently, but the percentage of subjects from each stratum in the total sample is not proportionate to the percent contributed by these strata to the entire population. Stratifying may result in a very small number of cases in one or two cells; this produces pressure to increase the size of the whole sample. An alternative is to oversample the very small subpopulations; the resulting sample is *disproportionate.* For instance, in order to insure a sufficient number of "two-parents-present" households in a study of use of health services by families on welfare, a population of cases, stratified by three assistance categories, was sampled in the proportions of 1.7% of Aid to Dependent Children cases, 5.3% of Temporary ADC cases, and 4.3% of Family Home Relief cases (Podell 1973). Selecting the same number of cases from all strata is another form of disproportionate sampling. Of course, after the data are obtained from a disproportionate sample, arithmetic adjustments are made to arrive at proportionate contributions in making generalizations about the population. Suppose that three assistance categories contributed to a population of mothers on welfare in the proportions of 85% AFDC, 10% TADC, and 5% General Assistance. Suppose also that, from a disproportionate sample, use of contraceptives was reported by 62% of the AFDC sample, 55% of the TADC sample, and 40% of the General Assistance sample. In order to make statements about the use of contraceptives by the population of mothers, a representative sample would be reconstituted, by weighting each cell appropriately so that its contribution to the final population estimate would be representative of its weight in the population. Sixty-two percent of the AFDC group, which contributes 85% of the population, would be estimated to use contraceptives; this cell would contribute, then, 62% of 85%, or 52.7% ($.62 \times .85 \times 100\%$) to the final population estimate. The TADC group would contribute 5.5% (55% of 10%), and the General Assistance group 2.0% (40% of 5%). The estimate for the entire population of mothers would be that 60.2% (52.7% + 5.5% + 2.0%) use contraceptives. In this estimate, the representativeness of the sample would be reconstituted, since the contribution of each stratum to the estimate would be proportionate to the number of mothers it contributed to the population.

In stratifying, the investigator needs to ask, Stratification with respect to what? The sample's representativeness with respect to the criterion variable must always be unknown. Stratifying may reflect social barriers relevant to the criterion variable, thus introducing an unsuspected or unintended bias into findings.

Systematic Random Sampling

In this modification, subjects or sampling units are selected sequentially from a list, at some fixed interval, as, for example, every other applicant for service, every fifth card in a file, every tenth name on a list. The starting point is determined by choice of a random number; the chosen interval is applied for selecting the second case, the third, and so on. The size of the interval to be used depends on the size of the population and on how much chance one decides to give each case to be chosen. If one wants each element to have a one-in-ten chance of inclusion, the sample size is to be one-tenth of the population. If this method were applied in a stratified population, the process would be applied separately within each stratum.

Systematic sampling approximates randomization *provided* that the interval at which cases are to be picked has nothing to do with the question being studied. Often it is safe to assume that the units of the population are arranged haphazardly, so far as the variables under study are concerned. It is, however, important to know how a list is made up. If the ordering of names reflects a trend, systematic sampling would introduce the trend itself into the sample, biasing it without possibility of detecting the trend itself as a source of bias. Suppose, for example, systematic sampling were applied to a list of school graduates to which graduates' names were added yearly as a group. If one entered the list near the top, the least recently graduated individuals would be more frequently chosen; if one entered it near the middle, the more recently graduated individuals would appear in greater numbers. In neither case would the sample represent the population on any characteristic strongly associated with recency of graduation. Seasonal variations, cyclical or other corresponding patterns may be reflected in lists or show up in other ways. Suppose one wished to study accuracy of face sheet data assembled by agency staff members, and decided to use every tenth face sheet completed. Slower workers would be underrepresented; if slowness were associated with more or less accuracy, the resulting sample would be biased in favor of, or against, slow workers.

Area Sampling and Cluster Sampling

These methods use groups of elements, rather than individual elements, as sampling units. From a complete listing of population groupings, called *clusters*, a *random sampling of clusters* is drawn. All subjects in each cluster are then studied. When nothing else is known about a population, and it is not totally listed, random sampling of the geographic area it occupies has proved an excellent way to get a representative sample. The U.S. Bureau of the Census employs area sampling, on noncensus years, to spotcheck particular developments. Public opinion polling also makes wide use of area sampling. More thorough study by a relatively small number of trained investigators without loss of representativeness can be cheaper than wider coverage with less disciplined observers.

A listing of clusters that are social units, such as schools, families, hospitals, may be sampled as well as geographic clusters of a population such as states, city blocks, dwelling units. Once a sample of clusters has been drawn, listed subclusters or strata within the selected clusters may be randomly subsampled. In such *multistage* sampling, each successive listing of clusters, subclusters, and so on is randomly sampled. Estimates of sampling error must be modified to fit cluster sampling.

Purposive or Judgment Sampling

In early stages of knowledge development, when insights that lead to the discovery of variables or to hypothesis formulation are the intent, purposive sampling may be employed. Cases are selected on the basis of their likelihood of stimulating insights within the investigator. In such research, the position is taken that the sample's representativeness is not an issue. The selection made is a selection of "insight-stimulating" cases, situations, or individuals (Selltiz et al. 1959).

THE RESEARCH DESIGN AND THE SAMPLING PLAN

Choice of a particular sampling plan is naturally related to a study's overall strategy. Representativeness, control of investigator bias, and adequate size are important in all research that employs samples. Sampling for relationships introduces requirements for control that are absent where sampling is used primarily with descriptive intent. This section deals with application of sampling in studies of relationships.

In such inquiries, the study question concerns the existence of some critical difference between otherwise matched, or equivalent, sample groups. The investigator seeks to know whether the samples represent populations that differ with respect to the factor being studied, or whether they represent, rather, two large divisions of the same population.

The required assumption that the sample groups are equivalent on factors presumed relevant to the critical variable, or criterion variable, is commonly achieved by one of three methods: *precision matching by pairs* of cases, *frequency distribution matching*, and *random assignment* of cases to different sample groups.

Matching in an Ex Post Facto Design

In this design, where an experiment is simulated, the investigator locates two large groups with a known difference and draws a sample from each. On the factor of known difference, the samples cannot help but be representative of their larger groups. With respect to other factors that might influence the criterion variable, the samples must be made as much alike as possible.

Chapin (1947) has illustrated and discussed extensively the use of both precision matching and frequency distribution matching to achieve control in ex post facto studies. Briefly, a set of selection criteria, usually chosen on grounds of reality factors, is first applied to both study populations, providing two "pools" in which the investigator looks for cases that go together. In matching by pairs, each case drawn from one pool is matched with a case from the other that is identical on all the factors that are being controlled. Achieving such homogeneity of samples on the matching factors typically leads, however, to tremendous loss of cases and to samples that are *atypical of the larger groups from which they came*, since the imposition of each control factor screens out cases that make for heterogeneity in the original pools. To reduce sampling attenuation and the high cost of such precision, investigators often settle for less rigorous control by frequency distribution matching. Here, samples are so constituted as to contain similar proportions of cases on each control factor. For example, if sex, employment status, and race were being controlled, the samples would show similar proportions, say, of men and women, employed and unemployed, black and nonblack subjects. The risk in such matching is that the samples may not in actuality be as "equal" as they appear to be; the risk may be considered acceptable since an ex post facto study is a simulated rather than an actual experiment anyhow (see chapter 3).

The decision as to which factors should be selected for matching has to come from the investigator's familiarity with his subject matter. It would be a waste of time to control for a factor that could be only remotely connected with the criterion variable. Thus, if one were studying whether mothers in a Head Start program conferred more often with children's teachers than mothers in a commercial day care program, one would not, presumably, try to control for mothers' preferences for a given brand of soap.

In such a design, the study populations are frequently considered to be themselves samples of a larger population. If the variables under study are of a very high level of generality, representativeness with respect to the factor on which the samples were known to be different is all that is required. It is also useful to start with study populations with a very strong, or definite, known difference, since this is how the "known cause" or "known effect" is introduced in ex post facto designs.

Matching in a Projected Design

The preferred method of sampling in most projected studies is by random assignment of individuals or cases to different sample groups. Investigator bias, stemming from knowledge of the stimulus to be introduced, is controlled. Experience is generally that randomization produces two groups fairly evenly matched not only on factors known or suspected to be relevant to the variable under study, but also on *factors the researcher may not know about*. Initial differences between the groups will be due to chance alone; just as many chance factors will probably be included in one group as in another. The criterion of representativeness, implying the exclusion of nonrandom differences between experimental and control groups, tends to be enhanced through random assignment to different groups, and if samples are so chosen as to be representative of an underlying population, they will resemble each other. Statistical tests of significance for differences between estimates from different sample groups, applied after exposure to different stimuli, are designed to take account of chance errors introduced through randomization. Results are thus considered more trustworthy, within the limits set by the population definition.

We have noted above the limitations on representativeness that may accompany precision and frequency distribution matching. Because these methods increase the "sensitivity" of the experiment to very small differences in responses of samples exposed to different stimuli, they are sometimes used in projected experiments. If subanalysis of particular subsamples or subvariables is planned, precision matching by pairs will yield more dependable results, as control on factors that might have produced the results being studied is tighter. This, of course, can be done only in a situation in which a good deal of information is available about the individual cases, on all the relevant variables. Prediction from study of samples, however, depends on representativeness, and matching by pairs or by distribution is intended to supplement randomization rather than to replace it.

FINAL REFLECTIONS

This chapter has been an effort to discuss some of the principles and methods of sampling which we believe to be important to students and practitioners. It was not feasible to include more illustrations of the application of sampling theory from the growing number of excellent studies by social work practitioners and teachers. For those of our readers who would go further than this chapter has gone in explaining sampling, we suggest they consult the sources listed below.

REFERENCES

Ackoff, R. L. 1953. *The design of social research*. Chicago: Univ. of Chicago Press.

Chapin, F. S. 1947. *Experimental designs in sociological research.* New York: Harper.

Diamond, S. 1959. *Information and Error.* New York: Basic Books.

Festinger, L., and Katz, D., eds. 1953. *Research methods in the behavioral sciences.* New York: Dryden.

Geismar, L. 1973. *555 families: A social-psychological study of young families in transition.* New Brunswick, N.J.: Transaction.

Goode, W. J., and Hatt, P. K. 1952. *Methods in social research.* New York: McGraw-Hill.

Henshel, A. M. 1972. *The forgotten ones.* Austin: Univ. of Texas Press.

Kinsey, A. C., et al. 1953. *Sexual Behavior in the human female.* Philadelphia: Saunders.

Kish, L. 1965. *Survey sampling.* New York: Wiley.

Mead, M. 1953. *Sex and temperament in three primitive societies.* New York: Morrow.

Moynihan, D. P. 1965. The Negro family: The case for national action. In Rainwater, L., and Yancey, W. L. 1967. *The Moynihan report and the politics of controversy.* Cambridge, Mass.: MIT Press.

Podell, L. 1973. Family planning by mothers on welfare. *Bulletin of the New York Academy of Medicine* 49: 931–37.

Ruby, L. 1954. *The art of making sense.* New York: Lippincott.

Selltiz, C., et al. 1964. *Research methods in social relations.* Rev. ed. New York: Holt, Rinehard, & Winston.

Silverstein, C. 1973. Even psychiatry can profit from its past mistakes. Manuscript. New York: Institute for Human Identity.

U.S. Public Health Service. 1962. *Highlights and developments in public health.* Washington, D.C.: U.S. Department of Health, Education, and Welfare.

Weiner, H. J.; Akabas, S. H.; and Grynbaum, B. 1964. *Demand for rehabilitation in a labor union population,* part 1. New York: Sidney Hillman Health Center.

5

Exploiting
Available
Information

Ann W. Shyne

For many a researcher a projected design is the most desirable, as he can then collect data of the exact kind needed to answer the questions or test the hypotheses he poses. Even more elegant is the projected experiment, with control not only of data but of experimental conditions. But such a bias is dangerous, as it may lead the researcher to dream an impossible dream. Some problems simply do not lend themselves to projected designs, and reliance on information already available is the only choice. Other problems lend themselves to such design but data collection is too expensive and time-consuming. The funds or the research staff are exhausted or the question loses relevance before the research is completed. It therefore behooves the researcher to be imaginative in exploiting available information to the maximum degree.

SOURCES OF AVAILABLE INFORMATION

"Available information" for the purposes of this chapter includes not only compilations of statistical data but also unassembled quantitative data and narrative reports, published and unpublished.

Statistical compilations are issued by innumerable public and private organizations on a variety of social and demographic variables. The material published by the United States Bureau of the Census is listed in a quarterly *Bureau of the Census Catalog,* which should be available in a university library, along with the major Census Bureau reports. In addition to the regular volumes reporting the basic data of the censuses of population and of housing, the Census Bureau issues several series of periodic releases presenting national and state data on population estimates, special censuses, the labor force, consumer income, etc. It publishes separate bulletins of statistics on each census tract. If the published reports do not suffice, the tenacious researcher can obtain unpublished tabulations from the Bureau of the Census at modest cost.

The Department of Health, Education, and Welfare has two major sources of statistics relevant to social work research. The National Center for Social Statistics issues reports on public assistance, child welfare, adoption, and juvenile delinquency, among other subjects. The National Center for Health Statistics, probably best known as the source of vital statistics (birth, death, marriage, and divorce), publishes extensive data on health resources, health expenditures, morbidity, and so forth. The Bureau of Labor Statistics in the Department of Labor is the source of the Consumer Price Index, which appears in a monthly *Handbook of Basic Economic Statistics*, along with data on employment, wages, and hours. The Federal Bureau of Investigation publishes a quarterly, *Uniform Crime Reporting*, based on statistics from police agencies throughout the country.

National voluntary agencies are another important source of data. For teachers' salaries we turn to the reports of the National Education Association; for community fund contributions, to the United Way; for enrollment in schools of social work, to the Council on Social Work Education. Somewhat further from our usual range of inquiry are the National Industrial Conference Board and the larger labor unions, whose operations include extensive data collection.

Many of these organizations, public and private, have state and local counterparts. These may be very helpful in study of a particular geographic area. In many cities, community councils, local planning bodies, economic research bureaus, and other organizations collect and collate data on population, housing, economic status, and other matters relevant to local problems and needs. Taking advantage of their resources avoids duplication of effort.

Rare is the researcher who has at his fingertips knowledge of the precise source of all of the available compilations he may possibly have occasion to use. However, every researcher should be sufficiently acquainted with the major sources of data relevant to his general field of inquiry to know where to turn for further information. He should keep a card file of sources he locates. A good reference librarian is an invaluable guide.

Statistical compilations in published form are more accessible and easier to use than other kinds of material that can comprise important data for the social work researcher. However, their abundance should not divert the researcher from less obvious sources of material. Agencies in their day-to-day operations provide for recording, often in reasonably accessible form, material that is not subsequently compiled or analyzed. Individual record forms carry data expressed both in quantitative terms (age, income, height, hemoglobin, duration of marriage, psychological test scores) and nominal scales (type of problem presented, psychiatric diagnosis, disposition of case). National bodies and local coordinating agencies collect data about the characteristics of their member organizations (size of staff, budgets, types of service, etc.) comparable to the data the local service agency has on file about its clientele. Such unassembled data may be harder to use but just as dependable as compilations whose previous publication lends them an aura of accuracy.

Least readily susceptible to statistical treatment but essential to study of many issues is descriptive or narrative material. The staff member's recording of his transactions with a particular client or group is probably the most frequently used source of narrative data in social work research. The range of available material also includes laws, legal opinions, and administrative rulings; minutes and reports of board, staff, and committee meetings; agency annual reports and interpretative publications; statements of theory and philosophy in professional literature; and public interpretation in the popular press.

USES OF AVAILABLE DATA

Available material plays important roles *preliminary* to a research endeavor in providing background and in helping to identify and clarify the questions for study. It may serve an essential *supplementary* function by supplying data for comparison with the findings of original research. Secondary analysis of available data may permit *indirect measurement* of a variable one cannot target in on directly. In many instances reliance on available information may be dictated by *practical considerations* of time, cost, or effect on agency operations, which preclude collection of original data. Finally, it constitutes the only possible data base for a variety of important research endeavors: historical research, syntheses or critical reviews of research which may expand knowledge substantially, and efforts to cast light on urgent questions that have not been anticipated.

In Planning Research

Reviewing related research and other professional publications can be extremely useful in identifying questions for investigation and suggesting avenues of approach. The professional literature is replete with hypotheses and evidence supporting them in an individual case, group, agency, or community. Agency reports, minutes of staff meetings, and the like similarly carry many assumptions, hunches, and convictions. As Margaret Blenkner once said, "if we listen to what the practitioner says works . . . , we may then build hypotheses from his hunches and test them through research" (Blenkner 1959, p. 105).

Individual case records may help in sharpening an area of inquiry, developing hypotheses, and creating data-collecting instruments. For example, in planning a prospective study of the circumstances under which certain types of adoption placements are more or less likely to work out well, one should review the records of a number of successes and failures —this would be a good way to get clues to pursue systematically.

Administrative statistics often suggest questions for study, questions that may have implications for theory as well as for administration. About twenty-five years ago, family service agencies began to be uneasy about the high proportion of brief-service cases that showed up in statistical reports. What did these mean? Were the agencies accomplishing remarkable results with very few contacts, or were they losing cases before service was even started, or what? The statistical reports stimulated a body of research on short-term service that has had important implications for practice.

In planning research, the researcher must be well informed of what has gone before. The proliferation of research and of publications makes this very difficult, but the concurrent proliferation of abstracting services keeps it within the realm of possibility (Reid 1968). Failure to review related work may be due to the fact that the researcher is precipitated into a project with such pressure for completion that he feels forced to bypass seemingly expendable preliminaries. Here haste certainly makes waste, for old ground may be trod unnecessarily, methods that have proved unrewarding applied again with similarly unrewarding results, and no cognizance taken of advances in method that could contribute greatly to the success of the project at hand.

As a Basis for Comparison

An important function of available data is to provide a frame of reference for study findings. Many social work research projects concern a particular agency, community, or client group. Unless the findings can be generalized beyond the population studied, they have little practical or theoretical value. Suppose an agency finds that it has had a substantial increase in the proportion of Puerto Rican clients in its case load. Does this mean it has become more effective in reaching the Puerto Rican community? The first thing it needs to know is whether there has been an increase in the proportion of Puerto Ricans in its area. Or suppose an agency has a sharp decrease in adoptions. Is this unique to the agency, or have other agencies experienced the same thing?

Comparison with available data from other settings may also stimulate questions about the validity of one's conclusions or about whether a crucial element has been neglected in one's investigations. Suppose a community fund has attempted to identify the factors determining level of giving in the community. It needs to do so to predict probable support of its constituent agencies from year to year. Further, suppose that it has found a close relation between campaign contributions and the prosperity of the community. Data on community chest contributions and at least some economic indices will be available from other communities. If the relation of contributions to economic level is lower than in other comparable communities, it behooves the investigator to look into such other factors as local public attitudes toward community services. These may be a good deal more amenable to change than the economic level of the community.

Social Indicators

Analysis of available statistics may provide approximate answers to complex questions. Suppose a state legislature wants to know how adequate the state's child welfare services are. Really to answer this question requires an elaborate analysis of the extent, nature, and outcome of the services. But per capita expenditures for child welfare services tell quite a bit about their adequacy. If the state is spending only a third as much as the national figure, its services are likely to be grossly inadequate, even though such a conclusion ignores variations in cost, skill, efficiency, and level of need.

An important use of social statistics is in constructing composite indices to measure significant trends. An early effort was the work of Bradley Buell and his associates in the 1930s on the Social Breakdown Index as a general measure of the effectiveness of community welfare services (Community Chests and Councils 1939). The appropriateness of some of the components was immediately questioned. For example, does a rise in admissions to mental hospitals reflect an increase in "social breakdown," an increase in the adequacy of hospital facilities, or a change in public attitudes toward the use of psychiatric services? As a result, this index was used only to a limited extent; but the use of statistical data to develop indices of need for service has played an important part in community studies (see, e.g., Jenkins 1963). Such indices have utilized data on population density, ethnic distribution, family composition, mean rental, rate of home ownership, proportion of houses in disrepair, birth and death rates, infant and maternal mortality, incidence of divorce, juvenile court appearances, and many others.

Theoretical work on the development of social indicators has expanded greatly since 1960 to become a specialized field. It has received impetus from the federal government, through the National Science Foundation (1969) and other units, and also from the Russell Sage Foundation (Sheldon and Moore 1968). In 1972, a bibliography of over one thousand items was published (Wilcox et al. 1972), and in early 1973 the Social Science Research Council established a Center for Coordination of Research on Social Indicators. The quantity of publication is far disproportionate to the practical indices that have been developed, but then the social indicators "movement" is relatively recent.

The current activity in this area that appears most closely related to social work is the work of Leonard S. Kogan on child health and welfare indicators, a project funded by the U.S. Office of Child Development. The opening paragraph of a progress report on this project may be useful not only in indicating its purposes but in conveying the general intent of work on social indicators.

> The major purpose of this research program is to develop a set of indicators which can be used to represent the quality of child health and welfare for varying sampling units. . . . Although compiling of statistical data is almost epidemic in the fields of health and welfare, there has been little attempt to study the interrelationships and patterning among the multiplicity of statistics published each year. The present research has therefore sought to cast a relatively wide but systematic net for hypothetically useful variables so that their interrelationships can be examined with the aim of reducing their multiplicity and increasing their utility for understanding of the phenomena involved, prediction of future trends, and program planning [Kogan 1972].

Expediency of Use of Existing Data

Since data collection is very expensive in time and money, it is obviously inefficient to engage in it if available data will serve the purpose just as well. Because of the limits on research funds and manpower, it is often necessary to settle for existing data if they will yield approximate answers. For example, to compare social work salaries with salaries in other professions, it would be nice to collect information on salaries, education, years of experience, and so on, from a representative sample of members of the various professions of interest. However, the cost of such an undertaking might well be prohibitive. Most professional associations have some information on salaries. Why not use their data?

Collection of original data may also so prolong a study that the question at issue may have ceased to be important by the time the study is completed. For instance, in examining the relation of certain attributes of service to its outcome, the researcher has the choice of trying to get the service data from existing records of closed cases or undertaking a projected study in which new cases are followed until service is terminated. The latter approach may be preferable for obtaining the specific data desired, but it is clearly not feasible if the study's purpose is to provide the basis for an immediate policy decision about eligibility requirements for, or staffing of, the service.

Another practical consideration is the effect that carrying out a research project may have on an agency's service operation. Collecting new data frequently necessitates the service staff's participation. If this participation consists merely of noting a few factual items that are ordinarily known to such personnel, it will not seriously disrupt service. If, however, it requires a substantial amount of staff time to furnish the necessary data, via questionnaire or interview, then the time available for service is reduced. Even with the best will in the world on the part of administration

and staff, it may simply not be possible for an agency to make the necessary time available without shortchanging clients.

Suppose staff are asked not only to complete special recording forms
but to secure information about the individuals, groups, or organizations
they serve beyond that usually obtained for service purposes. Their participation then not only takes time but alters the way they relate to the
informants, and this may be disruptive in varying degrees both to practice
and to the research. In other words, the very fact of additional contacts
and discussion of particular topics alters the mode of practice and affects
the subjects of study.

Since demand for service usually exceeds staff resources and agencies
are often pressed by the community to increase the "productivity" of their
personnel, extensive participation by the service staff may be very difficult
to arrange. The use of available quantitative or qualitative material, for
all its limitations, obviates the problem of interference with service operations.

Historical Research

Reliance on available data is not always a matter of expediency; it may
be dictated by the nature of the problem, as in historical research. Historical research, by definition, is concerned with what has gone before
and must be based on existing records. These may then be supplemented
by the recollections and judgments of those who have lived through the
events under study. Such historical research is beautifully illustrated by
Margaret Rich's history of family social work (1956), and by the series
of studies of the history of the public social services conducted at the
University of Chicago (e.g., Linford 1949).

Critical Reviews of Prior Research

One of the most useful ways in which researchers contribute to the extension of knowledge and understanding is by major syntheses and critical
reviews of previous work. Such reviews may be directed to methodological or substantive issues. Meehl pursued rather effectively the question of
the comparative efficiency of clinical and actuarial prediction through
analyzing data from a number of studies in which predictions had been
made on both clinical and actuarial bases (Meehl 1954). Elizabeth Herzog's classic publication, *Some Guide Lines for Evaluative Research*,
which is both a "state-of-the-art" paper and a miniature textbook on
evaluative research methodology, was based on an extensive survey of
the literature (Herzog 1959).

Reviews directed to substantive issues may be broadly or narrowly
focused. The two reviews of research edited by Henry Maas provide
excellent overviews of what has been and what has not been learned in

broad fields of social service (Maas 1966, 1971). They are very useful both to researchers and to administrative and service personnel. Critical reviews of research in delimited areas are more common, but good ones are in short supply. The hazards are well illustrated by the methodological criticisms brought against Eysenck's early effort to evaluate the effects of psychotherapy by drawing on data from a number of published reports, most of which gave insufficient information for comparative purposes on the nature of the subjects, the therapy and the change measures (Eysenck 1952). Fischer's much more recent review of research and his conclusion that social casework is ineffective (Fischer 1973) have raised similar questions (Alexander and Siman 1973). A successful effort to distinguish among fact, myth, and untested assumption in a controversial area through a comprehensive and scholarly review of research is exemplified by Herzog and Sudia's work on the effect on boys of being reared in fatherless homes (Herzog and Sudia 1970).

Answering Unanticipated Questions

There are many questions of theoretical as well as practical concern that can be approached only through study of such data as are already at hand. We are not sufficiently clairvoyant, even in this day of computerized information systems, to anticipate questions that will arise some day and to plan ahead for systematic recording of the data that would be desirable for answering them. If a new policy, such as charging fees, is initiated, it is well to project a study of its effect on agency intake. However, if the question of its effect on intake arises six months later, at least a partial answer may be obtained by comparing already recorded data on number of applications, source of referral, and service requested during a period prior to and a period subsequent to the inauguration of the policy. One can easily think of innumerable subjects for studies of this sort—the role of administrative decisions in the development of public assistance law; the relation of changes in a community center program to a decrease in "in-migration" or to changes in the ethnic composition of the neighborhood; changes in the problems prompting application to a casework agency over a period of changing economic conditions; differences in the content of service associated with changes in the theoretical orientation of staff. Such retrospective or ex post facto studies must rely heavily on available data, although some original data may be gathered through interviews with knowledgeable people about their recollections and opinions of past events.

PROBLEMS IN THE USE OF AVAILABLE MATERIAL

Whether one is using quantitative data on individual cases, compilations of quantitative data, or narrative records, there are two problems: Can you find the material that you think you want? Is the material you find what it appears to be? The first may be called *consistent availability*; the second involves the familiar problems of *reliability* and *validity*.

Consistent Availability

If the researcher attempts to compile data on agency clients over a period of time from forms ordinarily filled out on each client, such as age, education, or income, he is likely to find a particular datum missing for an appreciable number of clients. Completed schedules are likely to be sprinkled with "unknowns." This problem is illustrated by recent research at the Child Welfare League of America on factors associated with placement and nonplacement decisions. Seemingly important information about the child's behavior and the parent's handling of the child was frequently not known to the workers responsible for case decisions. As a result, the focus of the research shifted to the development of an intake procedure that would help to ensure that such information would be collected in every case (Phillips et al. 1971, 1972). Similarly, a study of available records for the caseworker's statement of his service goals may run aground if the agency expectation that such a statement will be included in all records is not fulfilled in practice. Obviously, committee process cannot be deduced from minutes, some of which include only decisions made; and trends in the volume of cases cannot be examined unless such data have been compiled regularly over the period of interest. This point may seem too obvious or elementary to mention; however, it is easy to be trapped into assuming that data important to one's study plan will be available simply because the agency has intended that a record be kept.

Preliminary spot-checking of the sources to be used will give one an idea of the consistency with which the data are available and a basis for deciding whether the extent of missing data will allow too great a margin of error in the research proposed. Not only should the extent of missing data be considered but also the possibility of a bias in their omission or inclusion; for example, is age more likely to be determined and recorded for persons near the extremes of the eligible age group than for others? Is acting-out behavior more likely to be known and recorded than withdrawn behavior? The danger of missing observations is magnified if there is a likelihood of bias in the omissions, since one ordinarily handles data as though missing observations were distributed in the same way as available observations.

When one is dealing with compilations of quantitative data and wants to compare several sets of data for a given date or a series over a period of time, the problem of consistent availability takes on another dimension —comparability in time and content. Comparability of time is particularly important on a rapidly changing variable like professional salaries. The reference date is, of course, but one of many aspects in which the series to be compared need to match. Data on salary ranges are not directly comparable with data on actual salaries; data based on samples including part-time employees are not comparable with those based on full-time employees; and so forth.

The point is a simple and obvious one, but it seems to deserve some emphasis because the researcher is frequently asked by an administrator or other nonresearcher to analyze ostensibly comparable data. The researcher must then examine the data, try to determine how consistent they are, and decide whether the probable degree of consistency is such as to admit of meaningful use.

Reliability and Validity

If we assume that the necessary data are consistently available, there remains the more difficult question of whether the data are what they seem to be. First, let us consider quantitative data. How well defined were the units? How accurately were they reported? Do they represent what they purport to represent? On rare occasions one has the happy experience of having some evidence of the reliability and validity of the material with which one is dealing; more often, this is a matter of judgment or an educated guess on the basis of what is known of the method of data collection, the sample used, the capability of the enumerators, the possible bias of the collecting agency, and other contingencies that may affect the end result.

Data on juvenile arrests and detentions may be highly reliable. However, they are notoriously poor measures of juvenile delinquency, because many factors besides a youth's behavior, such as his race and social class, determine whether he is apprehended and what official action is taken if he is. The number of children known to psychiatric clinics may be reported accurately, but comparative rates for different communities are a much better reflection of the availability of clinic service than of the incidence of psychiatric impairment.

A subject of common interest to agencies is the relative effectiveness of their services. But comparison of the proportion of clients reported as showing improvement has little meaning unless a good deal is known about the criteria. Precisely how was "improvement" defined by the various reporting agencies? By whom was the definition applied? Who exactly are "clients"? All the applicants to the agency, all applicants accepted for service, all applicants accepted for service who continue with the agency for a given length of time, or what? Were the clients comparable in severity of problem?

Variation in the samples studied, the definitions used, and the data assembled preclude any simple summation of findings of different studies or compilations of data. In view of the relative dearth of tested knowledge in the field of social work, however, such bits and pieces of information as are produced should not be disregarded. Through careful scrutiny of the data and of whatever can be learned about the method of collection and analysis, tentative impressions may be drawn as partial guides to practical action and as clues to questions to be pursued more rigorously.

In the case of narrative data, the basic question concerns the dependability of the narrative as a record of whatever it purports to record—a casework interview, an activity group session, or a committee meeting. This problem does not arise, of course, if one is interested in the *content of the document itself*, as, for example, the relative amount of space given to client versus worker activity. Much more often, however, the researcher uses the written document as the best available approximation of the actual life situation described. Discrepancies between the document and the event or situation described occur because the recorder's own conceptions, beliefs, and standards affect what he observes and records, because the human being has limitations as a processor of information (Hunt 1959). One can measure the degree of distortion only if the dictated record can be compared with a verbatim report of the same transaction in at least a sample of cases. This was illustrated by a comparison of measures of tension expressed by the client, obtained from both dictated and electronic records of interviews. Incidentally, the correlation of measures derived from the two sources was estimated to be .80 (Kogan 1951). Of course, if one is using existing records, it is impossible to secure in retrospect tape recordings of the transactions already documented. A comparison of verbatim and dictated records of current cases by the same personnel would give some indication of the accuracy of the older records, but this would introduce another set of problems.

If tape recordings are available, as is increasingly true, the problem of the validity of the record is taken care of, but other problems arise. Under some circumstances, knowledge that the transaction is being recorded may affect the content. This is less worrisome, however, than the practical problem that verbatim reports are extremely costly to transcribe and extremely time-consuming to read or to listen to.

Despite the difficulties in dealing with available narrative documents, whether summarized or verbatim, they have distinct advantages in some situations. If the researcher collects qualitative, judgmental, or subjective data directly from a therapist or group leader about a client or group, he has no way of checking the reliability of the reporter's judgments. If on the other hand a narrative record of the client interview or group meeting is available, judgments can be obtained from a number of judges and the degree of agreement determined.

Even if it is not possible in the context of a particular study to determine the accuracy of the documents used, the researcher should be aware of the many complex factors that affect the reliability of documents. He should consider the purpose of the documents and the possible bias of the recorders very carefully. He should avoid undue certitude about and generalization from his findings.

STATISTICAL REPORTING PLANS

Two matters of particular concern to social work researchers have been selected for discussion in the remainder of this chapter—the operation of statistical reporting plans, and analysis of the content of documentary material.

Between the use of quantitative data collected, processed, and issued by other organizations or persons, and the collection of original data through field investigation, there is a kind of twilight zone. There lie the statistical reporting plans of community councils, national voluntary agencies, federal and state departments, and the like, through which they assemble data compiled by their affiliates.

In the ten years since the first version of this chapter was written, there has been quite a bit of motion and commotion about statistical reporting plans. Computer technology has made possible more comprehensive systems of data collection and much more sophisticated analysis of the data collected within agencies and across agencies. "Statistical systems" have become just a part of MIS (management information systems) as the voice of EDP (electronic data processing) has been heard across the land, and "information systems" now merit a full chapter in this edition (see chapter 10). By the time it is published, these acronyms may well be replaced by others, but there is little doubt that the quantity of available statistical data will increase. If the computerized systems can be developed jointly by personnel who understand the field and personnel who understand the technology, the quality of the data may also improve.

Central reporting is undertaken to provide data as a basis for program planning, formulation of policy in deployment of resources, standard setting, and interpretation to the public using and supporting the service, to financing bodies, and to the schools training staff. These purposes may be served by information about such matters as the proportion of the population with access to service, trends in volume and type of service, composition of staff, size of work load, income, and expenditures. If such data from different agencies are to be added together or used for interagency or intercommunity comparison, obviously they must be consistently available, based on identical units of count, and compiled accurately.

Most of what follows applies both to the traditional manual reporting system and the sophisticated computerized system, but there are some differences. In general, computerized systems greatly increase the amount of data and the detail of cross-tabulations that can be handled. They do not solve the problems of determining which variables are relevant, defining and classifying them sensibly, and the like. And they carry a risk of generating a mass of data that gives an illusion of accuracy. If the reporting organizations use a system identical internally, with central compilation and analysis, such as that initiated by the Chicago Council for Community Services in its *Childata* (1972), the probability of error is reduced enormously. There is still the matter of ensuring that the information fed into the system is complete and accurate.

Clarity of purpose is the first essential. If the researcher is clear about why he is collecting data, he will collect only what he is likely to be able to use, and his selectiveness will lessen the burden on the agencies submitting data. His use of the data and his reports should clarify, for the participating organizations, the purpose of data collection and increase their efforts to report responsibly.

Familiarity with agency operation is essential if the researcher is to select items of information that are important enough to the participating agencies to be compiled regularly by them. However, even if the general categories of information seem generally applicable, they will not be interpreted in the same way by different reporting units unless clear definitions and instructions are provided and the importance of adherence to them communicated effectively. Here the dilemma is whether to supply detailed instructions—which may be ignored—or to sacrifice precision for brevity and readability. Variables that seem simple on first thought may lend themselves to quite different interpretations. For instance, "applications from prospective adoptive parents" for some agencies include all persons who inquire about adopting a child and for other agencies only persons who submit a formal application. If data are to be compiled on this item, it is essential that all agencies count the same thing. We at the Child Welfare League decided it was easier to drop the item than to achieve uniformity.

How is the researcher to know if definitions and instructions are followed? Clues may be found in the internal consistency of reports, if the reporting forms show the steps by which the final figures are obtained. Such forms may be less acceptable to the reporting agencies on first inspection than are very brief forms, but the apparent simplicity of the brief form is often illusory. The spadework has had to be done elsewhere to arrive at the few figures on the innocuous-looking report. A detailed form may thus be no more trouble to the respondent, and it has the advantage of enabling the recipient to make an additional check. Other clues to the degree of adherence to prescribed reporting methods may be found in the comparability of items from agency to agency. If the experience of one agency appears to be markedly out of line, it is worthwhile to inquire whether this represents a deviation in experience or simply a deviation in reporting.

One headache in carrying out a statistical reporting plan is caused by its relative inflexibility. Any change in definitions or in selection of items to be reported tends to disturb trend data, but to cling to outmoded items and definitions negates the usefulness of the plan. Furthermore, changes that seem appropriate to some agencies may create problems for others. Striking a balance between rigidity and capriciousness is a matter of judgment. If changes are made, there are devices for lessening their ill effects.

If the definition of "casework interview" is expanded from the face-to-face conversation to include interviews by telephone, a change in numbers of interviews reported will have been caused by change in definition. A simple solution is to obtain separate counts of face-to-face and telephone interviews. This would avoid disturbance of trend data and also lessen the problem that arises if not all reporting units are able to supply the additional counts immediately.

Subtle changes in definitions make it difficult to differentiate trends from artifacts of the change in definition. The effect of the change may be determinable only if data are reported for a time according to both definitions, but this is burdensome. Sometimes it is feasible to arrange for selected agencies particularly interested in the new method of reporting to carry this burden.

The fact that organizations may participate in more than one reporting system (e.g., local council, state welfare department, and national agency) may contribute to the ossification of such systems, for alteration of one is disruptive to others, and simultaneous modification of several is very hard to achieve. Or the systems may break down altogether, as agencies rebel at trying to meet the varying expectations.

If the reporting plan does not provide for total coverage, it is important to consider this fact in drawing inferences from the data collected. How representative are the reporting units?

Another question is how the data can be summated meaningfully. The use of aggregate figures may be misleading when a few large agencies dominate the total. Presentation of trends in terms of the proportion of agencies showing increases or decreases, or in terms of the median rate of change, may be more informative than a rate based on aggregates.

A statistical reporting system will have little value to participants unless there is constant effort to ensure understanding of its purpose and limitations and adherence to the definitions and rules by the reporting units, and unless it is recognized that the resulting data will not stand alone but must be accompanied by interpretative material and suggestions for use.

ANALYSIS OF THE CONTENT OF WRITTEN DOCUMENTS

If narrative documents are to serve as more than descriptive accounts of historical events or illustrative examples of the population or events under consideration, their content must be reduced to quantitative terms that will permit summation or comparison. Any attempt to categorize and summarize the contents of narrative records, minutes, or reports is a form of quantification of narrative material. This is true whether one is counting the number of group members to whom reference is made in a group work record, classifying the types of problems that a client or a committee discusses, categorizing the kinds of service offered by the caseworker or the kind of role played by the group leader, estimating the intensity of given attitudes or responses, or measuring change in client or group.

Propaganda analysis was the focus of early formal work on the quantification of narrative material—study of the dissemination of ideas through analysis of the content of newspapers and magazines. Some studies involved only classification of news and measurement of the space devoted to each category. Others included analysis of methods of presentation and evaluation of the quality of newspapers against rating schemes or criteria of merit (Kingsbury, Hart et al. 1937).

The general approach has been developed and refined into "a research technique for the objective, systematic and quantitative description of the manifest content of communication," to quote Berelson, who gives a good description of the elements of this technique (1954, p. 489). The interested reader will find another useful discussion of content analysis in Jahoda, Deutsch, and Cook (1951). In addition to its use in studies of the content and the effect of mass media on public opinion, this technique has been applied to other kinds of narrative documents, including records of group behavior and of individual psychotherapeutic and casework interviews. Among the better known work in psychotherapy is that of Carl Rogers and his associates, who have studied such factors as change in self-concept and behavior accompanying therapy through content analysis of electrically recorded case material (Rogers 1951).

The use of content analysis in social casework is of particular relevance to the social work researcher. Dollard and Mowrer are believed to have been the first to apply formal content analysis in casework research (Dollard and Mowrer 1947). They were interested in developing an instrument to measure the effects of social casework by analysis of the case record. They postulated that the effect of casework would be reflected in a reduction of tension in the client during his exposure to service, and that that reduction in tension would show in a change in the relative proportions of verbal expressions of discomfort (or distress) and expressions of relief from distress. They devised detailed instructions for classifying the emotional tone of units of the record as indicative of discomfort, of relief, or of neither. They experimented with words, sentences, and clauses as the unit of count. By dividing the record into parts, they could measure the change in the Distress-Relief Quotient (distress clauses divided by the sum of distress and relief clauses) during the life of the case. (The reader may be interested to know that this highly reliable instrument was unfortunately found to have little relation to other indices of client progress.)

During the past decade, methods for content analysis of process records and verbatim interview tapes were developed by Hollis and by Reid and Shyne to illuminate the nature of the casework process. Hollis applied to processed records a method she had devised for coding both worker and client communications according to the classification of casework techniques she had developed and according to the change objective of each communication (Hollis 1968, chap. 10, 1972). This method permits analysis of variations in the proportionate use of different techniques and the extent of client participation, as well as the interaction of client and worker.

Drawing heavily on Hollis's work, Reid and Shyne developed and used a slightly different system for classifying caseworker interventions in order to compare worker activity in planned short-term and open-ended service (Reid and Shyne 1969). Two interview analysts listened independently to over 120 taped interviews and classified each caseworker response according to this scheme. In addition to the overall comparison of the two types of service under study, variations in worker style as well as variations in worker techniques at different points in the sequence of service were examined.

Approaching a pile of case records with no more explicit purpose than to mine what is conceived as a rich lode of valuable material will not yield very useful results. It is essential, as in any research, to be clear about the purpose of the study, and to specify the variables that seem relevant.

Although there is nothing unique to the problem of sampling in content analysis of documents, a special word of caution may be in order. Because this method of analyzing information is extremely time-consuming and therefore costly, the researcher may have to be very selective in choosing the documents to be analyzed. It is important that, although fascinated by the analytic process, the researcher not lose track or let his reader lose track of how the sample was drawn and what it can be expected to represent.

If the relatively unstructured content of a record of one or more casework interviews, activity group sessions, or committee meetings is to be quantified, a central problem is the development of definitions and a classification or coding system that ensures uniform classification of the content by different analysts or by the same analyst at different times.

Definition and Classification

Gross income, source of referral, educational level are relatively easy to define. Behavior and attitudes are much harder. The more complex the property, the more spadework that is required to arrive at a definition.

The work of Hunt and his associates in developing a definition of "movement" is a good illustration. Caseworkers were asked to write the reasons for their unstructured ratings of movement or "improvement" in a group of cases. Analysis of their reasons served to show the criteria they shared as differentiated from those peculiar to each caseworker. The definition of movement was then formulated in terms of the commonly used criteria, with other factors explicitly excluded (Hunt and Kogan 1952, pp. 11–17).

Once each variable has been clearly defined, the next question is how to classify or rate it. Categories of analysis may be set up in advance on a logical basis or derived from the documents reviewed. For example, types of referral sources may be listed from general knowledge, and the analyst merely asked to check the appropriate one. Or the analyst may be asked to write out each specific source; the classification is then developed from these statements. The former procedure obviously saves a step, and should be followed when there is sufficient knowledge of the range and type of information to permit it. Classifications used in other studies have the advantage of permitting comparison with the findings of the other studies. However, prior use does not necessarily mean that a classification scheme is a good analytic tool. Classification of problems prompting applications to social agencies had been tackled in innumerable studies, but to no one's entire satisfaction, when Ripple and her associates conducted their casework research at Chicago. They therefore devoted considerable work to analyzing narrative statements of the problem as perceived by case record judges and deriving a classification scheme from these statements (Ripple and Alexander 1956).

If variables are to be rated on ordinal or interval scales, as is likely with degree of motivation, level of functioning, adequacy of parental care, and so forth, it is desirable to provide the rater with illustrations for key positions on the scale. These are appropriately called *anchoring illustrations*, as they anchor the rater's numerical judgments to concrete criteria and reduce bias toward optimistic or pessimistic ratings.

Instructions for classifying or coding are often relatively brief at the start, but for variables of any degree of complexity they rarely stay that way. A little practice in their use reveals points that need to be clarified and contingencies that need to be covered. For example, the judges who applied the scheme for classifying caseworker intervention in the Reid-Shyne study (1969) were provided with an eighteen-page manual of definitions and instructions.

Reliability

Written definitions and instructions for the case analyst are necessary but not sufficient for reliable content analysis. Training and practice are also important. One of the advantages of using documentary material is the possibility of using several judges on the same material and comparing their judgments. When judges are trained, it is usual to have them analyze one or more cases, compare their ratings, and discuss their disagreements with a view to achieving a common understanding of the task. Instructions can often be sharpened and additional illustrative material developed as a result of the training and review sessions.

On subjective material no two judges can be expected to agree completely on their interpretations of every item in every case. But if they do not agree at all in their interpretations, their analyses are of little use unless the case material is serving as a kind of projective test for the judges! Further practice and training sessions may reduce disagreements, but there comes a time when one must drop the item (or the judge) if serious disagreement persists. When is the point reached? How well do judges have to agree for their judgments to be useful as data?

A categorical answer to this question is not possible. Decision about the acceptable level in any study is arbitrary. The percentage of agreement on paired ratings—that is, the percent of cases in which two judges rate or classify a variable the same way—is widely used with both nominal and ordinal scales. Generally, use of items on which agreement is less than 75 percent or 80 percent is questionable. This is a slippery matter. For example, on an eleven-step scale, if ratings are widely dispersed over the full range of the scale, it may be satisfactory if 80 percent of the paired judgments fall on adjacent steps of the scale; that is, if the paired ratings are not more than one step apart on 80 percent of the cases. However, if the scale has only five steps, or if the ratings are clustered within a narrow band on a more extended scale, it is wise to require exact agreement on a similar proportion of cases.

When interval scales are applied, interjudge reliability can be estimated by computing intercorrelations of the ratings and determining whether the correlations are statistically significant. However, a significant correlation simply means that patterning of the judges' ratings is more alike than would be expected by chance in the absence of any agreement—and that is not very reassuring. High correlations are greatly to be desired in this context. It should be remembered that a correlation is a measure of relative, not absolute, agreement. It is desirable, therefore, to compare the mean ratings of judges to determine whether some tend to give consistently higher or lower ratings than the average for the group. Another useful index of the comparability of judgments is provided by a comparison of the standard deviations of the judges' ratings. Is one judge spreading out his judgments more widely than the other?

One problem sometimes confronted in assessing reliability of judgment is the concentration of judgments in one category or at one step in a rating scale. Application of most measures for expressing reliability depends on a distribution of judgments along the scale on which the variable is rated. If an item is rated uniformly across cases (e.g., parental care is "adequate" in practically all cases), reliability is indeterminate. That is less important than the fact that items rated uniformly have little utility in prediction, or in a study of interrelationships, and might as well be discarded.

Lack of agreement may arise from a variety of sources—absence of sufficient information in the records to provide an adequate basis for judgment; lack of clarity of definitions and instructions for coding; insufficient familiarity of the judges with the instructional material; and differences among the judges in such respects as knowledge of the subject matter, sophistication about the task of judgment, and any characteristic leaning toward optimism or pessimism (see chapter 7). If interjudge agreement on an initial group of cases falls below the standard established for the study, there are several possible courses of action. Definitions and instructions can be modified for greater clarity and specificity. Global concepts may be broken down into more specific components. Additional anchoring cases can be provided to illustrate selected steps on rating scales. Further training may help. If certain items continue to be coded unreliably on successive groups of cases, in spite of such measures, then it will be necessary to drop these items, devoted though the researcher may be to them.

Combining Judgments

In the happy situation in which a high level of agreement is achieved in application of the instrument, single judges may be used in subsequent coding of records. Use of two or more judges and combination of their judgments permit use of items with only moderate reliability, since combined judgments may be assumed to have higher reliability than those of individual judges. Judgments can be combined in various ways, each of which has advantages and disadvantages (Ripple 1959). Using an average or composite rating is economical but has the disadvantage of reducing the dispersion of ratings. The majority rating of three or more judges can be utilized, but one may not be able to afford three judges and one cannot count on majority agreement except on a dichotomous scale. A third possibility is reconciliation of interjudge differences through conferences among the judges; however, the conference method is time-consuming and it may result not in reconciliation of differences but in tacit agreement to accept the assessment of the dominant judge. Although it is desirable to test empirically the efficiency of various methods of combining judgments, the choice is usually determined by the predilections of the investigator and the feasibility of the method. In one study it was planned to resolve differences between pairs of judges by the conference method, but this procedure was found to be extremely time-consuming.

Since the initial conferences had usually resulted in a compromise, a system of simply averaging ratings was substituted for conferences (Shyne and Kogan 1957, p. 13).

Available information should not be treated as a second-class citizen in social work research. It has had an important role over the years and it retains that role, despite the increased sophistication of research design and methods of data collection and analysis. Use of available information should not be downgraded as an easy way out, for it has enough problems of its own to evoke the imagination and intellectual vigor of any researcher.

REFERENCES

Alexander, Leslie B., and Siman, Alan. 1973. Points and viewpoints. *Social work* 18:104–6.

Berelson, Bernard. 1954. Content analysis. In *Handbook of social psychology*, ed. G. Lindzey, pp. 488–522. Cambridge, Mass.: Addison-Wesley.

Blenkner, Margaret. 1959. Comments. In *Use of judgments as data in social work research*, ed. A. W. Shyne, p. 105. New York: National Assoc. of Social Workers.

Community Chests and Councils, Inc. 1939. Social breakdown: a plan for measurement and control. *Community planning bulletin* 101.

Council for Community Services in Metropolitan Chicago. 1972. *Childata: Case reporting manual*. Chicago.

Dollard, John, and Mowrer, O. H. 1947. A method of measuring tension in written documents. *Journal of abnormal and social psychology* 42: 3–22.

Eysenck, H. J. 1952. The effects of psychotherapy: An evaluation. *Journal of consulting psychology* 16:319–24.

Fischer, Joel. 1973. Is casework effective? *Social work* 18:5–20.

Herzog, Elizabeth. 1959. *Some guide lines for evaluative research*. Washington, D.C.: Children's Bureau, U.S. Department of Health, Education, and Welfare.

————, and Sudia, Cecelia E. 1970. *Boys in fatherless families*. Washington, D.C.: Children's Bureau, U.S. Department of Health, Education, and Welfare.

Hollis, Florence. 1968. *A typology of casework treatment*. New York: Family Service Assoc. of America.

————. 1972. *Casework: a psychosocial therapy*. 2d ed. New York: Random House.

Hunt, J. McV. 1959. On the judgment of social workers as a source of information in social work research. In *Use of judgments as data in social work research*, ed. A. W. Shyne, pp. 38–52. New York: National Assoc. of Social Workers.

————, and Kogan, L. S. 1952. *Measuring results in social casework: A manual on judging movement.* Rev. ed. New York: Family Service Assoc. of America.

Jahoda, Marie; Deutsch, M.; and Cook, S. W. 1951. *Research methods in social relations.* New York: Dryden.

Jenkins, Shirley. 1963. *Comparative recreation needs and services in New York neighborhoods.* New York: Community Council of Greater New York.

Kingsbury, Susan M.; Hart, H.; et al. 1937. *Newspapers and the news: an objective measurement of ethical and unethical behavior of representative newspapers.* New York: Putnam.

Kogan, L. S. 1951. The distress-relief quotient (DRQ) in dictated and verbatim social casework interviews. *Journal of abnormal and social psychology* 46:236–39.

————. 1972. Progress report: indicators of child health and welfare. Mimeographed. Center for Social Research, City University of New York.

Linford, Alton A. 1949. *Old age assistance in Massachusetts.* Chicago: Univ. of Chicago Press.

Maas, Henry S., ed. 1966. *Five fields of social service: Reviews of research.* New York: National Assoc. of Social Workers.

————, ed. 1971. *Research in the social services: A five-year review.* New York: National Assoc. of Social Workers.

Meehl, P. E. 1954. *Clinical versus statistical prediction.* Minneapolis: Univ. of Minnesota Press.

National Science Foundation. 1969. Knowledge into action: Improving the nation's use of the social sciences. *Report of the special commission on the social sciences of the National Science Board.* Washington, D.C.

Phillips, Michael, et al. 1972. *A model for intake decisions in child welfare.* New York: Child Welfare League of America.

————, et al. 1971. *Factors associated with placement decisions in child welfare.* New York: Child Welfare League of America.

Reid, William J. 1968. *A social worker's guide to abstracts publications.* New York: National Assoc. of Social Workers.

————, and Shyne, Ann W. 1969. *Brief and extended casework.* New York: Columbia Univ. Press.

Rich, Margaret. 1956. *A belief in people: A history of family social work.* New York: Family Service Assoc. of America.

Ripple, Lilian. 1959. Plans for obtaining judgment data. In *Use of judgments as data in social work research*, ed. A. W. Shyne, pp. 55–65. New York: National Assoc. of Social Workers.

————, and Alexander, Ernestina. 1956. Motivation, capacity, and opportunity as related to the use of casework service: Nature of the client's problem. *Social service review* 30:38–54.

Rogers, C. R. 1951. *Client-centered therapy*. Boston: Houghton Mifflin.

Sheldon, Eleanor B., and Moore, Wilbert E. 1968. *Indicators of social change*. New York: Russell Sage Foundation.

Shyne, Ann W., and Kogan, L. S. 1957. *A study of components of movement*. New York: Community Service Society.

Wilcox, Leslie D., et al., eds. 1972. *Social indicators and societal monitoring: An annotated bibliography*. San Francisco: Jossey-Bass.

6
Collecting Data by Questionnaire and Interview

Shirley Jenkins

Research has been called the art of asking the right question. How to phrase the question, whom to ask, who should do the asking, where to ask, when to ask, and how to record the answer are all part of this art.

There are many ways to learn about phenomena under investigation— observation and review of available data are discussed elsewhere in this book. Asking, the method examined here, is a universal way to find out about something. What generally distinguishes the research question from other kinds of questions is that information is being sought to help solve a carefully formulated problem, the wording is clear and specific, the respondents are believed to represent a representative sample, and responses are amenable to systematic classification and analysis.

The decision to collect data by means of written or oral questions stems from the nature of the research task. The methods of data collection decided upon depend on the way the study problem is formulated, which in turn influences the characteristics of the research design and the kinds of research methods used.

In practice, the determination of method of data collection in a given study is rarely an "either/or" decision. Although a variety of procedures will often be incorporated in a particular study, it is usually possible to identify the predominant data-collecting method. Collection of desired data through the use of questionnaires and interviews is perhaps the most popular way. One group of investigators (Webb et al. 1966, p. 1) have even estimated that this is the method used in 90 percent of all social research. The survey is particularly appropriate for much social work research, considering the nature of the problems commonly studied and the heavy reliance of social work practice on verbal communication. It need not be the only way, however. Sieber (1973) has argued for the integration of survey methods with participant observation, use of available records, and other fieldwork approaches.

QUESTIONNAIRE OR INTERVIEW?

If a decision is made to collect original data from respondents, one must decide whether to use a self-administered questionnaire or an interview.

For example: You wish to evaluate occupational outcome of an undergraduate social welfare program which has been in existence for five years. Graduates are working over a wide geographical area in many different settings, and their addresses are available from the alumni office. You want to know how many are working in the field; what jobs they are doing; if some have gone into graduate school; and how they evaluate their undergraduate work. With a wide geographical dispersion of potential respondents, an almost inevitable choice is the use of a mailed questionnaire. Supporting this choice is the fact that the respondents are a homogeneous group, they are literate, and they all have some presumed investment in the subject under study. For these reasons a relatively high response rate may be anticipated.

For example: From hospital data you have the names of a sample of young women in a metropolitan area each of whom gave birth to her first out-of-wedlock child, kept and cared for the infant, and was willing to talk with social workers. The literature on unmarried mothers has stressed problems of adoption and surrender, but you want to know more about women who keep their babies, how they manage in the community, what services they use or need, and how this type of single-parent family functions (Sauber and Rubinstein 1965). The appropriate respondents are the mothers themselves, the situation requires confidentiality, and, furthermore, mothers who care for their babies are tied down. Data collection by means of interviews of mothers in the privacy of their own homes is indicated.

Sometimes choice of research method is fairly obvious, as in the two examples given. At other times a careful weighing of costs and benefits is needed. In most cases some compromise is reached on methods of data collection.

For example: The United States Census, the major data collection operation in the country, operated for decades by sending census enumerators to each home where face-to-face responses were secured from residents. In 1960, as a transition measure, census forms were sent by mail to homes, and were collected and checked out by enumerators. By 1970, after extensive pretesting, the new procedure of having self-administered census forms, mailed to homes with return by mail requested, was instituted throughout the country. This was supplemented by a follow-up, primarily through home visits, to obtain forms from nonrespondents.

An extensive evaluation of the new procedure is being undertaken. Among the criteria, cost will certainly be an important factor, as well as quality of responses and extent of nonrespondents. The last can only be estimated by reference to various sample surveys and other kinds of projections. If nonresponses are random, occurring by chance alone throughout the population, these will not seriously affect the results because of the size of the population. But if failure to obtain satisfactory returns of the mailed forms occurs significantly more often among the poor, the less educated, the non-English-speaking, and the migratory population, then the data could result in biased or nonrepresentative findings. The question for study is not, Was bias introduced by the change in method? but rather, How can the biases introduced by each of the methods in 1950, 1960, and 1970 be compared? Which set of returns appears to be valid and closest to the "truth," and at what cost and for what benefit? No method is infallible; the research goal is to minimize error.

There are advantages and disadvantages to the use of either the self-administered questionnaire or the personal interview. The questionnaire is far less expensive to administer. It can be sent through the mail and reach respondents in a wide geographic area, nationally or even internationally. It can also be distributed to groups of almost any size—for example, in classes, meetings, or audiences. The standardization of the instrument makes it possible to precode answers, and this results in ease of tabulation. Since responses are on forms and not given in person, there can be real anonymity if unsigned questionnaires are permissible.

The advantages of the self-administered form also breed disadvantages. Unless the form is given to a captive group such as a college class, there is a problem of response rates. A mailed questionnaire will not get a high rate of return unless there is a strong incentive for the respondent to comply. In almost all such cases the researcher should analyze the characteristics of the nonrespondents, and estimate the representativeness of the returns. In the survey of alumni of an undergraduate social welfare program, for example, it would be anticipated that those graduates who remained in the field, who went on to graduate school, or who got good jobs would be more likely to answer than those who were either not employed or had moved to other fields.

The precoded form, with all alternatives clearly indicated, is good for reliability but gives no opportunity for respondents to explain answers or to introduce new ideas. Depth may thus be sacrificed for specificity. Ability to complete the self-administered form depends on the literacy of the respondent. With respondents of low educational level, with disturbed or disoriented persons, or with children, use of such instruments is limited. Anonymity is another mixed blessing, in that it precludes follow-up and does not allow for comparisons of individual responses with data collected from other sources.

The major alternative to the use of a self-administered questionnaire is the person-to-person interview, where verbal interaction occurs between respondent and interviewer. The advantages of the interview are its appropriateness to complex and sensitive subjects which are often of concern to social work researchers. Information in depth can be secured by trained interviewers, and the flexibility of the in-person situation allows for probes and exploration of respondent experiences. A better percentage of responses is usually secured from personal interviews than from questionnaires. The interview can be used with children, nonliterate persons, and those with limited capacities. In the "person-to-person" situation, non-verbal responses can be incorporated, and hesitation, tone, and affect can be noted. Although the typical interview is on a one-to-one basis, the family and group interview, where the interviewer seeks information from an assembled set of selected respondents, can often contribute a new dimension to data collection. Respondents often stimulate each other, whether by reinforcement or disagreement, and for certain purposes this is a useful technique for obtaining information.

To collect data economically from certain populations, the telephone has been found to be a useful method of communication. In a study where child welfare workers were the respondents, nearly a thousand telephone interviews were conducted, and needed information was secured at far less cost than personal interviews would have involved (Shapiro 1972, p. 21). An added bonus of this technique is that the use of the telephone ties up the respondent and eliminates a major source of inter-ruption in a personal interview of a busy professional—telephone calls. When using this procedure, it is helpful to have a prearranged appoint-ment for a block of telephone time, and to alert the respondent to mate-rials that may be needed for reference, such as case records.

The interview, like the questionnaire, has built-in limitations. Its very flexibility can also mean looseness and unreliability, since each interview situation has different components, and interaction between respondent and interviewer can affect results. The interview is time-consuming and expensive, and requires training and skill for field application.

In an experimental study comparing the use of interviews with ques-tionnaires to measure mothers' attitudes toward sex and aggression, Sears found both approaches to be useful, but for different reasons (1965). Interview measures correlated more highly with measures of child be-havior, but the questionnaire results correlated more highly with mothers' observed behavior in interaction with their children.

Although questionnaires and interviews are usually associated with sample survey research, in fact both techniques are used in all research designs including experimental methods. An example of use of a question-naire in an experiment may be the before and after completion of a questionnaire on social attitudes by two randomly selected samples from a population of welfare recipients who are exposed to different methods of establishing eligibility.

STRUCTURED OR UNSTRUCTURED INSTRUMENTS, OPEN- OR CLOSED-ENDED QUESTIONS

Once the decision has been made on whether to use a questionnaire or an interview, the kind of data sought will help determine the type of instrument to develop. The usual distinction between types of instruments is between those which are structured and those which are unstructured.

For example: On a survey of undergraduates designed to measure attitudes toward social work, there was a series of structured questions such as:

As far as you know, would you say there are (check one)

    (1) more job openings than social workers
    (2) about as many job openings as social workers
    (3) fewer job openings than social workers
    (4) don't know, or can't say

In a structured question, all respondents have the same possible choices, all questions are worded in exactly the same way, and the questions are presented to the respondent in the same order. Instructions and explanations are fixed, and there is no opportunity for the respondent to seek further clarification. This format can be used in both questionnaires and interviews. However, it tends to be more closely associated with questionnaires, since there are fewer options when there is no in-person contact.

At the other extreme is the unstructured instrument with open-ended questions. Such an instrument may be totally nondirective, with elaboration entirely up to the respondent. For example, the question may be, "How do you feel about your neighborhood?" or ". . . your job?" or ". . . your wife?" The entire interview content could then follow the lead of the respondent, with the interviewer simply encouraging further verbalization. This kind of interview, with vocally active respondents, can produce interesting if unstandardized data. The nondirective interview is an especially useful device for exploratory research, where the purpose is to secure new ideas and insights preliminary to more structured investigation.

More commonly used in social research is the focused interview (Merton, Fiske, and Kendall 1956), in which persons interviewed have been involved in a particular situation which has been analyzed by the researcher. The interview is focused on the subjective experiences of the respondents, to ascertain their definitions of the situation. In still another approach, useful with knowledgeable informants, an interview guide is prepared in which the respondent is introduced to a topic and encouraged to speak freely. The interviewer can redirect attention to the area under study, and probe where needed.

For example: In an exploratory interview study of executives of child welfare agencies on new developments and problems in their field, respondents spoke freely on many subjects (Kroll 1967). If they did not spontaneously mention an area of concern to the study, interviewers would direct their attention to it. Thus issues of staff, program, funding, and quality of service were among those covered, although with varying emphasis depending on individual interest on the part of the respondent.

In many social research interview studies, the full interview may contain both structured and unstructured items and sections. The instrument has defined topics, and some of the questions are closed with fixed alternatives, whereas others are open-ended to allow for freedom in response. The extent to which the instrument leans to structure or openness is based on the problem under study and the investigator's judgment of the most effective data collection procedure. There are advantages and disadvantages to both open- and closed-ended questions. If there are questions with fixed alternative answers, all respondents are exposed to the same stimulus, error is thereby reduced, and reliability is presumably strengthened. Tabulation and analysis of data are also expedited.

Problems for investigation in social work research may be in sensitive areas, and researchers often assume that more depth in responses is achieved when the respondent can speak freely without the constraints of the closed question. Where open questions are used, the researcher has the added task of developing reliable categories in which to classify answers, since unless responses are to be used only in an illustrative or anecdotal way, quantitative data are needed—something has to be counted so that characteristics of respondents may be described or differences between groups can be measured.

A question such as the popular, If you had three wishes, what would they be? for example, can present many difficulties in coding and categorizing answers. Any number of different approaches may be used to classify answers, depending on the population and the research interests of the investigator. You may want to know about "self and others" and categorize responses according to whether wishes are for the respondent, for family members, for society as a whole. You may want to know about the nature of wishes—for property, for health, for relationships. You may be concerned with a time concept, and want to know if wishes are for redressing the past, for present satisfactions, for future blessings.

Open-ended questions are generally easy to ask but hard to process for analysis. The researcher must utilize criteria of reliability and validity in justifying the scoring of responses. The answers may be subjected to the same kind of content analysis as discussed in chapter 5 in relation to use of available data. Judges can be utilized to measure agreement on categories, and items which cannot be rated with good agreement among judges may have to be eliminated because reliability has not been established. The procedures would be similar to those discussed in chapter 7 relating to interobserver reliability.

The hypothesis that questions involving depth and feeling can be handled only in open-ended questions is not necessarily valid. In a controlled study to test the effects of open versus closed questions on response quality, Dohrenwend (1965) found that open questions were less efficient than closed questions, and there was no evidence that they produced answers of more depth or more validity. Where interviewee resistance was experienced, objective questions yielded more valid results. The structured question, however, works best when the question being asked is measurable along specific dimensions and the conceptual framework is clear. The preparation of such questions can involve extensive work. Dohrenwend cites one study where eight pretests, each involving twenty-six interviews, were done before an appropriate closed question could be phrased.

One way the sophisticated researcher can straddle the choice between developing and pretesting closed questions and using open questions—which are hard to quantify—is to embed in the instrument sets of items with closed-ended format that have been previously used extensively to get at underlying dimensions. The advantage is that norms are available for comparative purposes. Srole (1956) developed a five-item scale for measuring the concept of alienation or, as he termed it, "anomia." The concept refers to a sense of powerlessness, normlessness, isolation, and self-estrangement. The items simply call for agreement or disagreement. One item is, "In spite of what people say, the lot of the average man is getting worse, not better." Another is, "It's hardly fair to bring children into the world the way things look for the future." The five items have been used in hundreds of studies, and the responses have been found to provide a score which correlates strongly with social class and other relevant variables. Lengthy open-ended questions exploring the same subject might be less reliable in producing an alienation measure than the brief five-item scale.

Social workers have been slow to utilize formal tests in research, but the literature in psychology, sociology, and education contains a substantial body of instruments which are applicable to many of the areas under study in social work research. The use of such tests improves the reliability of the data and also gives a basis for comparison of findings with those in other studies.

CONTENT AREAS FOR INSTRUMENT CONSTRUCTION

Once the decisions have been made on the kind of data collection procedure to be followed and the relative degree of structure to be used, the researcher proceeds to the actual development of the instrument. Initial attention should not be to the clever question or the gimmick to arouse interest, but to carefully laying out each phase of the research problem and specifying the information needed to answer each question or test each hypothesis. The number of variables to be studied to answer each question can be as few or as many as the investigator and the resources will allow. It is the rare investigator who sticks to the bare outlines of a research question. Typically the reasoning is, "If I'm going into the field, I might as well find out about x and about y, even though they are not particularly critical to the study. But I've always wanted to know about *x* and *y* and this is my chance." This approach must be looked at with caution, but some indulgence. If you go too far afield from your basic problem, you will overextend yourself and end with a vast body of unrelated and probably irrelevant information. If you stick to the bare bones, however, you may miss some interesting leads and the chance for serendipitous findings which may give new insights. At the very least, the investigator must be certain that the data obtained will in fact have bearing on the central hypothesis, and that the so-called "dross rate" (Webb et al. 1966, pp. 32–33), or interview conversation irrelevant to the subject at hand, will be minimized.

There are many different ways to classify the kinds of content usually included in a research instrument. Three categories are noted here.

1. Demographic and descriptive data. Few instruments do not include certain basic demographic and descriptive data about respondents and their characteristics. This information is needed not only to describe the group studied but to provide the basis for cross-tabulation among variables in the study. Among the kinds of information usually obtained are data on age, sex, ethnicity, birthplace, marital status, number of children, educational level, occupation, place of residence, and other factual areas. This is not to say that all such "facts" are easily obtained or even categorized. Does "religion," for example, mean religion of birth or religion practiced? Does "married" mean a legal certificate or does it include a common-law or consensual union? Corresponding to demographic information obtained about individuals, a study of agencies or programs would include other basic factual data such as sponsorship, funding, population served, fee structure, and program categories. For a community survey, the data could include geographic area, population, income, and social statistics such as crime rates, venereal disease and housing density.

2. Experiential and behavioral data. Behavior and experiences, past and present, constitute the second kind of content usually collected. This content explores what in fact has happened, been seen or heard, in current or previous circumstances. It differs from demographic and descriptive information in that it is problem or topic related. It differs from the attitudinal and feeling data in that it primarily refers to the experience and behavior of the respondent rather than the affective or emotional response. Findings in which mothers report on children's behavior, workers report on case loads, or clients describe services fall in this category.

3. Attitudinal and feeling data. A third content area in social research is concerned with beliefs, attitudes, values, and feelings. This research draws heavily on work by psychologists and sociologists. What people believe, how they are predisposed to act, and what their feelings are in role performance constitute a substantial part of social research, and the findings may contribute to both policy and practice. In the attitudinal areas, in particular, the use of standardized instruments is appropriate.

The distinctions among the three kinds of content noted are by no means fixed in relation to subject matter. Marital status, for example, can be an item which is checked as demographic data, can be a topic of intensive study with respect to experiential or behavioral content, or can be the subject of a standardized attitude scale. An important aspect of the distinction for the researcher concerns the reliability and validity of the responses. There may be special difficulties, for example, in evaluating inaccuracies, as distinct from falsifications, or distortions arising from emotional reactions to the subject matter.

CLARITY IN VARIABLES AND REDUCTION OF ERROR

The basic purposes of the research instrument are to get the information you want, and to be sure of what you have—a simple restatement of the need for validity and reliability. There is no greater contributor to error than lack of clarity in concepts. If different respondents interpret the same question in different ways, all the statistical manipulation available will not help the research either to get what is wanted or to be sure of what is reported.

Translating all major concepts in a study into operational definitions is important not only with reference to problem formulation but as a frame of reference for instrument construction. Such clarity and specificity are necessary to secure appropriate information content. This is important in interviews and even more important in self-administered questionnaires, where there is no opportunity for in-person explanations. Often a term that seems obvious can be subject to a range of interpretation. The question, "What is your income?" is a good example. Does this mean gross or net? Before or after taxes? Individual earnings or combined family income? Earned salary only or income from all sources, including interest, pensions, and benefits? Income per hour, day, week, month, or year? For a self-employed doctor, annual income may be easily determined; for a clerical worker, the weekly pay may be useful; for a plumber, the hourly rate may be appropriate. For a study of seasonal workers, both the hourly or daily rate, and how many days the worker is employed per year, are necessary.

Another concept on which clarity is often assumed, but confusion reigns, is that of family. If a respondent is asked, "Who are the members of your family?" it should be clear whether the reference is to the family of origin (own parents and siblings) or the family of procreation (the respondent's spouse and own children), or even to the so-called extended family. Only if the purpose of the question is to see how the respondent interprets "family" should no definitions be offered.

It is usually not possible to forecast all contingencies, but the author of an instrument should try to predict the main ways a question can be answered. A recent housing survey, for example, asked for mortgage payments and upkeep costs if the respondent were an owner, or rent if he were a renter. For the owners of cooperative apartments, who pay monthly maintenance which is neither rent nor mortgage, there was no place on the form. Since all contingencies cannot be foreseen by the researcher, it is generally important to include space for "other" and "not ascertainable" answers. This is less frustrating to the respondent and more satisfying for data tabulation and analysis, since blank spaces on a form can mean many things, including "no answer to the question," or that the question itself was overlooked.

Another important dimension, critical for many responses, is the time frame for a question. For example, in response to the question, "Do you spank your child?" respondents may be asked to check either "never," "sometimes," or "often." "Never" is clear, but "sometimes" may be often for some parents; "often" may be sometimes for others. It would be better to specify the frequency saying, "sometimes, like once a month," and "often, like once a week."

One further way to be specific about time frame is to ask for time-limited responses. In a study of health behavior, for example, the questionnaire stated, "We are interested in illness during the last two weeks. That is the period from Monday _____ to Sunday _____" (dates are inserted). A printed calendar was shown to respondents so that the exact days can be noted (Population Health Survey). Subsequent questions about the nature of illness, visits to doctors, and time lost from work all applied to the specified two-week period. The period specified may differ, however, when the interview turns to exploration of hospital experience. There respondents were asked to report all hospitalizations for the past year. Hospital admissions are infrequent and more likely to be recalled than visits to the doctor's office, so that a longer time span was needed to capture information, and defensible as well.

In addition to a time frame, a particular question may need some frame for designating intensity. In an attitudinal question (a comparable question to the behavioral one above), such as "How do you feel about spanking a child?" with the alternate responses being "very opposed," "opposed," "neither for nor against," "favorable," "very favorable," the inclusion of anchoring references would be helpful. Respondents might express extent of agreement more reliably if the alternatives were, for example, as follows: "very opposed: I would call a policeman if I saw an adult spank a child," or "opposed: I would never spank my own child, but what others do is their own business."

STRATEGIES FOR OBTAINING RESPONSES

Research workers experienced in constructing instruments have developed many strategies for securing information. One is called the "funnel" technique, which means the interview opens with a broad, general inquiry and then proceeds to narrow it down to more specific question areas. This is good for establishing initial rapport, breaking new ground, and gaining confidence of the respondent before getting to what may be more difficult, sensitive, and specific areas.

There are a number of techniques that are useful in the wording of questions. It is sometimes helpful when asking about problem areas to imply that you know that other people have problems as well. For example, "A lot of people have difficulties and disappointments with their children. What have been your major problems?" Another approach would be to balance the social desirability of the alternative responses: "In some families women work outside the home, and in others they do not, and most people feel there are advantages and disadvantages in both cases. What is your situation?" Euphemisms for value-loaded concepts are often used in phrasing questions. Students may be "counseled out" rather than failed. A respondent should be given a chance to praise as well as to criticize, whether the subject is another person, a worker, or a social service program. An example is the pair of questions, "What do you like best about your child?" and "What is the greatest problem?" This gives a balance to the responses, allows for mixed reactions, and helps the respondent give what may be unfavorable or critical answers. A study of some experimental interviewing techniques on the amount and quality of information obtained during a health interview found that "verbal reinforcement," that is, appreciative comments by the interviewer following fruitful recall by the respondent, was very effective in producing data (U.S. Department of Health, Education, and Welfare, Public Health Service, Health Services and Mental Health Administration 1971).

It is unwise to try for an answer to a question the respondent could not possibly answer. If you are interested in a comparison between ghetto and suburban living, you should not ask people in the ghetto how life there compares with life in the country. Having never lived in the country, many could not comment on the basis of direct experience. On the other hand, you could ask them what they think life is like in the country, to study their fantasies and beliefs. Sometimes researchers can compare actual data with respondents' estimates. In a neighborhood experiencing change in ethnic composition, for instance, it can be hypothesized that residents opposed to change are likely to overestimate the magnitude of change which has actually occurred. Thus the gap between fact and fantasy can be a measure of respondent attitudes.

Projective techniques are indirect methods of securing information, in which the respondents react to relatively unstructured stimuli. The assumption is that respondents will organize and structure stimuli in such a way that they will reveal some of their own feelings or attitudes. This is the basis for highly developed tests as the Rorschach or the TAT (Thematic Apperception Test), in which responses are made to ink blots or to pictures. Analyses of responses from thousands of cases have resulted in scoring procedures and norms which presumably reveal underlying psychological dimensions. Even in unstandardized items it is possible to utilize some projective or indirect methods. For example, a respondent could be asked, "If you had a friend whose son was on drugs, what would you advise your friend to do?" The assumption is that respondents will speak more freely with regard to the case of a hypothetical friend, but that the answers will in fact be revealing of the respondent's own feelings. Another kind of indirect method is sentence completion, in which a sentence is begun and the respondent is asked to complete it. An example of this in a recent study of biological parents with children in foster care (Jenkins and Norman 1972) was the request to complete the pair of sentences, "To a mother a child is _____," and "To a father a child is _____." The two were asked of both parents. The responses of mothers and fathers reveal differences in perceptions of maternal and paternal roles.

A more elaborate use of this technique is the introduction of incomplete stories. In a study of potential for return-to-school instruction of handicapped homebound children, a series of incomplete stories were given to the youngsters. They were asked to finish the narrative (Jenkins and Rusalem 1961). Analysis of the made-up endings revealed the children's own fears, concerns, and anxieties, which they could not state directly.

In constructing an instrument, investigators may seek to improve responses in many ways. Reliability is presumably improved by fixed wording of interview questions. This is especially appropriate for a homogeneous sample—all college graduates, all ten-year-old white middle-class children. But in a survey on health services, for instance, where respondents may range from illiterate recipients to practitioners of medicine, data collection may be impaired if all respondents are asked exactly the same questions. Issues such as access, availability, and quality of services may be explored for the whole sample, but questions may be worded differently for subsamples of respondent groups. There are dangers in such an approach—of patronizing the less knowledgeable or of making unfounded assumptions—but there are also dangers of losing data if the full capabilities and experience of all respondent groups are not appropriately tapped.

There are numerous other ways in which reliability can be improved through manipulation of order and style. For example, respondents are often asked to check items on a list to indicate agreement or disagreement. Studies have shown there is a tendency to agree with more of the items at the beginning of a list, which probably measures not agreement but fatigue from having read a long list. The avoidance of what has been called list-order bias can be accomplished by rearranging the items so that questionnaires with differing orders of presentation of items may be randomly assigned to different respondents. Then responses will be to the content of the item rather than the order, since list-order bias will be randomized among respondents.

An example of the opening question of a semistructured instrument used in a longitudinal study is cited here to illustrate one approach to securing data, using the funnel technique of an open-ended question followed by specific probes (Jenkins and Norman 1972). In this study, repeated in-depth interviews of about three hundred mothers whose children had been placed in foster care were undertaken by trained social workers. They visited mothers in their homes, explained the study purpose, obtained consent, and then opened the interview as follows, recording answers in as close to verbatim fashion as possible:

Main question	*Probe if not* *spontaneously answered*
I. *Respondent's statement of* *problem*	

1. First of all, would you tell me in your own words what brought about the placement of _____ away from home in foster care.	A. Who first had the idea to place _____?
	  1. Did anyone oppose it or disagree with it?
	    If yes:
	    a. Who?
	    b. Why?
	
	B. Were any attempts made to make other arrangements for _____ other than placement?
	    If yes:
	  1. What?
	  2. Who did this?
	  3. Why didn't it work out?

I. *Respondent's statement of problem* (continued)
   1.   (continued)

C. Was there anyone whom you usually depend on who couldn't or didn't help out?
   If yes:
   1. Who? (relationship)
   2. Why not?

D. Did all your children who were in your home go into placement at that time?
   If no:
   1. Which children were not placed at that time (name, age, sex, father)?
   2. Why weren't they placed?

E. Who was caring for _____ just before he was placed?
   If other than natural mother:
   1. For how long had she been caring for _____?
   2. Why was she caring for him (rather than his mother)?

If sample child two years or older, ask F:

F. Was _____ told that he was going into placement?
   If yes:
   1. By whom? What was he told?
   If no:
   2. What was the reason for that?

G. Was _____ prepared for placement in any (other) way?
   If yes:
   1. By whom? In what way(s)?
   If no:
   2. What was the reason for that?

H. Did anyone help you get ready for _____ going into placement away from home?
   If yes:
   1. Who? In what way(s)?

I. *Respondent's statement of*
problem (continued)
  1.   (continued)

                             I. Who actually took _____ to
                                 the agency the day he went into
                                 placement?

  2. From all you have told me,   A. When would you say this
      what would you say was the   problem *first* started?
      one main reason for _____
      going into foster care?

  3. And what would you say was   A. When would you say this
      the next most important   problem *first* started?
      reason for _____ going into
      foster care?

The total instrument, which required approximately a two-hour inter-view, was thirty-four pages long. It incorporated both open-ended and precoded structured items, including checklists and attitudinal scales. Question areas covered the placement experience, attitudes and experiences regarding agencies, general social attitudes and feelings about placement, family functioning, role preferences and performances, and socioeconomic and demographic information. Finally, judgments and reactions to the respondents' cooperativeness in the interview situation were requested. This opening portion of this interview schedule has been cited to illustrate the use of a long, complicated, and mixed type of instrument to collect extensive data with a variety of depth and focus.

Sociometric Measures

Where special subjects are under investigation, such as interviewing elites, e.g., Nobel laureates (Zuckerman 1972) or obtaining life histories (Roff and Ricks 1970), special methods of data collection have sometimes been developed to secure desired information. Sociometric measures, which are designed to gather information about social choices and interactions among people, arose to meet the needs of group research. Although the field of sociometry may be broadly defined as dealing with measurement of social behavior, the term "sociometric measures" relates primarily to the work of Moreno and Jennings, who developed this line of investigation (Lindzey and Byrne 1968). Basically, sociometric measures assess attractions and/or repulsions within a given group. In a classroom, for example, children may be asked to list in order of preference, the classmates they would choose to sit next to them. The question is easy enough. The interest lies in the analysis of who is chosen, who rejected, and by whom. Patterns of social interaction, leadership, clustering, cliques, and allegiances can be studied from the responses to just such a simple device.

One fairly common use of sociometric measures is in the evaluation of changes in peer group relations of children who are assigned to varying therapy groups or other forms of intervention.

APPLYING THE INSTRUMENT

Once an instrument has been developed and pretested, there are other matters to decide before data are collected. These include: (1) Who shall be the respondents? (2) How shall responses be gathered? (3) Who shall collect the data? (4) How shall they be recorded?

Determination of respondents is essentially part of the sampling plan discussed elsewhere in this book. This is critical in evaluating the importance of the findings, since the extent to which findings can be generalized depends on how representative the sample is of the population to be studied. Clarity in designation of respondents is the task of the researcher and should not be left to the field staff. Samples are defined in different ways, with varying specificity. In a quota sample, an interviewer could stand on a certain street corner with instructions to interview a specified number of passersby in certain categories, e.g., men, women, young people, Blacks, Whites, and so forth. In a neighborhood cluster sample, the interviewer may be instructed to seek any adult at a particular address and, if there is no one home, to try the neighbors on either side. In a follow-up study of a selected sample, the respondent is identified by name and must be reached in person. In general, scientific sample surveys do not permit substitution of designated households or respondents by the interviewers. Their substituting more accessible respondents for those hard to reach may render the sample unrepresentative.

The content of the data sought affects the designation of respondent. In the study, discussed above, of biological parents with children in foster care, some of the questions, such as living circumstances or demographics, could be answered by any adult member of the household. For other content areas, such as maternal feelings on placement, the only acceptable respondent was the mother herself.

Every investigator seeks to minimize nonresponse. Since mailed questionnaires typically have high nonresponse rates, devices such as the inclusion of a stamped self-addressed envelope, an offer to share findings, a bonus gift, and even a fee payable on receipt of the completed form have been used, with varying results. The ethics and advantages of cash payments to respondents are a controversial subject; if biased responses will result from such payments, then obviously findings will be contaminated. But if the content of responses is unaffected, it is not unreasonable to consider the time expended by respondents answering questions in a funded study as having cash value, as does the time of the interviewer and of the researcher.

Arrangements for interviews vary. Interviewers may telephone to make appointments, thereby easing entry. There are limitations here, since there are groups whose members do not all have telephones. Furthermore, there is a good chance of getting a quick refusal on the phone, whereas a friendly person at the door, showing credentials, may have a better chance to secure the interview. If the respondent must be a specific person, repeat visits will be needed before all respondents are reached—an important item in interview budgets.

In a personal interview study, the setting of the contact should be the same or comparable for all respondents, so that variations in locale do not affect responses. Interviews in the respondents' homes may provide more privacy, and thus result in more frankness in answers, than an office setting. On the other hand, privacy may be hard to achieve if the respondent is part of a large family living in crowded quarters. There are no prescriptions; there is no "right" way to interview. Subject content, nature of sample, need for privacy, the length of the contact, the cost of the operation, and the style of the researcher all affect the field approach.

In general—although not stressed in this chapter—interviewers should be trained so that they operate in comparable ways and can deal with unforeseen contingencies. In some studies the interviewers contribute their judgments as data, and in such cases training is especially important. Interviewers' experiences in the carrying out of survey sampling are described in a recent book which may be useful for training purposes (Converse and Schuman 1973).

SOCIAL WORKER AS RESEARCH INTERVIEWER

The social worker, trained in relating to people, in empathizing in problem situations, in encouraging responsiveness, and in communication skills, would at first consideration appear to be an excellent choice for research interviewer. As Kadushin states, "interviewing is the most consistently and frequently employed social work technique" (1972, pp. 1–2). Furthermore, their knowledge of personal and social needs and reactions makes them particularly appropriate interviewers for studies in sensitive areas (Hamovitch 1963). But there are important differences between the social work interview, whether intake, diagnostic, or therapeutic, and the research interview. These differences need to be made explicit in the training of social workers who embark on research (Wasser 1957, 1962).

Service to the client is the main concern of the social worker; the research interviewer wants to secure data relevant to the study. Research may confer deferred benefits to clients, or benefit future rather than present clients, but immediate services are not the primary goal. The social worker seeks to establish ongoing relationships with clients; the research interviewer often performs a one-time assignment and avoids deep involvement. The social worker represents help to be offered to the client; the research interviewer cannot make promises or commitments. At most, except in emergencies, he can refer clients to other resources. The social worker may be flexible in any one interview responding to the client's mood, interests, and leads; the research interviewer is more limited and needs to conform to such structure as is required by the study instrument, since it is usually "now or never" for data collection. Confidentiality may also be interpreted differently—the social worker uses information for case planning and treatment; the research interviewer, only for completion of the schedule. The researcher usually analyzes data for groups, not for individuals.

Where the differences in social work and research interviews are recognized and made explicit in a training process, the professional worker can make an important contribution to field research. However, trained workers are expensive, and it is valid to ask what level of training is needed for different tasks. This depends on the interview content, the population, and the resources available. Non-social work interviewers do well in many studies—in fact, they are used far more often than social workers. All kinds of interview personnel have been used successfully—college students, community people, paraprofessionals, social work moonlighters. There is some evidence that personality factors are more predictive of interview performance than is the social status of the interviewer (Summers and Beck 1973). Where feasible and appropriate, however, filling the role of research interviewer is one way for the practitioner to contribute to social work research.

MATCHING INTERVIEWER AND RESPONDENT

A major issue in relation to collecting data is that of "matching" respondents and interview staff. This can involve factors such as ethnic group, sex, age, class, and life experience. Research has shown there are differences in replies when respondents talk to people with whom they can identify. In an early report on effects of race of interviewers on responses, Hyman (1954) showed that, where Black respondents were randomly assigned to Black and White interviewers, there were substantial differences in results. The findings showed a more passive view of Black aspirations and problems when reports came from White rather than Black interviewers. Later studies showed that race-of-interviewer effects tend to be strongest where questions are related to specific issues of race relations, whereas questions about living circumstances and family show minimal interviewer effects (Schuman and Converse 1971). Brieland (1969) studied the preference of Blacks in relation to race of service givers, using both Black and White interviewers. He found that Blacks seeking or receiving service in one low-income neighborhood preferred service from

Blacks, given equal competence. This preference, however, was expressed more strongly when the interviewer was Black than when the interviewer was White.

There are other areas of matching which are important—the most obvious one is language (Welch, Comer, and Steinman 1973). Bilingual interviewers are needed if respondents are more comfortable in a language other than English, e.g., Spanish or Chinese. Interview instruments also must be carefully translated, and reliability must be established so that words and phrases have comparable meanings in all languages used. The best instrument construction would involve a bilingual team, so that concepts germane to different cultural groups would be incorporated in the initial version.

Sex difference between interviewer and respondent can also affect responses. An extreme example has been the nature of information elicited from rape victims when women interviewers are used. But the principle applies where any sensitive area is involved. In cases of special life experiences, rapport may be better achieved by interviewers with like backgrounds to interviewees. Studies of drug abuse, for example, have used former addicts to interview and to assist in instrument development, so that language meaningful to the respondents will be used. In research interviewing with low-income families, Geismar and La Sorte (1963) found that more abstract and conceptually difficult questions had more response failures, but that there was readiness to share personal matters with research interviewers. In measuring reliability, they concluded that on some items the researchers secured more reliable data than was entered on official records.

In his discussions of cross-cultural interviewing, Kadushin reports numerous studies whose findings support the need for consideration of "matching" (1972, pp. 219–60). He goes on, however, to raise the issue of "homophily," or the concept that people who have shared experiences will be more culturally at home with each other. The dangers of direct transference of this principle to research studies are apparent—overidentification, lack of control of bias, and confusion of roles are possible consequences of overemphasis on matching. Weiss (1968–69), in a study of welfare mothers' responses where both interviewers and respondents were Black, analyzed validity in terms of social distance and rapport. She found that status similarity, rather than disparity, was associated with bias, and that respondents rated highest in rapport were the most biased. There is a distinction between "total involvement" by the interviewer, which may be related to rapport, and "task involvement," which may be related to validity (Hyman 1954, pp. 138–50). Dohrenwend, Colombotos, and Dohrenwend (1968) found that both too little and too much social distance produced biasing effects.

In summary, issues of matching are important, and differences owing to race, sex, age, and life experience need to be recognized. Latent bias, racism, sexism, and different value systems must be examined and explicated. Where matching occurs, overidentification must be carefully controlled, since bias is a factor which can operate in at least two directions —positive and negative. Both empathy and appreciation of differences, as well as adherence to principles of scientific inquiry, are in order.

RECORDING THE DATA

A final phase of the collection process is the recording of data. In the self-administered questionnaire, questions are typically precoded, responses are derived from checks, circles, or underlinings, and the operation moves directly to data processing. The interview schedule, with open-ended questions, presents other problems (Crittenden and Hill 1971). The interviewer rarely takes shorthand and has few options. One is not to record but to try to recall, after the interview, what has been said. This is risky at best, fallacious at worst. Another procedure is to get down as much as possible verbatim—even, on occasion, slowing down the interviewing with a comment such as, "That was an important answer, I want to get it down." A third alternative, coming more into vogue with improved equipment, is the tape recorder which captures what is actually said. A pioneer study in the use of electrical recording of casework interviews was made by Kogan (1950), who found that clients were not resistant to the process. The tape recorder has been successfully used in studies of follow-up interviews with adoptive parents (Jaffe and Fanshel 1970; Kadushin 1967). Fanshel and Moss (1971) utilized tape recordings of clinical interviews as a basis for research interviews with the agency therapist about her role in treatment. These sessions were also recorded. Consent for the study was secured from both clients and therapist. Published materials include edited tapes and typescripts of the clinical interviews and transcriptions of the playback sessions. This study was a methodological innovation in that it presented data from both clinical interviews and research interviews and thus analyzed both content and process.

An obvious advantage of the use of tape recordings is accuracy. There are some problems in using mechanical devices and obtaining consent of respondents, but these are not critical. One weakness is that the procedure involves a great deal of time expended in the process of preparing usable typescripts or using the recordings themselves for research analysis. Nevertheless, the availability of recorded interviews makes it possible for data to be reanalyzed along different dimensions which may emerge after an initial analysis.

SUMMARY AND RIGHTS OF SUBJECTS

In collecting original data by questionnaire or interview, the decision on what method to use depends on the research problem, the population to be studied, and the study resources. The self-administered questionnaire can be widely applied, less expensively administered, and easily precoded for data analysis. The personal interview can deal at greater length with sensitive subjects, explore areas in depth, and produce new insights. Research instruments can be constructed in various ways, from closed-ended structured questions to unstructured nondirective guides. Where the conceptual framework is clear and the dimensions to be measured are defined, closed-ended questions which have been pretested are more likely to produce reliable data for analysis than open-ended questions.

There is a range of issues which are part of the research task, including designation of the respondent, selection of interviewers, and method of recording responses. As would be expected, researchers not only explore social and social work problems, they also investigate research methods. There is a substantial literature on the effects that various designs of questionnaires and interview schedules, as well as techniques used in the field training of interviewers, have on data collection.

The concern with protecting human subjects from possibly harmful experimentation has been extended to cover all kinds of investigations. Most funded studies in universities and elsewhere that involve people, even if only as respondents to interviews, must satisfy institutional review committees and file statements with the funding agency about steps taken to protect human subjects (U.S. Department of Health, Education, and Welfare, Public Health Service, National Institutes of Health 1971).

Interview and questionnaire forms are subject to scrutiny in this regard, as are arrangements for confidentiality of data. The investigator is typically asked to specify anticipated risks to respondents and to justify these in relation to the potential benefits of the research. Methods used to obtain informed consent must also be described. Thus the respondent to the research interview is presumably protected by institutional arrangements, just as the social work client is presumably protected by agency reputation and professional ethics.

Techniques and methods of data collection have become more knowledgeable and sophisticated, but the ideal method and the right question often escape formulation. In general there is no one "right" way—only considered decisions based on informed judgments. One conclusion that can be drawn from shared experiences, however, is that there rarely is a study in which collection procedures do not produce far more data than can easily be handled or reported. That is the time for the researcher to move on from methods of data collection to techniques for data reduction.

REFERENCES

Brieland, D. 1969. Black identity and the helping person. *Children* 16: 170–76.

City University of New York, Graduate Center, Center for Social Research. 1969. *Population health survey.* New York.

Converse, J. M., and Schuman, H. 1973. *Conversations at random: Survey research as interviewers see it.* New York: Wiley.

Crittenden, K. S., and Hill, R. J. 1971. Coding reliability and validity of interview data. *American Sociological Review* 36:1073–80.

Dohrenwend, B. S. 1965. Some effects of open and closed questions on respondents' answers. *Human Organization* 24:175–84.

———; Colombotos, J.; and Dohrenwend, B. P. 1968. Social distance and interview effects. *Public Opinion Quarterly* 32:410–22.

Fanshel, D., and Moss, F. 1971. *Playback: A marriage in jeopardy examined.* New York: Columbia Univ. Press.

Geismar, L. L., and La Sorte, M. A. 1963. Research interviewing with low-income families. *Social Work* 8:10–13.

Hamovitch, M. B. 1963. Research interviewing in terminal illness. *Social Work* 8:4–9.

Hyman, H. H. 1954. *Interviewing in social research.* Chicago: Univ. of Chicago Press.

Jaffee, B., and Fanshel, D. 1970. *How they fared in adoption: A follow-up study.* New York: Columbia Univ. Press.

Jenkins, S., and Norman, E. 1972. *Filial deprivation and foster care.* New York: Columbia Univ. Press.

———, and Rusalem, H. 1960. Attitudes of homebound students toward return to regular classroom attendance. *Exceptional Children* 28:71–74.

Kadushin, A. 1967. An experience in tape recording interviews: Report of an adoptive follow-up study. *Journal of Jewish Communal Services* 43:327–33.

———. 1972. *The social work interview.* New York: Columbia Univ. Press.

Kogan, L. 1950. The electrical recording of social casework interviews. *Social Casework* 31:371–78.

Kroll, F. 1967. *Perspectives on foster care in New York City: A report of a field interview survey of executives of fifty-eight child-caring agencies.* New York: Columbia University School of Social Work.

Lindzey, G., and Byrne, D. 1968. Measurement of social choice and interpersonal attractiveness. In *Handbook of social psychology,* 2d ed., ed. G. Lindzey and E. Aronson, pp. 452–525. Reading, Mass.: Addison-Wesley.

Merton, R. K.; Fiske, M.; and Kendall, P. 1956. *The focused interview.* Glencoe, Ill.: Free Press.

Richardson, S. A.; Dohrenwend, B. S.; and Klein, D. 1965. *Interviewing: Its forms and functions.* New York: Basic Books.

Roff, M., and Ricks, D. F., eds. 1970. *Life history research in psychopathology.* Minneapolis: Univ. of Minnesota Press.

Sauber, M., and Rubinstein, E. 1965. *Experiences of the unwed mother as a parent: A longitudinal study of unmarried mothers who keep their first-born.* New York: Community Council of Greater New York.

Schuman, H., and Converse, J. M. 1971. The effects of black and white interviewers on black responses in 1968. *Public Opinion Quarterly* 35: 44–68.

Sears, R. R. 1965. Comparison of interviews with questionnaires for measuring mothers' attitudes toward sex and aggression. *Journal of Personality and Social Psychology* 2:37–44.

Shapiro, D. 1972. Agency investment in foster care: a study. *Social Work* 17:20–28.

Sieber, S. D. 1973. The integration of fieldwork and survey methods. *American Journal of Sociology* 78:1335–59.

Srole, L. 1956. Social integration and certain corollaries: An exploratory study. *American Sociological Review* 21:706–16.

Summers, G. F., and Beck, E. M. 1973. Social status and personality factors in predicting interviewer performance. *Sociological Methods and Research* 2:111–22.

U.S. Department of Health, Education, and Welfare, Public Health Service, Health Services and Mental Health Administration. 1971. *Effect of some experimental interviewing techniques on reporting in the health interview survey.* Vital and Health Statistics, Data Evaluation and Methods Research, Series 2. Washington, D.C.: U.S. Government Printing Office.

U.S. Department of Health, Education, and Welfare. Public Health Service, National Institutes of Health. 1971. *The institutional guide to DHEW policy on protection of human subjects.* Washington, D.C.: U.S. Government Printing Office.

Wasser, E. 1957. The caseworker as research interviewer in follow-up studies. *Social Casework* 38:423–30.

———. 1962. Research interviewing in social work research: Some formulations. *Social Service Review* 36:286–94.

Webb, E., et al. 1966. *Unobtrusive measures: Nonreactive research in the social sciences.* Chicago: Rand McNally.

Weiss, C. H. 1968–69. Validity of welfare mothers' interview responses. *Public Opinion Quarterly* 32:622–33.

Welch, S.; Comer, J.; and Steinman, M. 1973. Interviewing in a Mexican-American community: An investigation of some potential sources of response bias. *Public Opinion Quarterly* 37:115–26.

Zuckerman, H. 1972. Interviewing an ultra-elite. *Public Opinion Quarterly* 36:159–75.

7
Observation
of Social
Interaction

Sidney Rosen
and Norman A. Polansky

To observe social interaction is to take note systematically of behaviors occurring among two or more people who are typically compresent physically and psychologically. In this chapter, we shall usually have reference to observation of groups, including families.

Studies utilizing techniques of group observation have been conducted in the United States for about half a century. Dorothy Swain Thomas reported a study of interaction among young children in 1929. Her work was followed most notably by the classic studies of Kurt Lewin and his students. Investigations by Lippitt (1940), French (1944), and others effectively launched the organized scrutiny of group dynamics. Work by Barker, Dembo, and Lewin (1941), Meyers (1944), Wright (1942), and colleagues also helped establish direct observation and the laboratory experiment in the burgeoning fields of child development, family dynamics, and psychological ecology. Indeed, it is now two decades since some of the best known summarizations concerning observational methods appeared (Bales 1950; Heyns and Lippitt 1954; Heyns and Zander 1953; Leary 1957). Many craftsmen have since contributed technical advances and refinements. To this extensive literature, we can give only an overview.

SCIENTIFIC VERSUS CASUAL OBSERVATION

Our definition of the observation of social interaction suggests that any normally functioning adult is a qualified, certainly an experienced, observer. After all, he has been involved since early childhood in learning social behavior. Why, then, bother telling the would-be researcher about matters in which he is already expert? We do so because there are fundamental differences in emphasis between casual, or "natural," and scientific observation.

Compared to the casual observation of ordinary living, that for research purposes is more deliberately selective and geared to hypothesis testing; it involves greater skepticism about how representative a single event is of either the actor or the group situation; it occurs with greater awareness that the observer, himself, may be a faulty recording instrument. And, as elsewhere in science, the logical standards by which observations are used for inferring causal connections are far more rigorous.

REASONS FOR USING DIRECT OBSERVATION

Direct observation has the same ultimate goal as do all other methods of scientific data collection: to discover those regularities in social structure and process that make possible efficient prediction and treatment. Why choose this technology?

Some behavioral scientists place a higher credence in data obtained by observation than in those obtained by interview. We believe, however, that most civilized adults are adept at masking their motives in behavior quite as well as in words. In fact, there are complicated family intrigues about which one prefers to have both verbal reports and direct observation. And if the family members later say they felt one way, but were seen to act another, which record is the more valid? Valid for what?

Data on group behavior are typically more costly, time-consuming, and tedious to collect and analyze than are verbal reports. It is naïve to expect that they are thereby more "true." The chief reason for using direct observation is to measure something which it would be difficult or impossible to get at in some other way. Another major reason is as a validity check on measures obtained by other methods—e.g., by interview or projective testing.

Polansky, Lippitt, and Redl (1950) and Lippitt, Polansky, and Rosen (1952) studied the relationship between prestige and social influence among cabin groups of preadolescent campers. In the latter study, "prestige" was defined as "perceived position in the group's power hierarchy." To measure it, each of the eight or so boys in each cabin was asked to rank-order the group on, Who is best at getting the others to do what he wants? The study showed there is typically high agreement among group members in making this ranking; the average member ranks himself fairly close to where he is placed by his cabin mates; and rankings by the boys correspond closely to those by their adult leaders.

Nevertheless, the question remained, These perceptions of the power structure are widely shared, but are they valid? Specially trained research assistants were attached to each cabin for four or more hours each day. They recorded, among other things, every instance in which one boy tried to get another, or others, to follow his wishes. Whether or not the attempt succeeded was next recorded. Using these data, they could then rank the boys on such measures as number of successful influence attempts, and even on the *percentage* of attempts that proved successful.

Rank ordering of the group on social influence as *observed* could now be compared to that *attributed*. As one would hope, the two measures were significantly associated. Therefore, they worked to *validate each other* as adequate alternative operational definitions of group power structure. In later related studies, one could use the verbal, near-sociometric measure of power position with more confidence, with or without systematic observational affirmation (Blum 1962; Rosen, Levinger, and Lippitt 1960).

However, the researchers had a more theoretical question. Is prestige in one's group associated with one's being imitated by others without urging on one's part? Episodes of contagion of behavior are spontaneous; those involved are often unaware they have been subject to contagion and from whom. So, the only way to establish which boys were more frequently sources of contagion, and which less, was to observe the groups on this dimension. What had long been theorized was finally empirically demonstrated. In nearly every group, there was a positive correlation (averaging about $+.5$) between the boys' rank order on prestige and their being used as behavioral role models by their groups. It was concluded that the adage, "The rotten apple spoils the barrel," does not apply in treatment settings unless the "rotten apple" also has high prestige! Thus, we see that group observation is indispensable when the phenomena of interest are too subtle for the participants to report on them satisfactorily, especially when the participants are not even conscious of them. We also see that observation is often more fruitfully used in combination with other methods.

OPPORTUNITIES FOR OBSERVATION

Observational methods are familiarly associated with certain conditions or settings. These will be discussed roughly in the order of the degree of control over extraneous variables to which each lends itself.

Natural settings. Group interaction ordinarily occurs in natural settings. Even when it is under professional auspices, it does not usually take place for research purposes. Such settings range from a family quarrel at home to a second-grade picnic, from ceremonial dances to agency board meetings. The ethnographers refined a technique of unobtrusive data collection known as *participant observation.* The observer melts into the tribal meeting, either as onlooker or participant, later writing down his recollections of what transpired. The same method was used to study a millennial movement (a group who predicted the end of the world). The researchers, who infiltrated the group, periodically sneaked off to the bathroom to make their field notes (Festinger, Riecken, and Schachter 1956). Process recordings in casework and group workers' logs are also products of participant observation.

Controlled settings. A "controlled" setting is one so devised that the interactions that interest us have a good chance of being observed, and we have a reasonable idea of how the setting, itself, is affecting them. There is more hope of discerning the relationship between a couple when they are seen in a clinic than when they are observed amidst the bustle of children, neighbors, and TV in their living room. Yet, how will the fact of being in an unfamiliar office affect them? At least we know how others have acted at the clinic, and this provides a measure of constancy for assessing what goes on. A variety of *situational effects* have been demonstrated.

For instance, numerous studies have shown that strangers who share the same physical enclosure or facilities are more likely to become acquainted and talk to each other than those who do not share them (Barnlund 1968; Deutsch and Collins 1965; Festinger, Schachter, and Back 1950; Gullahorn 1952). In a study done for the navy, Altman and Haythorn (1965) found that when two strangers are confined to the same enclosure and not permitted much contact with the outside world, they disclose a greater variety of things, and more intimate things, about themselves than do those permitted more contact with the outside. Fellow travelers who are unacquainted, but come from the same corner of the world, are much more likely to interact freely in a setting strange and stressful to both (e.g., in a foreign country) than they do at home (Cozby 1973). Bringing a couple into the clinic may actually facilitate frank talking between them rather than deter it.

We know, too, that people who face each other are more likely to interact (Steinzor 1950) and to use a more informal language (Moscovici 1967) than if they sit side by side. "Undermanned" behavioral settings induce members to share more of the activity load. Thus, in a small high school, students interact more and are involved in a greater variety of the volunteer activities than do students in larger schools (Barker 1968). Our purpose in citing this small sampling of effects caused by settings is to suggest that, since much is now known about such effects, we can introduce refinement into data collection simply by controlling the setting in which the interaction will occur.

Situational tests. Further control is established when the types of activities of the group members are also prescribed. To sample a person's "intelligent" behaviors, a psychometrician presents him with a situational test consisting of a series of tasks and puzzles. Analogously, situational tests have been developed to bring a variety of social interaction processes into clear focus. To take an example from social work research, Sharlin and Polansky (1972) were interested in the way a mother's *infantilization* of her retarded child might bring about a further deficit in functioning. Subjects, aged eight to twelve, were brought to a clinic and given a series of puzzles to work on, with their mothers present. Children whose IQs had dropped additionally within the past year were observed to turn and look at their mothers more frequently than did an equally retarded comparison group whose IQs had not dropped. The looking toward mother was interpreted as visual clinging, evidence the children were being *in-fantilized*.

Group tasks. Many group tasks have been devised for researching social interaction. Some emphasize cognitive activity, such as arithmetic problems (Shaw 1955). Others emphasize physical activity, such as French's frustrating ball-and-spiral problem (1944). Some tasks are relatively structured, as in groups organized solely to discuss the Great Books (Davis 1961). Therapy groups are relatively unstructured. Some groups are provided with only one type of task. Others are given a variety, either to maintain interest or to permit more than one "specialist" to emerge.

A group task that has come into frequent use is Strodtbeck's *revealed difference technique*. In an early version (Strodtbeck 1951), Navaho, Texan, and Mormon married couples were each asked to pick three families that they knew well. Each husband and each wife was then separately and individually asked to decide which one of the three families came closest to fitting each of twenty-six characteristics, such as having the happiest children, being the most religious, etc. After their answers had been examined, the couples were confronted with items on which their private judgments were in disagreement and asked to discuss and try to reconcile these differences. Their interaction was categorized by means of Bales's Interaction Process Analysis system. Strodtbeck showed that Navaho wives exerted the most influence and Mormon wives the least, in keeping with expectations regarding husband-wife roles in the subcultures. Also, the spouse who talked more influenced more decisions. The technique was revised later (Strodtbeck 1954) to study power relations in three-person families (father, mother, adolescent child). This revision was recently adapted by Mishler and Waxler (1968) to study whether interaction in three-person families varies systematically when one of the participants is a schizophrenic or a normal child.

A therapy group serves for diagnosis as well as treatment. When used diagnostically, it is also a kind of situational test. Ganter and Polansky (1964) reported factors predictive of treatability in psychotherapy that were rated by a group worker in activity therapy groups at a child guidance center.

Laboratory experiments. Experiments conducted in the laboratory offer distinct advantages as observational studies. By using contrasting experimental conditions, the investigator can deliberately introduce and manipulate independent variables of theoretical interest. Subjects' characteristics can be equated by precise matching or, more typically, random assignment. Arrangements can be tailored to suit one's observational purposes.

But, although the laboratory offers a high degree of control, it is a *foreign* setting for the participants—thus stressful and conducive to atypical behavior. It does not necessarily follow that the results will not generalize to the "rest of life"; they may or may not. After all, to what extent can one generalize a man's behavior from seeing him in the unusual security of his own living room, a supposedly "natural" setting? The question of artificiality thus becomes a major argument for preferring *field experiments*. These, too, involve planned interventions, with contrasting groups. However, because they take place in natural settings, there is usually less control over subjects' characteristics and other variables, and it is often inconvenient to observe the whole process.

In conducting experiments it is desirable to institute a *validity check*, to see if the experimental variation occurred as planned. An early study by Lippitt (1940) concerned the influence of varying adult leadership styles on the social climates in boys' groups. Initially, democratic leadership was to be compared with autocratic. The boys were observed, of course, to see how they were reacting; but the leaders' actions were also recorded to see whether, in fact, they sustained the roles they were supposed to. When some odd results occurred, it developed that one leader had interpreted "democracy" as requiring a passive, detached sort of conduct on his part, and the boys responded unfavorably to this. Making a virtue of necessity, the investigators compared *three* leadership styles in their subsequent studies: democratic, autocratic, and laissez faire (an instance of serendipity).

Measures of the personalities and backgrounds of one's subjects, if conceptually relevant to what is being observed, are desirable additions to any experimental design. Lippitt's study went beyond noting the response of an "average expectable boy" to differing adult leadership. He asked, Does one's family background affect preferences? In contrast to most, a boy whose father was a regular army officer preferred the autocratic group to the democratic. Thus, the *interaction* of social situation with personal background can be determined.

There are various aspects from which one can intervene experimentally. The group as a whole may be subjected to an external stimulus. Pepitone and Reichling (1955) had an outside instigator make scathing remarks to a group he had just met. The group, itself, may constitute the causal factor. Asch (1951) made a classic study of the effects of consensus on judgments. Lone naïve subjects were confronted with the unanimous yet clearly mistaken judgments of collaborators posing as fellow subjects. The experimental manipulation may occur at the beginning, presumably playing a pervasive subsequent role. Groups have been made more, and less, cohesive by being given impressions of what to expect from each other before they had even met (Back 1951). Or the stimulus may be introduced steadily throughout the meeting. Whatever the technique, we should bear in mind that experiments basically provide unusually controlled opportunities for observing interaction.

FORMS IN WHICH INTERACTION IS RECORDED

Once a researcher has selected what he is interested in observing, his next step is to decide how to register his observations. His choice should be guided by the kinds of measures or indices that he wishes to construct from the raw data. An observer's impressions may be expressed in one or more of three basic forms, each of which has its particular virtues and shortcomings: (a) narrative accounts; (b) scales (rating or ranking); and (c) category systems.

Narrative accounts. The observer may decide to keep a verbal running account of the interaction. Such a narrative could emphasize pure description, with a minimum of interpretation and inference about the underlying dynamics. Or, it could emphasize interpretation. Both sorts of narratives were utilized in Lippitt's study. The advantage of a free-flowing narrative lies in its being a source of rich insights and flavor. However, it permits the observer latitude in exercising biases, and is relatively difficult to quantify later for statistical analysis.

Scales. Scales usually range from 5 to 11 gradations, since raters have difficulty working with finer gradations. Rating scale data typically reflect biases. For instance, raters tend to avoid making extreme judgments, such as labeling behavior as either "extremely friendly" or "extremely unfriendly." Also, ratings are often plagued by "elevation" bias—the tendency to use only one side of a scale, particularly the complimentary end. Another bias is the "halo effect," the tendency to assign a subject the same rating on *all* of several different scales.

Some investigators prefer to rank-order rather than to rate the members (or other segments) of a group. Ranking, like rating, is subject to halo effect. But it is less affected either by elevation biases or by the tendency to avoid extremes, especially if the observer is urged not to assign tied ranks. Both rating and ranking scales are easy to quantify. Ratings possess the added virtue of permitting the use of parametric statistics. On the other hand, there is the danger that the rating assigned may be taken too literally. "Best athlete" in one group may be poorest in another.

Category systems. Category systems are designed to tap certain classes or areas of interaction that the investigator considers to be theoretically interesting or relevant for his purposes. When using a category system, the observer tallies each separate instance of interaction occurring during the observational time frame which satisfies the definition of some particular category or subcategory of that system. He may record not simply that a particular type of act occurred but also who initiated it and toward whom it was directed.

In one of our field studies on influence behavior (Lippitt, Polansky, and Rosen 1952), we were partly interested in identifying the child who initiated each particular influence attempt (designated "Act" for Actor), also the child he tried to influence (labeled "Rec" for Recipient). Furthermore, we were interested in the *manner* in which one child tried to influence another, i.e., through the use of or threat of physical force (Frc), in a directive or bossy manner (Dir), in the form of a suggestion or request (Sur), or in a pleading manner (Pld). Of course, we were also interested in the fate of the attempt, such as whether the target responded with direct, overt rejection (OvR), by seeming to ignore the actor (Ign), by acceptance with modification (MAc), by tactful rejection (TRj), by excused rejection (ERj), or by complete acceptance (CAc). All this information concerning a particular event was entered by the observer on one line of a specially prepared coding sheet (see figure 1).

FIGURE 1. FORM FOR RECORDING INFLUENCE ATTEMPTS

Act	Rec	F r c	D i r	S u r	P l d	O v R	I g n	M A c	T R j	E R j	C A c
4	6			/		/					
2	6			/							/

Subcategories were identified by symbols to save space and to keep the variables from being transparent to the children. Similarly, the children were identified on the coding sheet by code numbers, both for convenience and to avoid giving the show away entirely. Row 1 indicates that Child No. 4 tried, in a rather directive manner, to get Child No. 6 to do something, but was overtly rebuffed. Notice that this particular category system is completely indifferent to what the influence attempter tried to get No. 6 to do. It may have been to slip rocks into the counselor's bunk, to stop picking on a third child, or whatever. The content of the attempt was not part of our research objective, but this does not necessarily mean that it did not merit investigation. You cannot study everything at once!

Does this atomistic representation of influence behavior capture anything meaningful about people? The procedure of counting up single acts implies that it is in the data-processing phase rather than in the observation that the search for meaning begins in earnest. That being the case, why not refrain from recording anything until the observation period is over, and then summarize the overall impressions through the use of scales or a narrative account? Paradoxically, the errors of judgment committed through counting are less likely to be serious than those committed through overall impressions expressed in rating scales or narrative accounts. The focus on only the isolated act as it occurs serves to minimize biases, for the trained observer is absorbed with the here-and-now-and-relevant. Furthermore, since it is through many acts that the researcher hopes to obtain a representative sample of interaction, a mistake in judgment or a careless error in tallying one act is less likely to distort the sample than is a single rating based on a mistaken overall impression.

Devices for preserving the interaction. The paper-and-pencil tally sheet or rating form has long been the workhorse in recording interaction. Because of its low cost and ease, it is likely to remain so. Still, there has been vast improvement in both fidelity and proficiency of electrical devices. The great advantage of taped audio recordings is that one can replay the recording at leisure. When observations are made from the taped recording alone, this possibility of replay increases the proportion retained of verbal utterances that could otherwise fail to be recorded. In very small groups it may be practical to assign one unidirectional microphone and recording channel to each group member. This is especially useful for distinguishing who is saying what when several talk at once. Videotape recordings are helpful in adding nonverbal information (e.g., eye contact) and share the advantages of being replayable. A frequent practice is to prepare a typescript from a tape recording and categorize behavior from that. Mishler and Waxler (1968) added the refinement of having their coders listen to the tape while coding from the typescript. Instead of using the tape recorder merely to pick up speech for later processing, some observers also dictate their judgments of what is happening directly into a microphone while watching the group.

ASPECTS OF RECORDED BEHAVIOR

Three main kinds of social behavior are recorded: verbal interaction, paraverbal behavior, and nonverbal behavior. Verbal interaction deals with *what* is being said, the ideas that participants communicate to one another through words. Paraverbal behavior deals with *how* things are said. Nonverbal behavior has to do with the bodily activity of the interacting individuals. Few investigators attempt to capture all three aspects. We shall touch briefly on them. For a more extended discussion, see the excellent paper by Weick (1968).

Verbal interaction systems. Among the various systematic approaches to verbal interaction, the most widely used is Bales's IPA (Interaction Process Analysis) system, developed in 1950. Six of its twelve categories deal with emotionally toned (social-emotional, expressive) acts, three of which are positive (shows solidarity, shows tension release, agrees), and three negative (shows antagonism, shows tension, disagrees). The remaining six categories concern relatively neutral (instrumental, task-oriented) acts, of which three deal with *giving* answers (gives suggestion, opinion, or orientation), and three with *seeking* answers (asks for suggestion, opinion, or orientation). While the IPA was intended to capture nonverbal behavior, too, in practice this tends to go underrecorded. Bales recently (1970) revised the IPA, but the revisions have not yet achieved general use.

The IPA has been used principally with adult discussion groups. Another early verbally oriented system is the Leary "wheel" (Freedman et al. 1951; Leary 1957). This sixteen- to twenty-category system is not unlike the IPA, although it is couched in a language of "interpersonal mechanisms." It was frequently used during the 1950s in research on psychotherapy. Another verbal system is Mills's (1964) three-category SPA (Sign Process Analysis) system, which focuses on the emotional (positive, neutral, or negative) connotations of each verbal remark. A six-category system currently in use is Borgatta's BSs (Behavior System scores). Its key factors involve an assertive-unassertive dimension and a sociable-surly dimension (Borgatta and Crowther 1965).

Paraverbal behavior. This kind of behavior may or may not be intended by the actor to communicate anything to others. Nevertheless, it may tell us a great deal. One cluster of such behaviors involves the linguistic style in which an idea may be expressed (Moscovici 1967). A second consists of timing variables, whose importance was originally recognized by Chapple (1939). They include the duration of an utterance, successful and unsuccessful interruptions, simultaneous conversations, significant pauses and silences, the latency of response (Willard and Strodtbeck 1972), and last, but perhaps most important and most researched, participation rate. Still another cluster involves vocal tonal qualities. An additional cluster concerns the extent to which speech is fragmented as opposed to organized (Mahl 1956).

Nonverbal behavior. There has recently been a surge of interest in responses that appear to convey interpersonal messages independent of the use of words. One cluster involves movement and spatial orientation of the torso (Birdwhistell 1952; Ekman 1965). Another deals with facial expressions (Leventhal and Sharp 1965). Perhaps the most popular cluster involves eye contact (see Argyle and Dean 1965; Exline and Winters 1965). While many investigators of nonverbal behavior have relied on the naked eye for recording, a more precise alternative involves the use of electronic and photographic devices. At present, such devices are best suited for observing stationary groups of minimal size, and operating and maintenance costs may be substantial.

PROBLEMS OF INFERENCE

When behavior is to be categorized, it is necessary to decide, From whose point of view? One possibility would be to avoid making inferences. While this sounds easy, note that it is easier to record, "He made a threatening gesture," than "He moved closer, with one hand lowered, one raised, his lips tightened, face flushed . . ."

Behavior and its meaning can be coded from three standpoints: that of the actor, that of the person addressed, and that of some onlooker or third person. Whatever the stance selected, all agree that the system of observation employed should include explicit criteria for inferring meanings and the *point of view* from which they will be judged (Heyns and Lippitt 1954).

It is often useful, in clinical work, to check how one is feeling, and then ask whether this may not be what the client is trying to evoke. Similarly, in interpreting group behavior, Bales (1950) suggested the observer put himself in the position of the target, using only the immediate context of the act, for judging how to categorize it. Failing that, the observer was instructed to take the stance of a "generalized other." Actions would be interpreted in terms of their commonly accepted meaning in the culture. On the whole, we would recommend this stance in most studies of social interaction.

Perhaps most controversial are judgments made about what a person *intended* when he did what he did. Weick (1968) distinguishes between investigators who want observers to make inferences about intent (i.e., about the actor's motives), and those who would have observers focus simply on the *effect* or social consequence of the behavior (e.g., taking the role of the "generalized other"). Those who prefer to focus on *effects* may argue that it would take considerable empathic ability and knowledge of the person observed to judge his intention, and that, furthermore, behavioral effects can be judged more easily and reliably than intentions. Yet intent can be judged. Moreover, complex interactions pose knotty problems for those who would prefer to judge effects. For example, in a study of social influence (Lippitt, Polansky, and Rosen 1952), it was not too difficult to identify an explicit influence attempt, but often harder to judge whether or not it was successful. Had the would-be influencer been refused or ignored, or was a delayed or grudging compliance under way before it was obscured by other group events? The strategy adopted was to judge success by the immediate verbal response of the target of the attempt.

It is clear that an overriding desire to be clinical can make for an observational system that is far too broad to permit reliable categorization. In stark contrast, an obsession with precision and objectivity can make for an observational system that will yield meaningless bits and pieces of events. Between these two extremes, there are a surprising variety of acceptable choices.

General versus Specialized Observational Schemes

Several experts have promoted systems and instruments for observing social interaction which would be applicable, it is hoped, to a wide range of problems, under most conditions. Rather than develop his own scheme to suit each study, the investigator is encouraged to apply a general-purpose instrument. The most notable example of such an instrument is Bales's IPA (1950; 1970).

There are cogent reasons for adopting an established instrument. Definitions of categories have been ironed out and potential interobserver reliability (see below) is known; there is usually evidence of validity. Since it is not easy to invent dimensions and categories that tap the most significant aspects of group events, adopting another's instrument saves effort. Using identical instruments makes it more likely one's research can have an additive impact with others'.

But there are limitations. The wheel for characterizing interpersonal mechanisms, proposed by Freedman et al. in 1951, was like a compass. North was Dominate; south, Submit; east, Love; west, Hate; points between were also labeled (e.g., due northwest was Reject), so that there were sixteen variations on the two main themes. Chance and Atkinson (1955) modified this scheme to investigate changes therapists predicted would occur in a group of patients who were mothers of disturbed children. For analysis, however, the scheme was reduced to four simple categories: positive active, positive passive, negative active, negative passive. Inexperienced therapists proved more optimistic than experienced ones. They predicted more positive change in their patients as a result of therapy.

Because they pretend to broad coverage, general-purpose systems for encoding behavior can almost always be reduced to a couple of global dimensions, assertiveness-nonassertiveness (or dominance-submission) and friendly-unfriendly (or, simply, positive-negative). Bales has more recently proposed a third dimension, "in-out," referring to whether the person is engaged or disengaged from the group's activity, but little has been reported on whether detachment can be reliably assessed. So, a system proposed as universal may prove inefficient for studying a particular hypothesis and miss the main point altogether.

Mishler and Waxler (1968) studied family power relations. They tried a number of different schemes for coding tape recordings of family interactions, and eventually came up with two broad typologies of "strategies." One, labeled "attention-controlling strategies," included sheer rate of participation, duration of sentences, and an interesting nonverbal indicator —extent to which the actor monopolized everyone's attention by not looking at any one person while talking. The "person-controlling strategy," on the other hand, was *asking questions*, which they grouped with *interrupting*. In the collegiate problem-solving groups studied by Bales, however, asking a question had been treated as a phase of problem clarification. The advantages of established instruments are often outweighed by their limitations for a specific study, in line with the general principle: *Method follows problem!* Any instrument has an implicit theory underlying it, and its implicit conceptions may be irrelevant or trivial with respect to the immediate problem.

THE PROBLEM OF UNIT SIZE

Anyone who proposes to develop a system for observing interaction must decide on how small a slice of interaction process he will accept as the irreducible unit. There is considerable variation in the sizes of units that have been employed. Borgatta and Crowther (1965, p. 2) cite several: "the smallest discernible change, . . . a coherent communication (thought), a sentence, an arbitrary time interval." The grosser units tend to be used more by those who prefer to describe interaction through scales or in narrative form, while the smaller units tend to be employed by those who prefer to tally, then count. More recently, Bales (1970, p. 68) defined the unit to be scored through the IPA as the single act which "in its context may be understood by another member as equivalent to a single simple sentence." Thus, the complex statement, "I love you dearly, but your giggling really revolts me," would be broken down by the observer into two simple sentences, the first of which seems friendly and the second unfriendly.

Some investigators are especially interested in sequences. One such sequence is labeled the "interact" and consists of the statement made by one participant *and* the response of another participant to that statement. Act sequences have been investigated to shed light on such matters as familial structure (Waxler and Mishler 1970), and responsiveness to others in schizophrenic and nonschizophrenic families (Mishler and Waxler 1968). They have also been studied to determine mothers' attentiveness, language complexity, and instructional techniques in interacting with their preschool children (Baldwin and Baldwin 1973).

There are also temporal units. Most investigators use fixed intervals during which to tally, rank, rate, or narrate that which is of particular relevance. Lippitt, Polansky, and Rosen used fifteen- to twenty-minute blocks in their 1952 influence study. The unit may involve only a few seconds. Bishop (1951) used five-second intervals to tally parent-child interaction, while Medley and Norton (1971) used twenty-five-second intervals to record classroom behavior. Another use of the temporal unit is to designate in advance the particular participant who will be the special object of observer attention. The aim is to ensure that the observer will not overlook the quieter and less mobile participants. Lippitt, Polansky, and Rosen used this focal person method.

Small verbal units simplify the training of observers. They reduce the necessity for making inferences about what is going on, and the likelihood of biases. In addition, they provide the researcher with maximum flexibility, since he can later combine and recombine the units into molar units or unit sequences to suit multiple objectives. It is easier to achieve satisfactory reliabilities with a large number of small units than with a small number of large units. It is possible to restore a surprising amount of meaning by counting up seemingly atomistic units. Also, some may say the more important events tend to be those that recur.

It is clear that systems that involve small units are more exhausting to use, particularly when observing on the scene, than those involving large units. Nevertheless, in view of the above considerations, it would be desirable to use a unit that is as small as feasible, but that is still meaningful.

Issues Confronting the Observer

On-the-spot versus after-the-fact recording and coding. A generation ago we would have unequivocally advised on-the-spot observation and recording. Nowadays we recommend that each investigator engage in his own cost-benefit analysis before deciding. Given a small group that sits and mostly talks, a good fidelity audio recorder can pick up most verbal interaction and paraverbal behavior better than the harried observer, a video tape can add nonverbal aspects, and further precision can be obtained through a typescript prepared from and used with such tapes. If, however, the group is mobile and physically active but not very talkative, if the members frown on tape recording, if the observation form is simple, if one lacks time, good recording equipment, or a good typist, then on-the-spot human recording is indicated. Some investigators hedge their bets by doing both. But very few rely on memory to provide the raw data for scientific analysis.

Choice of form for observing. We have already given reasons for preferring the category system approach most, scales next, and narration least, despite the fact that the costs in effort, concentration, and money are in that same rank order. Here, too, some find it useful to employ two (Mishler and Waxler used narration and category systems), or all three (e.g., Lippitt and White 1943).

Effects of knowing one is being observed. Most early students of inter-action tended, on subjective grounds, to dismiss this issue; a minority, on equally subjective grounds, took an alarmist position. We now know, through empirical research, that the answer lies somewhere in between. For instance, the presence (actual or imagined) of a passive audience affects what people say and do, especially when the performers worry about how "good" their performance is (Cottrell 1972; Zajonc 1965). This is true in laboratory experiments and in organizational settings. It is certainly true when the audience consists of practitioners. One way people cope with these fears is to try to please the researcher by engaging in the kinds of behavior they *think* he wants (Orne 1962), including saying the "right" things. For instance, Roberts and Renzaglia (1965) found that clients, during counseling sessions, said the nicest things about them-selves when a tape recorder was visible and running, but were most self-critical when they thought no recording was going on. Sometimes group members respond by "uncooperative" or aggressive acts, as Miller (1954) found in a factory, and Polansky and colleagues (1949) found in one camp study. If aggression is directed at fellow members, this should not delude the observer (Bishop 1951) into thinking this necessarily means he, himself, has rapport with the group.

By and large, the effects of being observed are apt to be most severe during the earlier part of a group session, or during a lull, or when the group is to meet for just one session. It would be foolhardy, particularly with an ongoing group, to try to deceive them for long, nowadays, into believing their responses are not being recorded, and to assume that one's professional ethics will go unchallenged. If you intend to use a one-way vision screen, tell them so. Tell them they are being observed. A screen may reduce the likelihood that the group will try to draw the observer into the conversation. But it cuts down on what he can see and hear and is useless with a highly mobile group.

How does one deal with observer effects? When one is comparing dif-ferent groups or different individuals in the same group, it does not matter, since one can argue that the audience is a constant. You can ask them whether they were bothered by your presence, but as the Sherifs (1956) suggest, do not believe them if they say they were not.

The observer's conduct. In commenting on the aggression encountered by Polansky and colleagues (1949), Heyns and Zander (1953) suggested that those were special circumstances which justified violating the rule that the observer behave like a piece of furniture. Today we would say that, in the small ongoing group, as on the international scene, the participants do not really believe there is a neutral observer. They can tell the difference between you and the furniture! Rapport is never permanently established. Moreover, in organization settings, many segments of the organization—not just those you are studying—worry whether you think they are doing a good job, even the administrators of therapeutic milieus! The observer must learn to cope with others' anxieties.

As a general set of prescriptions, we suggest that you behave as a *friendly* neutral; that you expect, nevertheless, that your credibility will be challenged repeatedly; and that you define the boundaries of your neutrality. Anticipate that the participants will be curious about your hypotheses—the more so if you are secretive. Tell them you will not reveal specific hypotheses, and why. Promise feedback on the general results (but not who did what, specifically). Keep that promise!

Reliability in Observing Social Interaction

The prospective researcher gains the impression that reliability is a good thing. Actually, it is a characteristic of measurement that is usually desirable, but not always. Much depends on the form of reliability at stake. The varied meanings of the term are unusually well exposed in relation to group observation, but the discussion that follows has relevance to all data collection.

Three types of reliability problems can be sorted out: (*a*) the reliability of the phenomenon; (*b*) the reliability of the instrument; and (*c*) the reliability of the observer.

The reliability of the phenomenon. Is the aspect of group process something stable? Is it likely to recur? We think of intelligence as a stable personality trait. We would be disappointed, therefore, with an intelligence test that put people in very different rank orders when administered the first time and when repeated a year later. We want this measurement to show high *test-retest reliability*. But, how about group morale? Is morale something fixed, or do we expect it to fluctuate? We would be unimpressed with a test that showed a group's morale as always the same. High test-retest reliability is desirable with respect to some group characteristics and not others.

When the phenomenon being observed is conceived as stable, and its associated behaviors as recurring, it is a *structured* element in the group's interaction. To speak of a group's "power structure" is to say that, over a series of episodes and on the average, some individuals will be found exerting more, and some less, influence over their mates.

Instrument reliability. We define this as the extent to which a system for collecting and encoding data could be depended upon to produce the same classifications on a given set of behaviors, if these same behaviors were to repeat themselves, or if the instrument were to be reapplied to the same set of behaviors. A category system will possess poor reliability to the extent that its categories are defined in vague or ambiguous terms, and the rules or instructions for applying them are also vague.

Strictly speaking, if precise statements are to be made about the reliability of a particular instrument, that instrument should first be tested on different samples of the phenomena to which the instrument applies. Also, if much competency is required, then the testing should be done by a representative sample of well-trained technicians, working independently of each other. Obviously, we would learn little about the reliability of a particular surveyor's transit if we asked a small boy or a blind man to test it out in the dark, during an earthquake. By the same token, we are not apt to learn much about the reliability of a complex instrument for measuring emotional interaction from trying it on a group that proved to be silent and unemotional at the time. The fewer the samples of a phenomenon and the narrower their range, the more any estimate of instrument reliability is likely to be influenced by the reliability of the phenomenon, as sampled. Similarly, if we use only two or three observers to establish instrument reliability, the estimate of reliability is likely to be influenced by how reliable the particular observers are.

For instance, it is a common practice to establish the extent of interobserver reliability or agreement and to use that as an estimate of instrument reliability. But if the observers are still green or have been poorly trained and show low interobserver reliability, do we blame the low reliability on the instrument or on the observers? Conversely, even with the best training, the maximum interobserver reliability will be limited by the intrinsic unreliability of the instrument. Still, when high interobserver reliability is demonstrated, it is probably safe to infer that the instrument is clear, has appropriate definitions and instructions, and deals with phenomena that can be reliably observed.

Observer reliability. When a single observer is involved, observer reliability has to do with the *consistency* with which he uses an instrument, assuming he is confronted again with the same phenomenon. Interobserver reliability, of course, has to do with the agreement that exists among observers in their independent observations of the same phenomenon by means of the same instrument. We will focus below on interobserver reliability.

MEASURING INTEROBSERVER RELIABILITY

1. Procedure. When data are on video tapes, it is easy to have the observers or judges encode the same events, then compare their records. Two judges can even observe at separate times. But when the encoding is done on the spot, from live interaction, the observers being tested must be positioned to get equivalent views of the group. To avoid bogging a group down with observers, one usually assigns no more than two at any one time. Consequently, if it becomes necessary to calibrate *three* or more observers, they may have to be assigned in pairs until all possible couples have been run, e.g., AB, AC, BC. Overall interobserver reliability can then be calculated by averaging the reliability estimates of the various pairs. For the sake of simplicity, we shall confine the rest of this discussion to a single pair of observers using a precategorized instrument to observe live interaction on the spot. Just as there is more than one kind of reliability, so there are a number of levels (the senior author has identified at least six) at which interobserver reliability can be checked. Here we shall discuss three levels.

2. Unitizing. No one can encode all the social interaction that occurs while observing; our "complete" record is at best a sample. Reliability of unitizing refers to whether our observers (coders, judges) agree on the sheer number of relevant acts that occurred during the time interval. Suppose that, in comparing the data on two groups, we find that Observer A noted forty "problem-solving" acts in one group while Observer B noted twenty-five such acts in the second group. Is one group less active than the others, or is the difference attributable to discrepancies between observers?

There are a number of sources of unreliability in unitizing. A may see a particular act as one long unit, while B may see what occurred as two distinguishable units. A may be slower. By the time he gets around to recording an act, a second has occurred. While he is pondering how to categorize what he just saw, three more relevant bits of behavior have gone by.

A simple way to test for similarity in unitizing is to expose the observers to the same group and then compare their totals. If the instrument dealt with direct attempts at influencing, we could ask: How many attempts did A record as compared with B? The significance of the difference between two or more observers can be tested by appropriate use of the chi-square test, with the expected frequencies being simply the average number of each. (This is the $1 \times k$ version of chi-square.) Or one can very appropriately use the *binomial test* (Siegel 1956) for the special case of only two observers, especially when the expected totals are small. If the difference in rate of unitizing proves significant, to our sorrow, it will be necessary to give the observers more training; perhaps one will have to be replaced.

3. Ordering categories. Total number of acts recorded is the simplest matter in unitizing. It is often of greater moment whether one's coders have systematic biases in utilizing certain *categories*. Does A see a higher proportion of "demanding behavior" than does B? Is B more likely to compensate by seeing more instances of "commanding"? Where the hypothesis requires comparing *proportions* of behavior under different group conditions, systematic discrepancies among judges become especially important.

A control is to rotate the observers among all groups, so that each contributes his biases equally to the data on every group. There would be less measurement error if the observers operated identically, but at least we will have equalized the error among the experimental conditions. Rotating the data may permit us to draw conclusions on the theoretical issues we set out to investigate. Indeed, there are statistical ways to extract error caused by observer bias, provided the observers have been rotated systematically.

4. Ordering persons. Apart from interobserver reliability in ordering *categories*, there is the parallel issue of the extent to which *persons* in our group are similarly ordered, or ranked. One can also rank members of a group on dimensions as simple as, Who is most active? or To whom are the most remarks addressed? Both measures are connected to status in the group.

To compute reliability at this level, it is customary to use the product moment correlation coefficient, Pearson's *r*. However, when the group is relatively small, containing as few as twelve members, then Spearman's *rho*, the rank-difference correlation is just as appropriate. The level of significance of *rho* for various sizes of *N* has been tabled. As before, the first question is: Does the amount of agreement exceed that expectable by chance? If it does not, one's instrument is highly unreliable. Beyond that, one usually asks: Just how strong is the *degree* of agreement? In areas that have been well researched, we expect our instruments to yield interobserver reliabilities of $+.80$ or so with respect to rank-ordering members on significant aspects of interaction.

5. Act-by-act reliability. We may also be concerned (some consider it paramount) about whether the observers can take a given event and categorize it identically. This is no longer the issue of how they do overall; it is a question of how well they do in the particular instance. To test reliability at this level of precision, it is necessary to ensure that two observers are coding the same act. When data are videotaped, synchronization is easy. In live observation, they sit side by side, and the problem of unitizing—ensuring that what has just happened is judged by both—is solved by placing one person in charge who says, Now! Then, both categorize that particular act, and the response to it. From one or two hours of joint work a sample results, containing a series of acts, each identified precisely and categorized by both. The next question is: How close are the two records?

A generation ago, the standard procedure for assessing act-by-act reliability was to calculate a *percent-agreement* score. An "agreement" was defined as an instance in which both judges placed the act observed in the same category. If they did not, they were said to be in "disagreement." The percent-agreement score was then computed by the formula:

$$\% \text{ Agreement} = \frac{\text{Number of agreements}}{\text{Total number of acts judged}}$$

A percent-agreement score can be computed for each subset of categories on an instrument (e.g., manner of the direct attempt at influencing). By keeping track of the errors, we can also detect which categories are causing trouble—e.g., whether "requests" is often confused with "suggests." Scrutinizing the sources of unreliability can result in improvements in the instrument.

The percent-agreement score is in wide use. Unfortunately, it is potentially affected by the number of categories employed, and by each judge's emphasis or bias in choosing among them. Suppose one were testing a simple two-category system for assessing outcome of influence attempts, judging them either as successes or failures. Suppose A categorized half of all the attempts as successes; the other half, as failures. B also divided his observations into two equal halves. The two judges might then have agreed fifty percent of the time by *chance alone*, regardless of how they were perceiving the interactions. In a three-category system, with each judge using all categories evenly, the percent-agreement score potentially attributable to chance alone would be 33⅓%. Hence, an obtained reliability of sixty % with the three-category system would be much more respectable than would the same score for a two-category.

Experience also shows that any given judge may tend to use some categories more than he does others. Consider again the two-category example. A sees 90% of the attempts as successes; B also sees 90% of the attempts the same way. By the operation of chance, they would be in agreement 82% of the time—a situation that is most disturbing, since we would not know whether to attribute their achievement to precise observing or common bias. If their biases were in opposite directions, e.g., A considered 90% of attempts to be successes, B considered 90% to be failures, then the potential effect of chance would be at the other extreme.

Attempts have been made to devise estimates of act-by-act agreement corrected for chance. The most popular is that pioneered by Cohen (1960) which he calls k (for kappa). The coefficient takes into account both the number of categories and the bias of each judge in using them. Cohen's k can yield a negative value, too, indicating that the agreement obtained was less than one would have expected by chance (see also chapters 5 and 6).

There are no rules that tell us what level of reliability one should demand of an instrument as long as agreement attained is well beyond chance. So far as act-by-act reliability is concerned, Mishler and Waxler (1968) set themselves the goal of having every interaction system they used in their family study yield an agreement of at least 85%. They were able to achieve this on all but two of the systems they used, during training, and then maintained it in the actual study. It is of interest that one of their two exceptions proved to be Bales's IPA system, where the mean agreement was 64%. Perhaps this illustrates our earlier point, that a system developed for one purpose and under one set of conditions may prove inadequate under others.

TRAINING IN OBSERVATION

The prospective observer cannot expect to learn the skills of scientific observation merely by reading. Sooner or later he must undergo direct training.

Qualifications for Observing

Whether the researcher is interested in verbal, paraverbal, or nonverbal interaction, his instructions are likely to be verbal. It seems desirable, therefore, that the trainee have had some college education to increase the likelihood that he or she will readily grasp oral and written instructions. People with a great deal of knowledge in the behavioral sciences may not make top-notch users of a new observational system, since it may be difficult for them to refrain from importing previous learning.

Several other qualities are also highly desirable but difficult to determine in advance. The observer should be flexible enough to "check his customary observational biases at the door," and to refrain from substituting his understanding of what certain words ordinarily mean for the special meanings the investigator may attach to them. On the other hand, a person who is so flexible he cannot bring himself to decide how to categorize or rate even a trivial act hardly makes a good prospect.

People who are alert to what is going on, who are "with it," *and* who can quickly record what they see, make particularly good on-the-scene observers, especially for tallying discrete acts. Years ago, the senior author was one of several graduate students who, together with a secretary, received training in the IPA. The secretary became the most prolific tally producer, while the least prolific was a student intellectual who often seemed lost in thought. In the influence study, although it was critically necessary that periods of watching be timed, one observer managed to lose his watch. Fortunately, the junior author (then project director) had had the foresight to bring spare watches. That observer then broke his glasses. Both of these well-meaning, but gauche, observers are now professors.

On-the-scene observation also requires sustained effort and concentration. A person who tires rapidly, or who quickly loses patience with this sort of activity, will not make a first-rate observer. A clinically oriented worker may find it difficult to restrain habitual "looking beneath the surface."

Steps in Training

There are opposing views about what the observer should be told in the beginning. One view, more prevalent in the 1950s (cf. Heyns and Zander 1953), was that the trainee should be thoroughly indoctrinated in the theory and objectives of the study, to enhance motivation and competence. The alternative view was more recently exemplified in Mishler and Waxler's training of coders (1968): "Coders were not explicitly told the hypotheses of the study nor the exact purpose of our expectations about the codes. They were also not told the type of family being coded" (p. 332). The latter view is in line with concerns regarding influence that knowledge of the theory may have on the data collected. Rosenthal (1963) showed that, if an experimenter's assistant knows what the experimenter wants, he tends, often unwittingly, to fulfill the experimenter's prophecy.

Trainees should be provided at the outset with a *code book* or *manual of instructions*. It should define, conceptually and by illustration, what the unit of observation is to be—the simple sentence, the entire utterance, the action, etc. It should also carefully define categories and subcategories, and provide concrete illustrations. Rules should be included to help the categorizer or coder decide how to deal with events which fall near the border between two categories.

For on-the-scene observation, trainee exposure to live interaction should be gradual. Preferably, trainees ought to begin practicing with a typescript containing material like what they will encounter in actual observation. Their first practice should be on unitizing acts. After they show progress in unitizing, it is desirable if they begin to categorize, from typescript. Discrepancies from the trainer's version are then noted and discussed. The trainer will need to remain responsive to new possibilities and to the desirability of adding conventions to the manual, to handle problems brought to his attention by his observers.

The next step may well be an hour or so of role playing, which has two aims. It begins the process of switching from typescript to live process. Also, the investigator or his assistants can show vividly what is meant by a particular coding category by acting it out, pretending to be a group under observation. Trainees can also join in—for example, by demonstrating acts that appear to them to fall on the boundary between two categories, thus challenging the researcher to refine his instrument.

Following this phase of training, it is now beneficial if the trainees are permitted to watch a live group, comparable to the one(s) whose interaction they will be asked to encode. Next, they are ready to practice their new skill on this live group. If the research objective includes the identification of both the initiator and the target of interaction, it will be judicious to give the trainees practice first in merely listing the initiator of each act, then both the initiator and target, and finally, the initiator, target, and nature of each act. "A big advance in the scoring process comes when they learn not to get frustrated when they have missed or misclassified an act. One secret of progress seems to be the acquiring of an ability to inhibit all but the present context of acts, and to avoid jamming incoming stimuli with internal reflections" (Bales 1950, p. 86).

The concluding phase of training consists of a series of *reliability checks*. Two observers use the instrument for a two-hour stretch on a live group. Their interobserver reliability will then be computed, according to one or more of the methods given above. An effort is made to identify the particular interactions that result in disagreement. If the researcher is by now satisfied with his instrument and definitions, it is up to the trainees to learn to use them consistently. So, after additional training, another reliability sample is obtained. The process is repeated until a satisfactory level of reliability is reached, since attaining proficiency in observing is like acquiring any other skill—golfing, typing, painting. Training stops and the study proper can begin when either the level of reliability has reached the goal set or the researcher can afford no more training time. Mishler and Waxler spent four weeks training coders on Bales's IPA without achieving the desired act-by-act reliability. Fortunately, other coders required only a week of training to achieve their goal of 85 percent agreement.

Every effort should be made to interpolate at least one, preferably several, reliability checks into the actual study period, to ensure that the observers have not drifted apart on use of the system. One researcher (Reid 1970) advocates continuous monitoring, since he found his observers' data were more accurate when they thought they were being checked than when they did not.

VALIDITY

The validity of any system for encoding social interaction must be thought about in terms of the meaning given to what has been recorded (see chapter 3). By "meaning," we refer to the classical question: How well does this operational definition fit the concept? A related matter comes to mind: To what concept is this particular observation relevant? It will be recalled that question asking was treated as a kind of clarifying act when Bales was emphasizing problem solving; Mishler and Waxler, immersed in family dynamics, cited it as an attention-controlling maneuver. Validity is assessed in three main ways in observational studies.

1. Concurrent validity. One method for testing adequacy of an operational definition is to compare it with an alternative operational definition of the same concept. When both measurements occur at about the same time, we think of this method as concurrent validity (see table 4 in chapter 3). While the two measurements are conceptual siblings, we like them to come from two quite independent sources that use divergent means of data collection. In the social influence study, boys' oral reports of the power structures in their groups were significantly associated with the influence structure observed. The first time this was checked, no observer had prior knowledge of the near-sociometric interview data.

2. Predictive validity. Extending the same logic, we come to the more rigorous and convincing method of predictive validity. An observation is made now and filed away; later, we see whether it correlates with another operational definition, obtained independently of the first. If professors are kept in the dark about Scholastic Aptitude Test scores, then it is worthwhile to see whether the SAT predicts subsequent success in college. Both are presumed to reflect the same underlying ability. The predictive mode was applied in social work when Ripple (1957) demonstrated that the way a client related to his worker in the first interview proved predictive of whether he continued five sessions or not. Both measures are related to the client's motivation to continue the relationship.

When the variables measured have no obvious, common-sense connections to one another, and are obtained quite independently, then predictive validity shades into construct validity.

3. Construct validity. In construct validity, the fact that one has advanced a theory, made measurements, and successfully predicted his results is used to demonstrate the solidity of the whole process. Sharlin and Polansky's (1972) study of retarded children has been mentioned. Recall that a drop in IQ was seen as reflecting infantilization in the home. The prediction, that infantilization would also be evident in the social-emotional sphere, specifically in the form of visual clinging by those retardates whose IQ had dropped, was fulfilled. Finding an anticipated connection between two seemingly unrelated variables such as IQ decrement and visual clinging serves to validate both the theory and the methods of data collection.

Of the three methods, construct and predictive validity are considered to be the more "respectable." Construct validity has been, perhaps, the primary basis for confidence in observational data when such data were obtained in the course of field studies. Predictive validity has, as one may expect, been the principal basis for confidence when such data were obtained in laboratory and field experiments on groups.

We can only end this chapter with a reprise of a theme with which it began. Observation of social interaction is one among a number of valuable methods. As is now evident, it is not without its pitfalls. But there are a great many problems which can be approached meaningfully in no other way.

References

Altman, I., and Haythorn, W. W. 1965. Interpersonal exchange in isolation. *Sociometry* 28:411–26.

Argyle, M., and Dean, J. 1965. Eye-contact, distance, and affiliation. *Sociometry* 28:289–304.

Asch, S. 1951. Effects of group pressure upon the modification and distortion of judgment. In *Groups, leadership, and men,* ed. H. Guetzkow, pp. 177–90. Pittsburgh: Carnegie Press.

Back, K. 1951. Influence through social communication. *Journal of Abnormal and Social Psychology* 46:9–23.

Baldwin, A. L., and Baldwin, C. P. 1973. The study of mother-child interaction. *American Scientist* 61:714–21.

Bales, R. F. 1950. *Interaction process analysis.* Cambridge, Mass.: Addison-Wesley.

———. 1970. *Personality and interpersonal behavior.* New York: Holt, Rinehart & Winston.

Barker, R. G. 1968. *Ecological psychology.* Stanford: Stanford Univ. Press.

———; Dembo, T.; and Lewin, K. 1941. Frustration and regression: An experiment with young children. *University of Iowa Studies in Child Welfare* 18 (1):1–314.

Barnlund, D. C., ed. 1968. *Interpersonal communication: Survey and studies.* Boston: Houghton Mifflin.

Birdwhistell, R. L. 1952. *Introduction to kinesics.* Louisville, Ky.: Univ. of Louisville.

Bishop, B. M. 1951. Mother-child interaction and the social behavior of children. *Psychological Monographs* 65, no. 11 (whole no. 328).

Blum, A. 1962. Peer group structure and a child's verbal accessibility in a treatment institution. *Social Service Review* 36:385–95.

Borgatta, E. F., and Crowther, B. 1965. *A workbook for the study of social interaction processes: Direct observation procedures in the study of individual and group.* Chicago: Rand McNally.

Chance, E., and Atkinson, S. E. 1955. Some interpersonal characteristics of individual treatment. *International Journal of Social Psychiatry* 1:5–22.

Chapple, E. D. 1939. Quantitative analysis of the interaction of individuals. *Proceedings of the National Academy of Sciences* 25:58–67.

Cohen, J. 1960. A coefficient of agreement for nominal scales. *Educational and Psychological Measurement* 20:37–46.

Cottrell, N. 1972. Social facilitation. In *Experimental social psychology*, ed. C. McClintock. New York: Holt, Rinehart & Winston.

Cozby, P. C. 1973. Self-disclosure: A literature review. *Psychological Bulletin* 79:73–91.

Davis, J. A. 1961. Compositional effects, role systems, and the survival of small discussion groups. *Public Opinion Quarterly* 25:574–84.

Deutsch, M., and Collins, M. E. 1965. The effects of public policy in housing projects upon interracial attitudes. In *Basic studies in social psychology*, ed. H. Proshansky and B. Seidenberg, pp. 646–57. New York: Holt, Rinehart & Winston.

Ekman, P. 1965. Differential communication of affect by head and body cues. *Journal of Personality and Social Psychology* 2:726–35.

Exline, R. V., and Winters, L. C. 1965. Affective relations and mutual glances in dyads. In *Affect, cognition, and personality*, ed. S. S. Tompkins and C. E. Izard, pp. 319–50. New York: Springer.

Festinger, L.; Riecken, H.; and Schachter, S. 1956. *When prophecy fails.* Minneapolis: Univ. of Minnesota Press.

————; Schachter, S.; and Back, K. 1950. *Social pressures in informal groups: A study of a housing project.* New York: Harper.

Freedman, M. B.; Leary, T. F.; Ossorio, A. G.; and Coffey, H. S. 1951. The interpersonal dimension of personality. *Journal of Personality* 20:143–61.

French, J. R. P., Jr. 1944. Organized and unorganized groups under fear and frustration. *University of Iowa Studies in Child Welfare* 20:231–308.

Ganter, G., and Polansky, N. A. 1964. Predicting the child's accessibility to individual treatment from diagnostic groups. *Social Work* 9:56–63.

Gullahorn, J. 1952. Distance and friendship as factors in the gross interaction matrix. *Sociometry* 15:123–34.

Heyns, R. W., and Lippitt, R. 1954. Systematic observational techniques. In *Handbook of social psychology*, ed. G. Lindzey, 1:370–404. Cambridge, Mass.: Addison-Wesley.

Heyns, R. W., and Zander, A. F. 1953. Observation of group behavior. In *Research methods in the behavioral sciences*, ed. L. Festinger and D. Katz, pp. 381–417. New York: Holt, Rinehart & Winston.

Leary, T. F. 1957. *Interpersonal diagnosis of personality.* New York: Ronald.

Leventhal, H., and Sharp, E. 1965. Facial expressions as indicators of distress. In *Affect, cognition, and personality*, ed. S. S. Tomkins and C. E. Izard, pp. 296–318. New York: Springer.

Lippitt, R. 1940. An experimental study of the effect of democratic and authoritarian group atmospheres. *University of Iowa Studies in Child Welfare* 16:43–195.

————; Polansky, N.; and Rosen, S. 1952. The dynamics of power: A field study of social influence in groups of children. *Human Relations* 5:37–64.

————, and White, R. K. 1943. The "social climate" of children's groups. In *Child behavior and development*, ed. R. G. Barker, J. S. Kounin, and H. F. Wright, pp. 485–508. New York: McGraw-Hill.

Mahl, G. F. 1956. Disturbances and silences in the patient's speech in psychotherapy. *Journal of Abnormal and Social Psychology* 53:1–15.

Medley, D. M., and Norton, D. P. 1971. The concept of reliability as it applies to behavior records. Paper presented at the meeting of the American Psychological Assoc., Washington, D.C.

Meyers, C. E. 1944. The effect of conflicting authority on the child. *University of Iowa Studies in Child Welfare* 20:31–98.

Miller, F. B. 1954. "Resistentialism" in applied social research. *Human Organization* 12:5–8.

Mills, T. M. 1964. *Group transformation: An analysis of a learning group*. Englewood Cliffs, N.J.: Prentice-Hall.

Mishler, E. G., and Waxler, N. E. 1968. *Interaction in families: An experimental study of family processes and schizophrenia*. New York: John Wiley.

Moscovici, S. 1967. Communication process and the properties of language. In *Advances in experimental social psychology*, ed. L. Berkowitz, 3:225–70. New York: Academic Press.

Orne, M. T. 1962. On the social psychology of the psychological experiment, with particular reference to demand characteristics and their implications. *American Psychologist* 17:776–83.

Pepitone, A., and Reichling, G. 1955. Group cohesiveness and the expression of hostility. *Human Relations* 8:327–37.

Polansky, N.; Freeman, W.; Horowitz, M.; Irwin, L.; Papania, N.; Rapaport, D.; and Whaley, F. 1949. Problems of interpersonal relations in research on groups. *Human Relations* 2:281–91.

————; Lippitt, R.; and Redl, F. 1950. An investigation of behavioral contagion in groups. *Human Relations* 3:319–48.

Reid, J. B. 1970. Reliability assessment of observation data: A possible methodological problem. *Child Development* 41:1143–50.

Ripple, L. 1957. Factors associated with continuance in casework service. *Social Work* 2:87–94.

Roberts, R. R., and Renzaglia, G. A. 1965. The influence of tape recording on counseling. *Journal of Counseling Psychology* 12:10–16.

Rosen, S.; Levinger, G.; and Lippitt, R. 1960. Desired change in self and others as a function of resource ownership. *Human Relations* 13:187–93.

Rosenthal, R. 1963. On the social psychology of the psychological experiment: The experimenter's hypothesis as unintended determinant of experimental results. *American Scientist* 51:268–83.

Sharlin, S. A., and Polansky, N. A. 1972. The process of infantilization. *American Journal of Orthopsychiatry* 42:92–102.

Shaw, M. E. 1955. A comparison of two types of leadership in various communication nets. *Journal of Abnormal and Social Psychology* 50:127–34.

Sherif, M., and Sherif, W. W. 1956. *An outline of social psychology.* New York: Harper & Row.

Siegel, S. 1956. *Nonparametric statistics for the behavioral sciences.* New York: McGraw-Hill.

Steinzor, B. 1950. The spatial factor in face-to-face discussion groups. *Journal of Abnormal and Social Psychology* 45:552–55.

Strodtbeck, F. L. 1951. Husband-wife interaction over revealed differences. *American Sociological Review* 16:468–73.

———. 1954. The family as a three-person group. *American Sociological Review* 19:23–29.

Thomas, D. S. 1929. *Some new techniques for studying social behavior.* Child Development Monographs, no. 1. New York: Teachers' College.

Waxler, N. E., and Mishler, E. G. 1970. Sequential patterning in family interaction: A methodological note. *Family Process* 9:211–20.

Weick, K. E. 1968. Systematic observational methods. In *Handbook of social psychology,* 2d ed., ed. G. Lindzey and E. Aronson, 2:357–451. Reading, Mass.: Addison-Wesley.

Willard, D., and Strodtbeck, F. L. 1972. Latency of verbal response and participation in small groups. *Sociometry* 35:161–75.

Wright, M. E. 1942. Constructiveness of play as affected by group organization and frustration. *Character and Personality* 11:40–49.

Zajonc, R. B. 1965. Social facilitation. *Science* 149:269–74.

8
Evaluation

Ruth E. Weber
and Norman A. Polansky

Evaluative research in social work addresses itself to a brusque and fundamental question: Are you doing any good? The question is simple and direct, but answering it may prove complex and difficult. It is not a comfortable issue to contemplate when one is already working hard, but especially if he is not.

Nonetheless, evaluation has traditionally been a major motivation for social work research. Newer trends have reinforced the historical concern. The supporting public, spending ever more funds, is demanding that social workers be accountable for the value of their services and programs. *Accountability* means we are held responsible for the worth of what we do, and therefore must maintain a reporting system that describes, analyzes, and justifies our efforts. A related, influential thrust is the emphasis on cost-benefit ratios at the federal level, reflecting attempts to rationalize management in industry and elsewhere. Cost-benefit analysis, of course, has to do with the matter of whether one is getting the best bargain. For beyond the question of whether one is doing any good is the efficiency issue: Are you doing the most good we can expect for our expenditure? Thus, our concerns as dedicated persons and craftsmen combine with external incentives to evaluate our effectiveness.

Few major matters of design or method are unique to evaluative research. The logic of design, sampling, and measurement, and the techniques of data collection are all equally applicable here. However, as with any focused endeavor, the attempt to measure effectiveness has opened up its own specialized problems requiring solutions one may not otherwise have had to devise. In short, there is by now a body of knowledge and technology concerning evaluation per se, and to these the present chapter will be directed.

SCOPE OF EVALUATIVE RESEARCH

In 1853 Charles Loring Brace, a graduate of the Yale Divinity School, became the first head of the Children's Aid Society of New York. He was a dedicated man, unusually enlightened for his day, and tried to do much for the destitute and often vagrant children of New York City. Soon, he became convinced that the best solution was to send as many of them as possible to the homes of farmers in the West. For reasons ranging from religious and philanthropic ones to the wish for cheap help, numerous farmers took them in—often with no greater acquaintanceship than could be acquired by looking over a group left standing forlornly on a railroad platform after having been delivered to the local committee. It is estimated that as many as fifty thousand youngsters were placed in this fashion. Brace was sure emigration was a better fate than the children would have found in the congregate institutions of his time—which seems very believable. Yet, later in the century, criticisms arose regarding the whole program. Brace handled these by trying to learn how the youngsters had turned out. Attempts were made to locate them years after their placement. Statistics were cited to show that only a small proportion, for example, were *known* to be in prison. But Brace's evaluation of his own program—well-meaning and useful a man as he was—becomes harder to accept when one discovers the substantial percentage of the children who, at a later date, had disappeared and could not be traced at all (Brieland 1971).

Brace's was a simple, descriptive follow-up study, open to unconscious bias because the person assessing the program was the man who founded and preached it. Evaluating social service intervention involves much more than just trying to find out what happened to the recipient of a particular service. Ideally, it involves delineating: *what exactly was done; with whom; under what circumstances; by whom; at what point in time; with what results; from whose perspective;* and *whether the benefits were worth the price paid.*

All of us who are engaged in service are constantly appraising effectiveness in others and ourselves. But we do not think of all such judging as "evaluative research." Informal evaluation is necessary; otherwise, one would not be in position even to decide whether one could, in good conscience, refer a client to another agency or individual. The assessments made informally may be objective, accurate, and incisive, but the odds are only fair that they will be. Hence evaluative research applies the scientific method. Its aim, as in all science, is to contribute to a body of verifiable knowledge. At a minimum, evaluative research should offer an objective assessment of a social work intervention in one agency. Ideally, it should contribute to knowledge for the field at large, that is, it should contribute to practice theory. It follows that the generalizability of results from evaluative research is also dependent on the present state of the theory of practice.

RESISTANCE TO EVALUATION

Testing the results of one's interventions may seem like an obvious step in the direction of excellence, but it is not universally welcomed, of course. The practitioner often has enough trouble with the daily effort he is making to offer help without raising fundamental doubt in his mind about the efficacy of his whole undertaking. As was noted in chapter 1, belief in and commitment to a common approach may serve to integrate and improve a service. Hence it is not surprising that, while the president of the board of an agency may cheerfully call for its evaluation, there may be considerable resistance to this among his staff (Blenkner 1950; Merton 1957). So, conceptions of the process cannot be divorced from its motivational, interpersonal, organizational, and political contexts.

Among individuals (and groups) resisting evaluative research are those who oppose specifying exactly what they do, and identifying its intended result. They prefer to leave their work unstructured, insisting that casework, for example, is too complex, too much an art, to be pinned down in this fashion. Others will be found who have hidden agendas or latent objectives which they do not want subjected to close scrutiny. An administrator who has loaded his staff with favorites and sycophants is unlikely to welcome close observation of any kind by outsiders—let alone evaluation. Some professionals welcome change as an end in itself; if one is automatically against the status quo, there is hardly any reason to assess it scientifically. There are always people who have already condemned an approach informally and would resist having their biases questioned. Some, convinced that only by revolution can the lot of man be improved, associate casework and group work with "adjusting the client to the system," and would like to see them abolished. Such an attitude may be held in spite of the fact that available evidence strongly suggests that the rate of occurrence of various forms of mental illness is rather similar regardless of the form of government of a society.

Finally, there are those so committed to a particular approach that they cannot consider alternatives. Campbell (1969) identified two types of administrators with whom the researcher may find himself engaged, the "trapped" and the "experimental." The experimentalist, he says, justifies the giving of service on the basis that the problems are important and warrant help. Since the form of the help, however, is not frozen in his mind, he is open to alternatives, and therefore will be more likely to support a study using experimental and quasi-experimental designs. The trapped administrator is not able to be so playful. Executives who make their agencies extensions of their own narcissism are typically defensive not only about the overall structure but about every detail of it. Such a person could not accept results that go against his needs. Therefore, Campbell recommends he be fed "Favorably biased analyses, grateful testimonials, and confounding selection and treatment" (p. 428). The mature and experienced researcher has all these social and psychological realities in mind when entering a situation in which he is to do evaluative research. They affect his decision about whether responsible work is possible in the setting; they also affect the manner in which—and how quickly —results of his study can be utilized in feedback to staff and board.

FOCUSES OF EVALUATION

The follow-up study by Charles Loring Brace sought to reply to the query: How did it all come out? But the weaknesses in such a well-meant effort should be quickly apparent to those who have come this far in our text. Many children were not located some years after placement. Is it not likely that those who were lost had lives less happy than those who were found—in other words, that the sample located is unrepresentative of the sample placed? How convincing is it to be told that few of them were in prisons or other institutions? Is this a satisfactory criterion for success?

And how might their lives have been had they never been placed? No control group was studied. Was removal to farm communities the treatment of choice for *all* these youngsters? Were they really so uniform, or might there have been a type for whom it were better had they never left New York? Were some families better for one kind of youngster than another? Did Brace look for such interaction effects?

From questions like these, cogent and yet so quickly raised, we become more fully aware that, if it is to be optimally useful, evaluative research is far more complicated than it at first appears. Indeed, our thinking about it has undergone a rather long development which is typified most recently in writings by Freeman and Sherwood (1965), Kiesler (1971), Paul (1966), and Katz and colleagues (1972). Probably the most sophisticated and clearest delineation of evaluative research is that by De Geyndt (1970), who wrote on assessing the quality of health care. Five approaches were distinguished, namely, assessment (1) of content; (2) of process; (3) of structure; (4) of outcome; and (5) of impact.

Focus on *content* addresses the question of whether services are being "properly delivered." But, what is "proper"? Currently accepted practice becomes the standard by which content is judged. Thus, specific techniques and procedures are identified and checked in depth. Content studies help to police practice for quality control. In a field like medicine, there is good reason to believe that, if strict antisepsis is maintained in an operating room, more patients will survive. This does not mean, however, that because a mode of practice is widely accepted it is effective. Family agency practice used to be evaluated in part on the basis of whether process recording was kept of client interviews. Such recording may be an aid to supervision and training, but there is little evidence that clients' movement is affected by their case records. In short, for content evaluation to be meaningful, practice theory in a profession has to be well advanced and verified (Breedlove 1972).

Evaluation of *process* also appraises the manner in which service is given. Rather than scrutinizing details, however, it typically focuses on "the whole person" and on the sequence and pattern by which services are made available. "An important assumption underlying the rationale of the process approach is that good coordination of the teamwork in a logical sequence of the various elements in the care process will result in better health of the recipient" (De Geyndt 1970, p. 27). Again, the assumption is only partly credible. No one questions that smooth teamwork is a positive element in getting any job done. But which would one prefer for a cholera epidemic—an informal group armed with antibiotics or a finely disciplined crew who bring aspirin and computers?

Assessment of *structure* focuses on two elements thought crucial in meeting the needs of a community, namely, facilities and manpower. Of course, it is impossible to minister to health needs without staff and hospitals. Yet the knowledge and skill of personnel also make an enormous difference. A surprising number of evaluative surveys, especially in the field of health care, consist of bed counts and head counts. Sheer numbers of facilities and staff may be, like the issues already covered, necessary but not sufficient conditions for getting the job done.

Concentration on *outcome* posits that the ultimate criterion to be used in judging social work services should be the net alteration or change in the individual recipient. Most agree that this is a highly acceptable locus for evaluative research, since improving the client, or at least stabilizing him, is the professed aim of most help offered. The critical issues in *outcome* evaluation are two: (*a*) Are the measures of success, the objective and subjective criterion variables, satisfactory? (*b*) Do we have reason to believe that the action taken ought to affect these variables? In other words, is the state of practice theory adequate to support use of outcome as the focus of evaluation? We shall discuss these problems at greater length below.

Assessment of *impact* focuses on an entire target population rather than the individual. The question, one may say, is not whether psychodrama as a technique does any good, but whether it is a method that is likely to have an important impact on the prevalence of mental illness in a whole community. Hence, in De Geyndt's formulation, impact studies go beyond clinical and even epidemiological considerations to deal with such matters as the availability, acceptability, and accessibility of services provided. The notion of impact serves to broaden our vision of what is hoped for. However, it is so complex a matter to study that, to quote De Geyndt, "No studies are as yet available using this composite approach" (p. 34). Which is not to say that impact studies are totally out of the question. For example, it is quite reasonable to hope that methadone programs may reduce the incidence, the numbers of new cases, of drug addiction. If they do this by making it less necessary for current addicts to set up in business as peddlers, we would have an example of a case where a technique may prove better from the standpoint of impact than of outcome, if we mean, by the latter, "curing the individual addict."

De Geyndt makes us aware that there are various approaches from which evaluative research can begin. While each seems reasonable, it also has limitations. Subsequent authors have recommended multilevel intervention and evaluation, going forward simultaneously, as closer to the ideal (Mullen and Dumpson 1972). The numbers of evaluators may well exceed those of practitioners in such a project, but the principle involved is not without its appeal.

Because of the complexities of which De Geyndt's listing makes us aware, efforts have been made to find alternatives to evaluative research, utilizing experimental designs. Suggested are such familiar modes as correlational studies, trend analyses, and the version of systems analysis popular during the Johnson administration, the PPBS (planning-programming-budgeting system). An obvious way to keep an eye on impact is to watch certain social indicators, like crime or unemployment rates. But here, too, cautions become necessary. As Campbell has noted, "The social indicators' approach will tend to make the indicators themselves the goal of social action, rather than the social problems they but imperfectly indicate. There are apt to be tendencies to legislate changes in the indicators, *per se*, rather than changes in the social problems" (1969, pp. 416 f.). As this is being written, the United States is undergoing a major shortage of gasoline. We are told that, because of the lowered speed limits for cars, the number of highway fatalities is down 23 percent. However, since the total amount of highway driving is down 20 percent, the cause of the drop in deaths is obscure. It is also obvious that our crime rate could be lessened if a number of victimless crimes now on the books could be eliminated. While this nicely illustrates Campbell's point, it is not exactly the factor we want evaluated! As was suggested in chapter 2, when it comes to drawing conclusions about cause-effect relationships, experimental designs are hard to beat.

SELECTION OF THE CRITERION

No issue is more important to evaluative research than selection of the criterion, the standard by which success or failure is to be judged. The issue goes beyond formal evaluation in a professional field. After all, as Kurt Lewin pointed out, "Without a measuring stick there can be no learning." All progress requires a criterion if it is to be rationally guided. There is no standard solution to what some authors have aptly termed "the criterion crisis" (Stern, Stein and Bloom 1956). We shall simply list some criteria for the selection of a criterion.

As with any measure, it is desirable that the variables chosen meet the requirements of reliability, especially interobserver reliability. They must also be reasonably sensitive to change over time. Economy is always a consideration. If it costs more to measure the effectiveness of a service than to offer it, questions will be raised.

The biggest concern, of course, is appropriateness. Do we have reason to believe the particular service introduced will produce changes on the dimension used as a criterion? At the moment, a number of persons are dismayed that once-a-week interviews with a caseworker have not been shown to be effective deterrents among youngsters with a tendency toward delinquency rooted in lifelong character traits. It would be nice if such miracles occurred, but most experienced therapists never find one. Unquestionably, the major source of disappointment in evaluative research lies in the hope that one can get, if not something for nothing, at least large payoffs for miniscule investments.

Intelligent choice of criterion variables requires a practice theory which is willing to make commitments about what it is hoped will be achieved. It also requires reasonably good knowledge, or preliminary scouting, of the content area being researched. Timing may make a difference. Studies of relocating elderly people have shown that the maximum effects occur during the first three months or so. Hence an investigation of such relocation that fails to measure during that time period will yield the end result of a process but no image of the process itself.

Another feature relates to the principle of indeterminacy in science. This principle says that, in the course of measuring a thing, we inevitably change it. Even inserting a thermometer in a tubful of water will very slightly alter the temperature of the water, unless the temperatures of both were identical to begin with. A follow-up interview with a client may be experienced as a reflection of continued interest in his welfare that could make him report more favorably on his opinion of an agency. Or, if he did not like his experience, he could regard it as further intrusion on his privacy, and give an even more negative judgment. One evaluative study that included a means for considering the effect of the assessment process was that of Katz and colleagues (1972). In their research community, public health nursing was offered on an experimental basis. The investigators concluded that repeated research interviews, combined with solicitous nursing, resulted in *unfavorable* scores on social functioning as measured by return to employment, resumption of role as homemaker, use of physician services, etc. The added attention, they believe, "tended to reenforce the sick role" (p. 85). On the other hand, it would be hard to conceive that our locating a particular man in the state prison is the cause of his being there. In studies with a contrast group design, criterion measures must also be feasible for use with the untreated, or unserved, group.

In some studies, it seems desirable to have repeated measurements, in order to follow a process in detail. However, this gives rise to difficulties, too. Repeated administration of the same test yields "practice effects," improvement owing to familiarity with the test. There is, also, "practice fatigue," in which scores subtly deteriorate because of boredom or the like. A traditional solution for these problems is the use of two matched forms of the same instrument, equivalent but not identical. Unfortunately, this solution is not possible in all studies. There are only so many ways of asking, How are you feeling now? And establishing equivalence on more complicated instruments is a time-consuming, expensive exercise. The desirability of avoiding practice effects may influence the study's design. Rather than risk them, one may measure his experimental and control groups only *after* service is given, without the elegance of equating them on measures taken before or the advantages of change scores in measuring effects (see chapter 2).

In any event, it has become evident that the criterion used should permit *deterioration* to show itself. In their study of the use of services with the aged, Blenkner, Jahn, and Wasser (1964) did something unusual. Until then, the factors of death, unwillingness to be interviewed, and being unable to be located were regarded simply as sources of unfortunate attrition in a sample. But Blenkner and colleagues found that aged people, carefully persuaded to leave their homes for the better care of an institution, were somewhat more likely to die than persons not served—and so not moved. If every cause has an effect, every service has a consequence —whether or not it is the one anticipated, and whether or not we have looked in the right place for it. Bergin (1971) has also identified deterioration effects in psychotherapy. The estimate is that 10 percent of patients actually get worse while in therapy.

Mention must also be made of subjective evaluation. Here we have reference especially to the feelings of the recipients, as well as the community at large, about a service. For a long time there was justifiable doubt about how to regard testimonials. Too many clients, who objectively were not improved, expressed exaggerated gratitude—whether out of a dependent tie to the helper, or as a reaction formation against bitterness for not having been helped. However, the emphasis on accountability to consumers and the community has lately led to some alteration in how we view subjective data. In the private sector, where there is freedom of choice, citizen attitudes may be measured in part by where they put their dollars. For services about which one has no choice, client satisfaction or lack of it may be measured only by research surveys.

Moreover, community attitudes as influenced by word-of-mouth advertisement may affect a program's spread and accessibility. So, in De Geyndt's terminology, while a testimonial may be an invalid index of *outcome*, it can be highly relevant about *impact*. An associated idea has to do with multilevel evaluation, which De Geyndt's listing also suggests. In assessing a protective service, for example, one may find that, whereas the workers' dedication has pushed them to remove a number of children from their natural parents to protect the children, this very occasional action has given the workers a reputation as baby-snatchers in the whole neighborhood where they operate (Varon 1964). Indeed, it is difficult now to envisage a multilevel evaluation which would *not* contain data on consumer attitudes toward the program along with other measures. Multilevel evaluation implies multilevel criteria.

STUDY DESIGNS

As noted, the logic by which conclusions are to be drawn in this area is not unique. The direction of research is more charged because it is frankly evaluative. But this does not alter the basic scientific aim, which is to establish precise relationships among phenomena and to determine at times that a relation suspected does not, in fact, exist. Here, as elsewhere, the study design usually best calculated to permit concise conclusions is the projected experiment adequately controlled and with multifactorial design. And here, as elsewhere, the level of design required to increase our knowledge depends to a considerable extent on the current state of knowledge in the field. Such information is better than no information at all, even if the conclusion drawn must be cautiously qualified.

There is one general rule which can be stated at the outset. The stimulus variable, the cause of change, the social work intervention, must always be clearly identified and described. This, after all, is what is being evaluated. One type of evaluative study has been given the label "black box." In this sort of study, we are told that a client of a certain type was given "treatment"; subsequently, we are told how he came out and whether he showed improvement over his state at the beginning. The exact nature of the treatment and the whole process gone through are not described in enough detail that someone else could repeat them. Even if such a study reports positive results, its replicability and general usefulness to the field are nil. Close to the black box studies are those that make unwarranted assumptions about uniformity. Thus, we are told the clients were offered a group work program or that "community organization services were provided." No experienced practitioner needs to be reminded of how wide a range of activities can, and should, be covered by either term. Hence, evidence that such a program failed tells us little about what to stop doing; even worse, evidence that one succeeded does not tell us what to continue! Another unwarranted uniformity assumption has to do with the clientele. We shall return to this issue. As stated earlier, any responsible design must try to describe precisely *what* was done, to whom, by whom. These are principles applicable throughout the succinct listing below.

Experimental Designs

1. Simple before-after. This is perhaps the most common design implicit in informal evaluation, at least. A community organizer enters a situation, makes a diagnostic appraisal, offers a service for a period of time, and then tries to judge whether things have improved because of his efforts. Objection to awarding him sole credit is all too familiar. What would have happened had there been no community organization? Suppose the economy had been on an upswing, anyhow? Might not all the related social indicators also have improved without his intervention? In studying psychotherapy, we are aware of spontaneous remissions, self-healing that occurs anyway.

Both the design and its limitations are familiar, but they do not rule out the design's usefulness completely. Often, for example, a suitable control group cannot be located. Try to match two communities; then try to match two whole *samples* of communities! When a sophisticated researcher has confirmed for himself how unsatisfactory attempts to match whole communities are, he may settle for a before-after design as better than nothing, and at least not an expensive exercise in hypocrisy. Somewhat similar problems arise, by the way, in offering help to individuals. In this instance, the issue is not whether you can achieve reasonable matching, but whether the kind of information about their attitudes and backgrounds which clients give in treatment is at the same level as that offered by an untreated group seen only "for research." So, the potentialities of logic and statistical analyses ought not blind us to the realities we know so well as practitioners.

Simple before-after design also seems appropriate in studies that are still highly exploratory, and do not pretend to more. An example is the research on "the intermediary treatment of inaccessible children" done by Ganter, Yeakel, and Polansky (1967). The study reports work with forty-seven children at a child guidance clinic who were considered to be untreatable as outpatients and recommended for institutional treatment. Since, as is not atypical, such care was unlikely to be available, a program was set up aimed at bringing the youngsters and their families along to a point at which they could be, if not certainly treatable, at least accessible to outpatient treatment. This program made extensive use of clinical group work, with both the youngsters and their families. There was a very explicit theory involved, specifying the "target dependent variable" in the child as his *verbal accessibility* and other personality dimensions which, it was hypothesized, would lead to favorable changes on that one. In order to effect change, a number of programs and methods of intervention had to be adapted and, in fact, invented for this experimental program. Some of these had evolved in preceding pilot research. Therefore, an important feature of the report was the detailed specification not only of the measure of outcome but also of the nature of the help offered and vicissitudes experienced in trying to carry out the helping process. For nothing ever goes exactly according to plan, and the discovery that certain possible interventions cannot actually be carried out may be as useful as knowing which other techniques were able to be offered but had no discernible effect!

The results were appraised in terms of ratings on verbal accessibility achieved by the subjects in later actual attempts to treat them individually as outpatients. It was concluded that about two-thirds had benefited from the program. An attempt was made to identify those who could not benefit. Now, was this success? What can we conclude in the absence of a control group? The answer must be taken from the use of a hypothetical control. From what is known already, the thing most to be expected if help had not been offered was further deterioration of the child and his family relationships. Spontaneous remissions were not to be anticipated in a group on whom the clinic had, in effect, given up. Hence, as we say, The case was his own control.

Rather similar logic can be used with respect to programs instituted in whole communities to reduce delinquency—to cite a well-financed but still mythical example. Even if no other community exactly matches the one entered, if the delinquency rate for all communities of that size had reportedly increased but the target community has even remained constant, one could conclude that the program is having its desired effect just on the basis of measures taken before and after the program was instituted.

2. Contrast group designs

(a) Ex post facto experiments. In social work, as in medicine, there has been reluctance to set up experiments with control subjects, that is, clients supposedly in need from whom treatment is deliberately withheld. The ethical issue is obvious to any sensitive professional with no wish to play god or devil. Reluctance has been reduced only as two related issues have been clarified: the service to be given was something extra, which would not have been available to the experimental subjects unless there were a study; and, since the whole purpose of the project was to evaluate a service, it was not known whether the control group were losing anything. Negative results in a number of studies have suggested, alas, that control groups were often not substantially deprived.

One way out of the difficulty is especially attractive because it combines a high moral tone with relative cheapness. Why not isolate, after the fact, an experiment which has already occurred in nature? Locate a group of subjects who have been offered a service, such as admission to a public housing project. Then, find a group comparable to the first in all respects except one key matter. For extraneous reasons, such as the limited housing available, they did not receive the service. Thus, the ex post facto experimental design is lent to evaluative research. The basic idea was stated and illustrated by Chapin (1947) in a standard book on the sociological method of the time. There are so many examples of ex post facto research in the literature, including the first edition of this book, that it does not require another illustration here.

However, its major handicap should be pointed out. The problem is that of *confounding selection of subjects with treatment.* If there are two groups of people equally in difficulties and one received casework but the other did not, the researcher must be extremely careful to establish that the reason for the difference has nothing to do with the issue being studied. Was the so-called control group offered treatment, but declined it? Were the treated group clients with enough initiative and intactness to seek help? In the latter instance, if the treated group proved to be doing better, we would not know whether the cause were in the treatment received or in the fact that they were in a better state to begin with. And how well they are psychologically is hardly determined by such things as their sex, age, race or even socioeconomic status—the sorts of demographic variables on which subjects are often matched. Hence, the potential confounding of treatment and subject variables has proved the insurmountable drawback to evaluation via the ex post facto study. One would not abandon this design—but one would not use it uncritically, either.

(*b*) *Projected contrast group designs.* One is led, therefore, to the very real advantages of the projected experimental design. In this, subjects can be precision-matched or, more feasibly, matched by random assignment to treatment groups. Moreover, one can overcome still another logical problem of ex post facto researches. Control groups are assumed to be persons to whom, in effect, nothing too relevant happens while the experimental group is being served. The assumption is most dubious. They may spontaneously seek out treatment superior to that being offered in the project, to cite one alternative. If many in the control group do that, a very useful social work service may appear worse than "nothing"! The fact is that we are *contrasting* two groups, one given a known treatment, the other, a treatment either not known or at least not precisely described. In evaluative research, this problem takes on great significance, of course. Thus Blenkner (1962) points out that, while the locus, administration, amount, and duration of the service provided the experimental group may be controlled, this is no assurance the service was in fact different from that received by the controls.

The same issue is exacerbated by the phenomenon of *leakage.* In one state hospital, two wards were selected for additional service in the form of vocational guidance counselling. Two comparable wards were unserved, "controls." However, the fact that the first two were receiving something extra bestirred the staff of the control wards to efforts not at all typical of them. The leakage of the improved ward atmospheres and staff ambitiousness showed itself in improved discharge rates from *both* sets of wards. The experiment? "Results were inconclusive." The patients got better, but Science was not served.

The late Margaret Blenkner did much to introduce projected contrast group designs into evaluative research in social work, so it seems only fitting to describe a study she led (Blenkner, Bloom, and Nielson 1971). The population studied comprised noninstitutionalized older persons (i.e., sixty or older) living in the Cleveland SMSA who were likely to come to the attention of health and welfare agencies and need protective services. Such need was defined, in part, as present in a person "whose behavior indicates that he is mentally incapable of caring for himself and his interests without serious consequences to himself and others" (p. 483). The sample consisted of 164 older persons meeting the definition and referred by a total of 13 local agencies. Seventy-six were assigned to the experimental treatment at random, and eighty-eight served as controls. All were interviewed at intervals of three months, six months, and one year following intake. The group served were offered social casework on a "social therapy" model and various legal, medical, and supportive services. The control group received the services ordinarily provided persons in their situation in the community.

Effort expended on the served group was significantly greater—more concrete assistance, better, varied services, and a better physical environment, because of home aides and the institutionalization of a greater proportion. So *content* was favorably evaluated. How about the ultimate goals of the program? While the service relieved the anxiety of family and friends, it did not result in more favorable scores on participants' functioning, mood, or *survival*. Indeed, detailed analysis of data on death rates slightly favored the controls and those not institutionalized. The negative survival effect resulting from institutionalization dissipated after four years. On the other hand, an excellent study by Goldberg (1970) in Great Britain suggests that a served group of aged persons profited from social work.

Another justifiably well-known study is that which Reid and Shyne (1969) conducted at the Community Service Society of New York. The cases included were limited to those coming to this family agency for help for marital conflict and/or parent-child relationship problems. A multifactorial design involved assigning cases at random in terms of three variations: supportive vs. modifying methods of casework; individual interviews combined with joint conferences; and the usual open-ended continued service vs. planned short-term service, defined as one to be rendered within not more than eight in-person client interviews and within no more than three months after the completion of intake. The various combinations of these three dichotomized variables permitted a total of eight possible treatment conditions. Each case included was seen by a research caseworker at the beginning, at the end, and six months following treatment.

Of the three experimental variations, only that between planned short-term service and continued service proved statistically significant. The results, especially as measured in client attitudes, favored the short term, and thus go against the prevailing wisdom and practice in the field. The study illustrates well the increased power of a multifactorial design in which, for little added expense, several variables can be investigated at once. Moreover, unless one uses all possible combinations, such a design offers the only opportunity to study interaction effects—e.g., to answer such a question as whether short-term practice may be better combined with supportive casework but worse when modifying techniques are used. Missing from the results is still another factor, the possible influence of client personality, which can also be studied in a multifactorial design. But no study does everything, and this is one of the most elegant we have had thus far.

(c) *Placebo effects.* These consist in getting the right result for the wrong reason. They refer to the observation that patients in serious straits may respond to any special attention, particularly one offering them hope of recovery. Hence, when some patients were administered a new pill, but others were not, the question was whether improvement was due to their medication or their morale. That there was reason for concern was demonstrated when a number of patients, in several experiments, showed improvement when on placebos (pills containing a bit of sugar and otherwise biochemically inert). One can control for this extraneous variable in large measure by concealing from the patients who is getting the active, and who the inactive, drug. Comparable controls are hard to establish when one is offering a whole program of special services, of course.

Paul (1967) has offered a sensible solution to this problem, in a paper reprinted by Fellin, Tripodi, and Meyer (1969). His basic idea was to compare the effectiveness of a densensitization technique with very brief "insight therapy" for college students afraid of public speaking. Accordingly, he set up groups offered desensitization, and compared them with subjects offered insight. To see whether either treatment was better than nothing, he introduced a control group. And to study the placebo effect, he had a group given an equivalent amount of attention but with no structured treatment. An important feature of his design was the effort made to follow up as many participants as possible. Sure enough, it was shown that those unavailable for follow-up were in the greater difficulties to begin with; hence, the sample actually *found* would be favorably biased.

According to Paul's measures, two years after the brief treatment, those given desensitization treatment were most favorably affected; those offered insight treatment were equally well off with those given the attention placebo; while the untreated group was significantly worse off than the other three. In short, on objective measures the placebo treatment was weaker than his best condition, but still better than the control. However, to pick up a thread dropped earlier in this chapter on *self-reported* improvement, all three treated groups scored about the same but better than the control. Paul's is one study among many showing the placebo effect is no speculation; it demonstrates a design by which the effect may be usefully taken into account in assessing the net advantages of an intervention. Unfortunately, it is as hard to design a social work placebo as to sustain the state of nothingness we used to consider "control"!

Other Designs

Some information, as we have said, is better than none. There is evaluative research less rigorous in design than the experiment which nevertheless proves highly valuable to the field. For brevity, we shall cover only descriptive follow-up studies, demonstrations, and clinical research.

A follow-up study which both authors know intimately is reported in Allerhand, Weber, and Haug's *Adaptation and Adaptability: the Bellefaire Followup Study* (1966). Bellefaire is an institution in Cleveland for the treatment of emotionally disturbed boys and girls up to the age of around sixteen. The study was instituted in 1960, and its aim was to follow a group of fifty youngsters, who had been at the institution at least six months, between one and two years after their discharge. The difficulties of following up a group from even one community deserve a chapter in themselves (Paul 1967; Geismar 1973, pp. 22–24). Clients came from all over the country and were contacted in their home communities through the senior researcher's extensive traveling. He had tape-recorded interviews with them. The study measured the success of the treatment program in terms of the boy's ability to fulfill various functions expectable of a person in his role in his setting. However, it constituted an advance over most comparable researches in that it related postdischarge adaptation to status on admission and to a number of measures of how the course of treatment had gone. The latter feature became possible because the follow-up was linked to ongoing research on factors influencing a child's accessibility that was concurrently being conducted at the institution (Polansky, Weiss, and Blum 1961; Weber 1963). Therefore it was possible to raise, and give at least some tentative answer to, the question which any sophisticated practitioner would offer: For *which* sort of youngster is this particular type of treatment evidently effective? Thus, an outstanding feature of the research is that it does *not* fall victim to the uniformity assumption common to most follow-ups. Incidentally, many of the mothers complained that, while their sons seemed better, they were "detached." Observing this inadvertent effect of prolonged separation foreshadows phenomena later systematized by Bowlby (1973) in attachment theory, but we were unable to grasp its general significance at the time. It becomes for us a personal experience of the principle that discoveries are made by those prepared with a theoretical framework to make them.

Another kind of evaluation frequently accompanies what are termed demonstrations. A demonstration grant should be obtained for the purpose of installing a new service which one already knows how to conduct and which needs only to be demonstrated to the local officials for them to become enthused and institutionalize it in their community. Evaluation research is built into the package in order to provide objective evidence of usefulness and increase the probability that the project will not end, when, say, the federal funding does. In practice, and leaving out the unwillingness of local citizens to support services for the poor unless the money seemingly comes from out of town, many such projects are not nearly at such a stage of certainty. The basic service may well be in its beginnings (e.g., client advocacy). Furthermore, installing it in a strange setting with a new staff requires an extended period of training and shakedown before the program is actually operative. In other words, the evaluation of demonstration projects, if it is a serious endeavor, ought to be realistically timed so that what is to be assessed has some chance of being in existence (see the "validity check" in group experiments mentioned in chapter 7).

Finally, there is a type of experimental work in a practitioner field that may do well to dispense with formal evaluation altogether. We refer to *clinical research*, in which an investigator sets forth on a voyage of discovery to see if he can devise some means of helping a particular client group. As he goes, he should keep some sort of log, totting up the ideas for intervention that never got off the ground because they seemed good in theory but could not be carried out in practice. He may get a hunch that a technique currently tried has promise, even though it is not yet sufficiently refined or strong in its effects to overcome the measurement error endemic among criterion instruments. In other words, when invention and discovery are the goals, it is shortsighted of granting agencies to weight a project with rigorous tests of efficiency. These can come later, and indeed ought to come later if the discovery has merit and its spread is being touted. The argument between the creative practitioners, aware that the evaluators almost never offer suggestions but only critiques, and the hard-nosed enthusiasts of research methodology cannot scientifically be resolved in favor of either. It has been pointed out, for example, that after millions of man-hours devoted to the development and promulgation of learning theory (which underlies behavior modification), we still do not know how to teach reading—and that is where the whole enterprise began. The efficacy of the classical technique has also been subjected to severe questioning, and so deservedly so that it is not so often used any more even by psychoanalysts. From a scientific standpoint, there are adequate grounds for humility for all.

The Dissemination and Utilization of Evaluative Research

Closing the gap between the production of evaluative research and its use has been the subject of numerous publications and conferences. Plans for dissemination and utilization of results of a project should be built into the study from its inception. Moreover, transferability, feasibility, and adoption of the findings should be evaluated in a final stage of the project (Weber 1973).

Application is a two-pronged process involving *dissemination* and *utilization*. The dissemination of research findings requires that one identify significant results and translate them into the language of the users. It also requires packaging and conveying results to potential users. Thus, abstracts, periodic reviews, progress reports, handbooks, central data banks, and retrieval systems are all emphasized.

Research utilization, on the other hand, is fundamentally a matter of adopting a different idea or approach, albeit one that has survived empirical testing. Utilization involves change in one or more systems, but one must first develop openness to change and "change capability." Change may be brought about by an inside change agent who, convinced of the value of the research findings, has the power to effect their adoption. Typically, the staff must respect him as being knowledgeable and also not see him as too "far out" or too conservative.

Even so, however, he may still not be able to overcome barriers to change. It is often most effective to expose the staff to an outside change agent who reinforces the efforts of the inside change agent. A research utilization specialist whose role is that of a middleman between the researcher and the user may be such an agent.

To offset the isolation and inertia of the researcher who would waste time on dissemination and utilization, and to overcome the negative attitude of the practitioner toward the elitism of the scientist, another approach is suggested. This requires the collaborative efforts of the researchers and practitioners conducting a demonstration. Such personnel would be committed to the importance of feedback to potential users, trained in research dissemination, and interested in evaluating the transportability and generalizability of their findings (Weber 1973).

Several models detailing the theory and techniques of research utilization have been identified. Foremost among the behavioral scientists are staff members of the Center for Research on Utilization of Scientific

Knowledge of the Institute for Social Research at the University of Michigan (Havelock 1969), and Glaser and associates at the Human Interaction Research Institute in Los Angeles (Glaser and Taylor 1969).

The prototype of early approaches to knowledge utilization was the Cooperative Extension Service, affiliated with agricultural departments in land-grant universities and employing county agricultural agents. The Cooperative Extension Service approach was borrowed by the National Aeronautics and Space Administration (NASA). Especially noteworthy among NASA innovations was information storage through the development of efficient coding systems, as well as methods for selectively disseminating information. Subsequent experience, however, has shown that human service problems present far more difficult and diverse barriers to knowledge utilization than does engineering or agriculture.

New organizational arrangements have been promulgated and are now under examination. They include the Social Problems Research Institute, recommended by the Special Commission of the National Science Board (1969), and the Regional Social Welfare Research Institutes spearheaded by the Social and Rehabilitation Services. Other approaches launched by the Social and Rehabilitation Services include the establishment of a research utilization specialist based in the state office of the Vocational Rehabilitation Agency and the funding of research utilization laboratories (Engstrom 1970).

Research utilization is a challenging new field promising a more viable rapprochement between science and practice than has obtained in the past. The exchange should be rewarding and stimulating.

REFERENCES

Allerhand, M. E.; Weber, R. E.; and Haug, M. A. 1966. *Adaptation and adaptability: The Bellefaire followup study.* New York: Child Welfare League of America.

Bergin, A. E. 1971. The evaluation of therapeutic outcomes. In *Handbook of psychotherapy and behavior change,* ed. A. E. Bergin and S. L. Garfield, pp. 217–70. New York: Wiley.

Blenkner, M. 1950. Obstacles to evaluative research in casework. *Social Casework* 31:54–60, 97–105.

———. 1962. Control groups and the placebo effect in evaluative research. *Social Work* 7:52–58.

———; Bloom, M.; and Nielsen, M. A. 1971. A research and demonstration project of protective services. *Social Casework* 52:483–99.

Blenkner, M.; Jahn, J.; and Wasser, E. 1964. Serving the aging: An experiment in social work and public health nursing. Mimeographed. New York: Community Service Society.

Bowlby, J. 1973. *Separation anxiety and anger.* New York: Basic Books.

Breedlove, J. L. 1972. Theory development as a task for the evaluator. In *Evaluation of social intervention,* ed. E. J. Mullen, J. R. Dumpson, and Associates. San Francisco: Jossey-Bass.

Brieland, D. G. 1971. Charles Loring Brace (1826–1890). In *Encyclopedia of social Work,* ed. Robert Morris, pp. 83–84. New York: National Assoc. of Social Workers.

Campbell, D. T. 1969. Reforms as experiments. *American Psychologist* 24:409–29.

Chapin, F. S. 1947. *Experimental designs in sociological research.* New York: Harper.

De Geyndt, W. 1970. Five approaches for assessing quality of care. *Hospital Administration* 15:21–41.

Engstrom, G. A. 1970. Research utilization, the challenge of applying SRS research. *Welfare in Review* 8:1–7.

Fellin, P.; Tripodi, T.; and Meyer, H. J. 1969. *Exemplars of social research.* Itasca, Ill.: F. E. Peacock.

Freeman, H., and Sherwood, C. 1965. Research in large-scale intervention programs. *Journal of Social Issues* 21:11–28.

Ganter, G.; Yeakel, M.; and Polansky, N. A. 1967. *Retrieval from limbo: the intermediary group treatment of inaccessible children.* New York: Child Welfare League of America.

Geismar, L. L. 1973. *555 families: A social-psychological study of young families in transition.* New Brunswick, N.J.: Transaction.

Glaser, E. M., and Taylor, S. H. 1969. *Factors influencing the success of applied research: A study of ten NIMH-funded projects.* Los Angeles: Human Interaction Research Institute.

Goldberg, E. M. 1970. *Helping the aged: A field experiment in Social Work.* London: George Allen & Unwin.

Havelock, R. G. 1969. *Planning for innovation through dissemination and utilization of knowledge.* Ann Arbor, Mich.: Institute for Social Research, Univ. of Michigan.

Katz, S.; Ford, A. B.; Downs, T. D.; Adams, M.; and Rusby, D. I. 1972. *Effects of continued care: A study of chronic illness in the home.* Department of Health, Education, and Welfare, Health Services and Mental Health Administration, National Center for Health Services Research and Development. Washington, D.C.: U.S. Government Printing Office.

Kiesler, D. J. 1971. Experimental designs in psychotherapy research. In *Handbook of psychotherapy and behavior change,* ed. A. E. Bergin and S. L. Garfield, pp. 36–74. New York: Wiley.

Merton, R. K. 1957. Role of the intellectual in public bureaucracy. In *Social theory and social structure,* ed. R. K. Merton, pp. 207–24. Rev. ed. New York: Free Press of Glencoe.

Mullen, E. J., Dumpson, J. R., and Associates. 1972. *Evaluation of social intervention*. San Francisco: Jossey-Bass.

Paul, G. 1967. Insight versus desensitization in psychotherapy two years after termination. *Journal of Consulting Psychology* 31:333–48.

Polansky, N. A.; Weiss, E. W.; and Blum, A. 1961. Children's verbal accessibility as a function of content and personality. *American Journal of Orthopsychiatry* 31:153–69.

Reid, W. J., and Shyne, A. W. 1969. *Brief and extended casework*. New York: Columbia Univ. Press.

Special Commission on the Social Sciences of the National Science Board. 1969. *Knowledge into action: Improving the nation's use of the social sciences*. Washington, D.C.: National Science Foundation.

Stern, G. G.; Stein, M. I.; and Bloom, B. S. 1956. *Methods in personality assessment*. Glencoe, Ill.: Free Press.

Varon, E. 1964. Communication: Client, community, and agency. *Social Work* 9:51–57.

Weber, R. E. 1963. Children's verbal accessibility as a predictor of treatment outcome. DSW dissertation. Case Western Reserve University.

————. 1973. Evaluative research: Community mental health services for the aged. Prepared for the Subcommittee on Evaluative Research of the Committee on Research and Development Goals in Social Gerontology, Miami.

Roger R. Miller

9
Statistical
Analysis of Data

The prominence of statistics in a field of inquiry seems to vary inversely with the command enjoyed by an investigator over his subject matter. The physical scientist, who is relatively advantaged in his ability to isolate, manipulate, and measure, and who also has the benefit of relatively adequate theory, may rarely use elaborate statistical tools. In contrast, the social scientist needs a variety of statistical tools to organize and sift raw data in order to grasp the results of his work. Like other social scientists, social work researchers rely on statistical tools to cope with some of the problems in design, sampling, and measurement that derive from our present limited command of our subject.

The statistics in general use in social work research can be divided into three groups according to the different issues they address. One group, called descriptive statistics, consists for the most part of simple tools that condense and summarize data. Essentially they help to answer the question, What was found? Descriptive statistics, which have an ancient history, were developed to handle practical problems of administration and commerce. In character, simple descriptive statistics are as straightforward, utilitarian, and dependable as the German and British mercantile interests they were designed to serve.

A second group of statistics, denoted as inferential or predictive statistics, reflects quite a different lineage. In pursuit of their passion for gambling, some of the French nobility sought help from mathematicians in order to illuminate the outcome of games of chance. Inferential statistics, the product of this work, provide tools for the calculation of chance or probability. Inferential statistics all make use of one or another probability model against which obtained data are studied. That is, to the straightforward, empirical description of actual data, inferential statistics add the elegance of hypothetical models.

The third group of statistics, which makes varied use of both inferential and descriptive approaches, consists of techniques for combining, partializing, and sifting data. These tools, some of which are elaborate and complex, are designed to help answer the question, What more can be learned about the meaning of the findings?

The three groups of statistics are coherent with each other and are used in concert. Indeed, a statistical analysis routinely initially pursues a description of data, expressed in terms that lend themselves to an inferential analysis. An inferential analysis can in turn become the basis for more elaborate or refined analysis. Together, statistics from these three branches provide means for summarizing data, for drawing logically correct inferences about the place of error in the data, and for appraising further the meaning of data.

Statistical tools provide the basis for solving analytic problems that would otherwise exceed the capacity of the human mind. Unfortunately, statistical processing can also distort and obscure. The major hazard in statistical processing derives not from the possibility of computational error, which can be checked and corrected, but from another source. Statistical distortion is chiefly the product of incompatibility between the characteristics of actual data and the logic of a particular statistical procedure. Statistical *technology* is wholly blind to this issue. Effective statistical analysis thus rests on the selection of an analytic program that best fits the characteristics of the study data and allows the study questions to be addressed efficiently.

The aim of this chapter is to provide perspective on a range of statistical tools. As an extensive literature on computational procedures exists, no attempt is made to consider step-by-step calculations. Instead, the logic underlying the use of various statistical tools is emphasized.

Descriptive Statistics

Describing a Sample

Both the social work practitioner and the researcher are confronted regularly with a bewildering volume of data; both collect more information than can be absorbed and appraised conveniently. The practitioner's solution to the problem of too much data is a complex, artistic, and poorly understood one. In contrast, the researcher's solution to too much data is almost embarrassingly simple. When the data take the form of measurements such as, for example, the number of interviews held with each of a hundred cases, two general ways of reducing this information to manageable size are open to him. Either the measurements can be organized and described by categories, or some characteristic properties can be abstracted from the measurements. The procedures, described below, have the common-sense objective of simplifying the data to the point where they can be grasped.

Description by categorization. A simple, straightforward way of ordering and describing data is the familiar frequency distribution table. Relevant, exhaustive, and mutually exclusive categories are selected to provide a convenient number of intervals, and a simple count is made of the number of cases which fall in each category. For example, the responses of social workers to this article may be summarized by table 1.

TABLE 1
DISTRIBUTION OF READERS' TOLERANCE FOR "STATISTICAL ANALYSIS OF DATA" REFLECTED IN NUMBER OF PAGES READ

Number of Pages Read	Readers	
	Number	Percent
Under 3 pages	17	8.9
3 to 5 pages	68	35.6
6 to 8 pages	23	12.3
9 to 11 pages	19	9.5
12 to 14 pages	64	33.5

For more convenient visual presentation, these data could be described pictorially by means of the familiar bar chart (histogram), as in figure 1, or by line chart (frequency polygon), as in figure 2. Whichever technique is used, the result is a picture of where the typical or average score lies, the amount of variability in the series, and the general shape of the distribution of the measurements. In each of these methods of presentation, we note that almost half of the readers gave up somewhere short of six pages, but the remainder tended to stick it out until the bitter end. These data, which were assumed, undoubtedly represent an overly optimistic estimate of the tolerance of readers.

Tabular and graphic organization of data makes it possible to describe a lot of information quite simply. It is important to note, however, that a price has been paid for this convenience. Some of the information has been obscured or thrown away, i.e., the exact number of pages each reader tolerated. This loss would be less serious if the size of the class intervals were reduced (say, from three pages to one page). However, the smaller the class interval, the more the goal of simplification and economy is defeated. Every table and chart represents a compromise between precision and simplicity.

Description by abstraction. To avoid some of the loss of precision that is inevitable in description by categorization, it is often practical to abstract or summarize certain properties of a set of measurements for purposes of description. Indications of central tendency and of variability are the most commonly abstracted characteristics of measurements.

Central tendency. A central value, or *average*, is a single number which tells something about an entire set of numbers. The central value is easily understood and easily computed, and can be a remarkably economical way of saying a great deal about a whole series of measurements. The *mean* (the sum of the measurements divided by the number of measurements) identifies the "center of gravity" of a distribution of scores. The *median* is the point on a scale of ordered measurements above which exactly half of the measurements lie and below which the other half fall. The *mode* is the most frequently occurring value or score. Whichever indication of the central value is used, the result is a single number which characterizes, at least to some degree, the entire set of measurements and represents the ultimate in simplification.

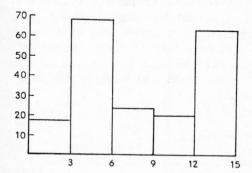

FIGURE 1.
DISTRIBUTION OF READERS' TOLERANCE BY PAGES READ

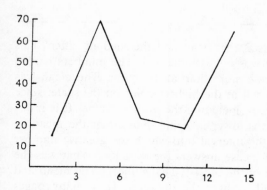

FIGURE 2.
DISTRIBUTION OF READERS' TOLERANCE BY PAGES READ

The mean, median, and mode of a series do not ordinarily coincide, although each is a way of expressing the "average." They are different measures and need to be used selectively. Which measure is the *appropriate* indicator of central value follows from the quality and characteristics of the measurements themselves. The reader will recall from chapter 3 that the mean may be most defensibly abstracted from interval and ratio scales (scales with a common unit of measurement, such as occurs in age, income, height). If the measurements lack this characteristic but are simply ranks (the tallest subject given a rank of 1, the next tallest the rank of 2, etc.), the arithmetic center of gravity (the mean) is senseless. For ordinal scales, then, the median is the appropriate measure of central value.

The mode may be derived from even a nominal scale, such as "male-female." The modal subject may be either male or female. In calculating the measure of reader masochism, described above, the data were drawn from a ratio scale. The number of pages read, like income, age, etc., is a "hard" number, allowing full mathematical treatment; and so it would be possible to extract a mean to reflect the central value of the readers' accomplishments. It would also be possible to make the other calculations of central tendency—the median and the mode. The results of this statistical abstracting are shown in table 2.

TABLE 2
CENTRAL VALUES REFLECTING READERS' INTEREST IN
"STATISTICAL ANALYSIS OF DATA"

Central Value	Number of Pages Read
Mean	7.32
Median	6.25
Crude mode	4.00

It will be noted that in table 2 the mean and the median differ. This occurs because the distribution was not symmetrical. The numbers tended to pile up at one end of the scale more than at the other. The mean was drawn toward the group which fell at the highest point on the scale, since the mean *is* sensitive to all scores, including the most extreme. It is interesting to note that the mode was lower in value than either the mean or median. The mode designates the interval into which the greatest number of subjects fell. The mode in this case answers the question, What was the actual reading accomplishment of the most typical subject? The mean and the median, on the other hand, answer the question, How many pages did a theoretical, "average," person read?

Variability. The variability (dispersion, scatter) of measurements, conveyed in a rough way by tabular or graphic organization of data, can also be expressed by a single number. Because the measure of central tendency gives no information except "location" of the distribution, a statistical description ordinarily includes both an indication of central value and an indication of the scatter or dispersion of the numbers.

The *range*, the simplest of the measures of dispersion, consists of the difference between the highest and lowest values in the series. This indication of scatter is frequently misleading, as it depends entirely on the two extreme values. Other indications are used in preference. *Variance*, the arithmetic mean of the squared deviations of measurements from their mean, does take into account every number in a series. The square root of the variance, the *standard deviation*, expresses the same information in more familiar form. The standard deviation is the most dependable indicator of scatter for most distributions and has the advantage of allowing further computation and certain interpretations related to the normal curve. The standard deviation identifies the range within which the central two-thirds of scores lie in a *normal distribution*.

As implied by the definition, the standard deviation is appropriate only to measurements from which a mean may be properly derived. For ordinal measurements (ranks) from which only a median can be drawn, another indicator of scatter is appropriate The *semi-interquartile range*, the mean distance between the first and third quartiles, is an available measure of dispersion around the median value.

To complete the description of the reading accomplishments of the subjects—it is hoped before too many have given up—the measures of dispersion are reported in table 3. Translating these measures of variability into the ideas they represent, we observe that the readers' tolerance varied from fewer than three pages to twelve to fourteen pages. The standard deviation of 4.7 defines the interval around the mean within which about two-thirds of the subjects are apt to fall, if the distribution is normal. That is, it would require an interval from 2.62 pages to 12.02 pages to encompass the accomplishments of two-thirds of these subjects, assuming a normal distribution. The standard deviation gives a numerical value to the obvious scatter in performance. The variance, reported here, is harder to grasp. Variance is simply the standard deviation squared. While used for further analysis, it is seldom reported as an indication of scatter. A variance of 22.4 seems very large. To interpret it, the reader needs to reduce the number to the ordinary unit of measurement by extracting the square root, the standard deviation. To save the reader this mental effort, scatter is generally described by the standard deviation.

TABLE 3
DISPERSION IN NUMBER OF PAGES OF "STATISTICAL ANALYSIS"
READ BY A SAMPLE OF 191 SUBJECTS

Range	14.0
Variance	22.4
Standard deviation	4.7
Semi-interquartile range	8.3

The wide scatter in the performance measured here is further documented by the semi-interquartile range. One-half of the range of the middle 50 percent of the subjects was more than eight pages.

Describing Association among Measurements

In many studies, interest centers on the relationship between variables. Does the client's dependence on the agency tend to increase with more prolonged service? Do adolescents tend to use neighborhood centers less as they grow older? Whether or not one set of measurements shows a systematic relationship with a second series of scores is of considerable practical importance. The discovery of association may provide insight into cause-effect relationships, on which all science is built. Moreover, measures of association index our ability to predict. That is, they show how much our knowledge of one variable reduces our uncertainty about another variable.

Picturing association. Association may be described in two general ways, pictorially and numerically. The pictorial method demands only a simple elaboration on the routine plotting of frequency distributions. Let us assume that we have measured the age and weekly attendance rate for a group of students who use a women's center; that is, we have secured paired measurements (age and frequency of contact) for each subject. Instead of picturing these scores in separate charts, we could easily set up a two-way frequency distribution or scatter diagram by placing one variable along each axis. In this way, each pair of measurements is represented by a single point. The results could look like figure 3, figure 4, or figure 5.

The distribution of the points in a *scattergram* give a picture of the shape, strength, and direction of association. In figure 3, the points fall near a straight line, indicating a *linear* association between participation

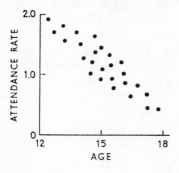

FIGURE 3.
AN EXAMPLE OF LINEAR ASSOCIATION

and age. In figure 4, however, we see a *curvilinear* relationship between age and weekly attendance rates. That is, the change in one variable does not bear a constant relationship to the change in the second variable. This figure shows that attendance diminishes with age among early adolescents but that it increases with age among the older adolescents.

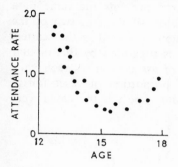

FIGURE 4.
AN EXAMPLE OF CURVILINEAR ASSOCIATION

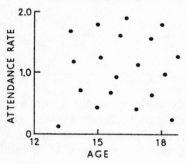

FIGURE 5.
AN EXAMPLE OF INDEPENDENCE

The strength of the relationship between variables is indicated by the extent to which the points on a scatter diagram cluster around a single smooth line drawn to approximate them. Figure 3 and figure 4 depict a strong relationship between variables, while figure 5 shows no systematic clustering along any line. Figure 5 is a graphic presentation of *independence between variables*; age and attendance show no relationship to each other. Put another way, a subject of fifteen could show any rate of attendance; knowing her age tells you nothing about the other variable.

The *direction* of association between variables is indicated by the slope of a line which would best approximate the position of the points. In figure 3, we see that increase in age is associated with decrease in attendance.

This is a picture of a *negative* association, an *inverse* relationship. A *positive* association would create a line running from the lower left of the figure to the upper right of the figure, termed a *direct* relationship.

A less detailed picture of association can be obtained by constructing a *contingency table*, which is really only a simplified scattergram. The two-by-two contingency table shown in table 4 presents the same data offered in figure 3. The concentration of the distribution in two of the four cells conveys some of the same information presented in the scattergram; that is, a strongly *negative* association is suggested by this tabular organization of the data. In contrast, a *lack of association* between variables would show itself by having the same proportion of cases fall in each of the four cells. This is what one would expect if the cases were distributed at random or by chance.

TABLE 4
FREQUENCY OF PARTICIPATION IN A WOMEN'S CENTER, BY AGE

	Age	
Frequency of Participation	Below 15	15 and Above
Less than once weekly	2	9
Once weekly or more	12	3

It should be evident that the contingency table is simply a two-way frequency distribution in tabular form. Each pair of measurements was represented by a point in the scattergram. The points falling within a designated area have simply been totaled and the numbers of points entered to form the contingency table. It must be obvious that a contingency table of any desired number of cells may be constructed. As with tabular presentation of simple frequency distributions, contingency tables represent a compromise between simplicity and precision.

Numerical Description of Association

Reduction in predictive error. The above pictures of association, in graphic or tabular form, provide the basis for an impressionistic appraisal of the joint occurrence of events. In order to achieve greater clarity, it is useful to supplement a picture with a numerical index of some sort reflecting the strength of the association. When the data are in the form of categories (nominal scales), an index of their association can be found through measuring the gain in our ability to predict a score on one variable from knowing what the person got on a second. For example, from the data in table 4, a prediction of participation could be made on the basis of the attendance rates alone. Of course, the best prediction for any one subject chosen at random would be "once weekly or more," the modal category. This prediction would obviously yield a number of errors or misclassifications. But if we already knew the age of the subject, errors in predicting attendance rate would be substantially reduced. Several measures of association show such a reduction in predictive error.

Lambda (λ) is an easy-to-calculate index of association for nominal categories. Varying from zero to 1.00, it reflects the gain in predictive accuracy resulting from the strength of relationship between joint classifications. In the above instance, a $\lambda = .58$ was obtained. *Tau* (τ), developed by Goodman and Kruskal, uses a different basis for computing expected error that is better suited to unbalanced distributions. It, too, ranges between zero and 1.00 and indexes the amount of reduction in predictive error.

Neither *Lambda* nor *Tau* takes advantage of the fact that the data in the illustration were partially ordered. Because the categories are ordered, a more *powerful* measure of their association can be used. *Gamma* (γ), the predictability of *order* among pairs of cases, takes advantage of these data. In its simplest form, for a two-by-two table, *Gamma* reduces to Yule's Q (the ratio of the difference between products of diagonal frequency to the sum of those products). Both *Gamma* and Q range in value between -1 and $+1$. For the problem above, a value of $-.89$ was obtained; the value is interpreted as the percentage of guessing errors eliminated by using a second variable to predict order in the first, while the *negative sign* is interpreted as it is for most correlation coefficients (see below).

Correlation indices. The association between two variables is frequently described by a mathematical abstraction, a coefficient of correlation. Most correlation coefficients indicate the strength and direction of linear association. Because a curvilinear relationship is underestimated or even undetected by an index designed to reflect straight line association, the measure of association should be selected to fit the shape of the actual distribution.

Measures of linear correlation are designed to yield scores that vary from -1 (perfect negative association) through 0 (no relationship) to $+1$ (perfect positive relationship) in value. The sign connected with a coefficient of correlation indicates the direction of association—it tells whether an increase in one scale accompanies an increase or decrease in the other scale. The size of the coefficient is an index of the strength of the relationship.

As with measures of central tendency and scatter, association can be expressed by a variety of techniques. The most sensitive measure of linear correlation for interval measurements is the *product moment correlation coefficient* (r) described in any statistical text. The *rank* difference correlation measure (*rho*), easier to compute in small samples, is appropriate for ranked data. In addition to these standard measures of relationship, there are a variety of techniques which allow the matehematical description of association in special situations. To measure the relationship between a variable, such as participation, and an attribute, such as sex (which could only be classified on a nominal scale: male-female) the *point biserial coefficient* (r_{pbi}) of correlation may be calculated. If both variables are dichotomous, such as right-wrong, the *phi coefficient* (ϕ) can be used to reflect the association. If a variable which is basically continuous has been artificially dichotomized, such as old-young, and the second variable is continuous, the *biserial correlation coefficient* (r_b) is an appropriate measure. A specialized but highly useful simplified measure of association is the *tetrachoric correlation* (r_t), easily computed if underlying normally distributed measurements are dichotomized around medians. The *correlation ratio* (*eta*) is the appropriate measure of association between variables when their relationship is not linear. Almost all linear measures of correlation vary between -1 and 1; the interpretation of all of these indices of association is similar. Weak correlations cluster around zero; strong correlations approach 1. Measures of nonlinear association are generally unsigned values.

The size of the correlation is an index of the strength of the relationship. However, the size of the correlation does not directly show the portion of variation on one scale that is explained by the other scale. A correlation of .5, for example, accounts for only 25 percent of the variation in scores. To convert a correlation coefficient to an estimate of reduction in predictive error, it is necessary to square the correlation coefficient.

DRAWING INFERENCES FROM DATA

The Logic of Statistical Inference

The problems. Accurate description of data often gives some clue about their meaning. Description alone, however, frequently fails to provide the basis for the interpretation of measurements; that is, the meaning of data is often not immediately apparent. This unhappy circumstance is the result of two basic and related problems which characterize many studies. Since these problems determine the logic of inferential statistics, they must be explicitly considered. Our interest is almost always in learning about a population or universe, but our object of study is usually only a sample.

For building a science, the individual case of a school phobia, for example, is of only incidental interest. For accumulating a body of verified, synthesized, and communicable knowledge, any comparable case or group of cases would serve as well. Our interest lies in learning about the universe of school phobias, for instance, and one "representative" sample of this universe could be as usable as another. Since we are almost never in a position to study all cases of this class, our point of access is the sample, a subset of the universe.

Thus far, we have considered a number of statistics, such as the mean, standard deviation, and correlation coefficient. *Statistics* are descriptive statements about samples. *Parameters*, on the other hand, are descriptive statements about populations. To restate, a problem which characterizes much of our work in research is that we want to learn parameters but must work with statistics. This situation would constitute no special stumbling block except for one additional fact—samples do not perfectly represent the universe from which they are drawn.

If, in a population of one hundred clients, fifty clients were pleased with the agency's service and fifty were not, a small sample, e.g., five of the cases selected for follow-up, might contain only those who were dissatisfied. Admittedly, this would be unlikely, but a less extreme misrepresentation of the universe would be well within the realm of probability. The fact is that, in the behavioral sciences, any given sample is not likely to be a perfect representation of the universe.

Solution to the problem of sampling variability: repeated sampling. There is one way out of the problem posed by sample misrepresentation or sampling variability. Instead of drawing one sample, we can draw repeated random samples from the same universe. By "random sample," we mean that each client had an equal chance to be selected. In repeated random samples, errors would tend to balance each other. On the average, we would get as many which overrepresented client enthusiasm about the agency as samples which underrepresented client acceptance. Further, we would expect only a small proportion of these samples to contain only satisfied or only dissatisfied clients; most samples would contain some mixture. Actually, *the distribution of the means of a large number of such samples would be close to a normal distribution.* If the opinion of the population were truly fifty-fifty, most of the samples would be divided equally or almost equally in opinion; few would be extreme misrepresentations of the universe. More important, the mode of this sampling distribution would approximate a parameter. Repeated random sampling, if extensive enough, would provide knowledge about the relative proportions in the universe. When the population parameters are unknown, which is the usual case, we can reverse this logic and draw inferences from the samples to the population. Thus, knowledge of the form of the *sampling distribution* is very important, for it enables us to infer the parameters of the population.

Use of a statistical model. Repeated sampling is an uneconomical and often unavailable method for determining a parameter. The concept of the sampling distribution, however, allows us to *estimate* a parameter from a single set of measurements. The estimated parameter lacks precision and certainty. However, the risk involved in such an estimation is determinable. For example, assume that the tabulation of the incomes of a single sample shows a mean income of $4,500. By using only the sample data, we could estimate that the mean of the universe probably falls between $4,409.84 and $4,590.16; moreover, the odds are nineteen to one that this interval would encompass the mean of the universe. The logic of such inferences rests on the properties of the normal curve; a brief detour to review this concept is in order.

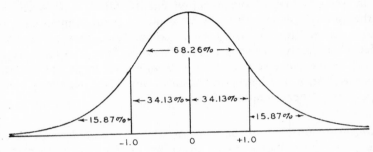

FIGURE 6.
NORMAL CURVE SHOWING PROPORTIONAL DIVISION OF AREA CREATED BY ORDINATES ERECTED AT A DISTANCE OF ONE STANDARD DEVIATION.

The normal curve. The normal curve is a symmetrical curve in which the mean, median, and mode coincide. The height of the curve declines slowly at first on either side of the mean, then rapidly, then slowly again. The tails of the curve never touch the base line; in principal, its range is unlimited.

In the *normal curve* shown in figure 6, the distances on the base line are expressed in terms of standard deviation units. This form has the advantage of allowing a comparison between the *theoretical model* and any obtained measurements, regardless of their particular mean and standard deviation. The characteristics of the normal curve are known, and tables have been prepared which allow easy use of the model. The tables designate the proportion of the total area which would fall on either side of a line erected anywhere along the base line. By consulting the table, one can determine the area falling between the mean and any cutting point, expressed in standard deviation units. Similarly, it is possible to determine the proportion of area between lines erected at any two points along the base. From the proportions identified within intervals such as these, statements about probability are derived.

Estimating parameters from statistics. If we drew repeated samples and calculated the mean of each, it would be easy to establish the variability, or standard deviation of these means. This variability, called the *standard error of the means*, can also be estimated from a single sample, because it is a function of the standard deviation of the sample and the size of the sample. That is, the standard error of the mean is estimated to equal the standard deviation of the *sample* divided by the square root of the number of cases in the sample. A sample mean, and from this an estimated standard error of the mean, can then be related to the normal curve to identify the range of values within which the population mean is very likely to lie. From knowledge of the areas of the normal curve, we know that 1.96 standard errors on each side of the mean will define the range within which 95% of the means of repeated samples will probably fall. We can thus conclude with 95 percent confidence that the population mean falls somewhere within that interval. To reduce the risk of misstatement, we could broaden the confidence limits to 2.58 standard error units and be 99% confident that the mean of the population would be included in this interval.

Let us return to the earlier example in which a mean of $4,500 was obtained from a single sample. The range within which the universe mean would be apt to fall was calculated by first determining a standard error of the mean. The estimated standard error was $46.00. Erecting confidence limits of 95 percent, or granting a 5 percent risk of error, we simply multiply the standard error by the number of standard error units (1.96) which will encompass 95 percent of the cases. Our result is a range of $90.16 on each side of the mean. From a single sample, we find that the mean of the universe will probably fall between $4,409.84 and $4,590.16, and we are assuming a risk of only 5 percent in this estimate.

Testing hypotheses about the population parameter. The logic used in estimating the interval within which a parameter may fall makes it possible to calculate as well the probability that a parameter will be of any fixed value we may elect. We can measure the distance between the observed mean and a hypothetical mean in standard error units and use the theoretical model of the normal curve to estimate probability. In practical terms, we simply calculate the number of times in a hundred the obtained sample would be drawn by chance from the hypothetical universe.

Testing substantive hypotheses: the null hypothesis. In addition to testing hypotheses about the compatibility of an obtained sample with hypothetical parameters, inferential analyses are used to test hypotheses about the relationship between two samples. A critical issue in much research concerns the significance of difference between two samples. In experimentation, for example, the difference between one sample (the experimental group) and another sample (the control group) is typically the major issue under study.

A statistical investigation of this issue is necessary because not every difference between samples is noteworthy. Some difference between samples would probably be found if they were randomly drawn from the same population. It is therefore possible that an obtained difference between samples reflects the random fluctuation of sampling rather than a true difference. That is, the study hypotheses must compete with a hypothesis concerning chance as an explanation for the evidence.

A hypothesis asserting chance, or sampling error, as an explanation for data is called a *null hypothesis*. For a comparison between two groups, the null hypothesis states that the obtained difference may occur through random error in sampling a common population. It is called the null hypothesis because the statistical investigation seeks to nullify it as an explanation. By calculating the probability that the evidence could have been drawn randomly from a single population, we can establish the tenability of this explanation. If a difference between samples actually obtained would rarely occur in repeated random sampling, the null hypothesis can be rejected and the study hypothesis retained. Only then is the difference between samples said to be *significant*.

Several of the more common tests for *significance of difference* between samples will be discussed subsequently. Here, it is pertinent to make clear that one method for determining significance consists of calculating, from the normal curve, the probability that scores drawn from a common universe will differ as much as the obtained measurements differ. All of the tests of significance involve the comparison of obtained scores by the use of some statistical model, of which the normal curve is one example.

Evaluating probabilities

Risks. It will be recalled that inferential statistics involve a degree of uncertainty, and that the conclusions reached contain some *risk*. For example, we may find that two samples will show an observed difference or a larger difference one time in twenty, by chance alone. The odds, therefore, are nineteen to one against the observed difference's being due to chance alone. However, the obtained measurements may represent the one time in twenty when sampling variability created an apparent difference. This fact highlights an important issue in inferential statistics. What weight of evidence should be demanded? How big a risk is appropriate? How good should the odds be before we take the results seriously? Should we accept a finding on odds of nineteen to one, or should we dismiss it as not supported by sufficient evidence?

Any decision to reject or accept a statistical hypothesis runs the risk of two kinds of error. These potential errors are so important that they have been given names. The first of these is known as a *Type I error*; it is the obvious one. A Type I error is the error of rejecting a null hypothesis when it is acceptable, i.e., taking chance results seriously. To reduce the risk of attributing significance to results which may be due to chance, it would be possible to set higher standards. We could, for example, decide to demand odds of 99 to 1, or even 999 to 1, against chance as an explanation for findings. In this manner, we would progressively reduce the risk of attaching meaning to chance results or of making a Type I error. However, we encounter a dilemma as we protect ourselves against this type of error. The more rigorous our demands become, the more we are likely to disregard "real" differences which fail to meet our arbitrary standards. The error of accepting a null hypothesis when it is wrong, i.e., dismissing a true difference as the product of chance, is known as a *Type II error.*

Balancing the risks. It is clear that, in evaluating evidence, we must find some reasonable balance in the risks of either accepting chance results as meaningful or ignoring important differences in our findings. That balance is formalized by specifying a region of acceptance and of rejection of the null hypothesis. Because, most commonly, our greater concern is decreasing the risk of a Type I error (attaching meaning to chance association), the odds are usually stacked in favor of accepting the null hypothesis. We demand a fair weight of evidence before we are willing to dismiss chance as an explanation.

In designating significance, we express conclusions in terms of *probability.* The results are said to be significant statistically if the probability that chance alone would account for the differences under consideration is lower than a selected value. The probability elected for designating significance thus controls the risk of a Type I error. In research, results are often described as "significant" if the probability that chance would explain the findings is less than five times in a hundred ($P < .05$) and "very significant" if the probability is less than one time in a hundred. On the other hand, some investigators report results which have a Type I error risk up to ten times in a hundred: ($P < .10$). When the risk exceeds the .05 standard, the results are usually described as showing "a tendency" to differ significantly rather than a clearly significant difference.

Determination of significance. The odds elected for assigning significance represent a region of acceptance and a region of rejection for the null hypothesis. If the results of the statistical test fall within the region of acceptance for the null hypothesis, we say that the difference may be due to variability found in random sampling. However, if the results fall beyond that region into the shaded area indicated in figure 7, we are willing to reject the explanation that sampling variability, i.e., "chance" alone, accounts for the difference.

Here, 95 percent of the area under the normal curve, falling between plus and minus 1.96 standard deviations, is taken as the region of acceptance within which chance alone may be accepted as an explanation for the differences in measurements. The 5 percent area, under the two tails of the distribution, is the region of rejection. Sometimes the discriminatory power of a test may be increased by placing the region of rejection in only one tail of the curve. This is done by stating a null hypothesis and an alternative hypothesis which specify the direction of expected differences. For example, if our interest were limited to deciding whether the mean age in sample A were greater than in sample B (rather than differing in

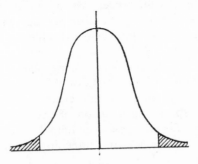

Figure 7.
The Two-Tailed Test of Significance for the Null Hypothesis: Mean 1 = Mean 2, or $M_1 - M_2 = 0$ in the population.

either direction), we would concentrate our test in one tail of the distribution and increase its power. Frequently, this allows us to reduce the risk of a Type II error without increasing the risk of a Type I error.

Overview of Inferential Techniques

Choice of statistical tests. Recent developments in the field of statistics have produced alternate techniques for testing objectively many of the hypotheses we encounter in social work research. It is important to know the alternatives available. Just as with descriptive techniques, there are more or less appropriate inferential techniques. Knowledge of the alternatives and the assumptions on which they rest will lead to a rational choice of the appropriate tool.

Tests of significance fall into two broad groups, designated as parametric and nonparametric. *Parametric* tests involve assumptions about the parameters of the population from which the samples were drawn; usually parametric tests assume an underlying continuous and normally distributed population. Additionally, parametric tests assume at least an interval scale. In contrast, *nonparametric* tests assume only that the underlying population is continuous or that there is a continuum underlying the measurements, without assuming that the population distribution is of a particular form. Further, nonparametric tests are applicable to nominal and ordinal scales as well as to interval and ratio measurements. Nearly all tests assume the sampling was random, as defined earlier.

As would be expected, the parametric tests, with their more rigorous demands on the data, are somewhat more powerful on the whole than nonparametric tests; that is, appropriate parametric tests are somewhat more likely to reject the null hypothesis when it should be rejected. Further, at present, certain complex inferential problems can be solved only by parametric methods. For these reasons, parametric tests are preferred when the data to be analyzed appear to meet the test requirements.

Although nonparametric tests are somewhat less powerful than those which make assumptions about the distribution of the population, they are probably more important to social work research than parametric techniques. Many of the scales with which we work are actually only nominal or ordinal. With crude measuring instruments, we are often certain that "A is greater than B, and B is greater than C," but we may not be certain how much greater A is than B, etc. For ranked data, and nominal classifications, no choice exists; only nonparametric tests are appropriate. Inferences drawn through the use of these techniques are exact and independent of the shape of the underlying population. An additional, rather important, appeal of the nonparametric tests is their simplicity. These tests are relatively easy to learn and to calculate.

Some theoretical models and their use. Reference has been made to the normal curve, a model basic to the estimation of probability. Through reference to the normal distribution, we may draw inferences about the significance of differences between two means, two proportions, and two correlations. However, the model of the normal curve is most applicable to large samples measured on interval or ratio scales. These are the very characteristics which are lacking in much social work research. In our field, greater use is made of three other distributions, designated as t, F, and *chi-square*. The t distribution, which resembles a flattened normal distribution, is accepted as a description of what is likely to happen to sample statistics when relatively small samples ($N < 30$) are drawn from an underlying normal population. By calculating a t ratio, we can draw inferences about the difference between two means, two correlations, and two standard deviations. F, named in honor of Fisher, is the distribution of variances among samples. Like the model of the normal curve, the t and F distributions are suitable for interval scales; all three are parametric models.

The most widely used nonparametric model is the chi-square distribution. It, too, consists of a series of distributions related to varying sample size. The chi-square model is basic to a series of nonparametric tests; probabilities about the difference between two medians, proportions, and correlations are derived from it. Variations based on the chi-square model make it a highly flexible technique adaptable to a wide range of problems. Specialized nonparametric models include the Mann-Whitney U test for the significance of a difference between two samples where data are in ranks, and the Kolmegorov-Smirnov test for the independence of two samples.

Examples of inferential technique. The simplest and most widely used statistical tools allow the comparison of two groups. The potentialities of the statistical techniques for such comparisons can be seen readily in examples. A problem may serve also as a review of the principles of inferential statistics thus far considered.

Significance of difference between means of independent samples. As part of a recent study, the educational priorities of social work students entering a practice sequence were explored. The students were asked to indicate their relative preferences for each of thirty items which sampled different content areas. The priorities they assigned to the ten items relevant to direct individual practice were summed, giving a mean score of 28.42 for the students enrolled in the regular sequence. However, it was found that the fifteen students enrolled in a new special intercity service sequence gave the same items a mean score of 32.40, indicating that the intercity project students placed a different priority on this content than did their classmates. It was necessary to investigate the meaning of this descriptive difference, because the aim of this research was to evaluate the new program against the ongoing program. Unless the students in each program were comparable at the beginning of their education, any differences in outcome could be due to differential selection rather than the effects of the program itself.

Is a difference in score of fewer than four units likely to occur on the basis of random sampling from a common population? To answer this question, we began by establishing a null hypothesis, that the observed differences could be accounted for by chance. Second, we selected a statistical test appropriate to the quality of the measurements and to the sample size. In this case, as often occurs, the choice of a test required thought. Because the partial rank ordering required by the questionnaire imposed a near normal distribution on each subject's array, it seemed acceptable to treat the summed ranks as interval data and to use Student's t distribution to investigate the null hypothesis. A review of the frequency distribution of the scores revealed that the measurements within each sample tended to cluster around the central values reported; a comparison on the basis of their means thus seemed appropriate. As the cluster around the means of both samples appeared similar, there was no reason to believe that the samples were drawn from nonnormal populations or populations with different variances.

A significance level was next elected. For this, the customary .05 level of significance was regarded as appropriate. By reference to the table distribution of t for samples of this size, we identified a region of rejection; that is, prior to conducting the test we knew the value of t which would be required to reject the null hypothesis.

The value was next computed for the t ratio of these samples. The t ratio is the ratio of the difference between means to the standard error of that difference. In this case, the difference between means, 3.98 units, was divided by 1.3, the standard error of the difference between values, calculated routinely from formulas found in any statistical test. The resulting t value of 3.06 fell within the region of rejection for the null hypothesis. It was concluded that the samples were not drawn randomly from the same population or that they were randomly drawn from different populations. The result of this statistical investigation was designated by the symbols: "$P < .05$ by t test"; that is, the probability that a difference this great or greater will occur by chance fluctuation in random sampling is less than five in one hundred.

The evidence that the two student groups differed in their initial educational orientation disappointed the investigator. Because direct comparison between the two groups of students could not be expected to clarify the influence of program differences, alternative ways of probing the study issue had to be sought.

Significance of difference in distribution. An example of the most widely used nonparametric test will show identical underlying logic. To check the hypothesis that participation in neighborhood self-help groups is related to the levels of aspiration—social and economic aspirations—of the members, the data shown in table 5 were collected. This illustration is drawn from a study of block clubs in Cleveland, Ohio, conducted by John Turner.

Does the participation status for the two aspiration levels differ so greatly that chance alone is unlikely to provide an explanation? Initially, we establish a null hypothesis that chance alone was operating here; that is, the differences in proportion of active and inactive participation of high and low aspiration levels is so small that chance alone would explain it. Next we select an appropriate test of significance. In this case the chi-square test seems most appropriate. Our interest is in testing the significance of difference in proportions. We have measurements drawn from an ordinal scale. The cases classified as active and inactive probably represent an underlying continuum, including cases which were extremely active, marginally active, marginally inactive, and clearly inactive. Where such a scale exists, dichotomization into active and inactive is suggested. A similar, underlying continuum may be assumed for the ratings of participation. To perform a chi-square test, one need not make assumptions about the form of the distribution of the underlying populations. Although the sample is a small one, there appear to be enough cases in each of the four cells to meet minimal standards for the chi-square test (an "expected frequency" of five or more in each cell).

Reference to the tabled value for chi-square for samples of this size identifies a region of rejection for the null hypothesis, at the .05 level of significance. Because we do not have sufficient basis to predict a *direction* of differences, we use the two-tailed test of significance.

For the chi-square test, the null hypothesis is made explicit in a parallel contingency table in which the numbers are redistributed as if chance alone had operated; that is, as if active and inactive participants were divided equitably among high and low aspiration levels. Chi-square involves the calculation of the difference between the observed frequencies, shown in table 5, and the *frequencies expected if chance alone were operative*. A short form of the test, for a four-cell contingency table as in this problem, makes the calculation very simple. The computation in this case yields a chi-square value of 4.2.

Reference to the tabled distribution of chi-square indicates that the value of this ratio falls within the region of rejection. This means that we

TABLE 5
BLOCK CLUB PARTICIPATION STATUS BY LEVEL OF ASPIRATION

	Aspiration	
Participation	High	Low
Active	12	5
Inactive	17	25

can reject the null hypothesis and accept as tenable the hypothesis that the two groups of clients were drawn from different populations or were not drawn at random from the same population. Our risk of error in this decision is 5 percent. A difference as great or greater than that seen in our samples could occur by chance alone not more than five times in one hundred. Participants tend to differ from inactive members in their levels of aspiration.

Analysis of variance. Analysis of variance is a system for sorting information into distinctive portions so as to address several null hypotheses simultaneously. Used chiefly in experimental inquiry where multiple groups are studied under multiple conditions, the statistic, an *F* ratio, yields a useful overall indication of whether anything systematic occurred. If so, the statistic also helps to locate the source of variance, according to its origin in study groups, in study conditions, or in the interaction between the study group and study condition. The concept of interaction designates a joint effort of two influences different from the effect of either influence acting alone. The capacity of this statistic to extract a measure of interaction distinguishes its yield from that obtainable by a series of *t* tests, for example. By means of statistical control, information can be abstracted from one set of data that would otherwise require a whole series of repeated experiments with minor variations.

The test assumes that the samples (preferably of identical size) have been drawn at random from a common population, that the measures are independent and are derived from interval or ratio scales, and that similar variance is found within each group.

Several nonparametric techniques parallel analysis of variance for measurements weaker than interval scales. The chi-square test accommodates the relationship of several independent groups measured on nominal scales. Where data consist of ranks, the Kruskal-Wallis H test provides a one-way analysis of variance. Where data are classified on nominal scales, the Cochran Q test for related samples may be used. For ordinal data, the Friedman two-way analysis of variance may be computed.

Other parameters. The logic used in drawing inferences about central values and dispersions is applicable also to measures of association. For convenience, the values of correlation coefficients significantly greater than zero are available in tables. The significance of the *difference* between two correlation coefficients can also be calculated.

Bayesian inferences. Classical inferential methods, surveyed in the previous section, combine obtained statistics with some statistical model in order to calculate the plausibility of a particular null hypothesis. The Bayesian extension of classical methods provides a system for supplementing the obtained data considered in drawing inferences and for calculating the compatibility of the sample with a range of parameters. In addition, Bayesian inferences lend themselves to the calculation of the risks and gains associated with acceptance or rejection of null hypotheses. Because this approach has been found useful in allied fields and appears to fit the social realities of our research, the investigator may find it a valuable supplement to classical inferential statistics.

Instead of a single calculation of probability, Bayesian approaches work with three separate probabilities. One is a *prior probability*, envisioned before the collection of new evidence is advanced; that is, the investigator draws on prior inquiry, theory, or even his own judgment to express mathematically his expectations about the true value of the population under study. In an earlier study of ten families of schizophrenics, three instances of marital skew were encountered. These data led to the prior probability estimate that marital skew will be found in about 30 percent of that population. In elementary Bayesian analysis, such evidence from a prior inquiry is reprocessed with the new evidence, a sample of fifty cases in which twenty instances of skew have been observed. That is, in a total of sixty families, twenty-three exhibited the phenomena of interest. From these combined data, a *posterior probability distribution* was obtained which located the parameter at 38 percent. The preliminary data were thus used in conjunction with additional evidence to calculate a posterior probability. In addition, a *likelihood function* or set of conditional probabilities may be calculated. The likelihood function expresses the probability that the sample information could derive from populations with a range of parameters. For making decisions about hypotheses, these probabilities can be weighted by a loss ratio, the expected loss associated with type I and type II errors. The conventional .05 level of significance is equivalent to assigning a loss value of 19:1 between type I and type II errors. Depending on the consequences of either error, different loss ratios can enter into scientific decision making. For example, research attempting to evaluate the efficacy of treatment by lobotomy, which presents a high cost associated with a type I error, may call for unusually conclusive proof of its effectiveness. Obtained data might appropriately be weighed by a loss ratio of 999:1. On the other hand, in evaluating the results of the service achievements of an AA program, the researcher may find that the loss associated with a type II error will deserve special attention. In view of the limited efficacy of alternative services and the negligible cost of a type I error, less conclusive evidence might well merit an endorsement of the program; a loss ratio of 2:1 might be adopted.

Although Bayesian methods are not yet available for routine application to all scientific problems, there is reason to expect that this obstacle will soon be overcome and that a Bayesian perspective will increasingly color our work. In particular, it challenges the investigator to clarify and state his prior expectations, to locate his original work in an ongoing process of inquiry, to view his findings as an addition to but not the final word on his subject, and to consider their implications in a social context.

These perspectives on data analysis fit well the stance shared by many investigators who perceive the derivation of statistical significance as less an outcome than a way station in responsible analysis. It has been widely recognized that statistical significance often corresponds poorly with social significance and, in fact, says only that chance is an unlikely explanation for particular findings. Consequently, it is usual to pursue analysis beyond the initial description and derivation of significance estimates to search for explanation and understanding. A number of analytic techniques are available to aid in the further examination of data.

DATA INTERPRETATION

When the results of a test of significance reveal that chance is an unlikely explanation for the observed data, the search can begin for understanding what systematic influences seem to be operating. And when chance *is* accepted as a likely explanation for the study results, the data can be examined for other clues about the study issue. One aim for such an analysis in either case is to check for the effects of confounding variables in the findings.

Confounding variables are influences that systematically, rather than randomly, accompany study variables. In an earlier example, the finding of a systematic difference between the learning priorities of two groups of students confounded a direct comparison of the results of the two programs they had entered. As in this example, much of the social behavior we study is far from random, but expresses instead constellations of interrelated influences. When the presence of confounding variables can be anticipated, the design can include provisions for their measurement, and the statistical investigation of their effects can then be undertaken. In addition, the data themselves can be used as a source for knowledge about unanticipated confounding variables.

Confounding variables may enter powerfully into the results of a test of significance, serving either to exaggerate or to minimize probability estimates. As a consequence, any outcome of a test of significance raises a question about whether the results speak to the study issue or instead to the effects of some systematic accompanying variable.

The search for possible confounding effects benefits from the interplay of knowledge about the study variables and about the data themselves. A reinspection of the data can be expected to reveal something about the sources contributing to significant outcomes or about the influences confounding the anticipated results. Reanalysis using purified subsamples and an inspection of extreme and deviant subgroups may provide additional clues about variables contained in the data. Clues derived from inspection and subanalyses, as well as directions gleaned from theory, may provide the basis for selective investigation of more complex interrelationship among variables.

Investigating the Relationship of Several Variables

Partial correlations. When there is reason to suspect that a correlation between two measures is influenced by a third variable, that possibility can be explored through the calculation of partial correlations. Partial correlations provide a method of controlling or holding constant one or more variables while examining the association of two others.

For example, delinquency rates in areas of a city may be found to vary with proximity to neighborhood youth centers. This association would not necessarily mean that youth centers were hotbeds of delinquency. The relation between these events might be the result of a third variable, such as the extent of deprivation in certain neighborhoods. If we control for the influence of this factor, the relationship between delinquency and agency-proximity may disappear. Partial correlations allow us to guard against a spurious association by nullifying the effect of an antecedent variable, without chopping up the data into small parts and having to compute independent correlations for each level of neighborhood deprivation. When one variable is held constant, the result is a first-order partial correlation. Two variables may be held constant, yielding a second-order partial correlation. Although partial correlation coefficients were originally derived for interval scales only, Kendall's partial correlation coefficient is a parallel measure available for solution of problems involving ordinal data.

Multiple correlations. A more common problem in research is the determination of the relationship between a dependent variable, like duration of client contact, and several independent variables considered simultaneously. Variables such as frequency of interviews, duration of the problem, and age of the client can be considered as influencing, to some extent, the duration of client contact. The coefficient of multiple correlation indicates the strength of the interrelationship, while controlling for the overlapping between the independent variables. For example, it is likely that age and duration of the problem may be correlated with each other. The overlapping effect here is taken into account in the calculation. The resulting coefficient indicates the proportion of variance in the dependent variable explained by the combined independent variables. The measurements, of course, must be derived from interval or ratio scales; there is no immediately parallel technique for ordinal scales, though Kendall's W yields an average of the correlations achieved across replicated rank orderings.

Factor analysis. Factorial methods provide an approach for discovering the intrinsic relationship among a number of variables; that is, factor analysis seeks to elicit underlying order to explain the relationships among measurements. The aim is to isolate a small number of factors or functional unities which account most economically and completely for the observed variability in measurements. The technique, which is appropriate for use with a large data pool drawn from refined interval or ratio scales, is differentiated from the investigation of multiple relationships in that it makes no prior assumptions about dependence and independence among variables. In this sense, it represents the least biased or most empirical form of statistical investigation. Although the approach has been advanced as appropriate for areas of study in which no firm hypothesis can be held prior to the investigation, the results of a factorial analysis are related to the adequacy and balance in the sample of data. Because of the demands of this powerful technique, it is less likely to be relevant to the post hoc exploration of available data than to the analysis of a study designed specifically with factor analysis in mind.

Use of a Statistical Consultant

To handle specialized problems that emerge in data analysis and interpretation, many investigators find it helpful to secure consultation. Such consultation is most likely to be useful when it is initiated at the design phase rather than after data have been collected. In making final decisions about the form and method of study prior to the initiation of data collection, one must make a review of the general plan for data analysis. At this point, a statistical consultant may be expected to help in plotting out the most efficient and objective route to the study goal. Because a study characteristically becomes more complex and confusing during data analysis, a blueprint of the major statistical steps to be taken will represent an economy of effort. And by anticipating the steps in data analysis, one can also check the efficacy of the planned system for retrieving and accumulating data. Time invested at this point often represents a considerable economy in the time required for subsequent processing of data.

In addition to contributing to plans for data analysis in the design phase, a statistical consultant may also be able to help determine the size of a sample needed. The pretesting and refinement of any measuring device may provide clues about the level of effects which will be reflected in the measurements. When it is possible to make guesses about the strengths of the effects under study, projections can be made about the number of cases needed to test the hypotheses adequately.

A statistical consultant may also be able to make a valuable contribution to dealing with some of the problems in analysis after data are collected. In general, the statistical consultant can be expected to save the investigator time and energy in selecting appropriate statistical programs, clarifying the questions each addresses, and appraising the results of statistical analyses.

Like the computer, the statistical consultant is best able to function as an aid to the investigator's understanding rather than as a substitute for it. A statistical consultant is usually not able to become familiar enough either with the data or with the theory underlying the inquiry to direct adequately the interpretive phase of data analysis. The investigator himself, who has a serious interest in extending his understanding of the study issue, is in the best position to use his knowledge of the data and of the substantive area in pursuit of the inquiry. And it must also be recognized that a statistical consultant is probably most able to help the investigator who needs him least. That is, a statistical consultant is most able to help the investigator who has acquired a working knowledge of statistics and can participate in an examination of data analysis issues.

It is hoped that this overview of data-processing possibilities will challenge the reader to extend his grasp of tools that can aid his efforts to learn from evidence.

References

Hays, W. L. 1973. *Statistics for the social sciences.* 2d ed. New York: Holt, Rinehart & Winston.

Koosis, D. J. 1972. *Statistics*. New York: Wiley.

McNemar, Q. 1973. *Psychological statistics*. 4th ed. New York: Holt, Rinehart & Winston.

Mueller, J. H.; Schuessler, K. F.; and Costner, H. L. 1970. *Statistical reasoning in sociology*. 2d ed. Boston: Houghton Mifflin.

Schmidt, S. A. 1969. *Measuring uncertainty: An elementary introduction to bayesian statistics*. Reading, Mass.: Addison-Wesley.

Siegel, S. 1956. *Nonparametric methods for the behavioral sciences*. New York: McGraw-Hill.

Wallis, W. A., and Robert, H. V. 1956. *Statistics: A new approach*. Glencoe, Ill.: Free Press.

Walsh, J. E. 1962. *A handbook of nonparametric statistics*. 2 vols. New York: Van Nostrand.

10
Applications of Computer Technology

William J. Reid

Major innovations in scientific hardware often appear to follow a certain pattern in their development and utilization. A device may be used initially by scientists to facilitate the kind of research they are accustomed to doing—the "normal science" of their discipline, to borrow an expression from Kuhn (1964, p. 10). As more sophisticated forms of the apparatus evolve, it begins to stimulate, and make possible, new areas of inquiry. Thus advances in the microscope have given rise to microbiology, and the development of the cyclotron has created new horizons for research in physics.

The computer may be following a similar course in social research. Since its introduction in the 1950s, it has been used primarily as a tool in conducting normal research, more specifically as an instrument for performing the calculations of the researcher. In this role the computer has functioned as an efficient but unobtrusive servant, used (not always wisely) to obtain a greater yield from the data produced by conventional designs.

The role of computers as supercalculators has continued to grow. At the same time, advances in computer technology and imaginative work in computer applications have begun to affect social research in more dramatic and substantial ways. Computers are now making possible forms of inquiry hitherto inconceivable.

This chapter is designed for the reader who wishes to gain a general orientation to the utilization and potentials of computer technology in social work research. We assume his needs can best be served by considering both the "old" and the "new" of computer applications in the field. To help him carry out typical studies of the present or to evaluate their products, we shall first consider how computers are used and misused in normal social work research. To help him understand, and perhaps participate in, emerging applications, we shall examine the newer uses of computers within two major contexts: information systems and clinical research.

The writer is indebted to two of his colleagues at the University of Chicago for their expert assistance with certain parts of this chapter: F. Dean Luse, for his help with the section on information systems; and Harold C. Bloom, for his aid with sections concerning computer programming.

COMPUTERS IN NORMAL RESEARCH

The critical role of computers in data analysis makes an understanding of their capacities and limitations essential to the researcher. A general knowledge of how computers work in normal research will also provide a basis for appreciating their potentials in new research applications.

The Computer-Centered Data-Processing System

Any use of computers occurs as a part of a larger system of data organization and processing—a system that is required in fact for computers to function. Divorced from such a system, the computer has no utility: it is simply a box of electronic circuits. We shall examine this system from the inside out, beginning with the computer and our means of instructing it.

Computers and programs. Computers may be viewed as data-storing and manipulating machines. (A very readable explanation of how computers operate may be found in Hamming 1972.) Their special advantages lie in their speed, accuracy, and economy. Since they perform their calculations with a rapidity approaching the speed of light, they can reduce to seconds computational tasks that would otherwise take days, weeks, or even longer to complete. Moreover, they perform these operations virtually without error. The "mistakes" attributed to computers almost invariably turn out to be the result of error elsewhere in the system. This combination of speed and accuracy results in enormous economy. For a few cents, a computer can duplicate what would be dollars' worth of computations if carried out by technicians on a hand calculator.

A computer performs its operations on orders from a *program*, which is basically a set of precise instructions supplied by the user. In this respect, the computer is not essentially different from a large variety of ordinary machines that we operate daily with simple "programs." For example, a soft-drink machine is programmed to provide a user with the product he selects and his correct change. The instructions given a computer are simply more complex.

The program provides the "language" to communicate instructions to the computer. Basic programs are written in special computer languages, such as FORTRAN (the one most commonly used for programming in social research). Since such languages are relatively complex and require some time to master, standard "program packages," which can be used with relatively simple instructions, have been developed. Two widely used packages are *Data-text* (Harvard University 1967) and the *Statistical Package for the Social Sciences* (Nie, Bent, and Hull 1970; illustrated below). Such packages permit users to carry out a range of standard analytic operations sufficient for most studies. Beginning facility with "canned" programs of this kind may be acquired through a few hours of instruction or directly from manuals.

Because researchers generally lack either the skill or the time to do their own programming, they usually employ programmers. Typically, the researcher tells the programmer in ordinary language what he wants from the computer. The programmer, in turn, tanslates these instructions into a computer language and puts the resulting program and the researcher's data into the computer. To do the job adequately, the programmer should have a working knowledge of the statistical methods being applied to the data. Ideally, he should be able to suggest ways in which the data can be analyzed so that the computer can be used to best advantage. If both the researcher and the programmer lack adequate statistical knowledge, the services of a statistical consultant with expertise in computer utilization may be needed.

Data processing. Not only must instructions about what is to be done with the data be translated into computer language—the data themselves must be put into a form that is acceptable to the computer, that is, into numerical form. (Data must be in this form for *digital* computers, the type generally used in social research.) This requirement brings additional actors and processes into the system.

If the raw data are in nonnumerical form, as in the case of answers to open-ended questions, the data must be categorized and numerals assigned to each category. Or, the raw data may already be in numerical form, as in the case of scaled ratings. In either case the numerals are then transposed to special sheets of paper (code sheets).

These processes are carried out by coders. Highly trained, knowledgeable coders may be needed to categorize unstructured data. The transposition of numerals onto coding sheets requires only clerical skills. Code books must be devised to instruct the coders on how the data are to be reduced to numerical form and recorded for further processing. More generally, the code book provides the basic informational link between the raw data of the study and the digits used by the computer.

The numerals on the code sheets are then usually "punched" onto cards by a key punch operator. For example, a "4" in a designated column on the card is "punched out" if the code sheet specifies a "4" for that column. This is a fairly rapid process: a skilled operator can keypunch 100 to 125 cards (each containing 80 columns of information) per hour. (The steps described thus far are not unique to computer-centered systems. More primitive data-processing systems, using such devices as counter-sorters and McBee cards, also require data to be coded in numerical form and transposed onto cards.)

A common shortcut in these operations is the precoded instrument. Numerals standing for given responses can be circled, checked, etc., by interviewers or respondents, and instructions to the key punch operator can be printed on the instrument itself, thus eliminating the step of transposing these data to code sheets. Even keypunching can be eliminated (though often at extra expense) by equipping the computer with devices to "read" pencil marks or even handwritten numerals on precoded instruments. Precoding is possible only with highly structured instruments and may not be worthwhile if last-minute changes in the items are a possibility.

After the data have been punched on cards they are "fed" into the computer, along with control cards which instruct the computer to perform whatever operations are desired. This step is accomplished by placing the cards in a "card reader" which translates the punches on the card into electronic signals and stores them for subsequent use. Once the data have been run in accordance with the desired programs, the results are printed out on a high-speed printing device attached to the computer.

The process usually does not move so rapidly or as smoothly as this summary may have suggested. One usually has to allow at least a day or two for programming, delivery of the data to the computation center, waiting for access to the computer, and retrieval of the final print-out— if all goes well. Frequently, jobs have to be rerun because of programming errors or misunderstandings between the programmer and the researcher. While "computer time" may be measured in milliseconds, the time it takes to use a computer is usually measured in days.

An illustration. The operations we have described will be illustrated by "tracking" a set of data through a computer-centered data-processing system. The example will also introduce additional detail on man-machine communications.

The data from which the example is drawn consist of the results of research interviews conducted with adolescents who had sought help at an agency serving primarily runaway youth (Fortune and Reid 1973). One of the informal hypotheses posed in the study was that runaways are more likely than nonrunaways to have had disagreements with their parents concerning rules and responsibilities in the home.

To test this hypothesis through computer analysis, it was necessary to assign numerals to the relevant data. Coders were instructed to designate *runaways* as *1* and *nonrunaways* as *2* on the coding sheets, basing their judgments on information about each adolescent's status when he applied to the agency and a definition of what constituted a runaway. In the research interviews, the adolescents were queried on problems in their relationship with their parents. The adolescents were encouraged to talk freely about these problems and their responses were probed by the interviewers. Coders then listened to tape recordings of the interviews and made judgments about whether or not given kinds of conflict were mentioned by the subjects. Disagreement with parents about rules and responsibilities in the home was one of the types of conflict considered. If the coder heard that type of conflict mentioned as either a major or a minor problem, he recorded a *1* for presence; if not, he recorded a *2* for absence. In this way, measurements on 145 adolescents were obtained.

For each adolescent, then, there were numerals signifying whether or not he was a runaway and whether or not he mentioned conflict around rules and responsibilities in the home. These numerals, together with an identifying number for the adolescent and, of course, a large number of other numerals signifying other kinds of data similarly coded, were punched on cards in the manner described above.

The programmer was asked, in effect, to carry out a particular analysis that would determine how the runaway and nonrunaway adolescents differed on this type of conflict. Since both variables were categoric, it was decided that a cross-tabulation was the proper statistical technique for testing this hypothesis. The program chosen was the Statistical Package for the Social Sciences (SPSS) (Nie, Bent, and Hull, 1970).

The programmer's task was to write the control statements that would allow SPSS to perform the desired calculations. These control statements contain such information as the names of the variables, their locations on the punch card, the number of cases in the data deck, and the type of desired statistical analysis. A simplified program and a description of what each control statement does follow:

RUN NAME   CROSSTAB OF RUNAWAY STATUS BY CONFLICT OVER RULES

This statement provides a title to be printed out at the top of each page of output. (Each statement is typed out on a card in English. The key punch machine automatically translates and punches the letters into a numeric code.)

VARIABLE LIST   RUNAWAY, CONFLICT

Tells the program the names of the variables to be read in.

INPUT FORMAT   FIXED(3X,F1.0,F1.0)

Tells the program to ignore the first three columns (used for the case identifying number), and that the variables RUNAWAY and CONFLICT are in columns 4 and 5.

VALUE LABELS   RUNAWAY (1) YES (2) NO/CONFLICT (1) PRESENT (2) ABSENT

Assigns labels to the values of the two variables.

OF CASES   145

There are 145 cases in the input data deck.

CROSS-TABS   CONFLICT BY RUNAWAY

Asks the program to perform a cross-tabulation of CONFLICT by RUNAWAY.

READ INPUT DATA

Signifies that the data cards immediately follow.

FINISH

Signals the end of this particular SPSS computer run.

After the SPSS program has been invoked, the control cards and data cards are read by the program, the cross-tabulation is computed, and the results are printed as shown below.

CROSSTAB OF
RUNAWAY STATUS BY CONFLICT OVER RULES

		CONFLICT OVER RULES			
		I PRESENT	I ABSENT	I ROW	
		I 1	I 2	I TOTAL	
RUNAWAY	1	I 35	I 42	I 77	COUNT
YES		I 44.5	I 54.5	53.1	ROW PCT
	2	I 17	I 51	I 70	
NO		I 25.0	I 75.0	46.9	
	COLUMN	52	93	145	
	TOTAL	35.9	64.1	100.0	

RAW CHI-SQUARE = 5.70922 WITH 1 DEGREE OF FREEDOM
SIGNIFICANCE = 0.02

As can be seen, the hypothesis is supported. The table has been simplified somewhat for purposes of presentation. Also, a dozen or so summary statistics following the chi-square data have been omitted. The table was actually one in a batch of about a hundred that were programmed (in an hour or so) and run off (in less than a minute) at the computation center.

On-line systems. We have described and illustrated the kind of automated data-processing system that social work researchers use today. The picture is changing, with greater application of newer devices for receiving and transmitting data and with the ever increasing capabilities of the computers themselves.

The technological advance with perhaps the greatest implication for social work research has been the development of data-processing systems which permit users to interact directly or "on-line" with the computer via remote access terminals (Kemeny 1972). Although the use of such systems is well established in many fields—most readers have seen them in operation in airline reservation counters—their impact is just beginning to be felt in social work and social research.

The typical terminal consists of a teletypewriter connected to the computer by telephone lines. Data and instructions can be "typed" directly into the computer on the teletypewriter, obviating the need for card punching. Results of analyses can be printed out on the same machine, on a printer attached to it, or on a higher-speed printer at the computation center or they can be displayed on a video apparatus with an accompanying photocopy, if needed. Moreover, these input and output processes can take place a considerable distance from the computer itself, eliminating not only the need to transport material to and from the computation center but also the usual requirement that a center be nearby.

Terminals are generally used with computers with sufficient capacity to operate on a time-sharing basis. In time-sharing systems, computers accommodate many users more or less simultaneously, rather than one at a time—thus the user can "interact" with the computer, obtain his results within seconds, and, on the basis of initial results, immediately instruct the computer to perform additional tasks. Some of the potentials of the interactive mode of computer utilization will be illustrated in the second part of the chapter.

If an on-line system had been used in the example of the study of adolescent runaways, the data on the 145 cases would have been typed (filed) into the computer's storage unit. Instead of instructing the computer through control cards, the user would guide the computer's operations through a teletyped dialogue which could begin (and could actually appear) as follows:

User: Get IDA.*

(After having previously typed an identification number to gain access to the computer, the user orders a particular package of programs.)

Computer: Good morning. IDA is ready. Need help?

(The computer informs the user that the requested program has been selected and asks him if he wants any explanation of it. The user can then ask for specified kinds of explanations or "prompts" which the computer will print out.)

User: No.

Computer: Mode of input: terminal or file?

(In this case the data are on file. Otherwise they could have been entered at this point.)

User: File.

Computer: Name of input file?

Such a dialogue, which so far has run about a minute or so, would continue until the variables had been named and the desired cross-tabulation run. Although holding a conversation with a machine may give one an eerie feeling, there is really nothing mysterious underneath it all. Statements as set forth in a manual are typed in by the user. They are automatically translated into numerical codes, as was done with the information on the punch card in the previous example. The computer is programmed

---

*"Interactive Data Analysis Package" developed by Robert Ling and Harry A. Roberts, Graduate School of Business, University of Chicago.

to respond in specific ways to all such statements—to carry out orders, give instructions, supply explanations, and so forth. One can think of the process as a machine-mediated interaction between users and programmers.

Research Applications

We have described the basic elements and processes of computer utilization. Now we shall consider how computers are applied to normal research undertakings in social work and some of the quandaries and problems involved in their use. Because most researchers still use "off-line" or noninteractive systems, our discussion will assume that level of technology.

Planning computer use. Although the computer is employed primarily in data analysis, how (or if) it is to be used must be considered during the planning stages of the study. If computers are to be used, then the researcher must make sure that relevant data can be cast into computer-acceptable form. This requirement, in turn, affects decisions about the instruments to be used and may even influence decisions about the design and questions of the investigation. Moreover, computer and programming costs usually constitute a sizable proportion of a research budget; these expenses must be planned for.

Decisions about whether or not to use a computer often arise, particularly in small-scale studies. There are no simple rules. The benefits in speed, accuracy, and possible complexity of analysis must be weighed against the time and costs of computer processing.

The quantity of data to be analyzed and the extensiveness of the analysis are the central factors to be taken into account (rather than the number of cases, as such, in the study). For example, if only a few simple analyses are to be performed with only a few items of information per case, hand analysis may be the more economical alternative, even with as many as a hundred cases. On the other hand, computer analysis may be the better choice if complex analyses are to be carried out with relatively large amounts of data, even if the sample is small. Such additional factors as the investigator's knowledge of programming and access to computer facilities also enter into the decision. Finally, it must be remembered that computer processing generally requires a cash outlay of some kind, at least for keypunching, computer time, and printing costs. Although the amount may be modest, any amount becomes a factor if the project has a "zero" budget, which is often the case in student research. Some schools of social work have small budgets for the computer costs of student research or are willing to make funds available on request. It is hoped that more schools will follow this pattern.

Often the investigator must decide whether to use the computer or hand methods to perform certain transformations of data preparatory to analysis, such as combining items into scales. For example, an instrument can be scored by hand and the scores entered into the computer, or the process can be carried out entirely by the computer. The temptation is to let the machine do such work. Before yielding, the investigator should consider the programming required for the necessary transformations of the data. Often seemingly simple manipulations require costly, elaborate programs vulnerable to programming errors and misunderstandings between the investigator and the programmer. Many times the job is more easily done by hand, particularly when involved manipulations are to be carried out on a modest amount of data.

When computers are used to do the bulk of the data processing in a project, there may be a tendency to ignore data that cannot be put into computer-acceptable form. Thus the investigator may have his interviewers ask working mothers an open-ended question to explore underlying feelings and attitudes about the child-care arrangements they use. A mother's responses may reveal some complex but identifiable patterns in her attitudes toward these arrangements. For instance, many mothers may say they are satisfied with the arrangement but at the same time manifest signs of guilt over not being at home with their children during the day. The investigator may not see this pattern in his review of a sample of responses to develop a coding scheme for computer processing or, if he does see the pattern, may decide it is too subtle to be coded reliably. In fact, the final coding scheme may well be some such simple reduction as: *degree of satisfaction with day care arrangements*: (1) very satisfied; (2) somewhat satisfied; (3) somewhat dissatisfied; (4) very dissatisfied. Easy for the computer to handle, but obviously superficial. A qualitative analysis of the responses may have detected a variety of patterns of this kind, but under pressure to put his data into a common, computer-acceptable mode, the investigator may well forego such analysis, perhaps with the intention (seldom realized) to do it "later on."

In this way the requirements of the computer may influence how data are treated and hence the findings and conclusions of the study. The decision to use the computer to do the bulk of data processing in a project does not mean that all the data must be handled that way.

Format for data analysis. If a computer is used, data analysis generally follows a certain format. One usually begins by obtaining frequency and percentage distributions for all the data on the cards. In addition to providing findings at a certain level, the distributions are used as a further check on coding errors and as a basis for planning additional analyses. Even though the "frequency print-outs" may run hundreds of pages and include information of little consequence, it is usually more convenient, and cheaper in programming time, to run "everything" than to be selective.

The kind of analyses then carried out will vary according to the research problem and the nature of the data but will generally consist of examination of relations among variables. This sort of inquiry is usually handled through already prepared or canned programs. The researcher specifies which variables he wants related and the method of analysis he wants. Then he (or his programmer) essentially instructs the computer to execute a stored program that will perform the desired analysis. If variables are to be cross-tabulated, then a cross-tabulation program is called for, as in the example given earlier; if they are to be correlated, then a correlation program is run, and so on. In addition to carrying out the analysis specified, the programs usually provide other information, such as the results of tests of significance and various measures of association.

With a large and increasing variety of canned programs available for use, researchers can readily carry out extensive, complex analyses that would be prohibitively costly if original programming had to be done. On the negative side, researchers tend to limit their analyses to available programs. Unless they possess (or can purchase) considerable programming skill, they are not likely to try to devise novel methods of statistical analysis.

Misuse of computers. The computer has made an incalculable contribution to data analysis. At the same time it has created, or aggravated, some problems. If computers are to be used to best advantage, researchers must be alert to ways in which they can be misused.

While computers have made the use of complex methods of analysis possible, they have, by the same token, made it easy for researchers to use statistical methods they do not fully understand. As a result, researchers may use methods inappropriately or may produce "findings" that they cannot properly interpret. In the precomputer era, investigators either did their own computations or had them done under their supervision; consequently they had a better grasp of what they were doing and tended to limit themselves to methods they knew reasonably well.

Ignorance of what goes into a method of analysis is no longer a barrier to its use. An investigator need know only that a method is generally relevant to his purposes. He can then call for its instant application. Thus he may whip his data through one or several factor analyses with only a hazy idea of the limitations of the technique or what the resulting printout really means. This kind of problem is regularly exposed in dissertation examinations when the student is unable to explain his more sophisticated methods. Fortunately, professional researchers do not have to undergo such detailed interrogations about their work.

It is probably unrealistic to expect either students or practicing researchers to understand fully the mathematical foundations or the intricate steps of methods of analyses the computer has made possible. A good working knowledge of the function and limitations of these methods seems to be a logical prerequisite to their use, however.

Another problem of the computer age may be seen in studies in which large quantities of data are collected and run through complicated programs "to see what turns up." Often the study questions and plan are poorly developed. The analytic prowess of the computer is expected to make up for deficiencies in problem formulation and research design. Sometimes it can, but usually the results are disappointing. More generally, the potentials of the computer can induce mental sluggishness in thinking through the problem to be studied, with consequent lack of focus in the analysis and findings.

The ease of conducting elaborate quantitative analyses can also lead researchers to carry their analysis beyond limits warranted by the quality of their measurement. Thus crude ordinal measures of phenomena may be manipulated as if they had the properties of ratio scales, or items may be arbitrarily combined through computer procedures into scales that have little inherent logic, and the scales may in turn be manipulated as variables. Or relations that are in fact curvilinear may be treated as if they were linear. Essentially the problem is lack of correspondence between what the original measures actually "map" and the mapping assumed to exist in the analytic models used in standard computer programs. One danger is the production of pseudofindings which may be artifacts of the "overapplication" of the analytic model. Another is that findings indicating lack of relations among variables may be interpreted literally to mean lack of association among the attributes measured, without taking into account the possibility that cumulative distortions in measurement and analysis may mask relationships which, in fact, exist. This kind of problem is not new to social work research. Our capacity to manipulate data has always exceeded our capacity to measure. Computers have widened this gap considerably.

With the computer's ability to digest endless quantities of data, analyses have become far more thorough. But this very thoroughness often makes it more difficult to distinguish between significant and chance results. The findings of primary interest in quantitative research are those which demonstrate a significant degree of statistical relationship between variables, such as in the example of the relation between runaway status and presence/absence of a particular kind of conflict with parents. Tests of significance are used to determine whether a given relationship is of sufficient magnitude to permit the researcher to reject the null hypothesis— that it is a chance occurrence.

As explained in chapter 9, a source of error in the interpretation of tests of statistical relationships "is taking chance findings seriously" (Type I error). The probability of Type I error increases in proportion to the

number of relationships tested; the greater the number of tests of significance that are run, the greater the likelihood that some of them will
produce spuriously significant results.

In the precomputer era, this problem, although serious, was controlled
by practical limitations on the number of statistical relations that could
be tested. The computer has removed this control. With a computer, it
takes only a little more effort and expense to examine a hundred relations
than a few. Increases in Type I error are thus inevitable. If researchers
then accept the significant results without taking into account the number
of tests that were run to produce them, as often happens, their findings
can be falsely interpreted.

EMERGING APPLICATIONS

Despite problems in their use, computers have been of enormous help to
researchers in pursuing their accustomed directions. But computers are
also creating new avenues for social research. These emerging applications
have been pushed ahead considerably by technological developments, in
particular on-line, time-sharing systems.

Rather than attempting to present an exhaustive review of how computers are stimulating novel approaches to research in social work, we
have decided to concentrate on two areas of particular importance: utilization of computers in agency information systems and in new forms of
clinical research. In examining these areas, we shall be able to consider
most of the major innovations that computers are bringing about.

Information Systems

Almost all social agencies routinely collect some form of data on their
clients and programs. The utilization of available agency data in social
work research was considered in chapter 5.

This kind of information is being collected in greater quantities than
ever before. The informational needs of agencies are growing in response
to demands that they provide a better accounting to their constituencies
(Reid 1974) and in response to the requirements of modern management
approaches, which place a strong emphasis on data in planning and decision making (Carter 1971). Computers are being used increasingly to
master these expanding aggregates of data. At the same time, the potentials of computer technology are stimulating agencies to collect greater
amounts and varieties of data, because computers enable agencies to use
such information much more effectively.

These trends are leading to the development of *information systems* in
which computers are used to process, store, retrieve, and analyze relatively
extensive data on the recipients, characteristics, costs, and outcomes of
agency services. Examples of information systems in operation or under

development can be found in most fields of social work practice: public assistance (Linnan 1971; Roache 1970); mental health (Cobb 1971; Kiresuk and Sherman 1968); family service (Child and Family Services of Connecticut 1972); corrections (Wenk, Gottfredson, and Radwin 1970); child welfare (Rothschild and Bedger 1974; Luse 1973; Jack 1972); and medical social services (Vanderwall 1972).

Information systems are making exciting new developments in both administration and research possible. Although the research side of these developments will be stressed here, the line between the use of information systems for research as opposed to administrative purposes is often difficult to discern.

Characteristics. An agency information system may be confined to a single organization or may span a number of organizations, such as state-funded mental health facilities or child welfare agencies in a particular community. Whatever its span, such a system can be described in terms of two essential features: its data base and its data-processing capability.

The more important is the data base, which defines the input for the system. Depending on the functions of the system, data may be collected on: (1) characteristics of clients or patients, sometimes including personal history information and results of diagnostic tests; (2) nature and costs of services or treatment; and (3) case outcome or disposition.

Data are normally obtained and recorded by line staff, although they also may be obtained directly from persons served by means of self-administered instruments or by research technicians through follow-up interviews or other methods. Whatever the means used, the data are *routinely* collected as a part of normal agency operations and *accumulated* over time, rather than being especially collected for limited periods, as is the case in usual research undertakings.

The data-processing capability of a system describes its capacity to convert its data base into usable forms. The methods of processing used are essentially those employed in the computer-centered data-processing systems described earlier. Because agencies may not have their own computers and because immediate data retrieval is of particular advantage, remote terminals connected to a time-sharing system are being used increasingly. An agency can rent a terminal and contract with a commercial computation center (service bureau) to pay for whatever computer time and storage it uses.

Once entered into the computer via the terminal, the agency's data are automatically stored. Stored data on each case or other unit can be readily updated or corrected as new information becomes available. In advanced systems using terminals and time sharing—the kind we have in mind in this section—stored information is at the user's fingertips. For example, all data accumulated on a given case or grouping of cases may be called for and printed out in seconds through a "direct access" search by the computer. Since he can interact with the computer through the terminal, the user can make successive inquiries, guided by the information he is receiving. He may also request that the system print out at regular intervals statistical tables containing specified kinds of data or, through a procedure known as "exception reporting," he may request, again at regular intervals, listing of cases that exceed certain limits—e.g., all cases that have been on a waiting list over one month.

An example. Childata is a multiagency information system developed under the auspices of the Chicago Council for Community Services (Rothschild and Bedger 1974; Luse 1973). A consortium of child-care agencies contribute data on each child under care. The data, initially recorded and updated on precoded forms by the caseworker, include demographic characteristics of the child and his family, diagnostic ratings of the child, type of care arrangement, services needed and planned, projections of adoption prospects, reasons for discharge, and outcome ratings (in terms of achievement of service goals). The data are then entered into a time-sharing computer system located in another city by means of a terminal in the Childata office. Retrieval of data and interaction with the computer are carried out at this terminal; results, including regular statistical reports, are sent to the participating agencies. (A next logical step would be for each agency to have its own terminal.) The system has been used by the agency staffs and by funding and planning organizations for such purposes as determining numbers and kinds of children awaiting adoption, types of services given to children with particular problems, the presence of service gaps, and the simple whereabouts of children under care.

Research potentials. Information systems are designed to produce data to answer questions put to them by users. It is difficult to say, in this process, when "fact finding" ends and "research" begins. Requests for information on individual cases or simple counts of cases in particular categories would probably not be considered research, but inquiries involving comparisons, say, of outcomes of different groups of cases, could be. The distinction is complicated by the fact that information systems permit users, including nonresearchers, to carry out fairly elaborate investigations without the usual collection and processing of data, that is, outside of the methodological frameworks within which research is usually conducted. Even if one objects to designating as "research" data retrieval and manipulation performed at computer terminals, it can hardly be denied that information systems can often enable users to achieve the *practical equivalent* of products yielded by conventional research undertakings.

In fact, information systems may frequently serve the data needs of users better than conventional research. There are several reasons why this may be so. (1) Information systems can make use of total data sets —for example, all clients served by a program since its inception; a study need not be restricted to samples. (2) Programs or other operations can be studied as they normally operate rather than under the exceptional conditions, or the spotlight, of special projects. (3) Data on interrelated elements can be examined simultaneously, thus permitting "systems-oriented" studies of agencies and programs. (4) Initial findings can be amplified readily through dialogues with the computer. (5) Results can be obtained far more quickly, sometimes in minutes as opposed to months or years— a critical advantage when research is used as the basis for short-range program planning or for responding to the emergency requests of fund-raising or legislative bodies. (6) Agency decision makers can ask questions directly of the information system when they want to and as often, a way of obtaining information that many of them would find infinitely superior to commissioning studies and collaborating with researchers.

Information systems clearly have the *potential* for delivering far greater amounts of useful data to agency decision makers than could ever be obtained through conventional research. Although few information systems are sufficiently advanced at present to realize this potential, a sizable number should be able to do so before the end of the decade.

Agency operations and agency-based research will change accordingly. Administrative approaches will become increasingly data-oriented, a trend already in evidence with the increasing utilization of "scientific management" approaches—management by objective, PPBS, systems analysis, and the like (Wiehe 1973; Lyden and Miller 1967).

The role of agency-based researchers will certainly be altered. An important function will be to help develop and operate information systems (Service, Mantel, and Reisman 1972). In carrying out this function, they will be designing and overseeing a perpetual "research machine" capable of producing an infinite variety of specific studies. In addition, they will use the information system to carry out, or assist with, more elaborate studies, particularly those involving more complex analyses of data. For example, multivariate programs can be used to assess the relative outcomes of alternative services while making statistical adjustments for initial differences in client groups treated by each; time series analyses can be carried out to determine changes in the amounts and kinds of service provided particular groups of clients; and so on. Despite their scope and complexity, such studies could conceivably be designed and completed in hours or days and at a fraction of the cost of comparable studies carried out through conventional methods.

The data base and hardware of information systems may also enable researchers to make use of computer simulations of program innovations (Fuller 1970; Sisson 1970). The essence of such simulations is to try out a projected innovation on the computer, making use of available data and certain assumptions. The benefits and costs of the innovation and its expected consequences for other components of the agency system can be estimated. Variations in the innovation can be systematically introduced and additional simulations run or alternative innovations simulated. The optimal plan for the agency's purpose can be selected—or it may be decided not to introduce any change at all. In short, simulations enable an organization to experiment on the computer before it commits its resources.

For example, suppose a family agency wished to eliminate its waiting list without sacrificing the quality of its service or restricting its intake. Let us assume that possible ways of achieving this end have been narrowed to two alternatives—increasing the number of caseworkers, or decreasing the amount of supervision of caseworkers, which would free the time of both supervisors and caseworkers for more direct service to clients.

Even if a computer or systematic information were lacking, some effort would normally be made to simulate these options, although it might be called "thinking through" the alternatives and might be carried out largely in someone's head or in a staff conference. Thus an attempt could be made to calculate the number of cases a new caseworker might take on or how much time would be freed for practice if time spent on supervision were decreased by a certain amount; various consequences, such as increased budget allocations for additional caseworkers, might be taken into account. The limitations of "scratch pad" simulations are obvious. There are seldom enough accessible data to make many accurate estimates; calculations become overwhelmingly voluminous and complex, as a large variety of factors are considered; and it is usually not feasible to develop a number of simulations based on different assumptions.

A computer simulation using data from an information system could carry the process much further. Projections of the case loads of additional workers could be based on data about productivity of new workers; the amount of time and money saved by a decrease in supervision could be calculated from data on how staff members allocate their time; and so on. Using such data, the computer could be programmed to answer such questions as how many new caseworkers would be needed, at what cost, to eliminate the waiting list if intake continued at the same rate. Obviously, such questions must be answered within the framework of certain assumptions, such as salaries to be paid for the additional staff and continuation of intake at past levels. In other words, the computer would generate *models* of given operations based on specified data and assumptions. Certain assumptions could then be altered—it might be assumed, for example, that intake during the coming year would double—and the model rerun. Clearly, such models would be only as good as the data and the assumptions. Important pieces of data may be missing, such as differences in outcome between supervised and unsupervised cases; and certain assumptions, such as the optimal quality of service, involve value considerations that cannot be reduced to quantitative terms.

Although computer simulations may leave many questions unanswered, they can serve as valuable tools in agency decision making. Their construction will become an important task for the researcher. When simulations are used, as in the example above, to test out alternative means of reaching some objective and involve consideration of how the alternatives may affect other parts of the organization, the job is more than a technical one. It requires a grasp of the interrelation among various components of the agency system and ability to organize data to show how these components may operate under specified conditions. That kind of study, appropriately referred to as a *systems analysis*, will be used increasingly with the development of automated information systems (see Blumstein, Kamrass, and Weiss 1970).

Finally, information systems can be utilized for research of a more theoretical nature. Much social work research, particularly the kind carried out in academic settings, is directed at testing hypotheses or answering questions that go beyond the interests of particular agencies. Because many of these investigations still make use of data on agency clients, practitioners, services, and outcomes, information systems can play an important role. In some cases, the data the researcher needs may already be within the system or he may be willing to tailor his needs in order to exploit the advantages of information systems research.

For example, suppose an investigator wished to determine the likelihood that offenders imprisoned for homicide would be returned to custody for the same offense during their first year of parole, and if this group were more likely to commit homicide than parolees originally imprisoned for some other felony, say, burglary. One can imagine an extensive study being conducted, requiring an elaborate sampling plan, coding of existing records, and possibly the collection of original data. If the study were nationwide in scope, data on thousands of cases would need to be obtained at a cost of thousands of dollars; several years might be required to do the job.

These questions were effectively answered through use of an information system which contained at the time over one hundred thousand records of individual parolees submitted by all fifty states, the great majority of which reported on their total parolee populations (Wenk, Gottfredson, and Radwin 1970). It was found, for example, that of all persons ($n = 4,177$) originally imprisoned for homicide, 1.9 percent were again arrested for murder during the first year, as opposed to 1.5 percent of parolees ($n = 15,620$) originally imprisoned for burglary. These questions were asked and answered in a few minutes' time. Computerized data files located in California were interrogated from a terminal in Massachusetts, as a part of a conference demonstration. Inquiries were typed in and results displayed on a video screen.

Limitations and problems. The most serious limitations on the usefulness of information systems for research are found in their data bases. The data needed to answer particular questions may not be in the base; if they are, they may be of poor quality. Since the bulk of data collection and reporting is usually carried out by agency staff as a subsidiary responsibility, data collection and reporting procedures must be relatively inexpensive (on a unit basis), uncomplicated, and not too time-consuming (see chapter 5). Since coding large quantities of data is quite costly, the information must usually be put into precoded, computer-acceptable form by those gathering it.

Given such constraints, data bases tend to be weighted heavily with things that can easily be counted or measured, such as biographical characteristics of the client, or with gross, unverified ratings of complex phenomena (such as case outcome) supplied by agency personnel, whose biases may result in serious distortions. Since data are normally collected without the controls of experimental designs, they usually cannot be used to establish the effectiveness of program inputs.

Such limitations are not totally irremediable, however. If data needed for research can be specified far enough in advance, they can be collected as a part of the system. The data base can be strengthened by obtaining routine follow-up information directly from recipients of service. The reliability of data can be ascertained and ultimately improved by cross-checking data from different sources, for example, by comparing practitioner ratings with client assessments or the practitioner's accounts of his treatment methods against tape-recorded samples of his interviews (see chapter 5). Moreover, there is no reason that research based on data from information systems cannot make use of certain experimental designs. For example, as Kiresuk and Sherman (1968) suggest, cases can be randomly assigned to alternative programs feeding data into the system.

Nevertheless information systems cannot be expected to supply all of an agency's research requirements. There will always be a need for studies that utilize more rigorous and innovative methodology than will ever be possible within the framework of information systems.

The use of information systems in research and management presents certain risks. The large aggregates of quickly retrievable data stored by computers are vulnerable to misuse. Noble (1971) has discussed threats to the confidentiality of the professional-client relationship and to the client's right of privacy posed by information systems in the health and welfare fields. The professionals may have cause for concern about their own status if bureaucratic hierarchies use information about their performance to enforce excessive compliance to "approved methods." Social agencies may run the risk of being judged unfairly, or of being judged without their knowledge, in comparisons based on information from multiorganizational systems.

Strong safeguards must be employed to control access to computerized information and the purposes for which it may be used. Different kinds of protections are possible. For example, the identity of client data can be disguised through code numbers; for many uses, including research, names of individuals are superfluous. Or agencies can control access to their own information even if it is a part of a multiorganizational system. Still, much work needs to be done, and much vigilance needs to be exercised, before we can ensure proper usage of the highly transmittable and often sensitive information on clients, practitioners, and agencies stored in computers.

Newer Applications in Clinical Research and Practice

Until recently, the computer has been used in clinical research, as in research of other kinds, almost exclusively as a tool in the analysis of large aggregates of data. Now other applications are beginning to develop (Abels 1972).

Many of these emerging research uses are related to increasing utilization of the computer in clinical practice, particularly for assessing and diagnosing clients and patients. For example, computers are being used to score and even administer and interpret diagnostic tests (Fowler 1969). Or they can place individuals in diagnostic categories, following programmed rules for evaluating the evidence submitted to them (Slettin et al. 1973; Spitzer and Endicott 1969). Computer processes employed for these purposes can also be used to generate data for research studies. Diagnostic and other data obtained from routine use of the computer in clinical work can be stored in information systems for subsequent investigations.

One of the more intriguing developments of this kind is the "automated questionnaire" used at the Stanford Medical Center (Stillman et al. 1969). The questionnaire is administered to psychiatric patients by an on-line computer. The computer prints out a question at the terminal ("Have you been hospitalized for mental problems?") and the patient then types out his response, usually "yes" or "no." A "branching" feature permits the computer to ask questions based on the patient's previous answers. For example, if the patient answered "yes" to the question about prior hospitalization, he would then be asked, "How many times?" If he answered "no," the computer would select the next question ("Do you feel sad or depressed?"), and so on. Sections of standard psychological tests can also be incorporated for all patients or given contingent on certain responses. In this fashion, data can be collected on each patient without expenditure of staff time. Complete uniformity in administration is ensured, as well as complete accuracy in recording results. This process may be impersonal, but that is not necessarily a disadvantage. A patient may be more inclined to reveal sensitive information to a machine than to a human interviewer and may well do so with greater comfort.

The development and application of this kind of technology in social work will become a new arena for research. Formerly content to generate schemes for categorizing clients, social work researchers will begin to attempt to construct computer programs which will make it possible to classify actual clients. Instead of just trying to demonstrate certain abstract relations between client attributes, treatment methods, and outcome, researchers will give their attention increasingly to devising means of providing practitioners with data-based probability estimates of outcomes to be expected if particular courses of treatment are pursued with given types of clients or in given case situations.

An example of work in this direction is reported by McEachern and Newman (1969). Their SIMBAD program simulates probable outcomes for a given juvenile offender under different disposition alternatives, such as institutionalization, foster placement, or returning home. The computer determines from stored data how offenders with similar characteristics have actually fared under different dispositions; on this basis, it calculates the probable outcome for the offender in each kind of disposition. Correction workers can ask for and obtain such outcome probabilities at a terminal in an on-line system.

In addition to their diagnostic and prognostic functions, computers are beginning to assume roles in the conduct of ongoing treatment and in research on the treatment process. In certain treatment approaches, such as behavior modification, the practitioner's interventions are guided by detailed observations of the client's behavior. Since these observations must be coded and analyzed quickly, computers can be used to excellent advantage. In one social work project (Thomas, Walter, and O'Flaherty 1974), problems exhibited by marital partners in live interactions are coded directly into the computer by an observer. In addition, the computer records other events, including duration of each client's responses and light signals by the therapist to express approval (green light) or disapproval (red light) of particular interchanges between the clients. Through computer analysis of the data, the therapist-experimenter gets rapid feedback on the effect of his signaling on the communication problems the partners are exhibiting in their interaction.

Clinical and research applications of this kind of technology to other treatment approaches can be readily imagined. Through terminals and other remote input devices, almost any kind of direct observations of client behavior or treatment interactions can be coded into a computer. In addition, the computer can record, by means of electronic signals, a range of reactions from workers and clients as they occur in treatment. Any data so received can be instantly analyzed or stored indefinitely.

There are any number of applications of computer technology in "pure" research on treatment processes, that is, research not carried on as part of a therapeutic operation. Let us mention two briefly.

One is the use of computers to carry out content analyses of recorded verbal communications among practitioners and clients in treatment situations. The communication of the participants, taken from narrative or tape recordings, can be punched directly on cards or into terminals. The computer is programmed to code or classify words or other units of speech according to a "dictionary." Thus, use of the first-person pronoun can be categorized as references to "self." Or particular sequences of words can be classified according to particular rules. Special purpose dictionaries, some of which have been used in the study of the processes of psychotherapy (Psathas, Cleeland, and Heller 1966), have been developed. A number of such programs have been assembled in one package —the General Inquirer (Stone et al. 1966). Whatever is coded can be analyzed rapidly and exhaustively by the computer.

A good deal of effort has been devoted to the analyses of the communications content in casework (see chapter 5). Much of this work, particularly the classification of complex treatment techniques, is beyond the present capabilities of automated content analysis. Nevertheless, there is still much here that computers may be able to do, such as identifying topics of discussion dwelt on by caseworker and client, and defining patterns in the practitioner's style as they may be revealed in the words he uses. Although the computer may analyze treatment content at a distressingly low level of abstraction, human judges operating at high levels of inference often produce data of distressingly poor levels of reliability.

The other development is the use of computers to simulate either the practitioner or the client in therapeutic interviews. The simulated interviews are conducted over terminals. If the client is being simulated, the practitioner types in his responses at a terminal and the computer prints out its replies; the client uses the computer in a similar fashion if the practitioner is simulated. The following excerpt is taken from an interview between a human interviewer and a simulated client (Starkweather 1968, p. 17):

Practitioner: What brings you in to see me today?
Computer: Well, my wife wanted me to come.
Practitioner: Go on.
Computer: It's not my idea, that's for sure. She told me I ought to see a psychiatrist. She said—she said she was going to leave if I didn't go.

Practitioner: Do you have any reason yourself for coming?
Computer: Hell, I don't know what to tell you. Ask me some questions. Then maybe you can figure out what's the matter.

Such simulations are based on the same principle used in automated content analysis. The computer is programmed to identify and code speech units in the communication of its human partner, as in content analysis, but in addition it prints out replies keyed to particular units. As the example illustrates, the resulting dialogues may be difficult to distinguish from the real thing.

The utility of the simulated interview for clinical learning is obvious, and its uses in clinical practice can easily be imagined, but what of its research potential? In general, simulated interviews permit study of the communications of practitioners and clients in treatment under conditions that are both controllable and begin to approximate the complexities of the interactional systems in which such communications occur. For example, there have been a number of studies of caseworker reactions to simulated clients, usually presented on paper, tape, or film (Reid 1966). The "client" presents a certain stimulus situation and the practitioner is asked to respond; it has not been feasible to ask what the practitioner would do next if the client reacted in a certain way. The computer can bring the simulated client to life by having him react. In this way, we can examine sequences or chains of practitioner interventions and how they may be altered by different kinds of feedback from the client.

These newer applications of computers to clinical practice and research are still highly experimental and largely confined to the fields of psychiatry and psychology. But here, as with other kinds of applications of computer technology, there is nothing to be gained by waiting until new developments trickle down into social work research. By trying these applications ourselves, we can bring the future a great deal closer to the present.

REFERENCES

Abels, P. 1972. Can computers do social work? *Social Work* 17:5–11.
Allen, B. R., and Horniman, A. B. 1969. *Child welfare and the computer: A projection of potential.* New York: Edwin Gould Foundation for Children.
Blumstein, A.; Kamrass, M.; and Weiss, A. B., eds. 1970. *Systems analysis for social problems.* Washington, D.C.: Washington Operations Research Council.
Carter, G. W. 1971. The challenge of accountability: How we measure the outcomes of our efforts. *Public Welfare* 27:267–77.
Child and Family Services of Connecticut, Inc. 1972. A service evaluation and information system for mental health and social services (SEVIN). Mimeographed. Hartford, Conn.

Cobb, C. W. 1971. A management information system for mental health planning and program evaluation: A developing model. *Comm. Mntl. Hlth. J.* 7:280–87.

Colby, K. M. 1966. Experimental treatment of neurotic computer programs. In *Psychotherapy research: Selected readings*, ed. G. S. Stollak, B. G. Guerney, Jr., and M. Rothberg, pp. 670–80. Chicago: Rand McNally.

Curran, W. J.; Laska, E. M.; Kaplan, H.; and Bank, R. 1973. Protection of privacy and confidentiality. *Science* 182:797–802.

Donohue, J. F. 1969. Computer-based study of mental retardation. *Computers and Automation* 18:50–52.

Eiduson, B. R.; Brooks, S. J.; Motto, R. L.; Platz, A.; and Carmichael, R. 1968. New strategy for psychiatric research, utilizing the psychiatric case history event system. In *Computers and electronic devices in psychiatry*, ed. N. S. Kline and E. Laska, pp. 45–58. New York: Grune & Stratton.

Fortune, A. E., and Reid, W. J. 1973. *Through the looking glass: Reflections on runaway youth.* Chicago: Travellers Aid Society.

Fowler, R. D., Jr. 1969. The current status of computer interpretation of psychological tests. *Amer. J. Psychiatry* 125:7, January supp., pp. 21–28.

Fuller, R. K. 1970. Computer utility in social work. *Social Casework* 51: 606–11.

Hamming, R. W. 1972. *Computers and society.* New York: McGraw-Hill, Paperback ed.

Harvard University. 1967. The data-text system: A computer language for social science research. Mimeographed preliminary manual prepared for the Department of Social Relations.

Harway, N. I., and Iker, H. P. 1966. Computer analysis of content in psychotherapy. In *Psychotherapy research: Selected readings*, ed. G. E. Stollak, B. G. Guerney, Jr., and M. Rothberg, pp. 667–69. Chicago: Rand McNally.

Jack, B. 1972. Social work accountability in a children and youth program. In *Accountability: A critical issue in social services*, ed. W. T. Hall and G. C. St. Denis, pp. 35–45. Pittsburgh: Graduate School of Public Health, Univ. of Pittsburgh and Maternal and Child Health Service, Health Services and Mental Health Administration.

Kemeny, J. G. 1972. *Man and the computer.* New York: Scribner.

Kiresuk, T. J., and Sherman, R. E. 1968. Goal attainment scaling: A general method for evaluating comprehensive community mental health programs. *Comm. Mntl. Hlth. J.* 4:443–53.

Kuhn, T. S. 1964. *The structure of scientific revolutions.* Chicago: Univ. of Chicago Press, Phoenix Books.

Linnan, J. K. 1971. Putting together a better welfare system. *Government Data Systems* 2:16–20.

Luse, F. D. 1973. Information systems for social agencies, part II— CHILDATA. Video tape lecture presented at the School of Social Service Administration, University of Chicago, 9 March 1973.

Lyden, F. J., and Miller, E. G., eds. 1967. *Planning, programming, budgeting: A systems approach to management.* Chicago: Markham Publishing.

McEachern, A. W., and Newman, J. R. 1969. A system for computer aided probation decision-making. *Journal of Research in Crime and Delinquency* 6:184–98.

Martin, J., and Norman, A. R. D. 1970. *The computerized society.* Englewood Cliffs, N.J.: Prentice-Hall.

Nie, N.; Bent, D. H.; and Hull, C. H. 1970. *SPSS: Statistical package for the social sciences.* New York: McGraw-Hill.

Noble, J. H., Jr. 1971. Protecting the public's privacy in computerized health and welfare information systems. *Social Work* 16:35–41.

Psathas, G.; Cleeland, C.; and Heller, K. 1966. Applications of a computer system of content analysis to therapy-analogue interviews. In *Psychotherapy research: Selected readings,* ed. G. E. Stollak, B. G. Guerney, Jr., and M. Rothberg, pp. 681–95. Chicago: Rand McNally.

Reid, W. J. 1966. The use of laboratory devices to investigate caseworkers' activities. In *Trends in social work practice and knowledge: NASW tenth anniversary symposium.* New York: National Assoc. of Social Workers.

———. 1974. Developments in one use of organized data. *Social Work* 19:585–93.

Roache, D. A. 1970. The nationwide demonstration program: An update. Paper read at 3d National Conference on Public Welfare, Data Processing Division on Administration, Data Processing Section, American Public Welfare Association, 22–24 July 1970, at Denver, Colorado.

Rothschild, A. W., and Bedger, J. E. 1974. A childata system can work. *Child Welfare* 53:1.

St. John, D. B.; Dobin, D. R.; and Flashner, B. A. 1973. An automated system for the regulation and medical review of long-term care facilities and patients. *Amer. J. of Pblc. Hlth.* 63:619–30.

Service, A. L.; Mantel, S. J., Jr.; and Reisman, A. 1972. Systems evaluation of social agencies. In *Systems approach and the city,* ed. M. D. Mesorovic and A. Reisman, pp. 343–74. Amsterdam: North Holland Publishing.

Sisson, R. L. 1970. Applying systems analysis to education. In *Systems analysis for social problems,* ed. A. Blumstein, M. Kamrass, and A. B. Weiss, pp. 151–61. Washington, D.C.: Washington Operations Research Council.

Slettin, I. W.; Altman, H.; Evenson, R. C.; and Cho, W. D. 1973. Computer assignment of psychotropic drugs. *Amer. J. Psychiatry* 130: 595–98.

Spitzer, R., and Endicott, J. 1969. Diagno II: Further developments in a computer program for psychiatric diagnosis. *Amer. J. Psychiatry* 125:7, January supp., pp. 12–21.

Starkweather, J. A. 1968. Computer simulation of psychiatric interviewing. In *Computers and electronic devices in psychiatry*, ed. N. S. Kline and E. Laska, pp. 12–19. New York: Grune & Stratton.

Stillman, R.; Roth, W. T.; Colby, K. M.; and Rosenbaum, C. P. 1969. An on-line computer system for initial psychiatric inventory. *Amer. J. Psychiatry* 125:7, January supp., pp. 8–11.

Stone, P. J.; Dunphy, D. C.; Smith, M. S.; and Ogilvie, D. M. 1966. *The General Inquirer: A computer approach to content analysis.* Cambridge, Mass.: MIT Press.

Thomas, E. J.; Walter, C. L.; and O'Flaherty, K. 1974. Computer assisted assessment and modification: Possibilities and illustrative data. *Social Service Review* 48:170–83.

Vanderwall, W. J. 1972. Accountability of social services in a health program: A working model. In *Accountability: A critical issue in social services*, ed. W. T. Hall and G. C. St. Denis, pp. 46–60. Pittsburgh: Graduate School of Public Health, Univ. of Pittsburgh and Maternal and Child Health Service, Health Services and Mental Health Administration.

Wenk, E. A.; Gottfredson, D. M.; and Radwin, M. S. 1970. A modern information system for uniform parole reports data. *Journal of Research in Crime and Delinquency* 7:58–70.

Wiehe, V. R. 1973. Management by objectives in a family service agency. *Social Casework* 54:142–46.

Edwin J. Thomas

11
Uses of Research Methods in Interpersonal Practice

Although knowledge of research methods is essential for conducting research, such knowledge is not ordinarily considered particularly relevant to interpersonal practice. Actually, the research methods of behavioral science may be effectively applied in connection with direct practice and may provide critical information to be employed in working toward service objectives. This is a relatively new emphasis, especially for interpersonal helping in social work, and much more work needs to be done to elaborate and specify it. The present chapter will be addressed to further exposition of this thesis, along with specification of selected applications of research technology in clinical work.

The Empirically Oriented Practitioner

The empirically oriented practitioner, as conceived here, makes strategic use of the ways of thinking and procedures of behavioral science research, along with the particular practice procedures of his method of helping, to help attain clinical and practice objectives. The objective of contributing to knowledge through conducting clinical research, as conventionally conceived, is secondary in this approach. The primary objective is to serve client needs, the principal method is a particular treatment modality and procedure, such as the behavioral or psychodynamic approach, and the place of research methodology is to enrich and strengthen the practice procedures. In this view, research methods do not replace practice procedures; rather, they augment and provide empirical grounding for the information dealt with in the practice. Again, the ultimate objective is service, not research.

However, it is important to observe that practice based on the regular and creative utilization of research methods will ultimately also make contributions to knowledge. These contributions will rest on empirical information relating to clinical description, the testing of clinical hypotheses, and the evaluating of outcome through single-case experimental designs. The experience of practitioners and agencies will consequently have

I wish to express my appreciation to Ms. Marilyn K. Moore for her competent assistance in preparing this manuscript.

a stronger empirical basis than it has had in the past, with the result that practice knowledge will be more informative and cumulative. There will be more rapid discarding of invalid ideas, better feedback to clients and practitioners concerning helping efforts, and better documentation and corroboration of what works and what does not. Unusual cases and novel procedures can more readily be described for colleagues and, if appropriate, reported in journals. Altogether, practice activities can be made more accountable to everyone involved.

Research methodology is relevant to interpersonal practice because interpersonal practice is based on information that, in principle, is largely or wholly factually verifiable. Practitioners need to collect two types of empirical information. The first is descriptive information about particular individual and family behavior, life situations, and environmental circumstances. The second involves possible interrelationships and interconnections between and among empirical events, such as are illustrated by data on conditions that originate, precipitate, or maintain desired or inappropriate behavior. Research methodology makes its contribution by providing leads to the practitioner about how to plan to gather data, how to obtain them, how to process and analyze the information, how to interpret the findings and make decisions about them, and how to record and report the results.

The direct relevance of research methodology to clinical practice was perhaps most clearly articulated and strongly advocated by the British psychologists Shapiro (1957) and Jones (1961). Although both focused on the use of psychological methods in clinical psychology, their positions are applicable more generally. Shapiro proposed the use of the experimental methods of psychology in the psychological description of the individual psychiatric patient. In regard to the methodology of psychological description, he proposed four "rules." The use of standardized methods was the first; the second was validation. The third was called "calibration," by which he meant the quantification of a given characteristic, such as a psychological attribute. The fourth rule was that it was possible to test a theory about an individual's behavior by using such a theory to predict how that behavior would vary from one circumstance to another. This use of the experimental method "enables us to reduce the error of the conclusions we come to, and to make discoveries about the mode of psychological function of our patients without waiting for leads from fundamental research" (p. 14). Shapiro saw no conflict between the demands of scientific method and service. He expressed this as follows:

> It seems to be incorrect to maintain that there is a divorce between the urgent needs of the psychiatric patient and the fulfillment of the most rigorous requirements of scientific method. On the contrary, there can, once we have decided to serve the patient's needs, be a complete iden-

tity of the interest of the patient with the most rigorous requirements of science [p. 24].

In elaborating this view, Jones (1961) claimed that, although the aim of clinical psychology was the improved welfare of the patient, psychological methods had more to contribute to clinical procedure than did the theories of psychology. Jones conceived of the clinical psychologist as an auxiliary scientist assisting the psychiatrist and others in the psychological appraisal of the patient—giving objective tests, conducting special experimental studies, using objective methods of observation, testing hypotheses, and, when necessary, conducting special studies with clinical cases to test more general hypotheses. Jones called this the experimental approach to applied abnormal psychology. Its objective was not only to assist in the appraisal of individual patients but also to engage in clinical studies with individual patients in order to extend the knowledge of psychological functioning more generally. Although this school of British clinical psychology led to many contributions to therapy and abnormal psychology and continues to flourish, the suggestions of these writers concerning the potentialities of the use of research methods in clinical procedure have not been fully realized.

Several recent developments suggest, however, that there will be increasing use of research methods in connection with interpersonal practice. Among these developments:

1. The initiation and productive use of single-case experimental methods allow the worker to retain individual service objectives and still employ a rigorous evaluation procedure. Single-case experimental evaluation has been advocated by Baer, Wolf, and Risley (1968) as a part of applied behavioral analysis; by Bijou et al. (1969) as part of a field experimental method; by Chassan (1967) and Thoresen (1972) as a component of intensive experimentation and design; by Risley (1969) as a component of experimental therapy; by Browning and Stover (1971) as an aspect of the experimental clinical method; by Carter (1972) as a central feature of case experimentation where the practitioner functions as his own outcome researcher; and by Howe (1974) as a component of casework self-evaluation in which single-subject designs are employed as a part of the practice of social casework.

2. There has been disenchantment with the results of control group-oriented clinical and behavioral research as applied to practice. This research has been very slow in coming and has often not been clinically applicable. The use of research methods as part of practice procedure allows the practitioner, as Shapiro (1957) and Jones (1961) have observed, to endeavor to answer empirical questions applicable to a particular person without having to wait for generalized knowledge to be generated. In a related context, Polansky (1958) has emphasized the

potential contributions of the individual practitioner to research on practice. He said:

> Caseworkers themselves have important opportunities to do a kind of research which is most sorely lacking in our field. This is thoughtful but courageous, systematic but imaginative research into new techniques for doing casework. Such research should come naturally to caseworkers. They have to do it for themselves. It will not be provided by those with an interest in general theory; it cannot take place merely by abstracting, in the university, from what is now going on [p. 275].

3. The success of many contemporary practice procedures derives in part from the use of empirical methods that have their counterparts in behavioral research methodology. Although other therapies could also be cited here, behavior therapy has been conspicuous in its emphasis on operational specification of variables, empirical assessment, and the monitoring and evaluation of therapeutic outcome. Indeed, it is probably fair to say that almost all practice procedures in the different treatment modalities have already been influenced to at least some extent by the availability of a large armamentarium of research methods and techniques.

4. There is disenchantment with vague and imprecise practice procedures and outcomes associated with some treatment modalities.

5. Practitioners have been increasingly aware that they are accountable to sponsors and consumers for the time, effort, and money devoted to interpersonal helping.

OVERVIEW OF CONTRIBUTIONS

The contributions of research methods to interpersonal practice may be divided conveniently into several components. The first involves a *scientific perspective* which consists of scientific attitudes, such as objectivity, parsimony, and emphasis on evidence rather than on faith or authority; scientific precepts, such as those relating to observation, operationism, and determinism; and the logic of science, which includes formal logic and the logic of experimental inference. A second component consists of the *methods per se*. These involve problem and hypothesis formulation; operational specification; standardization of procedure; recording; data-gathering designs, such as single-case experiments; data-gathering techniques, such as interviewing, observation, and the use of schedules and checklists; and data-processing techniques, such as statistics and procedures for data analysis. A third component consists of conventions involving *data interpretation*. The fourth involves practices of *research reporting*.

The practitioner familiar with these contributions would ideally have his practice skills enriched in important ways. The scientific perspective should enable the practitioner to be data-oriented, to think clearly and logically, and to avoid circular reasoning, reification, and pseudoexplanations. The methodology itself should enable the practitioner to make behavioral and environmental events operationally specific; to observe objectively; to employ standardized procedures; to keep accurate and up-to-date records; to use nonbiasing techniques of interviewing and of data collection; to create special data-gathering instruments when necessary; to formulate relevant, testable hypotheses for practice phenomena; to carry out the testing of clinical hypotheses; to design, conduct, and evaluate an assessment probe; and to design clinically useful outcome evaluations. The conventions of interpreting data should make the practitioner aware of some of the main data-biasing and intrusive effects of the practice procedures themselves, recognize the limitations of clinical data, interpret clinical data correctly, have the ability to evaluate the adequacy of clinical data for given practice objectives, and be able to take appropriate action and make decisions on the basis of the data obtained. The practices of research reporting should enable the practitioner to display data, e.g., in graphs or tables, and to describe practice procedures so that they could be replicated by others.

Thus, the potentialities are great, but much needs to be done to realize them. It will not be possible in the confines of this chapter to explicate the many possible contributions of research methods to interpersonal practice. Because the discussion must be limited, two important topics have been chosen for discussion. These are measurement and the uses of experimental methods.

MEASUREMENT

Measurement has application to a number of the activities of the practitioner as they involve the behaviors focused upon as well as the environmental conditions associated with the target behaviors. The practitioner may wish to employ measurement procedures in connection with the target responses of intervention; their level prior to, during, and after intervention; the conditions associated with the target responses; the history of the target responses; and the environmental and behavioral resources that may be of assistance in intervention. "Measurement" is broadly conceived here to include both operational specification of these phenomena and their calibration.

Operational Specification

Practitioners typically face the task of specifying target behavior in such areas as classroom study, study at home, interaction skills, emotional behavior, family communication, and child management. Specification for purposes of practice is very similar to, if not identical with, making operational definitions in research. That is, concrete and objectifiable events must be identified as representatives or indicators of the phenomena in question. Operational specification may take at least two forms. In the first, the specification consists of a sample or a sign of the behavior or environmental event. A sample of the time spent on homework would consist of the direct measurement of the amount of time the client spent doing homework for a given period. In contrast, an individual's subjective report concerning his physiological indications of anxiety would be an indirect indication, a sign, of the level of anxiety, as physiologically measured. Likewise, an individual's report concerning his alleged hallucinations would be a sign of the phenomena involved rather than a direct indicator.

Although the sample is preferred over the sign, other things being equal, there are occasions when one cannot sample behavior directly. This is most evident in the case of private events, such as hallucinations, many emotional and cognitive states, and physiological phenomena to which ready access by physiological measurement is not possible. Self-reports are often useful here. Self-reports, as indicators of other events, have not been shown to be any less reliable or valid than other types of measurement, with the possible exception of well-calibrated electromechanical devices. Self-reports have been shown to be valid indicators of verifiable information concerning the person (Walsh 1967, 1968). Self-reports may also be used as indicants or summaries of more than one event. Using pain-state reports of subjects that were compared with different physiological indicators and with pain-inducing stimuli, Hilgard (1969) found that pain reported verbally on a simple numerical scale yielded orderly and valid results. The reported pain bore a systematic relationship to the pain stimuli and the lawfulness of the relationship was supported by a fit with the power function that has been found to hold for other perceptual modalities (Stevens 1957). Concerning the relationship of the reports to the physiological indicators, Hilgard said "I wish to assert flatly that there is no physiological measure of pain which is either as discriminating of fine differences in stimulus conditions, as reliable upon repetition, or as lawfully related to change conditions, as the subject's verbal report" (p. 107).

Calibration in Scalar Value

Operational specification does not always precede and lead to measurement in the form of calibration in scalar value. That is, specification of an event, such as a suicide attempt, does not also require taking a numerical count for a six-month period extending into the future! One ordinarily would not bother to quantify events involved in emergency or crisis situations, infrequent, episodic, or nonconfirmable events (such as most stealing, lying, or drug taking), or behavioral deficits (such as low-frequency behaviors or behaviors that never have occurred). If we omit these exceptions, however, calibration is generally highly desirable, especially to establish the level of the target behavior prior to intervention, to monitor it during intervention, and to follow up on the effects afterward.

There are three very useful and widely employed types of measurement applicable to determining scalar values of behavior. These are frequency, duration, and intensity. The data for *frequency* measurement involve discrete events which are counted. Examples involve such events as sexual contacts of given types, attendance at work or school, cigarettes smoked, or instructions followed. Frequency is most useful for measuring events that cannot be readily divided and can be captured most meaningfully in terms of their number.

Duration, in contrast, is based on the amount of time the behavior is engaged in, and the operation consists simply of timing that behavior. Examples involve such things as the time spent doing homework, duration of time spouses discuss family matters, or when an adolescent comes home before or after curfew. Measures of duration are most appropriate for behaviors that continue for variable periods of time and cannot most readily be captured as frequency counts. It is important to note, however, that many behaviors may be counted as well as timed. When both aspects of the events would be informative, frequency counts and duration of each event should be obtained. Temper tantrums, for example, can be counted and timed. Sometimes it is the frequency that is problematic, sometimes the duration, sometimes both.

Intensity involves quantification of continuous gradations of response along a dimension ranging from zero to a high value. Intensity measurement is often particularly appropriate for emotional conditions of clients. Examples would be the amount of anger, sexual arousal, anxiety, or attraction to a group. Scales and ratings can often be used to measure intensity. For example, subjective ratings along a scale, say, of seven points can be used to measure the amount of client anger or anxiety in response to given events.

Sources of Data

The practitioner almost always has a choice of the source of data he will employ in measurement. The interview has been most frequently relied upon, despite the fact that there are many other sources of information. Among these are checklists and schedules, records, observation, and electromechanical devices. These others probably should be used more often than they have been. However, as a source of data, each has its prerequisites as well as its advantages and disadvantages.

The interview. The interview is a face-to-face verbal interchange. Among the distinguishing characteristics of the interview is that it is generally simultaneously a source of self-report about the interviewee, a medium of influence for both the interviewer and the interviewee, and a multichannel presentation in which each partner displays responses which are verbal, vocal, and nonverbal. As a source of information, the interview presupposes that the client has verbal facility, will cooperate in providing information, and will produce accurate self-reports. The interview also presupposes that the interviewer will have a nonbiasing and relatively neutral interviewing style. To the extent that these conditions are not met, the interview is likely to yield biased information which may be of little or no use to the practitioner. (For more information on bias and needless influence in interviews, the reader is referred to Thomas 1973a.)

Unfortunately, these prerequisites are often overlooked by practitioners because of the many advantages of the interview as a source of information. It is highly flexible and can be used for purposes of exploration or as a standardized device; and there are essentially no restrictions on the areas of content that may be examined, including complex and emotionally laden events that would be difficult to examine by other means. Furthermore, the interview is relatively easy to use—although disciplined, nonbiasing interviewing is in fact very challenging and the ability to conduct it is a skill not many possess. The interview can be used with large segments of the population and is especially useful in working with persons who may be unable to provide information in other ways. The interviewer can often check the validity and reliability of client self-report at various points during the interview itself and can examine the congruence or incongruence of the verbal, vocal, and nonverbal aspects of the client's behavior.

Schedules and checklists. Schedules and checklists generally consist of a fixed set of stimuli, such as questions, calling for client or observer responses within a given range. The responses involved may be indirectly indicative of other events, as illustrated by responses on a projective test, or may be samples of the behavior itself, as they are in the Fear Survey Schedule III of Wolpe and Lang (1964), in which the subject reports the level of his anxiety for each of a large number of stimulus situations. The use of schedules and checklists presupposes the prior isolation of defined areas of response, the availability of an instrument or the time and capability to construct one, the respondent's requisite reading and verbal skills, and the respondent's valid self-report where self-reporting responses are involved.

A distinctive advantage of schedules and checklists is that they provide a uniform response format for a given set of stimuli. Schedules and checklists are especially useful for obtaining information involving private responses as well as socially disapproved areas of behavior. These sources of data have a high degree of flexibility and can be developed for a large variety of areas of behavior. Furthermore, schedules and checklists are easy to give and score and require little expense or skill to administer.

Although self-reports have been shown to be valid and reliable for a large number of purposes, schedules and checklists are subject to invalidities and lack of reliability. Among the reasons for this are response biases of acquiescence, social acceptance, extreme responding, and cautiousness and evasiveness. Schedules and checklists would be an undesirable source of information where a high degree of situational specificity is required for the responses, where fixed response alternatives would not yield the desired information, or where the questions could be interpreted in different ways by respondents.

Records. Official, written records are sometimes available from which to obtain information about such events as hospital admissions and releases, school attendance, school performance, and court contacts. The utility of such records, of course, depends on whether the recording was done with fixed and unchanging response definitions, and whether the information is relevant to the practitioner.

One of the distinctive advantages of such records is their nonreactivity. That is, their measurement does not ordinarily affect the events recorded. Other advantages are that records are often economical to keep, afford the opportunity to obtain trends over time, do not always require the cooperation of participants, and can be used for cross-validating other sources of information. However, aside from their infrequent availability for certain kinds of response specification, records also have the disadvantages of often containing unknown invalidities and errors because of omissions, changing category definitions, and inconsistencies in recording.

Observation. The distinguishing characteristic of observation is that an observer can see the client respond in a laboratory or real-life situation. The observer may engage in participant observation, in which instance he is present and somehow part of the situation, or he may be observing as a nonparticipant or as a hidden observer. Observation presupposes (*a*) that the practitioner has access to the observational situation; (*b*) that the behaviors in question are in fact observable; (*c*) that there is a purpose for engaging in observation; and (*d*) that there are some categories to be used in observing.

Observation has a number of distinctive advantages. Like the interview, it is highly flexible in terms of the information that may be sought as well as the format that may be used. Observation characteristically affords the opportunity to learn about stimulus-response sequences, chains of response, and situational specificity for the response. Observation does not presuppose that those observed have the ability to report verbally, and the behaviors observed are direct samples of behavior as it occurs in the situation in question. Observation of behavior also provides a powerful basis for feedback to clients and can often be combined with client intervention in the observational situation.

As excellent as it is for some purposes, observation has some particular disadvantages. First, not all target behavior for the practitioner is observable—for example, sexual responding, and most irregular events and crises, are not. Information about history and behavioral and environmental resources is also difficult to obtain by observation. When behaviors can be observed, there are also problems having to do with attaining adequate reliability and maintaining it in the face of such threats as reactivity of the clients to the observer's presence, shift and drift of reliability, and observer expectancy. Finally, the costs involved in developing a code, training observers, and maintaining reliability can often be excessive.

Electromechanical devices. The distinguishing characteristic of electromechanical devices is that they are mechanical, electric, or electronic apparatuses that have at least a recording capability. Some also have stimulus output and data-displaying capabilities as well. Electromechanical devices include timers, counters, telemetric devices, transducers, cameras, audio magnetic tape recorders, video tape recorders, and chart recorders (Butterfield 1974; Schwitzgebel 1968). The use of such equipment, of course, presupposes instrumentation, the isolation and specification of the behavioral units to be measured, and the requisite training and knowledge of those who are to employ it.

Among the advantages of using electromechanical devices is that they may attain a superior level of measurement consisting of the absence or the reduction of human error, high accuracy, capability of recording a large number of responses, and the possibility of rapid calculation. They are often also useful where verbal report is not possible and for handling some private events, such as aspects of emotional responding. Some devices can monitor as well as modify and give data display, some are portable, and some are nonreactive and unobtrusive.

There are disadvantages to using electromechanical devices. For example, one must be very clear about the events to be measured. It is also sometimes difficult to explore with devices that require a high degree of precision and exactness. Furthermore, such devices do break down and malfunction. When instruments are not readily available, the cost of developing them is frequently excessive (see chapter 7).

Data Display

As an epilogue to this section on measurement, let us mention briefly the importance of data display. Data should be processed and displayed, because this serves to help bring the practitioner's practice activities under the control of the results. In addition to tables, data may be displayed in bar graphs, cumulative frequency curves, histograms, line graphs, frequency polygons, smoothed-frequency curves, and semilog and log graphs (see chapter 9).

An example of target behavior recorded for practice purposes is given in the line graphs of figure 1, taken from a report by Thomas and Carter (1971). A depressed client's periods of crying were recorded prior to, during, and after intervention in the periods of maintenance and follow-up. Progress in regard to the target behavior recorded can be readily monitored by inspection of the graph.

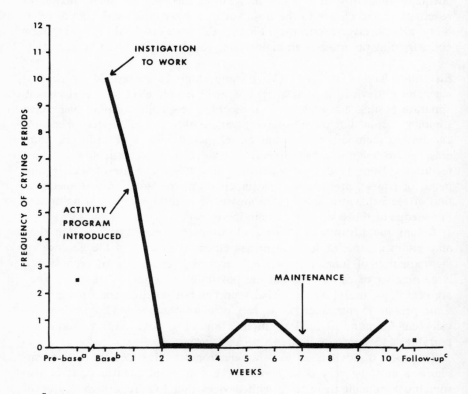

^aEstimate for a three-year period
^bSeven days of baseline
^cA five-week follow-up based upon client report

FIGURE 1.
PERIODS OF CRYING PER WEEK FOR A DEPRESSED WOMAN. From E. J. Thomas and R. D. Carter, "Instigative Modification with a Multiproblem Family," *Social Casework* 52: 444–55. Reproduced by permission of the publisher, Family Service Association of America.

Uses of Experimental Methods

Single-case experimental methods represent one of the most important developments in research methodology in recent years. These experimental methods allow the practitioner to conduct an experiment with a single case, in effect using the client as his own control. The purpose of such experiments is to produce information for practice purposes that would not ordinarily be available otherwise. Two applications of single-case experimental methods are considered here, the assessment probe and the single-case experimental method to evaluate intervention outcomes.

The Assessment Probe

The assessment probe is a miniexperiment in which the worker intervenes in the client's life situation, prior to beginning intervention proper, to obtain assessment information that would not otherwise be readily available. The probe generally takes the form of asking that the client engage in behavior not ordinarily requested during assessment. The information thus produced is carefully appraised and considered, along with other assessment data, in formulating an intervention plan. The assessment probe is a miniature experiment inasmuch as it has an objective, a design, a procedure, the collection and analysis of data, along with conclusions. It differs from other single-case experiments undertaken for research purposes principally because its objective is to produce information pertaining to assessment. And, in contrast to intervention proper, it is carried out prior to embarking on treatment.

I have found the assessment probe to be an especially useful tool in my own practice. Selected features of it are illustrated with information drawn from a probe conducted to learn about possible controlling conditions for the behavior as well as behavioral resources that may be employed in intervention. The illustration involves the use of self-monitoring in assessment to see whether self observation could be used to assist in monitoring or intervening in regard to the client's behavior. The results presented here are drawn from a study of an eighteen-year-old male with the multiple tics of *Gilles de la Tourette's* syndrome (Thomas, Abrams, and Johnson 1971). The most conspicuous and important tic was a bark-like vocalization. Prior to the probe, the assessment indicated that the presence of others may have been one of the conditions conducive to increased tic-ing. The probe was conducted in a room that allowed for unobtrusive observation, through a one-way mirror, of the client's bark. The client was asked to count his own tics using a simple wrist counter; in addition, the bark was also observed when the client worked alone, talked to a familiar therapist, and talked to a stranger.

As figure 2 indicates, self-monitoring with a portable counter produced the lowest rate of tic-ing. Because self-monitoring was incompatible with the tic-ing, it was used successfully, first to reduce the bark, and then, two other tics. Thus, in this instance, the probe disclosed a behavioral resource that was sufficiently promising to be employed in modification. The data from the probe also confirmed that the presence of others, particularly strangers, brought about a large increase in the tic-ing. This information was used in connection with another part of intervention, introduced later.

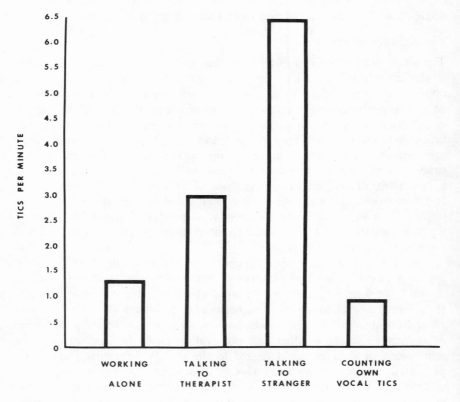

FIGURE 2.
VOCAL TICS PER MINUTE FOR PROBES CONDUCTED IN OBSERVATION ROOM. Length of observation periods were sixty minutes alone and nine, ten, and twenty minutes for the others, respectively. Reproduced with permission of the publisher from E. J. Thomas, K. S. Abrams, and J. B. Johnson, "Self-monitoring and Reciprocal Inhibition in the Modification of Multiple Tics of *Gilles de la Tourette's* Syndrome," *Journal of Behavior Therapy and Experimental Psychiatry* 2: 159–71. © 1971 Pergamon Press.

Probes may be conducted to learn more about controlling conditions for problem behavior and possible behavioral resources that may be utilized in intervention. Probes may also be undertaken to provide more adequate specification of target responses and to determine response levels for alleged response deficits. For more details on the assessment probe, the reader is referred to Thomas (1973b).

Outcome Evaluation

The behavior of the practitioner is, of course, directed toward attaining given practice goals. The information yielded by outcome evaluation should ideally serve to provide essential feedback to all involved about the success of the interventions. To conduct the evaluation, the practitioner needs special information—for obtaining which, single-case experimental methods are particularly useful.

The essential elements in outcome evaluation are fourfold. The target behavior must be specified in measurable terms. Procedures discussed earlier in this chapter and earlier in this volume would be particularly applicable here. Second, the target behavior prior to intervention must be measured. This preintervention measurement of the behavior informs the practitioner about its level, variability, and trend. It is also necessary to monitor the behavior during intervention, in order to have a basis for comparing the effects of the intervention with what occurred before. Third, the intervention itself must be sufficiently specific and identifiable so that it can be properly described and implemented. Fourth, there must be a criterion of success as a basis for judging the extent to which the intervention may or may not have accomplished the practice objective. Explicit criteria are better than implicit standards, inasmuch as the explicit standards are more public and unequivocal (see chapter 8).

Single-case experimental designs are particularly relevant to the enterprise of outcome evaluation. Such experimental methods may be applied to the specific actions of the individual client measured at various points in time. Thus, measurement of the target behavior before, during, and after intervention provides essential feedback to the practitioner concerning the success of his change effort as well as other changes that may occur in target behavior. The individual serves as his own control, inasmuch as past experience and individual differences are held equal in that particular evaluation instance. Treatment can be modified as necessary, depending on the outcome of the evaluation. The results of such single-case evaluations are more readily generalized to other practice situations than are the results of studies based on differences between averages for individuals. The possibility of replicating the evaluation in the same case or with others enables us to examine possible causal relationships more generally, thus affording us the opportunity to generalize more widely. For additional explication of the value of study in the single-case in clinical work, see Barlow and Herson (1973), Baer, Wolf, and Risley (1968), Browning and Stover (1971), Davidson and Costello (1969), Dukes (1965), Howe (1974), Kazdin (1973), and Leitenberg (1973).

Two strategies of evaluation. The emphasis in some prior writings on the relevance of single-case experimentation for outcome evaluation has tended to foster the false impression that single-case experimental methods may be employed in practice in very much the same way that they may be employed in research. The objectives of practice are usually quite different from those of research and these differences have important bearing on the evaluation. The objective of research is to evaluate the effects of one or more independent variables, whereas the objective of practice is to achieve change in given target behaviors. There are important differences in procedure that attend these objectives.

First, consider research. In his endeavor to evaluate the effects of an independent variable, the researcher will employ a design selected in advance of conducting the experiment. The design is implemented and departures are rarely made from it. The experimental condition is introduced and, irrespective of its effectiveness, the design is carried out as planned.

The practitioner, in contrast, is criterion-oriented and therefore focuses mainly on the effects of one or more interventions on changes in the target behavior. An intervention plan is implemented that calls for the introduction of a given intervention; but if this intervention fails to provide desired changes, others will generally be introduced. Furthermore, the practitioner tends to be opportunistic, inasmuch as any improvement in the client's situation will be exploited therapeutically and, if the conditions attending the improvement can be pinpointed, they will be strengthened. The practitioner retains or rejects interventions on the basis of client outcome and, if outcomes are not sufficiently favorable, other interventions will be introduced. The particular single-case design that is in fact implemented with criterion-oriented evaluation is more a result of whether a given treatment effort was successful than it is a fixed framework that is adhered to irrespective of a given intervention's effectiveness.

To highlight some of the above differences, consider the following example. If a researcher were employing an AB design (baseline measurement followed by intervention), the failure of the therapeutic stratagem to produce any demonstrable change over the baseline level of measurement would conclude the experiment. Using a fixed intervention strategy, the practitioner could select another design (e.g., another AB for which a new baseline would be required) and introduce it, or he could stop. Most practitioners, however, would find these alternatives unsatisfactory. Rather, the practitioner would follow what has here been called a criterion-oriented strategy. Thus, if the intervention in question did not work, the practitioner would sooner or later introduce another intervention and, if that failed, still another. If he were to introduce three such interventions (symbolized as B, C, and D) and only D were effective, the design, as reconstructed afterwards, would be an $ABCD$ design.

Fixed intervention strategy and criterion-oriented evaluation constitute two alternative models that the practitioner may employ in the outcome evaluation of practice activities. The fixed intervention strategy involves a fixed design and is best suited to practice research where the focus is on the evaluation of the effects of a particular intervention or group of interventions. Practitioners interested in the development and evaluation of new techniques should find fixed intervention-oriented evaluation particularly appropriate. The criterion-oriented strategy, in contrast, would appear to be most suitable for evaluation of practice outcomes for purposes of providing feedback to clients, the practitioner himself, colleagues, and sponsors. In addition to information on criterion attainment, criterion-oriented evaluation also provides some information concerning the efficacy of given interventions, albeit less rigorously than would design-oriented evaluation.

Intervention sets and criterion-oriented evaluation. Although the worker as well as the researcher generally implement a single intervention at any moment, the practitioner is willing to go on and introduce additional interventions if the first is not successful. It is therefore perhaps best to think of the practitioner as employing *intervention sets* rather than only a single intervention. The intervention set is one or more interventions introduced serially by the worker in order to achieve desirable outcomes in target responding. If one intervention is used, then the intervention set consists of this intervention; but if two are used, then the set consists of the two interventions; likewise, if five interventions are undertaken, then the intervention set consists of these five. Ordinarily, but not always, if the intervention set consists of more than one intervention, the results associated with the intervention introduced last meet the practitioner's criterion of success, whereas the interventions introduced before that do not, even if effective to a lesser extent.

For example, if a practitioner were endeavoring to work with poor interaction skills, he might first employ instructions concerning what the client might do in given life situations. If these failed, the practitioner might then turn to role playing to strengthen the skills. If that worked, he would then probably not introduce other interventions. In this example, the intervention set consists of two interventions, the second of which was effective.

The symbol adopted here for an intervention set will be X. A second, different set of interventions is symbolized by Y. Thus, AX means first a baseline and then a set of interventions, the latter consisting of one or more particular interventions. Table 2 presents a sample of single-case experimental designs for intervention sets consisting of designs involving intervention only, baseline intervention, reversal, and multiple baseline. These designs, discussed more fully below, along with those given in

TABLE 1
SELECTED SINGLE-CASE EXPERIMENTAL DESIGNS

Design Type and Examples	Design Procedures
Intervention-only	
B	Intervention-only
BC	Two successive interventions
Base line intervention	
AB	Baseline, intervention
ABC	Baseline and two different successive interventions
Reversal	
BAB	Intervention, baseline, intervention
ABA	Baseline, intervention, return to baseline
$ABAB$	Baseline, intervention, return to baseline, reinstatement of intervention
$ABAC$	Baseline, intervention, return to baseline, a different intervention
$ABACA$	Baseline, intervention, return to baseline, a different intervention, return to baseline
Changing criterion	
$B_1 \ldots B_n$	Successive application of the same intervention each with different criteria of behavioral performance
$AB_1 \ldots B_n$	Baseline followed by successive application of the same intervention each with different criteria of behavorial performance
Multiple Base line	
$A_1B\ B\ B$ $A_2A_2B\ B$ $A_3A_3A_3B$	Simultaneous baseline for three different behaviors in period one followed by introduction of intervention for the first while continuing the baseline for the other behaviors (A_2, A_3) in the second period, then introduction of the intervention for the second behavior while continuing the baseline for the remaining behavior (A_3) in the third period, with introduction of the intervention for the last behavior in the final period.
Construction	
$ABACA(BC) \ldots B, C, or (BC)$	For the intervention package (BC) systematic addition of each component alternated with baseline, ending with the component(s) that work most effectively.
Strip	
$(BC)ACABA \ldots B, C, or (BC)$	For the intervention package (BC) systematic substraction of each component alternated with baseline, ending with the component(s) that work most effectively.

TABLE 1 (CONTINUED)

Design Type and Examples	Design Procedures

Multiple factorial treatment
    BDC
    A   CBD . . . B, C, or D
    DCB
	Baseline alone at time one, interventions B, C, and D then each introduced in different situations or by different people at time two with a different order of the interventions at time three and still another at time four—ending with the use of the best intervention.

ACB
    BAC
    CBA
	Same as the one above except that here the baseline is part of the factorial arrangement.

TABLE 2
SELECTED INTERVENTION SET DESIGNS FOR SINGLE-CASE EXPERIMENTS

Design Type and Examples	Design Procedures

Intervention-only
    X
    XY
	Intervention set
	Two successive intervention sets

Baseline intervention
    AX
    AXY
	Baseline, intervention set
	Baseline and two successive intervention sets

Reversal
    XAX
    AXA
    AXAX
 	
    AXAY
 	
    AXAYA
	Intervention set, baseline, intervention set
	Baseline, intervention set, return to baseline
	Baseline, intervention set, return to baseline, reinstatement of intervention set
	Baseline, intervention set, return to baseline, a different intervention set
	Baseline, intervention set, return to baseline, a different intervention set, and return to baseline

Multiple baseline
    A_1XXX
    A_2A_2XX
    $A_3A_3A_3X$
	Same as multiple baseline in table 1, except that intervention sets replace single interventions

table 1, constitute a menu of design alternatives that may be employed for given purposes of outcome evaluation.

Evaluation objectives. There are at least four different objectives relating to outcome evaluation. These are effect detection, impact determination, comparative effect, and variable isolation.

Designs for effect detection. Evaluation directed toward detecting the effect of a given intervention involves determining that a given change has occurred following intervention and that this change is consistent with some criterion. The criterion generally involves improvement over the level of responding prior to intervention, but it can also involve achievement of a given standard. The detection of effect, while generally the practitioner's central evaluative concern, provides relatively little information about other objectives of evaluation, such as impact determination, comparative effect, or variable isolation.

Designs most suitable for effect detection consist mainly of intervention set paradigms. For example, the AX design given in table 2 involves a baseline followed by an intervention set. In this design, the interventions in the set are introduced in serial order and, as soon as the level of change that is desired has been achieved, no new interventions are introduced. The AXY design allows for the introduction of two successive intervention sets following baseline. Two different intervention sets are often administered, one as a part of intervention proper and another as part of maintenance. Also, the AXY design is useful when the X group fails and the Y group is turned to for alternatives.

Intervention-only designs are also relevant, as illustrated by the X design (see table 2). There an intervention set is introduced without a baseline. This design can be particularly useful in efforts to increase low-frequency behaviors that are near-deficits. For example, a home-token economy could be introduced to accelerate desirable behaviors for children in a family in which these behaviors were rarely exhibited prior to intervention. The X design, like its single-intervention counterpart, the B design, is most informative when there is an implicit or explicit criterion of target behavior to which obtained performance can be compared. The design is most informative when there are norms based on practice experience or research against which to compare outcomes. The X design is also particularly useful in situations where a baseline would be inappropriate or impossible to obtain. The related XY design involves two successive intervention sets without baseline.

Whether or not an effect has occurred can often be determined by visually inspecting the data points. However, more precise methods of determining an effect may call for the use of statistics. There is a growing literature on statistical tests applicable to single-case experimentation (Box and Tiao 1965; Gentile, Roden, and Klein 1972; Hannan 1960; Jones, Crowell, and Kapuniai 1969; Edgington 1967; Holtzman 1963; Nanboodiri 1972; Revusky 1967; Shine and Bower 1971).

None of the above designs calls for withdrawing or withholding help (see chapter 8), and they may be readily employed in a variety of practice situations and with a variety of treatment modalities. Their main limitation is that they ordinarily do not provide the practitioner with much confidence concerning what in fact occasioned the change or lack of it. Factors extraneous to the intervention but correlated with it may have confounded the results. These extraneous factors involve the effects of what Campbell and Stanley (1966) have called history, maturation, testing, statistical regression, and reactive arrangements. They also involve the interaction of the intervention with testing and with client selection, as well as the possible effects of multiple intervention interference. Even so, however, these designs do provide feedback to the practitioner about the possible efficacy of the interventions employed. Although weaker than the designs for impact determination, discussed below, the results of the above designs do provide a basis for self-correction.

Designs for impact determination. The focus of impact determination is on the effect of a given intervention or intervention set rather than merely on whether or not a change has occurred. If the practitioner is employing a criterion-oriented strategy, he will prefer to follow intervention set designs. Two types seem particularly applicable here. The first involves the reversal designs, as given in table 2. All these designs entail reversing an intervention set once it has been initiated. That is, the interventions in the set must be reversed or withdrawn as part of the design framework. This makes it possible to determine at a higher level of confidence the extent to which a particular intervention in the set may have been efficacious. For example, with the $AXAX$ design, the first intervention set is introduced until the appropriate positive change has been achieved or until no change has occurred in connection with any of the interventions. Then, after a return to baseline, there is reinstatement of the intervention set to determine whether or not the reintroduction produces the same effects that were found with the first application. If so, the practitioner has considerably greater confidence that the effects found were due to the impact of the intervention and not to other factors.

Reversal designs, of course, call for the withholding or reversal of interventions. This may not be possible, because some interventions are not erasable. Reversal also may not be possible because of the lack of the requisite time, experimental control, or client cooperation.

The multiple baseline design is an alternative to the reversal designs and is especially useful when reversals are not possible. A multiple baseline design for intervention sets is shown in table 2. In this design, an intervention set is introduced for the first target behavior while monitoring is undertaken for the second and third target behaviors until the change of the first target behavior meets the criterion. Then, the same intervention set is introduced for the second target behavior and, when concluded, it is again introduced for the third target behavior. If the same results are obtained for all three behaviors, the practitioner has very high confidence in what these results say about the efficacy of the intervention set. The ideal results, of course, consist of finding the intervention set effective when applied to each behavior.

If the worker has a clearly established criterion for the outcome, this is one of the most powerful designs that is also compatible with clinical objectives. In addition to allowing the practitioner to introduce one or more interventions to achieve the desired change in the target behavior, this design affords the practitioner a high degree of control by virtue of the time lags between applications of the intervention for different behaviors. The multiple baseline design, however, assumes that, if it is applied to different responses, there will be no response generalization over the different behaviors. It also assumes that the change is to some extent equally achievable for all behaviors (Etcheverry 1973). There are also limiting assumptions for the multiple baseline design when it is applied to different situations and persons (Kazdin 1973; Leitenberg 1973).

In addition to the criterion-oriented strategy, impact determination can be pursued with a fixed design intervention approach. The three groups of designs applicable here are the reversals, multiple baselines, and changing criterion designs, as illustrated in table 1. Of the reversal designs, the *ABAB* is the most powerful. The *BAB* design is a design fragment, inasmuch as the initial baseline condition is omitted; this design is most appropriate when it is not possible to obtain the initial baseline. The *ABA* design is also a fragment, inasmuch as the final reinstatement of the intervention is not undertaken; it is most appropriate when it is not possible or appropriate to reinstate the intervention. The *ABAC* and *ABACA* designs are perhaps most appropriate when the *B* intervention has not been shown to be effective and where it is possible to return to baseline again and to introduce a different intervention, *C*. Although the *ABACA* design is stronger than the *ABAC* because there is a return to baseline, these designs are essentially no different in power from the simple baseline intervention designs illustrated by the *AB* or *ABA* designs.

Altogether, however, if the interventions of the reversals are not effective, valuable time is wasted in following a fixed intervention strategy, inasmuch as therapeutic effort is invested in returning to baseline when other interventions could be introduced directly instead. This limitation also applies to single intervention multiple baseline designs.

The changing criterion design given in table 1 is applicable to impact determination, because this design calls for the successive application of the intervention to achieve different criterion levels of target behavior. For example, praise could be used to reinforce the criterion level of an eleven-year-old child, with doing homework for thirty minutes every night, as the first criterion; then, as the second, there would be praise for doing homework for forty-five minutes; the criterion would then be raised again, until finally two hours per night would be achieved. If the same reinforcement is used to achieve the criterion, at each level, this demonstrates very well the efficacy of the intervention. The failure of the praise to achieve the criterion at any level allows the practitioner to conclude provisionally that the intervention is to that extent not effective.

The designs mentioned in regard to impact determination are generally stronger than those specified as being applicable to effect detection. For example, the reversal (e.g., $ABAB$) and the multiple baseline designs generally protect against the validity threats of concomitant changes owing to history, client maturation, testing, instrumentation, and statistical regression. However, these designs may not so assuredly protect the practitioner against invalidities that may be associated with reactive arrangements, multiple treatment interference, and the interaction of the intervention with testing or with client selection. For additional details concerning the relevance of these threats to validity, see Campbell and Stanley (1966) and Etcheverry (1973).

The intervention set designs, as given in table 2, are not identical with their counterparts for single intervention, given in table 1. For example, compare an $ABAB$ with an $AXAX$, where X involves more than one intervention, the last of which is successful. In general, these two designs protect the practitioner about equally well in regard to most threats to validity except for multiple treatment interference or the interaction of treatment with testing or with selection of clients. In regard to the latter, the $ABAB$ would be more rigorous than the $AXAX$. Generally, invalidities caused by interaction and multiple treatment interference would probably be more likely to occur with the intervention set designs and with those involving single interventions. Altogether, from a research point of view, the single intervention designs are stronger than their counterparts for intervention sets.

Designs for comparative effects. The practitioner interested in the comparative effects of two or more interventions would wish to employ a design in which each of these interventions is somehow pitted against the other in terms of its possible effect upon a common outcome. The focus here is clearly on the efficacy of the different interventions and, therefore, the fixed intervention strategy, involving a fixed design, is most appropriate. A variation of a reversal design may be effectively employed to examine comparative effects. Consider the comparison of B and C in the following design: $ABACABACA$ . . . , terminating, for practice purposes, with A or C, whichever is most effective. Repeated reversals may not be appropriate, however, and may have some unintended side effects (Kazdin 1973).

Alternatives to this design are the factorial, multiple treatment designs in table 1. However, there appear to be limitations on when they may be employed. These designs require that there be either different situations or different people relating to the particular experimental conditions at different times. Thus, for the first factorial, multiple treatment design given in table 1, interventions *B*, *C*, and *D* would be made in different situations at time 1; at time 2, interventions *B*, *D*, and *C* would be made; and at time 3, interventions *C*, *D*, and *B* would be made. Consider an example in which *B* was praise for given desired behavior, *C* was disapproval of given undesirable behavior, and *D* was praise for desired behavior combined with disapproval of undesirable behavior. Then, in this type of design, a mother could use intervention *B* with her four-year-old child for the first week in the mornings, intervention *C* in the afternoons, intervention *D* in the evenings; in the second week, it could be *D* in the mornings, *B* in the afternoons, and *C* in the evenings; and in the third week, it could be *C* in the mornings, *D* in the afternoons, and *B* in the evenings. For additional details, see Browning (1967) and Browning and Stover (1971). In general, the comparative effects of interventions can be most validly examined through the use of group designs (Paul 1969), rather than with single-case paradigms.

Variable isolation designs. The purpose of variable-isolation designs is to examine interventional components of an *intervention package*. For this purpose I have proposed two designs, the construction and strip designs, as illustrated in table 1. Designating (*BC*) as the interventional package, the construction design assembles the intervention package by adding each component (*B* and *C*) one at a time, whereas the strip design disentangles the intervention package by removing each interventional component one at a time. In both designs, the interventional component or components found to be most effective are reinstituted at the end to provide the best intervention for the client.

In the construction and strip designs, the elements in a two-part interventional package could be praise for desired behavior, *B*, and disapproval for undesired behavior, *C*. Thus, in the case of construction, there would be baseline, praise for desirable behavior, return to baseline, disapproval of undesired behavior, return to baseline, and the intervention package of praise for desired behavior combined with disapproval of undesired behavior *ABACA*(*BC*). Then, the intervention left in operation finally would be that which was found to work best, which has been symbolized as *B*, *C*, or (*BC*).

If each of the interventional components in an intervention package can justifiably be examined for its effects on a given target behavior, then these two variable isolation designs are candidates for use in practice situations. It is important to note, however, that these designs involve as prerequisites the practitioner's ability to isolate the interventional components operationally and to introduce them and reverse them. The examples given in table 1 involve only two interventional components, and it is evident that even with these two, both the construction and strip designs involve a minimum of seven segments. If there are three or more interventional components, then clearly an extremely large and essentially unmanageable number of design segments would be called for in the series.

GENERALIZATION OF RESULTS

Results of studies based on groups of participants or single individuals frequently raise questions about the representativeness of the findings when applied to other individuals or under different conditions. A finding does not a generalization make. Or does it? The question is, To whom and under what conditions may findings from evaluative experiments be generalized? Although the problems of generalization are similar no matter what methodology is employed, evaluative experimentation with single cases typically involves some special strengths and limitations.

Among the strengths of single-case experiments conducted with clients, as described here, are the practice relevance of the intervention and the lack of artificiality of the evaluation. The intervention is carried out as part of an experimental design with a real client in a natural service context. Hence, the findings are typically directly applicable, or at least seem to be, to the real interventions and clientele of the practitioner. One is consequently tempted to generalize widely from such experiments. However, one must consider the limitations. Among them is the fact that the findings are based on a single individual or family rather than on a large sample, and that there may be particular methodological shortcomings, such as confounded order effects arising from the series of activities the practitioner carried out with the client. We mentioned some of the threats to validity in connection with particular designs and design types; the reader is encouraged to review these for any needed elaboration. Paul (1969) and Kazdin (1973) also discuss possible threats to validity for single-case experiments. These possible methodological shortcomings involve technical questions about whether the results of single-case experiments can, in fact, be attributed solely to the intervention or whether they may have arisen from factors extraneous to but coincident with it.

To begin with, the adequacy of $N = 1$ data depends in part on what one wants to conclude. Single-case experimentation oriented toward evaluation of interventions by the practicing worker is often adequate to provide the practitioner with useful empirical data on the effectiveness of his interventional efforts. Results of $N = 1$ experiments are thus probably most useful and valid when used to draw conclusions about a given practitioner's work with particular clientele. It should be remembered that this is extremely useful information that has not ordinarily been obtained in practice, as this chapter has emphasized.

Ordinarily, however, it is not safe to generalize widely from the results of an experiment conducted with a single case. But given valid results, there are special occasions when a sample of one would be adequate. These include the following: when between-individual variability for the phenomena under investigation is known to be negligible, making results from a second subject redundant; when one case in depth exemplifies many; when negative results from one case are sufficient to demand revision or rejection of an asserted or assumed universal relationship; when the behavior studied is very unusual and there is limited opportunity to study it; or when the practitioner wants to focus on a problem by defining questions and variables that may lead to more refined approaches. For more details see Dukes (1965), who discusses this.

When $N = 1$ is not enough, replication is called for. Intrasubject replication consists of repeating the experiment in the same way with the same subject and is suitable for endeavoring to establish the reliability of the experimental manipulation for a given subject. Intersubject replication involves repeating the experiment with different subjects and is appropriate for determining the reliability of the experimental innovation for a given group of subjects. In the case of practitioner-conducted experimentation, replication serves to make conclusions concerning the adequacy of the intervention for given clientele and case situations more plausible.

An important question for the practitioner is when to replicate. Replication within or across subjects is generally carried out in research on social work practice to learn more about the reliability of the intervention procedures and their applicability. The same applies to replication of single-case experiments conducted by practitioners for purposes of evaluation in practice, but there are some interesting twists. Thus, replication of positive results could be undertaken in those special cases where it would serve to persuade otherwise skeptical clients that the results initially obtained to help them were genuine and reproducible. Another time to replicate when positive outcomes are involved is when the worker suspects that the results obtained are false positives, i.e., are due to factors extraneous to the intervention. When the results of practice evaluation are negative, replication may be undertaken if the worker suspects that the results are atypical, as may happen during transitional or stressful life situations.

The results of replication may be essentially positive, in which case confidence in the reliability of the procedures used is greatly increased. Indeed, each successive, positive replication increases plausibility multiplicatively, because the chance occurrence of such results becomes much more improbable with each additional replication. The same may be said, of course, for replicated failures. Results involving mixed positive and negative outcomes pose special action alternatives. As Sidman has said, "successful replications . . . cannot be balanced out by any number of failures to replicate" (1960, p. 94). The practitioner's purpose in such instances is not to try to draw conclusions about some sample of clientele but, rather, to develop a more reliable intervention for those cases where the initial one failed. To quote Sidman again:

> If a datum fails to achieve consistent replication, the scientist cannot afford to ease his conscience with the rationalization that we live, after all, in a probabilistic world, where truth is only a relative matter. The proper inference to be drawn from variability is that one's control techniques are inadequate [1960, p. 94].

Mixed outcomes should lead to a temporary state of affairs during which the practitioner analyzes both failures and successes to try to learn about the conditions under which each outcome obtains.

STATISTICAL TESTS

It is appropriate to comment here on the use of statistics by practitioners engaged in experimental outcome evaluation with single cases. Single-case experimental work has relied heavily and will continue to rely on visual inspection of results and reliable replication as the bases of inferring whether procedures are adequate. Conventional inferential statistics have not been widely employed. One reason is that the objective of researchers in this tradition has been more to develop procedures to change behavior than to draw inferences about whether or not an effect was present, by statistical criteria. The evaluation of interventions in practice, using single-organism designs, should similarly be concerned primarily with developing effective interventions.

In keeping with this, the main criterion of change should be whether or not a *practical* difference has resulted from the intervention. Inspection of the data, without statistical tests, will ordinarily be enough to enable one to judge whether practically useful changes have occurred. After all, it doesn't matter that an outcome is statistically significant if it is practically meaningless. In a series of experiments or in the processing of data for a single case, the use of statistical tests may serve to increase plausibility, especially when the results are a mixture of positive and negative outcomes. However, the main conclusions, in any case, have to be that the intervention was not successful with all or most cases and, consequently, interventional refinement is required. No use of statistical tests will change this fact, and statistical tests are not a substitute for changing less than adequate procedures. Until bases of inference in single-case experimentation are more firmly agreed upon, the use of statistical tests for practice evaluation should probably be left to the option of the prac-

titioner. If such tests can be done easily, as in computer-assisted analysis
and evaluation, they should be done, because the results provide a useful
additional source of information.

SUMMARY AND CONCLUSION

The thesis of this chapter has been that research methods of behavioral
science can and should make a significant contribution to the practice
procedures of interpersonal helping. The empirically oriented practitioner
has been described as making use of the many contributions of research
technology to interpersonal practice in order to ground the practice more
firmly on empirical data and logical thinging. In addition to offering an
overview of the contributions research methods make to interpersonal
helping, this chapter has discussed two subjects in detail. The discussion
of measurement has included specification and quantification and a review
and appraisal of the following sources of data: interview, schedules and
checklists, observation, records, and electromechanical devices. The presentation on the uses of experimental methods has offered the assessment
probe and a variety of single-case experimental designs that may be used
in outcome evaluation. Designs have been specified for different objectives
of outcome evaluation and for two outcome evaluation strategies, namely,
the fixed intervention approach and a new viewpoint designated here as
the criterion-oriented approach.

The idea that the practitioner may be guided in large measure by empirical data and may employ research methods to collect and analyze
data deserves further elaboration and specification. Research methodology
complements practice procedures in very much the same way that interpersonal practice is enriched by theories of behavior and principles of
intervention.

REFERENCES

Baer, D. M.; Wolf, M. M.; and Risley, T. R. 1968. Some current dimen-
    sions of applied behavior analysis. *Journal of Applied Behavior Analy-
    sis* 1:91–97.
Barlow, D. H., and Hersen, N. 1973. Single-case experimental designs.
    Archives of General Psychiatry 29:319–25.
Bijou, S. W.; Peterson, R. F.; Harris, F. R.; Allen, K. E.; and Johnston,
    M. S. 1969. Methodology for experimental studies of young children
    in natural settings. *The Psychological Record* 19:117–210.
Box, G. E. P., and Tiao, G. C. 1965. A change in level of a nonstationary
    time series. *Biometrika* 52:181–92.

Browning, R. N. 1967. A same-subject design for simultaneous comparison of three reinforcement contingencies. *Behavior Research and Therapy* 5:237–43.

Browning, R. M., and Stover, D. O. 1971. *Behavior modification in child treatment: An experimental and clinical approach.* Chicago: Aldine-Atherton.

Butterfield, W. H. 1974. Instrumentation in behavior therapy. In *Behavior modification procedure: A source book*, ed. E. J. Thomas, pp. 265–305. Chicago: Aldine.

Campbell, D. T., and Stanley, J. C. 1966. *Experimental and quasi-experimental designs for research.* Chicago: Rand McNally.

Carter, R. D. 1972. Evaluating treatment outcomes in individual cases. Manuscript. Ann Arbor, Mich.: Univ. of Michigan School of Social Work.

Chassan, J. B. 1967. *Research designs in clinical psychology and psychiatry.* New York: Appleton-Century-Crofts.

Davidson, P., and Costello, C., eds. 1969. *N = 1: Experimental studies of single cases.* New York: Van Nostrand-Reinhold Co.

Dukes, W. F. 1965. N = 1. *Psychological Bulletin* 64:74–79.

Edgington, E. S. 1967. Statistical inference from N = 1 experiments. *Journal of psychology* 65:195–99.

Etcheverry, R. 1973. N:1 designs in clinical practice. Manuscript. Ann Arbor, Mich.: Univ. of Michigan School of Social Work.

Gentile, J. R.; Roden, A. H.; and Klein, R. D. 1972. An analysis-of-variance model for intra subject replication design. *Journal of Applied Behavior Analysis* 5:193–98.

Hannan, E. J. 1960. *Time series analysis.* London: Methuen.

Hilgard, E. R. 1971. Pain as a puzzle for psychology and physiology. *American Psychologist* 24:103–14.

Holtzman, W. H. 1963. Statistical models for the study of change in the single case. In *Problems in measuring change*, ed. C. W. Harris, pp. 199–211. Madison: Univ. of Wisconsin Press.

Howe, M. W. 1974. Casework self-evaluation: A single-subject approach. *Social Service Review* 48:1–24.

Jones, H. Gwynne. 1961. Applied abnormal psychology: the experimental approach. In *Handbook of abnormal psychology: An experimental approach*, ed. H. J. Eysenck, pp. 764–81. New York: Basic Books.

Jones, R. H.; Crowell, D. H.; and Kapuniai, L. E. 1969. Change detection model for serially correlated data. *Psychological Bulletin* 71:352–58.

Kazdin, A. E. 1973. Methodological and assessment considerations in evaluating reinforcement programs in applied settings. *Journal of Applied Behavior Analysis* 6:517–32.

Leitenberg, H. 1973. The use of single-case methodology in psychotherapy research. *Journal of Abnormal Psychology* 82:87–102.

Namboodiri, N. K. 1972. Experimental designs in which each subject is used repeatedly. *Psychological Bulletin* 77:54–64.

Paul, G. L. 1969. Behavior modification research: design and tactics. In *Behavior therapy: Appraisal and status*, ed. C. M. Franks, pp. 29–63. New York: McGraw-Hill.

Polansky, N. A. 1958. Getting down to cases in casework research. In *Ego psychology and dynamic casework*, ed. H. J. Parad, pp. 254–75. New York: Family Service Assoc. of America.

Risley, T. R. 1969. Behavior modification: an experimental-therapeutic endeavor. In *Behavior modification and ideal mental health services*, ed. L. A. Hamerlynck, P. O. Davidson, and L. E. Acker, pp. 103–27. Calgary, Alberta: Univ. of Calgary Press.

Revusky, S. H. 1967. Some statistical treatments compatible with individual organism methodology. *Journal of the Experimental Analysis of Behavior* 10:319–30.

Schwitzgebel, R. L. 1968. Survey of electromechanical devices for behavior modification. *Psychological Bulletin* 70:444–60.

Shapiro, M. B. 1957. Experimental method in the psychological description of the individual psychiatric patient. *International Journal of Social Psychiatry* 3:89–102.

Shine, L. C., II, and Bower, S. M. 1971. A one-way analysis of variance for single-subject designs. *Educational and Psychological Measurement* 31:105–13.

Sidman, M. 1960. *Tactics of scientific research: Evaluating experimental data in psychology*. New York: Basic Books.

Stevens, S. S. 1957. On the psychophysical law. *Psychological Review* 64: 153–82.

Thomas, E. J. 1973a. Bias and therapist influence in behavioral assessment. *Journal of Behavior Therapy and Experimental Psychiatry* 4: 107–11.

————. 1973b. The assessment probe. Manuscript. Ann Arbor, Mich.: University of Michigan School of Social Work.

————; Abrams, K. S.; and Johnson, J. B. 1971. Self-monitoring and reciprocal inhibition in the modification of multiple tics of *Gilles de la Tourette*'s syndrome. *Journal of Behavior Therapy and Experimental Psychiatry* 2:159–71.

Thomas, E. J., and Carter, R. D. 1971. Instigative modification with a multiproblem family. *Social Casework* 52:444–55.

Thoresen, C. E. The intensive design: An intimate approach to counseling research. Paper presented at the meeting of the American Educational Research Association, Chicago, April 1972.

Walsh, W. B. 1967. Validity of self-report. *Journal of Counseling Psychology* 14:18–23.

————. 1968. Validity of self-report: Another look. *Journal of Counseling Psychology* 15:180–36.

Wolpe, J., and Lang, P. J. 1964. A Fear Survey Schedule for use in behaviour therapy. *Behaviour Research and Therapy* 2:27–30.

12
Research
Reporting

Writing a research report is an important professional obligation. The social work researcher seeks knowledge, not for its own sake, but for the sake of people. Only as the researcher prepares careful reports of studies will the knowledge acquired become accessible for use by others.

Writing a research report is not an easy task, even for experienced research workers. That sense of exhilaration—or despair—that such workers experience when data analysis has been completed will usually be absent when they begin to write. Their own curiosity has been satisfied, at least up to a point, and probably they have run upon other questions they would like to explore immediately. It seems too bad to have to interrupt "creative" work for the task of writing a report. In the process of writing, however, the researcher may view the findings anew and may even discover that their import has not been fully understood. In asking the questions a reader may ask, the researcher may have to go back to the original data to make additional tabulations. From the effort to interpret the findings, the researcher may find new and exciting questions. From study of the flaws in what has been done may come fresh ideas about the design of the next study. Indeed, the very process of preparing the report may be transformed from a routine duty into an interesting and challenging opportunity to rethink the entire study and assess its possible value as the basis for further research. Experiences of this kind compensate for the hours of hard work that go into the planning and writing of even the simplest report.

This chapter deals with the content and structure of the research report and with some conventions of research reporting. It does not cover the mechanics of grammar, style, and usage. Doubtless the research worker already has a collection of favorite reference tools—a handbook of composition, a manual of style, and a good dictionary. Such a person does not need to be told how to construct sentences and paragraphs, but any beginning researcher needs to consider how to develop true skills in the creation of research reports.

The social work researcher may be required to prepare reports for many different audiences and for many different purposes. For example, in making a study in a family service agency, a research worker may prepare a detailed report for participating staff members, an interpretive summary for the agency board, a progress report for a supporting foundation, a general report for a meeting of a welfare council committee, an article for a professional journal, and a book or monograph which may be accompanied by a technical report. Some of the same material will be used in each of these reports, but the method of presentation and the amount of explanation and interpretation included will vary widely. In reports to staff and board members, for example, the research worker may assume that the potential readers already understand some aspects of agency policy that would have to be explained to outsiders. Similarly, members of the board will not be interested in certain matters that could concern the statistician who may read the technical report.

THE PARTS OF THE REPORT

Just as the research worker spends hours in planning the study before collecting data, so the writer of the research report spends time in planning the report. Such a writer considers first the purpose of the report and the audience for which it is being prepared, and then decides what material to include and in what order to present it.

In planning the report, the research worker can usually follow a model for a research report prepared for a professional journal. Such a report follows a logical sequence, which may be described most easily by a series of questions: What did the investigator study? How was the study made? What definitions and what materials were used? What methods were used? What were the results? What do the findings mean? How do they relate to the findings of other investigators? What questions are left unanswered?

The model used by a chemist or an engineer is equally useful to the writer of a report on a social work study. Although topics and research instruments vary widely, the sequence remains very much the same. The model presented on page 286 is often followed in articles for professional journals. (There are a number of manuals for writers of technical reports. The model used here was adapted from Trelease [1958].) With modifications, some of which are pointed out in this chapter, it may be used for other purposes.

Such a method of presentation has obvious advantages for the writer as well as the reader. Without trying to be clever, original, or inspiring, the writer simply tells what was done, how it was done, what was found, and perhaps what the findings mean. The reader is able to follow the logic of the study, to consider one phase of it at a time, and to understand and assess the findings as they are presented.

The model should be used flexibly. As indicated below, the writer of a report on a complex study may present material in stages. After the general introduction and description of the total study, the writer deals with each stage of the research almost as if it were a separate study. Each stage becomes a miniature of a research report, with an account of method and findings and a discussion of the findings.

Simple Model for a Research Report

Title
I. Introduction
  A. Nature of the problem and purpose of the study
  B. Scope and method of the investigation
  C. Nature of the findings
II. Materials and methods
  A. Definitions and instruments used
  B. Description of method
III. Presentation of findings
  A. Results of use of methods described above
  B. Statistical analysis of results
IV. Discussion of findings
  A. Conclusions to be drawn from findings
    (with reference to data supporting on each)
  B. Explanations of limitations or possible distortions of findings
  C. Comparison with findings of other studies
V. Summary

Model for a Report on a Study Consisting of Several Stages

Title
  I. General introduction
  II. General description of materials and methods
  III. Stage I
    A. Introduction
    B. Materials and methods
    C. Presentation of findings
    D. Discussion of findings
  IV. Stage II
    A. Introduction
    B. Materials and methods
    C. Presentation of findings
    D. Discussion of findings
  V. Stage III
    A. Introduction
    B. Materials and methods
    C. Presentation of findings
    D. Discussion of findings
  VI. General discussion

In the following pages, the various parts of the research report will be considered in detail.

Introduction

The introduction serves several purposes: to inform the reader about reasons for the study; to give certain facts about the auspices under which the research was carried out; to place the study within its theoretical context; and to prepare the reader for what is to follow. An introduction must include a brief statement of the purpose, scope, and method of the study. After reading the introduction, the reader should know enough about the study to decide whether to read the full account.

Nature of the problem and purpose of the study. The investigator need not describe to the reader all the painful steps involved in arriving at a clear statement of purpose or in delimiting the scope of the study. In some cases, however, it is important to state what the original question was and how it was reformulated for study. (For further discussion of problem formulation, see chapter 1.)

In some studies, the statement of the problem may be quite simple. For example, the following introduction to a welfare council study gives the reader a straightforward statement about the question studied:

In recent years the mounting rates of illegitimacy throughout the country have been a cause of public concern and efforts to study and understand the problem have proliferated in response to this concern. Interest in illegitimacy has grown to include not only the causes but also the characteristics and experiences of the mothers, fathers and babies who are involved. . . .

Although the literature pertaining to the unmarried mothers and children born out-of-wedlock is growing, little has been reported about these women who keep the child and their experiences as they raise the child in the community. The purpose of the current study has been to investigate the experience of the unwed mother *as a new parent.*

In New York City, as in many cities throughout the country, a variety of social services have been developed for the unwed woman who wishes to place her child for adoption—services to help her during pregnancy as well as with adoption arrangements. For the majority of unwed mothers, however, those four out of five who keep the child, few *specialized* services exist. General community programs are, of course, often available to help *all* mothers care for their children but practically no services have been designed and established specifically to aid the unwed mother who plans to raise her baby herself.

In order to determine if such specialized services are needed and what these services should provide, answers to a number of questions about these mothers and their babies are required. Do they have problems of basic financial support as a family without a responsible father

in the home? Do they have problems associated with economic deprivation and the personal situation of the mother? If the mother has had
to interrupt her education because of the pregnancy and wants to go
back to school, is it difficult, if not impossible, for her to do so because
of the need to care for the child? Does the responsibility for the care
of the child limit her employment possibilities, or is she handicapped
in employment because her education was interrupted by her pregnancy?
    The purpose of this study is to seek answers to these questions
through an analysis of the actual experiences of a group of these women
after the baby's birth [Sauber 1965, pp. 1–2].

In the report of a study dealing with a theoretical question, the statement of the problem may require a full section. Although more space is
to be given to the problem later on, the writer should make sure that the
introduction gives the reader at least a beginning understanding of the
problem.

Background of the problem. It may be necessary to give the reader some
information about the importance of the problem, its history, and the
state of information about it, but a long history or detailed review of
the literature is usually unnecessary and inappropriate.

At one time, the scientific article was expected to contain a full chron-
ological or topical review of the literature. More recently, this convention
has been changing. The writer who keeps the needs of the reader in mind
will probably include in the introduction references to only those parts of
the literature that apply immediately to matters considered there and will
make other references to the literature later, in the discussion of findings.

The fact that a long review of the literature is unnecessary does not
free the author from the obligation to make a painstaking review of earlier work and to refer the reader to relevant studies. All too often, writers
in social work journals create the impression that the subjects on which
they write have never been studied before.

Student writers of theses in schools of social work at one time considered it necessary to include a history of the agency in which a study had
been made and, in some cases, even of the locality served by the agency.
In most reports such information has little value. A footnote to some
easily obtainable source of history or other information will serve the
reader better. Explanation of a specific policy of an agency may be necessary if the report deals with that policy, but as a rule a full description
of agency structure and policy should not be included.

Scope and method of the study. The introductory statement on scope and
method should be brief and undetailed. For example, the writer may say
no more than that the data consisted of research interviews with a sample
of clients served during a specified time period. Sometimes it is necessary

to give a rationale for the use of that period, but in the introduction the writer will not embark on a long discussion of sample selection, design of schedules, or treatment of specific problems encountered during the study. One assumes that the reader knows how studies are conducted and needs no detailed chronology of the steps taken by the investigator in drafting schedules, writing instructions, developing coding plans, and working on analysis of data. In other words, the introduction gives a schematic and logical presentation of the study plan; it does not chronicle the researcher's daily life. Detailed analysis of schedules may come later.

The writer must decide whether definitions of terms are needed in the introduction. Sometimes a commonly accepted definition is so clear that no explanation is necessary. For example, the research worker who writes about a group of Girl Scouts need not give an elaborate definition of the term "member." In a study of a group of mental patients in a state hospital, a definition of "member" would be essential. If the study hinges on the definition of a concept—*movement*, for example—the writer may need to devote a later section of the report to an explanation of the definition used. It may be necessary to present the instruments employed and to give illustrations in order to make the concept clear to the reader, but such material would not appear as parts of the introduction.

Definitions used in analysis of a particular section of the study are often included later in the report. For example, in her study of unwed mothers, Sauber included in the introduction only a few questions covering the general content of the follow-up interviews. In later sections, as necessary, she included the precise wording of questions mothers were asked about their problems and needs. The questions were carefully placed at the points at which the reader was ready to consider the responses of the mothers (1965, p. 125).

The writer will tell the reader not only what the study purports to do but also what it does not do; that is, the limitations of the study will be made clear. By the manner in which data are handled later in the report, the writer will help the reader see specific limitations as well as flaws in methodology. In the introduction the writer says, in effect: "Do not expect too much. Be sure to notice that the study deals with this, not that." However, the writer need not apologize for the study. Readers will assess it for themselves.

Nature of the findings. The introduction may include a brief statement of findings. The reader who has been told the most significant result of an investigation is in a position to read more discriminatingly, to judge the evidence more carefully, to distinguish the essential from the incidental. Such a reader has perspective.

Often a social agency report prepared for use by policy-making bodies includes at the very beginning (before the introduction) a brief résumé of major findings. Such a device serves an important purpose. In many instances the report is prepared for persons who have taken part in the study or who have a good knowledge of the problem being studied. These busy people may not wish to read the entire report, but may wish to have the major findings available in simple form for quick reference. If they need supporting data or discussion of findings, they will turn to later parts of the report. Placement of major findings at the beginning of the report may arouse the curiosity of a reader who otherwise might not be interested in the report.

The introduction should give the reader a clear idea of what to expect in the remainder of the report. It need not give a full listing of all subsequent sections, but it should give a general plan.

If the report is one of a series, or a progress report, the introduction should let the reader know about other reports in the series. In a monograph or book, the information appears in a preface or on the title page. In an article, it may be included in either the introduction or in a footnote.

An introduction gives readers a clear idea of what to expect but need not satisfy their curiosity. It gives a brief description of the scope and method of the study. It sets forth what the study was and what it was not. In short, it gives the reader a sense of direction.

Description of Methods and Materials

In the description of methods and materials used, the writer gives a straightforward description of what was done and a definition of terms used. All the items in the questionnaire or schedule need not be included. It is appropriate, however, to give a general description of such instruments and, if necessary, to refer the reader to an appendix in which schedules and other supporting material may be found. Unless there is something unusual about the method, the author assumes that the reader will want only a general description of methodology and sources.

In a complex study, the writer may include in this section only a general description of methodology and present detailed material in the section on findings, along with the results of the use of the method. For example, if ratings of "improvement" were made, detailed information on how the ratings were made may be included in the section on findings. Then the reader will be in a position to assess the definitions, the method of rating, and the results without having to go back to earlier sections of the report to find out precisely how the ratings were made.

The writer explains how the sample was chosen and gives the rationale for the method used. The reader needs to know from what population the sample was chosen and the limitations set. Here, as elsewhere, the author adapts the material to the audience. In a report for research workers, material on sampling error may be placed in the text, in a technical note, or in an appendix, along with references to other sources of material on technical problems. In a report for a general audience, the author will be meticulous in pointing out the uncertainties created by using a part rather than the whole, but will use less technical terminology. A footnote indicating the source of further information may be added.

Presentation of Findings

The writer reports findings clearly and precisely. Rather than presenting them in the order in which they were produced, the author structures them so that they will make sense to the reader. Most often the writer begins work with a set of tables, some of which include material that is of little importance, while others throw light on the question studied. The author must consider carefully both the order of the main points and the weight to be given to each. Some findings are so simple that they may be understood without detailed explanation, yet they must be presented if other findings are to be understood. For example, a table giving age and sex of children in an institution may require little explanation, but the table must be included if the reader is to understand the findings about the outcome of treatment. A paper dealing with a group of clients often includes a section in which the population is described. This section is usually both brief and important. It gives the reader a background against which to assess all that follows.

A description of population need not be an impersonal recounting of the number of persons falling into certain categories. The writer selects those characteristics that seem to be relevant to the particular study and organizes the presentation to give a clear picture of the total group studied. For example, rather than presenting a series of tables on age, earnings, and education of a sample of clients, the writer may include simple averages. If the writer points out that the median age was seventeen years, that the median salary was $75 a week, and that three-fourths of the clients had not reached the eighth grade, the reader will rightly conclude that the typical client was young, poor, and educationally disadvantaged. The writer, of course, must guard against overgeneralization in description. For example, a student once wrote that "the typical client was half male and half female."

The findings should be presented as fully as necessary to make the results clear. Supporting data must be included so that the reader may assess the facts. Writers are likely to err in one of two directions. One may assume that something is so obvious that it need not be mentioned; another may go to the other extreme and give tedious details that have no bearing on the point to be made. The writer who focuses sharply on what the reader needs in order to understand the findings can usually strike a balance between skimpiness and excessive detail.

Sometimes the writer may forget that the reader does not understand the shorthand used in the course of the study. The reader will become confused by inadequate explanations of terms and symbols. No reader should be asked to take on faith the results of a classification process for which no explanation is offered. To tell the reader that "patterns were identified" or that "categories emerged" is to tell almost nothing. The writer must remember that telegraphic or highly abstract writing does not make a report "scientific."

If disappointed in what has happened to a favorite hypothesis, the researcher may be tempted to present material in such a way as to hide the disappointment. In such a situation, perhaps the best course is to state simply both the expectation and the outcome. Negative findings are important. The researcher who presents such findings clearly and without apology commands respect.

In the effort to present findings in an objective manner, the writer need not lean over backward to avoid pointing out to the reader that a certain finding tends to confirm or to deny some earlier statement or hypothesis; that is, the author should not draw too fine a line between findings and conclusions. The writer who takes the reader along by pointing out that a specific finding casts doubt on an earlier statement will be able to present his conclusions without undue repetition of findings.

In the section on findings, the author may use tables, graphs, charts, case illustrations, or other devices to make the findings clear.

Tables. The writer of a research report is often uncertain about how much tabular material to include in the text. A good general rule is to present only those tables that are essential to the reader.

The writer should consider each table carefully. The following questions may be asked:

Is the table necessary? Tables are costly; if only a simple total or proportion is needed, perhaps the table can be omitted. A table is of value if several figures are needed and if there are to be several references to the same figures. The reader cannot be expected to remember figures and certainly cannot be expected to enjoy reading long series of figures in the text.

Can the table be simplified so that it will be clearer to the reader? Will information be lost if the table is simplified? Is the gain in clarity worth the loss in detail? The writer must judge how much detail the reader can assimilate. The reader will tend to skip a table that appears too complicated.

Is the table consistent with others in the report? Too much variety in table form may confuse and irritate the reader.

Are the stubs, captions, and totals arranged to give proper emphasis to important elements? Items may be arranged in order of magnitude or in some other logical order. Totals may be at the top and the left to give emphasis. If totals are not important, they may go at the bottom and at the right. In some instances, totals may be omitted.

Is the title accurate? The title should tell the reader exactly what is in the table. If it is stated that all the tables in a report deal with the same cases, table titles may be simplified; the reader need not be told over and over that each table refers to Jolly Fun Settlement House participants during the year 1972–73.

Are the figures accurate? Totals must be free of errors in computation. Figures in the text and in the table must agree.

Are source notes and footnotes clear and accurate? Source notes are necessary only when material has been obtained from other sources. Footnotes are used to explain headings, to clarify apparent discrepancies, to report on tests of significance, or to give other information needed by the reader.

Is there sufficient comment in the text to help the reader understand the table? Each text table should be mentioned by number in the text. The reference should be clear and precise. Without repeating the figures given in the table, the writer emphasizes the points that the reader is expected to notice in the table. If the writer ignores a table, the reader will do likewise.

Graphs and charts. Like tables, graphs and charts should be included only when they are essential to the reader. Most of the questions about tables may also be asked about each graph or chart. A graphic illustration may help the reader to comprehend the findings more clearly than many pages of text. Yet graphs and charts, unless carefully presented and clearly explained in the text, may be misleading. The writer will consider the audience and decide what method of presentation is most appropriate.

Case material. Case material is rarely needed in a research report, but occasionally it may be useful. It was skillfully used by Hunt and Kogan, for example, in their effort to describe clients who received high and low *movement* scores (1952). It may be used at times to describe subgroups within the sample studied. If used, case material should be condensed to the bare essentials.

At the end of the section on findings, the reader should have a clear picture of what facts were uncovered or what relationships were found. If the section on findings has been well done, the reader has a good grasp of the facts and is ready to engage in silent conversation with the writer about their meaning and their relation to other facts.

Discussion of Findings

The writer attempts to explain the findings, to qualify them, to relate them to theory, and to show how they differ from findings by other investigators. There is no need to repeat details from the tables, but the writer may wish to select specific findings for detailed discussion.

If data are inconclusive, the writer points out their limitations and raises questions that should be studied. If the findings could possibly be explained in various ways, the writer considers possible explanations. For example, a finding may deviate from expectations or from the findings of another investigator. The writer need not claim to have the last word, but may point out how differences in time, locality, instruments, sampling method, or other factors may have influenced the result. It is appropriate to point out flaws in the study or possible distortions of the findings and to indicate what further study is required to resolve the uncertainty.

In discussing the findings, the writer attempts, above all, to qualify what has been done so that the reader will understand it more fully. It is important to make sure that the reader, who has not seen the raw material, is both informed and warned—informed about what may be done with the findings and warned not to stretch them beyond legitimate bounds.

Summary, Conclusions, and Recommendations

A report may end with a summary, which may or may not be accompanied by conclusions and recommendations. A summary is a brief résumé of major findings and the circumstances under which they were obtained. A conclusion is the writer's final assessment of what the data mean. A recommendation is the author's opinion about what action should be taken as a result of the conclusions drawn.

Every report of completed research needs a summary of some type. In a brief article, the summary may consist of only a sentence or two. In a study of the "action-research" type, the findings may be listed at the very beginning and may be repeated briefly at the end. The length and content of the summary will vary from one report to another.

The research worker may or may not include conclusions and recommendations. The worker employed by an agency may submit the findings to a board or committee, which will consider the report and make recommendations. In such a case, the research worker has a clear responsibility. Because the researcher may not be asked to appear before the policy-making body to interpret or discuss the findings, the report itself must be so complete and so clear that it is unlikely to be misunderstood. The author may point out the various conclusions that may be drawn on the basis of the findings. If the policy-making body is to act on the basis of a brief summary of the report, the writer must see to it that the summary presented gives an accurate report of the findings. If the decision made by the policy-making body seems to be based on a misunderstanding of the report, the researcher has an obligation to raise questions about the basis of the decision, to clarify whatever sections of the report may have been misleading, and to make every effort to see that the research findings are not distorted or misused.

Minor Parts of the Report

In addition to writing a clear and accurate report, the author must make a number of decisions about the format of the completed report. Many of these decisions seem relatively unimportant, yet neglect of any one of them may impair the usefulness of the report.

Title. The report or article must have a clear title which distinguishes it from other materials on the same or similar topics. The writer must choose a title that will be remembered and that describes the subject matter of the research. A colorful title that tells nothing of the content of the report may be misleading, and as a result the work may be improperly listed or catalogued. For example, *Patients Are People*, a book on medical social work, was shelved in the humor section in a large bookstore. Sometimes a brief and colorful title may be used with a more exact subtitle. For example, *Girls at Vocational High* is an easily remembered title; and the subtitle, *An Experiment in Social Work Intervention*, identifies the subject for the librarian and the prospective reader.

Author or authors. The report may carry the name of one or more authors or may be issued under the name of an agency. Many studies from government agencies are issued without designation of author, but a letter of transmittal may give the name of the author. On the other hand, the Children's Bureau has issued its major publications under the names of specific authors. In general, these principles apply:

The person or persons who directed the work must take responsibility for it.

The name of the senior author—the person who has taken primary responsibility for the work—should be listed first, even if a large part of the report has been written by the members of a research team.

Persons who have made contributions to the work—as consultants or as project staff members—may be given recognition in acknowledgments, but need not be listed as authors.

Agency progress reports and administrative reports—such as annual reports including service statistics—are issued under the name of the agency, not the person writing them. In some agencies, however, separate parts of the report are credited to staff members responsible for them.

Preface. A preface is not to be confused with an introduction. In social agencies, the preface of a research report is usually written by someone other than the technical author. It may provide the reader with an explanation of why the agency sponsored the study. It may place the report in context with published reports or others to be issued.

The author of a book may wish to use a preface as a means of acknowledging help received. In a less ambitious work, acknowledgments may be placed in footnotes. The author lists only those persons whose contributions have been real; a preface is not a place for name-dropping.

Table of contents and list of tables. A brief report may need no table of contents. A more extensive work should have an analytical table of contents giving not only chapter headings but subheadings and page references. Headings should be listed exactly as they appear in the body of the work. Appendix, bibliography, and index should be listed in the table of contents.

If extensive tabular material has been used, a list of tables and a list of figures should be included immediately following the table of contents.

Abstract. Some journals publish an abstract at the beginning or the end of each article. An abstract is a brief digest of the report. It helps the busy reader to know what new information can be obtained from the article. It makes clear precisely what was studied and what the major findings were. Models of abstracts may be found in *Psychological Abstracts* and *Abstracts for Social Workers*.

Bibliography. A list of references may or may not be needed in a brief report or a journal article. A bibliography is usually given in a monograph or a book. The purpose of the bibliography is to guide the reader, not to exhibit what the writer has read. A brief annotated bibliography is sometimes of more value than a long list of titles that give no basis for choice to the reader who wishes to explore the subject more fully.

Appendix. A research report may have one or more appendixes. An appendix is often used for technical material of sufficient importance to some readers to justify publication. For example, copies of research instruments may appropriately be included. Complicated tables that have no place in the text may be put in an appendix for the careful reader who wrants to verify details.

The extent of the material will vary. A journal article rarely has an appendix; a monograph is rarely without one. The research worker may avoid many queries by placing at least a schedule and basic definitions in an appendix. Sometimes a researcher may prepare a mimeographed technical report for persons who seek additional information.

Index. A long research monograph should have a detailed index. Indexing is a technical and time-consuming job. Although a publisher may be able to give the author help, the author must assume final responsibility for the index used. The author, who knows what key words in the monograph will have meaning for the reader, must check carefully to see that the index produced by a technical expert will serve the reader for whom the report was intended.

Writing and Revising the Report

Writing the research report requires straightforward presentation of material and careful attention to detail. The writer usually prepares a rough draft and as many revisions as are necessary.

Many writers dread to begin writing. The research worker, unlike the so-called creative writer, has clearly defined limits within which to work. A study must be reported. Upon visualizing the audience and trying to plan an outline that will be appropriate for that audience, the researcher may find that writing goes easily. With tables and working outline ready, the author tells what has been done and what has been found. Teachers of writing often suggest that, once writing has begun, the author should not stop to check mechanical matters such as spelling, precise references, and table titles. Like the artist who makes a rough sketch of a landscape before the light changes, the writer simply puts down the material without stopping to question matters that can be dealt with later. Some writers develop their own shorthand or systems of abbreviation to use during this stage of writing. The aim is to get material on paper quickly.

Unfortunately, some writers think a rough draft will do. They are surprised at the amount of reworking required in preparing a readable paper. Such labor may seem tedious, but few writers have such good working habits that they can submit a first draft without revision.

The writer will usually gain perspective through leaving the manuscript for a time before revising it. After a few days, the writer will view the material with a fresh eye. In some spots, the findings may seem unclear; in others, too many details may have been included. The writer at this stage can give attention to revisions without feeling that the entire paper must be rewritten.

Some teachers of writing suggest that the author follow a definite order in making revisions. The stages in revision may be summarized as follows:

Organization. Before wasting time on details of awkward phrasing, the writer should look carefully at the paper as a whole to be sure that it is well organized and that the parts are appropriately balanced. Length is not always a measure of importance, of course, but ordinarily the writer will not wish to give four pages to a minor point and one page to major findings. Sometimes a section must be expanded. More frequently, a lengthy section must be condensed. At this stage, irrelevant material may be dropped. At this stage, too, the writer may wish to consider subject headings for the final report. Sometimes flaws in organization or balance become apparent only when one sees that subject headings do not follow in logical order.

Paragraph and sentence structure. Once the general organization or structure of the report seems appropriate, the writer can pay attention to details of paragraphs and sentences. Each paragraph should be considered as a unit. Does it convey its central idea clearly? Does it include too much or too little? Do its parts belong together? The writer will also consider each sentence to be sure that it conveys exactly what was intended. This scrutiny of sentences cannot be left to the typist, who may detect flaws in logic or grammar but cannot be expected to do more.

Connectives. Once the paper seems to be in good form, the author should look at transitions throughout the paper. Simple connectives serve an important purpose in holding a paper together and showing the relationship of the various parts.

Accuracy. The author is responsible for giving the paper a final scrutiny to see that no errors or misinterpretations have crept in. All figures in tables should be checked against statements in the text. Footnote references should be verified.

Style. Although a research report must be well organized, precise, and accurate, there is no rule that it must be dull. Indeed, a well-written report can be lively, not for its style but for its substance. The writer tries hard to make the report interesting to the reader by making it understandable.

PREPARING THE REPORT FOR PUBLICATION

If an agency is publishing the report, the author will probably be consulted about the appropriate form of publication. More frequently, however, the report will be submitted to a journal or a publisher. Each journal has its own style, which the author is expected to follow. A journal may publish in each number a general statement about form of manuscripts. In addition, upon request a journal may provide a printed statement about the form in which materials should be submitted.

The writer submitting material to a journal will consider the following:

Subject matter. An article that may fit well in one journal may be completely unsuitable for another. For example, a study of the educational qualifications of the public assistance worker may be rejected by *Social Casework* and accepted eagerly by *Public Welfare*.

Permissions. Before submitting an article, the author must obtain permission from agencies whose material is to be included. Such permission is usually obtained early in the work on a study. In some cases, it will be necessary to disguise names of participants or even of agencies. All these matters should be taken care of before the manuscript is submitted.

Length. Some journals publish only relatively short articles. Others seek a few longer articles. Sometimes a research report can be presented as a series of articles, each part standing as a unit.

Technical content. Journals vary in the type of presentation expected and in the amount of technical statistical material used. A highly technical article on child guidance would be inappropriate in *Children Today*, which is addressed to a general audience, but might be accepted by *American Journal of Orthopsychiatry*.

Subject headings. Well-chosen subject headings serve as guides to the reader. The headings serve as labels for major subdivisions of a paper. Sometimes two or more levels of headings may be needed. The author who includes headings in the manuscript saves the editor hours of work.

Footnotes. Footnotes are used for two primary purposes, to provide references to sources and to give explanation or elaboration of the text.

A reference note gives the reader the exact source of material quoted or mentioned in the text. The source of every direct quotation must be identified accurately. Moreover, the writer should give the sources of facts or opinions used in the text, even when direct quotations are not used. Reference notes give the reader the source of additional information about something mentioned but not fully dealt with in the text. For example, after a mention of the *Movement Scale* in the text, the writer will use a footnote to refer the reader to the source of more information about the scale.

An explanatory note may be used in various ways. It may explain that an agency name will be abbreviated throughout the article; it may give additional information about an agency; it may provide a definition or an excerpt from a statute; it may tell what statistical test was used and what level of significance was accepted.

Footnotes should be used sparingly. One of the marks of the amateur is the overuse of reference notes.

The research worker must master footnote form and acquire a firm habit of making consistent and accurate notes. Once form has been mastered, the author will be able to proceed with confidence in preparing material for publication. Although form varies from journal to journal, the writer who has prepared footnotes carefully will have the essential information that can be adapted to meet the requirements of the journal to which the article is submitted.

PUBLISHING THE REPORT

While working on the report, the research worker has a particular audience in mind and has decided to submit the report for publication as a journal article or a monograph or to publish it independently or as an agency report.

Working with an editor. Sometimes writers wonder if they should ask the advice of the journal editor before submitting a manuscript. A query to the editor does no harm, but it may be a waste of time. Occasionally an editor will suggest that a paper be sent elsewhere. More often, the reply will be that the editor must see the manuscript before giving an opinion.

Often an editor may agree to accept a manuscript if the author is willing to make changes in it. Sometimes what has seemed clear to the writer is confusing to the reader. The editor may ask for clarification of obscure points, for condensation of sections in which there are excessive details, for a more forthright introduction, or for the simplification of elaborate or ornate writing.

Sometimes an editor will insist on technical changes in the article. In such a case, the editor refers to a manual of style which requires, for example, that accepted spelling, capitalization, and hyphenation be followed, that punctuation be consistent, and that footnotes be uniform in style. The author who understands what the editor is trying to do will not react personally to editorial suggestions and usually will not quibble over each editorial change. On the other hand, the author should go over the edited manuscript carefully to make sure that the editorial changes have not altered the meaning.

Independent publication. Occasionally, research workers in social agencies have found themselves in the publishing business. Many agencies—notably welfare councils and public welfare agencies—issue mimeographed reports. Others use job printers or state printers who take no responsibility beyond mechanical reproduction of material submitted by the issuing agency. In such situations the research worker, in addition to assuming full responsibility as editor of the report, may need to obtain financial estimates and to work with the jobber in preparing the report for the public.

Preparation of the duplicated report may present some technical difficulties, but they are not insuperable. An agency that prepares its own reports usually has a skilled clerical staff to assist in planning the format of the final report. Moreover, companies selling office equipment will provide on request special types of stencils and lettering equipment for use in designing covers, charts, maps, and other technical materials.

The research worker who plans to use a job printer will submit prepared material as the basis for a cost estimate. Before estimating the cost of printing, the jobber must know the length of the report, the number and type of tables and graphs, the type size, the quality of binding desired, and the number of copies required. Usually jobbers make no provisions for mailing or for publicizing a report.

The jobber can often suggest ways of making a report more attractive and of keeping costs down. On the other hand, use of a jobber rather than a regular channel for publication has its disadvantages. Primary among these, to the writer, is the fact that the jobber gives no editorial help and does not correct errors, but simply prints the material submitted. Hence the writer must be especially careful to see that the material is correct in every detail. (For suggestions about independent publication, see Ferguson [1958].) Moreover, the writer will have to assume responsibility for seeing that the report is made available to other research workers. Official publications of state agencies and of major welfare councils find their way into libraries and indexes, but reports privately printed or published by small agencies are often poorly publicized and difficult to obtain.

CRITERIA FOR A RESEARCH REPORT

The completed research report may be tested by use of the following questions:

Does the report include a careful statement of the problem?

Is there a clear account of the scope and method of the study?

Are the findings presented accurately and carefully so that the reader's questions are answered? Are tables and other illustrative materials used appropriately and carefully?

Does the author discuss the meaning or relevance of the findings? Are the conclusions supported by the data presented? Is the report free of distortion?

Are the limitations of the study made clear to the reader?

Is the report appropriate—in content and style—to the audience for which it was prepared?

Is the report written in simple, straightforward language? Is it interesting?

Does the author recognize and build upon the contributions of other research workers?

REFERENCES

Ferguson, R. 1958. *Editing the small magazine.* New York: Columbia Univ. Press.

Hunt, J. McV., and Kogan, L. S. 1952. *Measuring results in social casework: A manual on judging movement.* New York: Family Service Assoc. of America.

Sauber, M. 1965. *Experiences of the unwed mother as a parent.* New York: Community Council of Greater New York. (The passage quoted in the text above is used by permission of the publisher.)

Trelease, S. F. 1958. *How to write scientific and technical papers.* Baltimore: Williams & Wilkins.

Contributors

SAMUEL FINESTONE
Professor of Social Work (Research); and
Director, Center for Research and Demonstration
Columbia University School of Social Work

GRACE GANTER
Associate Professor
Temple University School for Social Administration

SHIRLEY JENKINS
Professor of Social Research; and
Chairman of the Doctoral Program
Columbia University School of Social Work

ALFRED J. KAHN
Professor (Social Policy and Planning)
Columbia University School of Social Work

LEONARD S. KOGAN
Professor of Psychology, and Director of the Center for Social Research
The City University of New York

RACHEL MARKS
Samuel Deutsch Professor Emeritus
School of Social Service Administration
University of Chicago

ROGER R. MILLER
Professor, and Director of Research
Smith College School for Social Work

NORMAN A. POLANSKY
Professor of Social Work and of Sociology
University of Georgia

WILLIAM J. REID
Professor
School of Social Service Administration
University of Chicago

SIDNEY ROSEN
Professor of Psychology, and
Chairman of the Doctoral Program in Social Psychology
University of Georgia

ANN W. SHYNE
Director of Research
Child Welfare League of America

EDWIN J. THOMAS
Professor of Social Work and of Psychology
University of Michigan

RUTH E. WEBER
Associate Professor of Social Work
University of Georgia

MARGARET YEAKEL
Associate Professor of Social Work
West Chester State College

Index of Names

Subject Index